TOIL, TURMOIL, &TRIUMPH

A Portrait of the Tennessee Labor Movement

TOIL, TURMOIL, & TRIUMPH

A Portrait of the Tennessee Labor Movement

PERRY C. COTHAM

HILLSBORO PRESS

Franklin, Tennessee

TENNESSEE HERITAGE LIBRARY
Bicentennial Collection

Printed in the United States of America

99   98   97   96   95   5   4   3   2   1

Library of Congress Card Catalog Number: 95-71978

ISBN: 1-881576-64-7

All scenes on the cover of this book are drawn from historic photographs of Tennesseans at work. Included in this collage are photos of the following: a shift heading for home from Nashville's Avco Manufacturing Corporation (especially on back cover); a cotton picker resting in a West Tennessee cotton field near Memphis; construction on the AEDC wind tunnel near Tullahoma; and miners employing drill and hand pick. All cover photos courtesy of Tennessee State Library and Archives.

Cover by Bozeman Design.

Published by
HILLSBORO PRESS
an imprint of
PROVIDENCE HOUSE PUBLISHERS
P.O. Box 158 • 238 Seaboard Lane
Franklin, Tennessee 37067
800-321-5692

IN RECOGNITION OF THEIR DEDICATED COMMITMENT to the welfare of Tennessee's citizens, their respect for the struggles of the past, their support for the cause of industrial peace providing economic and social justice, and their leadership into a future of promise, we respect-fully dedicate this volume to

James Neeley, President
and
Eddie Bryan, Secretary/Treasurer

Tennessee Labor Council, AFL-CIO

Contents

Foreword

This is a story about people. We wanted much of the story to be in their own words. When the Tennessee Center for Labor-Management Relations commissioned Dr. Perry Cotham to compile such a story, we envisioned an interesting and readable blend of recorded information from the files of yesterday with personal observations gleaned from as many living sources as possible. Dr. Cotham has met our expectations, and we thank him for the time and energies spent in libraries, union halls, newspaper files, and personal diaries. Perhaps we are most grateful for the numerous face to face personal interviews, collecting and recording an oral history that might otherwise have been lost forever.

The Tennessee Center for Labor-Management Relations is proud to present this segment of Tennessee's history as one gesture of our firm commitment to the people of Tennessee. We know that learning from the events and behaviors of yesterday will not only help us mold the present, but will be the foundation on which to build a positive and productive tomorrow.

—Douglas Davis, Director
Tennessee Center for Labor-Management Relations

Personal Note and Acknowledgments

With pleasure I note that this volume, published for Tennessee's Bicentennial year, narrates a story of the men and women and sometimes children whose persistent labors and concerns helped shape and build the Volunteer State. Some of this story includes these workers' relationship to the rapidly changing social and political forces swirling about them. And, as you will note, a major part of the story concerns laborers' efforts to organize for strength in negotiation so as to share more fully in the American dream.

My interest in the concerns of labor can be traced to the mid- and late sixties. My young family and I had separated ourselves from the green hills of Middle Tennessee to live and work in the heart of Detroit, Michigan, where I attended graduate school for six years. The people with whom I attended school, worked, socialized, and attended worship were, at least the vast majority of them, working-class people from working-class families. Most were native Northerners and Midwesterners; a great many, to my surprise, were transplanted Southerners who remained "southern" in heart even if it always seemed impractical to return to Dixie. These ordinary, but solid citizens knew both hard times and hard work. As I heard them describe and lament the stress and tedium of their jobs, this son of a preacher's family was anxious to learn more about their real work world.

Visits that I made to area industrial plants—I vividly recall the River Rouge steel mill, the Ford assembly line, a General Motors stamping plant, among others—were adrenaline-pumping experiences for me. I tried to relate to how these men and women labored in the heat and sweat, the long hours, and unrelenting and almost excruciatingly loud noise of machinery humming and metal clashing

11

against metal, but I knew that I could not fully relate to their situation.

Graduate studies in American history at Wayne State University during those years deepened my understanding of how profoundly the American worker was affected by the hard times of the 1920s and the Great Depression of the 1930s. One assigned reading in a graduate class in the early twentieth century America, Irving Bernstein's *The Lean Years*, greatly impacted my consciousness. I then began to read books about Franklin D. Roosevelt and the New Deal and learned how and why the four-time elected president expanded the federal government in unprecedented ways on behalf of industrial workers and farmers. Not only did Roosevelt bring some degree of management of the economy to prevent extreme swings in business cycles, but also, I learned, the New Deal style of government postured itself to protect individual citizens from the worst fallout of national economic failures. Research on a doctoral dissertation on Harry Hopkins, who directed several public welfare programs and became a close friend and adviser to Roosevelt, led me twice to visit the archives of the Roosevelt Library at Hyde Park, New York.

At this writing, the nation has given some modest note to the fiftieth anniversary of the death of Franklin Delano Roosevelt at his resort in Warm Springs, Georgia, April 12, 1945. The current congressional leader, House Speaker Newt Gingrich, has boldly appropriated FDR's phrases "the first one hundred days" and "bold, persistent experimentation" in service of a Republican "dismantling of the New Deal." There is no doubt that under FDR's leadership almost every hitherto oppressed segment of Tennesseans, Southerners, and Americans in general made advances toward equal opportunity and fair treatment—industrial laborers, impoverished farmers, blacks, and women. At this point there is a legitimate question of whether Gingrich's "first one hundred days" are in the interests of the same people. Sure enough, throughout the New Deal the rich stayed rich, but much of the lower class had, by the Eisenhower fifties, moved into the middle class. The struggles and strength of labor are so vitally a part of that story.

My years with the Tennessee Center for Labor-Management Relations as a Labor Education Specialist provided me with a marvelous opportunity to revive my interest in late nineteenth and twentieth century American history. My own interest in Tennessee labor was stimulated in 1987 when Dr. Douglas Davis, director of the Center, asked me to begin researching and writing a state labor history. The bulk of material which the reader finds in this volume was written in 1988 and 1989. My *Handbook of Labor History: The*

Tennessee Edition was published by the Center in 1989. The *Handbook*, intended for a much more limited audience and limited circulation, contains some key excerpts and photographs drawn for this book.

The process of collecting information, visiting sites, and talking to locals began in summer 1987. My first on-site visit led me to Overton and Fentress Counties, accompanied by Sue Glore, as pleasant and congenial co-worker as one will ever encounter. Sue's father, Joe Welch, had entered the coal mines around Wilder-Twinton-Davidson as a teenager and his own memories provided a wealth of information and folklore about a lifestyle which has all but vanished from Tennessee.

The three of us, traversing dusty, gravel roads in that state-owned Chevrolet station wagon, drove to abandoned mines and depression-era company houses. We searched for and discovered the humble grave site of Barney Graham amidst the thistles and weeds in the community cemetery. Anything that looked old and interesting occasioned my stopping the car, opening the door and aiming my camera. We quickly exited one area near the end of our day-long visit when several rather uninviting and intimidating mountaineer males slowly approached our vehicle. Though I must have seemed somewhat concerned, Mr. Welch seemed not the least perturbed. "Don't worry, Perry," he reassured me. "I've got a loaded pistol inside my overalls." That was a fact I had not known until that moment. "I'll never forget the look on Perry's face when Dad said that," Sue continues telling people to this day.

A number of people have offered assistance simply in the "line of duty" of their professions. I acknowledge gratefully the assistance given by Dr. Edwin S. Gleaves, state librarian and director, and his excellent staff at the Tennessee State Library and Archives for making accessible numerous primary and secondary materials; Genella Olker, Jacci Herrick and Bob DePriest were especially helpful to me on a regular basis. In more recent days I have been graciously assisted by Marilyn Hughes, Ann Alley, and Julia Rather. Equally invaluable has been the staff, especially archivist Peter Roberts, at the Southern Labor Archives (Special Collections Department), Georgia State University, Atlanta. Wanda Mathews, reference librarian at the Tennessee State University Williams (Downtown) campus has been particularly helpful in soliciting published material for me. My thanks go also to David Bryan, an economic analyst for the state, for helping me locate newspaper coverage of recent events in state labor history, and to Annette Morrison, librarian for the *Tennessean* for her general assistance.

Most of all, I have been personally blessed and brought to new understandings and perspectives through numerous visits and conversations with a significant and varied group of personalties who have played a role in Tennessee's labor history. I have discovered that labor people are generally very hospitable, cooperative, and highly anxious to tell their story in hope that younger generations will know something of their sacrifices and struggles.

I have some wonderful memories. Sitting in the home of Pauline and retired Senator Albert Gore, Senior, just above the banks of the Cumberland River, I knew that I was in the presence of a man who not only had served his state and his country well, but had conscientiously and courageously dared to openly dissent from his own president's policies in Vietnam; the courage of such convictions cost him his seat in the Senate. And sitting in a living room surrounded by much window glass with Myles Horton, a panoramic view of the Appalachian Mountains before us, I knew that I was in the midst not simply of mountain majesty but also of disarmingly simple human heroism. After my two visits in the home of Stanton Smith, I concluded that surely there could not be a kinder and more gracious gentleman. I have experienced the same feelings after visits with Jim Neeley and Eddie Bryan. On and on I could go.

Special thanks are due also to James Crutchfield, a friend and consultant who assisted in the final stage of production for this project, and also especially to Jo Jaworski and Trinda Cole, most efficient and congenial technical assistants of Providence House Publishers, for their expertise and many hours of work.

A final acknowledgement is richly deserved by my friend Carolyn Wilson, acquisitions and development librarian at Nashville's David Lipscomb University, whose many hours of technical assistance in locating source material are superceded in value only by her continual encouragement and personal support for this project.

Hopefully, TOIL, TURMOIL, AND TRIUMPH: A PORTRAIT OF THE TENNESSEE LABOR MOVEMENT can provide for general readership a valuable slice of the rich heritage of Tennessee history. Admittedly, this volume was written from the perspective of organized labor and unionism, but a sincere attempt has been made in the narratives and pictures to provide insight about all kinds of Tennesseans who toiled by the sweat of their brow. If this book provides a useful tool in the hands of teachers and students alike, as well as brings to Tennessee workers and their families some sense of their interesting and rich heritage, then this project will have accomplished its dual purpose.

CHAPTER 1

"... workers struggled for recognition as a collective unit, for basic rights and work-place democracy, and, most basic of all, for respect as real human beings ..."

Men, Women, and Sometimes Children

Any student or reader seeking a state labor history which typifies all the conflict, color, and drama of the American labor movement would not likely turn to Tennessee. Instead, one would turn to the Northeast or the Midwest, where unionism first took hold in this country and has wielded the strongest influence on public affairs and public policy. The socio-cultural climate of Tennessee, partaking fully of southern attitudes toward labor organizations, has never been conducive to the growth of a large and strong unionized labor movement.

Tennesseans have known the meaning of hard work, to be sure. The great seal of their state appropriately features agriculture and commerce. From the days that the earliest settlers crossed the mountains from the east to seek a new and better life in the rich and fertile lands of the Tennessee territory which had been vividly described by hunters and trappers, until about the time of the Second World War, the men and women of the Volunteer State have maintained their existence and earned their profits primarily from agricultural pursuits—tilling the ground, harvesting the crops, maintaining the livestock, and processing their farm and forest products.

Antebellum Tennesseans, not unlike citizens in other southern states, were more concerned about preserving their rich traditions than they were in welcoming the penetration of industrial manufacturing interests from the North. Though mining and manufacturing had begun in some elementary forms in various Tennessee locales prior to the Civil War, the values and ideology of Tennesseans clearly supported their faith in the moral and economic superiority of agriculture. Industrial work, clearly not welcomed by most of the

15

citizenry, was thought to degrade public and social morality. A case in point is the experience of an early industrialist, Asa Faulkner, who opened a cotton factory in McMinn County in 1847. Faulkner, a wool-carder by trade, may have felt that the masses of poor white mountain folk would beat a path to his factory door to find steady work and a regular wage in a progressive industry. Alas, such was not the case. Countering what he called "foolish prejudice," an either ingenious or desperate Faulkner eventually put his own family to work in the mill to demonstrate that there was nothing inherently evil or dangerous about industrial labor.

Early on from young statehood, small craft shops were opened in Tennessee's larger cities where skilled artisans plied their trade. And though the prejudice against industrial labor was deeply entrenched, the latter nineteenth-century and early twentieth-century Tennessee welcomed steady increases in industrial manufacturing, especially in mining, textiles, and iron manufacturing. Tennesseans who entered the mines, mills, and other factories, became increasingly concerned about their plight. Their search and their struggle for more control over their work situation and their destiny clashed mightily with a second powerful prejudice which was dominant among Tennessee's business and professional class and the state press—a persistent antipathy for labor unionism.

This book is not intended to be a history of all Tennessee workers. Such a history would be monumental indeed and would necessarily give substantial emphasis both to the state's agricultural workers as well as to the experience of slave laborers, the latter being employed primarily in the middle and western sectors of the state in antebellum days. Such a volume would also include a study of the business and professional workers, from the experiences of the earliest entrepreneurs to the latest independent researchers in the human sciences at Vanderbilt or the University of Tennessee.

The story of the men, women, and even children who entered Tennessee's mine shafts, tool shops, metal foundries and rolling mills, clothing factories, boot and shoe factories, grain mills, and the many other factories in order to earn an hourly wage, constitute the main concern of the study here. Even still, it is presumptuous to attempt in a single volume to cover exhaustively a subject as vast and complex as a state labor history. Instead, with a concern for general readership, this project has sought to bring together the major stories in Tennessee labor history, a history of the state's labor leaders and their organizations and

Tennessee has been known largely as an agricultural state. Mules and plows have been plentiful in Tennessee for decades. This early to mid-twentieth century scene was captured in the Tennessee Clinch River Valley. (Courtesy—Tennessee State Library and Archives)

political concerns, with some assessment of the labor movement on the state's political behavior. This book, therefore, is a beginning.

Rather than seeing this volume as a complete history, except in a generous use of the term, perhaps a more accurate description might be a portrait of the labor movement in Tennessee. Dates and places of events are reported whenever possible and relevant. Occasionally, statistical data are referenced. But more than collecting and reciting names, minutes of meetings, proceedings, and pertinent statistical data, the purpose of this study has been to dramatize the working condition of Tennessee workers, to examine the work-related issues that concern them, to report on the unions and affiliations they started, to bring to life some of those men and women who lived well and served their co-workers nobly or who struggled courageously against all odds to further the spirit of collectivism and foster economic justice or, in some cases, just to survive. All too often, this is a story of people who were both oppressed and exploited.

The stories and anecdotes that have made their way into these pages are but a sampling of ones which could have been recounted.

Tennessee saw mill hands at work. (Courtesy—Tennessee State Library and Archives)

As such, too many of the stories do not have a happy ending. The stories do have, of course, all the elements of labor-management clashes in other sectors of the nations—the problems of economic collapse (unemployment, poverty, relief); the issues of labor standards (low wages, long hours, child labor, job insecurity, poor and unsafe working conditions); and the fundamental issues of labor-management relations (the right to recognition as a working unit; the right to collective bargaining; the right to settle grievances by a fair procedure). Put succinctly, the workers struggled for recognition as a collective unit, for basic rights and workplace democracy, and, most basic of all, for respect as real human beings and not simply as "girls," "chalk-eyes," or "lint-heads."

That struggle was made difficult by the power weighted on the side of the management and ownership forces. Tennessee, like other states in the South, was sought by northern owners and investors as ripe territory to escape unionism; it was an advantage for which they were willing to fight tenaciously and deviously. Time after time, one sees where the managing class relied on the tried and devastatingly effective methods of intimidating wage-earning workers—weapons such as flat statements of refusal to recognize and negotiate with any union, the iron-clad (yellowdog) contract, blacklisting union members, firings, court injunction against certain union activities, recruiting strike breakers, espionage at union meetings, and even "Rambo guards."

Perhaps the most dominant theme running through this history is the power of the state of Tennessee pitted against the aims and strategies of the unionized workers. Whether one looks at the plight of miners in east Tennessee at Coal Creek in the 1890s, or in Wilder in the 1930s, or at the Steelworkers at Nashville Corporation in the 1940s, or at the Murray Ohio factory workers in the 1960s, the theme is clearly highlighted.

The theme is clear at various levels. One sees it in the rural and small town interests and votes of the Tennessee General Assembly in establishing a system of convict labor and in attempting to maintain the status quo. One sees it also in the decision of governors as politically varied as John Buchanan, Henry Horton, Gordon Browning, or even Frank Clement, to dispatch the National Guard or the state's highway patrol to maintain "law 'n order" at a strike scene—an action that, no matter its justification, was invariably interpreted by the workers as the state taking sides with the company against the union. One sees it in the lobbying influence of the business and industrial leaders against legislation favorable to organized labor.

Combined with the weight of power and array of weapons in the hands of company owners and managers, this collusion by state leaders and officials all too often placed organized labor in Tennessee in a desperately defensive position in which the workers fought resourcefully for their jobs, affiliations, and their respect. The sad plight of American unionism in general has been that its emphasis on collective protectionism and survival has obscured from workers the values of labor organization for forwarding progressive agendas from a position of strength and equality with management.

Toil. Turmoil. Yet there is another theme, however obscure at times, which underlies some of the Tennessee labor stories. It is a theme of triumph. The history of Tennessee labor would not be complete without acknowledging the genuine successes and achievements of the movement: the state's progressive move on child labor reform; the abolition of the convict labor system; the development of one of the South's most advanced trade union movements in nineteenth-century Memphis; the significant role given to women in labor organizing and business administration; the influence and direction of the Highlander Folk School in the compatible movements of southern unionism and southern desegregation; the beginning of two unions in Nashville which moved irrepressibly to a position of international strength.

Organized labor in Tennessee had a vital role in all these developments. Additionally, the labor force and work ethic of Tennessee have been cited as major factors in two corporate decisions of the 1980s—the decision by a Japanese automobile manufacturer and by an American automobile manufacturer each to make the largest single investment of their company, indeed, of their respective nations, in the Volunteer State.

Throughout all the conflict between labor and its friends and management and its friends in terms of values, beliefs, theories, backgrounds, and systems has been the emergence of genuine heroes who are seldom acclaimed in the standard general histories. This study has uncovered not a few of them, some of whom can be named, heroes such as Byron Graham, a mountaineer union president who was gunned down on the streets of Wilder in the midst of a battle to save the jobs of fellow miners; or such as Myles Horton, who fearlessly continued organizing and teaching in the face of intense local animosity and official persecution; or such as Eugene Merrill, a labor organizer who spoke eloquently and fervently for the rights of poverty-stricken miners against the rights of the company to replace them with leased convict labor; or such as Norman Smith, a fearless UAW organizer who was twice beaten on public streets in Memphis at the height of a city machine's antagonism toward industrial unionism; or Albert Hill, whose tireless dedication to the labor in Tennessee helped to establish a state federation which has grown to become labor's leading voice in the state. These pages will name others.

Realistically, most of the heroes of these stories cannot be named. Among their ranks are those unionists who were willing to risk life, limb, and job security for their cause; the labor leaders in the state's four major cities who, with no allies in the press, or business and professional community, entered politics and formed their own workingmen's parties to work within the system and demonstrate a commitment to the welfare of their toiling brothers and sisters; those miners willing to storm the stockades under cover of darkness and release the convict laborers and load them on a train for safe transport to the city; those young women who courageously signed union cards in the face of their manager's intimidation and threats; those leaders who called for reform of unconscionable labor conditions and standards; those employees who left their work stations to support brothers and sisters on a picket line in another county; and those labor educators who traveled to work sites with only a few dollars in their pockets, offering instruction and encouragement in order to enhance the workers' sense of effectiveness and solidarity. It is the memory of these sacrifices which must be maintained by the guardians of Tennessee's heritage.

There is no attempt here to whitewash the woeful shortsightedness of labor leaders or deny their devious complicity in the senseless labor violence of the labor wars of the recent past. Maintaining a sense of perfect balance is an admirable, if impossible, goal that has been kept in mind as these narratives have been reconstructed. And, as this portrait has developed, every effort has been made to place the Tennessee picture within the larger backdrop of the forces and developments of United States labor history in general. Each reader may decide how accurately and fairly the various persona, events, and movements at all levels have been blended.

Road crew working on Benton Pike in Southeast Tennessee (circa 1905-1910). Men were allowed to work on the road crew in lieu of paying cash for road taxes. (Courtesy—Tennessee State Library and Archives)

CHAPTER

2

". . . the frozen fingers of the North have been laid in the warm palms of the South, and a healthful, invigorating temperature pervades them both as one body. . . ."

Seeds of Unionism

The Origins and Early Concerns of the Tennessee Labor Movement

Tennesseans have never been strangers to hard work. Whether black or white, young or old, male or female, skilled or unskilled, mountaineer or lowlands resident, migrant or native-born son or daughter—from the time that pioneer homesteaders began coming over the mountains to settle in Tennessee, the state has been populated with men and women who understood the meaning of working with their hands.

Jobs in days of old were often difficult, back-breaking, and tedious. Yet they were almost always necessary for survival. Generations ago Tennesseans across the 432 mile-breadth of their state spent their waking hours in harsh daily toil and sweat—cutting timber, sawing lumber, building houses, erecting barns and smokehouses, digging wells, capturing game and fish in raw wilderness, planting crops, harvesting crops, preserving food, milling grain, shaping tools, mining precious minerals in the earth, raising livestock, slaughtering livestock, processing meats, making clothes, tanning hides and skins, making soap, mending clothes, building railroads, courthouses, churches, and schoolhouses, and distilling spirits.

In modern times within the 42,244 square miles of the state, Tennesseans have engaged in fairly sophisticated, technological work assignments. They have printed and bound all kinds of books and magazines, manufactured and processed film, built dams, tested aircraft in giant wind tunnels, harnessed nuclear energy, assembled large tractor-trailer trucks, built steel radial tires, and constructed aviation wings.

Most of that toil and sweat by Tennesseans has come through tilling the soil and harvesting the crops. Throughout most of her history, Tennessee has been first and foremost an agricultural state. From the small farms of east Tennessee, broken by numerous narrow valleys and steep ridges, to the Mississippi bottomlands of west Tennessee, some 120,000 working men were engaged in farming by 1860. By contrast, no more than ten percent of all working men in Tennessee prior to the Civil War earned their living by manufacturing. Even then, Tennessee manufactured goods were mostly of locally consumed necessities.[1]

In the antebellum days one could find the origins of industry which decades later would employ the time and energy of thousands of Tennesseans. The first established industry in Tennessee was milling. In 1775 a grist mill was set up on Buffalo Creek; meal and flour were shipped to the Atlantic coast and to New Orleans. Other mills followed: on White's Creek, Mill Creek, and on a barge in the Cumberland River near Nashville; on Little Limestone Creek in east Tennessee; a powder mill in Sumner County; a fulling mill on Yellow Creek.[2] Flour milling became an important industry with the rise of the wheat as one of the largest cash crops of the 1830s; its supremacy was short-lived due to the competition in wheat farming from the great prairie regions.[3]

The textile industry in Tennessee may be dated as far back as 1791 when John Hague, of Manchester, advertised in the Knoxville Gazette that the machines in his spinning mill on the Cumberland were "in order for carding, spinning and weaving." Dr. Frederick Ross of Kingsport launched an unsuccessful venture into the silkworm culture. As a cotton-growing state, it was only natural that cotton textile manufacturing would emerge. An early cotton mill in Lebanon by 1846 was operating 2,000 spindles, 21 carding machines, and 40 power looms, producing 1,000 yards of cloth a day.[4] Competition from the better cotton lands in the deep South led Tennessee farmers to try other crops, thus impeding growth of cotton textiles before the war. After the war, however, the textile industry revived with plants established and operating in several urban areas.[5] The textile manufacturing industry was destined to move up among Tennessee's top industries in the late nineteenth and early twentieth centuries.

After the Civil War voices were being raised on behalf of a "New South"—a South that would acknowledge the defeat and loss of an old economic order rooted in an agricultural economy and supported by slave labor and would embrace and develop a new system of industry and manufacturing comparable to that which functioned effectively in the victorious North. "Not the plow beam, but the cog wheel" became a favorite epigram of pro-industrialists. The urban press was an effective vehicle for this new gospel of salvation. Joining the press were the voices of civic leaders such as Arthur S. Colyar and Joseph B. Killebrew,[6] both of Nashville, and James E. Bailey of Clarksville. Their message: it's time to remove sectional animosities and be willing to forgive those Yankees who laid waste to our land if those northerners are willing to return with capital and manufacturing expertise.[7]

Within weeks of the Appomattox surrender, fortune seekers from the North entered Tennessee to establish new industries. Companies received new charters in petroleum, mining, and manufacturing. Some small towns became the sites for new manufacturing ventures, although most of the new industry went to urban areas, especially in Knoxville and Chattanooga. The amount of capital pumped into the state was less than some Tennesseans had hoped for, but in these early ventures the groundwork was laid for a new economic base and a new kind of worker.

Just as the land was the source of the agricultural economy and prosperity, it was also the foundation of much of the industrial economy and prosperity. The processing of iron accounted for some of Tennessee's earliest industries. Even as early as the late eighteenth century in the eastern sector of the state, small forges and bloomeries, supplied by crude mining operations, were manufacturing bar iron, tools, and nails.[8] Real expansion of the iron industry, however, did not begin until the discovery of coal; soon thereafter, Tennessee iron was shipped to South Pittsburg, Louisville, and Cincinnati where it could be used in the manufacture of steam boiler engines. After the development of a rail system, iron was sent to additional markets. By 1860 a total of 75 bloomeries and forges, 71 furnaces, and 4 rolling mills were in operation.[9] The iron industry boomed briefly in meeting the Confederacy's war demands and then was abruptly halted by Union occupation. By the late 1860s, the Knoxville Iron Company, which included a rolling mill, a foundry, a machine shop, a nail mill, and a railroad spike machine, was in full operation. Founded by a former federal military officer, the company was one of several northern-owned enterprises which made up one-sixth of the business properties in Knoxville.[10]

Despite impressive growth and improvement in Knoxville after the war, Chattanooga was the real boom town of the state. In 1860 Chattanooga's 22 small industries employed 214 men. Ten years later

58 industrial companies employed nearly 2,000 workers.[11] The mountain city experienced a boom in land sales. Speculators talked about a great future for Chattanooga. Local newspapers, particularly the *Times*, did not miss an opportunity to proclaim to all who would listen that the mineral resources of east Tennessee, north Georgia, and north Alabama were destined to be the heart of the industrial "New South" and that Chattanooga would quite naturally be the hub of all this glorious activity. A building boom followed. Seats for the opening performance at the opera house were auctioned to the highest bidders. By the late 1880s the Chattanooga, Rome, and Columbus Railroad was built (William Gibbs McAdoo turned the first spade of earth on the project) and the area's Iron, Coal and Manufacturers' Association was reorganized, later renamed the Chattanooga Chamber of Commerce. A spectacular project named the Chattanooga Land, Coal, Iron and Railway Company and supported by Adolph Ochs involved plans for coke ovens, blast furnaces, mines, large land tract purchases and possible oil and gas drilling. Talk of future assets of $50 million made the project "the most gigantic company yet organized in the South." The vision of Chattanooga investors, however, extended their reach—investors for this grandiose scheme were scarce and the enterprise never took off.[12]

ROANE AND ROCKWOOD

Among the companies which did succeed, the story of one is worth telling. John Thomas Wilder, often described as "the greatest of the carpetbaggers," was quite familiar with Tennessee when he came to Chattanooga in the 1860s. Wilder, who had operated a foundry and mills in his native Indiana, had developed an interest in east Tennessee mineral deposits by examining the area as a Union soldier during the war. After participating in Sherman's siege of Atlanta, Wilder fell ill, resigned his commission as a commander, and decided to remain in the South. With Hiram S. Chamberlain, an ex-Federal officer who served in east Tennessee, Wilder purchased over 900 acres of Roane County land. Wilder won the interest of a number of midwestern investors in a new company, the largest investor being W. O. Rockwood, and the village which emerged around the furnace was named after him. The Roane Iron Company was thus incorporated in 1867.[13]

Wilder soon brought the Southwestern Iron Company, a defunct company which had a rolling mill, into his own company. In the early 1870s, the Roane Iron Company began building a company town at

The construction of Tennessee Central Railroad in 1910 near a tunnel in Rockwood, which would connect mines with markets. This was considered a major engineering feat. (Courtesy—Tennessee State Library and Archives)

Rockwood. The population of the town grew from about 300 persons in 1868 to 2,305 in 1890.[14] European immigrants were absorbed into the local white population, and blacks composed about a quarter of the town's population by 1880.[15] The company owned a large store and accepted company scrip at face value and also owned the housing although workers were free to buy their own homes. Most men worked ten hours a day and wages were somewhat higher for coal miners than for ore miners and furnace hands. In 1878 the Roane Iron Company made use of the first open hearth furnace south of the Ohio River. That same year the company's assets reached one million dollars; its two blast furnaces at Rockwood could produce sixty tons of pig iron per day, most of which was shipped to Chattanooga where 600 mill hands produced large quantities of rail for the growing network of railroads.[16] Progress had arrived in east Tennessee, the editor for the *Chattanooga Daily Times* noted with pride:

> The frozen fingers of the North have been laid in the warm palms of the South, and a healthful, invigorating tempera-ture pervades them both as one body. They are moving in united thought—united action, placing wherever they tread some monument of their skill, industry, and patriotism, and garlanding the nation with their intelligence and virtue.[17]

Rockwood industry in the late 1800s; smoke is from a local iron company. (Courtesy—Tennessee State Library and Archives)

By 1887 the Roane company was producing steel rails by the Bessemer process, the first such accomplishment in the old Confederate states.[18] Early enthusiasm about the process began its decline with the drop in steel prices. Blast furnaces were slowed down periodically and iron works in other east Tennessee communities began to struggle. Civic and business leaders began to realize that their communities needed to diversify their manufacturing exports if they were to maintain economic health. In Rockwood that need was answered in 1905 by James Tarwater, who before purchasing stock in the Roane company had worked for the company for $1.25 per day. Settling on a plot that covered eight acres, Tarwater established the Rockwood mills. The new mill would produce hosiery and its work force would be drawn from the iron workers' wives and daughters. Supposedly, with females earning money and husbands making domestic concessions, there were fewer and more tame Saturday night brawls among the men and Rockwood became more of a typical southern community.[19] Rockwood Mills was destined some thirty years later to experience a bitter strike which would bring to the state's attention the name of a young union activist named Matt Lynch.

THE KNIGHTS OF LABOR IN TENNESSEE

The plight of the unskilled worker in the 1870s could hardly have been more desperate. To many in the general American public, the wage earner was only a member of a sub-community or lower class and any movement toward unionization was an outlaw activity. Despite this public disdain, perhaps because of it, one labor organization flourished—the Noble and Holy Order of the Knights of Labor, organized in December 1869 by nine Philadelphia tailors who had belonged to the local Garment Cutters Association. By 1875 membership in this secret organization had reached 5000; before 1880 that figure had quadrupled. Breaking with the membership on the issue of secrecy, Uriah Stephens was forced to resign his post of leadership and was replaced by Terence V. Powderly, a machinist, Greenback-Labor politician, reformer, and then-mayor of Scranton, Pennsylvania. Powderly moved beyond traditional areas of organization by trade or craft and worked to organize the unskilled industrial laborers. The Knights grew steadily and impressively. By 1886 the Knights of Labor had attracted over 700,000 workers nationwide. It was the dominant labor organization of the 1880s.[20]

In 1878 the Knights of Labor launched their first concerted southern organizing drive by sending fifteen organizers into the region. Most of the organizers worked in Alabama and Kentucky. The order was open to all who toiled for a living and the local assemblies admitted workers in a trade or unskilled workers or in mixed assemblies.

Compared with other southern states, the Knights were not strong in Tennessee. The success the Knights enjoyed in the Volunteer State was mainly among coal miners. The first local assembly of the Knights of Labor in Tennessee was formed among the miners of east Tennessee in 1873, according to James Dombrowski, an early teacher at Highlander Folk School.[21] The Knights' recruiters were particularly active among the coal miners in Anderson County in soliciting new members and organizing lodges. In 1890 the local newspapers carried a notice of a Knights of Labor picnic at Betterchance (near Briceville) and in 1893 there were newspaper notices of Clinch River Assembly No. 93 of the Knights, which met every Friday night in the hall above Hills' grocery store near Clinton.[22]

The Knights also enjoyed some strong successes in Grundy County, scene of some of the earliest coal mining in Tennessee. The Sewanee Mining Company, chartered in 1852 to develop Grundy's fabulous deposits, soon brought miners to a bleak coal camp which was named after New York capitalist Samuel F. Tracy, the company's first president. Tracy City became about the most thriving community between Nashville and Chattanooga.[23] In 1873 Samuel Jones built his famous Fiery Gizzard coke iron furnace in Tracy City at a cost of

The Tracy City depot, in the 1890s, looking north. Grundy County coal was hauled away by rail. (Courtesy—Tennessee State Library and Archives)

$3,000; the fifteen tons of iron the furnace produced was the first coke iron produced in Tennessee, demonstrating that Sewanee coal could be converted to iron-producing coke.[24] Tracy City's coal mines emerged as the most extensive in the state in the 1880s.

About 1884 the miners of the Tracy City district formed a local assembly and elected Tom Carrick the first Master Workman and Walter Patton as secretary. At one time the local claimed 400-500 men, or most of the free miners of the district. The early meetings were announced and conducted secretly in a railroad building east of Tracy City; passwords and grips were used for entrance.[25]

Grundy miners had plenty to discuss in their meetings. Their workday averaged eleven hours. Their working conditions were often hazardous and they typically worked on their knees or lying on their sides or backs while swinging the pick into the heart of a mountain. The Grundy miner was proud of his occupation. When asked what he earned he would always report the gross amount. What he did not report to outside observers was the costs of working as an independent miner—the purchase of picks, dynamite, fuses, the work clothing, the two-layered lunch box (one compartment for water and the other for food) and other essentials. The miner entered the shaft with a car which was 3 1/2 feet wide, six feet long, and twelve inches deep—supposedly holding a half-ton of coal—and toiled in the heat, sweat and black grime to fill it up with the precious mineral as rapidly as he could.[26] Drivers were paid $.80 a day and coal diggers received 20 to 25 cents per loaded car; when the men were given larger cars to

load their coal, their wages remained the same. Accidents were frequent. The miners were compelled to trade at the company store.
There was no compensation for injury. Miners were laid off arbitrarily
and given no reason for their discharge.[27] Most of all, miners in both
Grundy and Anderson Counties lived with the constant threat of convict laborers being handed their jobs and only source of livelihood.

Reaction among the coal company owners to the Knights' movement was categorically and predictably negative. At least one company dispatched undercover agents (called "stooges" by the miners)
to the union meetings to gain information. As soon as the identity of
union leaders was discovered, the union officials were fired. When
the policy of blacklisting Knights became known to union members,
the membership quickly dwindled to a handful of miners.
Embarrassingly, the Knights' charter and seal were recalled by the
national office and the balance of $700 in the local's treasury was
donated to the local school.[28] Despite the ultimate failure of the
Knights to sustain a movement among Tennessee coal miners, the
groundwork was laid for a stronger and more aggressive drive in
these same coalfields by the United Mineworkers of America.
Nonetheless, the Grundy County area was to remain a hotbed of
labor-management strife through the early 1960s.

THE GREAT WAR AND A BIG COMPANY TOWN

When distant European enemies broke out into open and armed
hostilities, the "Great War" took on a special meaning in the South.
The young industrial movement in Tennessee was affected in several
ways, but in no place was it affected more than on the 5000 acres at
Hadley's Bend on the Cumberland River, seven miles from Nashville.
The story of the E. I. DuPont Nemours Company coming to Middle
Tennessee in 1918 is one of the most phenomenal developments in all
of southern labor history. To discuss it in terms of a state labor movement eventually leads the outside observer to ask why no union was
ever started in the vast enterprise.

The demands of England, France, Belgium, Italy, and Russia for
powder and explosives with which to continue combat in the World
War had overtaxed their sources by 1916. The British Munitions Board
was already dependent upon the American DuPont munitions production. With the entry of the United States into the European war,

DuPont was called on for even greater production. Among the five projects initiated to meet this wartime need was the Old Hickory Munitions Project. In its complexity and speed of construction, the Old Hickory project surpassed any industrial venture which preceded it. At its peak the plant employed 50,000 workers and included a company town with housing facilities of all kinds for 30,000 workers in both management and labor.[29] The entire operation was built in nine months—a phenomenal achievement which was undergirded by both corporate opportunism and patriotic fervor.

In time, seven miles of railroad were laid to transport material to the work site. A 54-foot steel suspension bridge over the Cumberland River was built. Railway cars transported several thousand workers from Nashville daily. Miles of paved streets, sidewalks, water lines and sewers were laid. Some 1,112 buildings comprised the power plant itself.[30]

The U.S. Government had contracted with DuPont for the production of specific materials for wartime use. Sulfuric acid was being produced 67 days after groundbreaking and nitric acid 9 days later. Guncotton, the raw material of smokeless powder, was produced two weeks later and the first finished powder was granulated 116 days after the initiation of the project.[31]

There was an air of excitement throughout the Nashville community during the war days. The coming of the powder plant, it was believed, would provide a great stimulus for population and commercial growth of Nashville. "Watch us grow," boasted the *Nashville Tennessean* in January 1918:

> Many serious questions which have perplexed and concerned us as a city will now find satisfactory solution, if one and all, with cheerful, brave spirits, now dedicate themselves anew to the support of their country and incidental to this the commercial upbuilding of the city.[32]

Business and commercial leaders in Nashville rendered every service they could offer in order to support the project. Commuter train lines were established. "Jitney" buses ran between Nashville and Old Hickory. A wide range of support services were offered in Old Hickory. In turn, the Old Hickory project stimulated a boom in real estate values and a surge in sales at downtown stores, which soon offered special shopping hours to workers from Old Hickory.[33]

The impact of the DuPont powder plant on the Nashville labor scene was both immediate and significant. The plant needed laborers immediately. From the farms, stores, and households where they had toiled as farmers, clerks, and servants, people scurried to Old Hickory to apply for any one of a wide variety of jobs which paid more than they had previously earned. The powder plant was the scene of a social experiment as well. More than 10,000 women and 5,000 blacks found new job opportunities at Old Hickory, many of them moving into routine industrial work for the first time in their lives. One chronicler of Nashville history, Doyle, comments further:

> Along with the soldiers, these factory employees created a huge pool of mobile workers accustomed to working in large-scale, highly regimented organizations. Though local employers bemoaned the destabilization of the labor force at the time, the DuPont plant helped to create an indispensable ingredient to the industrial and clerical work force that would be required by Nashville's postwar economy.[34]

Through the experiences of one of the special services employees, social worker Lou Cretia Owen, insights into this grandiose social and labor experiment were gained. Owen kept a diary and, with access to a typewriter, recorded details on the human side of work and community life in Old Hickory during the early days. Throughout her personal chronicling, there was a sense of patriotic enthusiasm and pride permeating everything in which the workers were involved. Owen's diary opens on October 1, 1918: "Today I became one of the great army of war workers. My number is 3185. This number identifies me with the Women's Work Department of the Old Hickory Powder Plant near Nashville."[35] "Thrown into the midst of the drama here," Owen continues, "I feel that we are near to the war front. Men and women are making a fight to play their part in the war program."[36] The Star Spangled Banner was played regularly at work and the office force rose on cue. "Eyes glistened and heads bowed while outside the flag waved as we paid tribute to our country," Owen continued. "United we stand at Old Hickory behind the trenches to help win the war."[37]

Work could be relentless at the plant. Owen recorded that she reported for duty at 7:00 A.M. and, not being an hourly employee, would end her day anytime before midnight. ("We do not count hours here. Only those who check in their time do. . . . Sunday is the same as a week day here. Our work does not stop.")[38] Women wore uniforms, called "womanalls," made of a blouse and "knickers of khaki cloth" which were designed to keep from being caught by a machine. On call to check on a young woman injured in the sulfuric acid department, Owen passed through the gun cotton division and was impressed by what she saw:

> This is one of the most important sectors of the powder plant. The principal buildings of the gun cotton section include fourteen crude fibre houses, two mixing houses, seven drying buildings, nine nitration buildings, seven purification buildings, five acid storage houses, nine boiling tub houses and nine poacher houses.
>
> By the first of September 2000 men were employed on cotton production work in this division. Now there are more than 4000 employed in this section of the plant.
>
> Here the cotton is taken from its raw state and through the processes followed here is turned into a great explosive. First it must be purified, then boiled in a caustic solution under steam pressure for a certain time; the cotton is then bleached and goes to the drying buildings where it is treated with nitric and sulfuric acid.
>
> The cotton is carried to the nitrate building by telpherage, or a trolley on which a series of tanks are operated. From the nitrate building it is pumped to the boiling room tub houses and then again to the pulping house.
>
> There are forty-eight tubs in the boiling-tub house through which the cotton passes. Sometimes in cold water and sometimes in hot water. Girls stand by these tubs and watch the cotton when the times comes to press a lever and send it away as it reaches the proper temperature or has been there long enough. It required about forty-eight hours for the cotton to get through the boiling-tub house.
>
> From there it is sent to the pulping station and put through grinding machines and from here to the poacher house. Here it is washed and boiled for further purification and then sent to the final centrifugal wringers where a percentage of moisture is removed. This is the final stage for the gun cotton. From this point it goes to the dehydrating presses in the powder division.

> The guide assigned to our party refused to permit us to
> linger at any one place. This area is considered the most
> dangerous on the reservation. Men and women handle high
> explosives. They wear rubber gloves while working with
> the acid used in the purification process. They deny any fear
> of danger and stay by their machines, saying they are too
> busy to even think of an explosion.[39]

With such a diverse work force of displanted employees, little
wonder that the management was faced with a wide variety of social
problems. As expected, there were fatalities by death and serious
injury; report of the injuries was not widely circulated. DuPont
moved early to construct educational, recreational, and medical facilities in Old Hickory and maintain residential halls on a segregated
basis. Some 1,300 Hispanics were employed and they resided in the
Hispanic village; some were among the thirty who died the first
winter during the flu epidemic. Owen was charged with the responsibility of inspecting the living quarters for "single colored girls," and
"each girl without an assignment card was required to leave. We took
courage and a long jack knife." Logic and an appeal to patriotism was
effective with one female intruder:

> Speaking in the name of the DuPont Company, I explained
> that the housing facilities are inadequate and that we need
> all the space we have and appealed to her patriotism by
> playing square. She apoligized [sic]. The footsteps outside
> turned away.[40]

One day "the colorful life of the reservation brought two pleasure-
seeking girls from a western city," the diarist notes. "They arrived
without food or money thinking that this is a sort of El Dorado. . . . We
immediately wired their parents and advised them, that they are
here."[41] On another occasion, Owen recorded: "A man got his paycheck today and he celebrated the happy event by deserting his wife
and children. . . . He may be employed here under another name or
he may be gone to another industrial site. The woman is all broken up
and scared."[42]

When the Armistice was signed in November 1918, there was an
immediate sense of relief and elation felt in Old Hickory. The spontaneous celebration quickly turned into a hastily organized parade with

trucks made up as floats. Some workers went into the city to join a parade there. Within the following Armistice it began to dawn on the Old Hickory powder plant workers that they had also celebrated the abrupt end of the powder plant, their jobs, and the quickly gained surge of prosperity it had spawned in the Nashville community. Operations were shut down. Release notices began to be delivered immediately to the workers. Dormitories were closed. Staff members rode away. There was no certain promise of work in the future and many preferred not to linger until something positive developed. "This is the present DuPont is giving each employee on a wage. Salaried employees get a month's pay as a parting gift. It is rumored that most of the executives will be transferred to Wilmington or that the company is opening a plant in Cuba and send us there. We are just waiting."[43]

In one way the DuPont powder plant fit the pattern of other major industrial projects in the South of this era—eastern management had teamed with southern unskilled laborers. Many workers were fully aware of this reality and looked on this project as an "experiment in industry here."[44] On the other hand, there were some important differences in the DuPont-government project from other southern industrial enterprises which combined to deny unionism any chance to take root: (1) The project was conducted during wartime and many workers were proud simply to be a part of it; (2) Workers felt they were receiving relatively high wages and that the company was taking necessary measures to insure work safety; (3) The project was short-lived due to the end of the European war; (4) The work force was highly mixed by race, gender, and place of national origin; (5) A union movement in DuPont at this time would have been interpreted by some as subversive activity; (6) The DuPonts opposed labor unions.[45]

Actually, the DuPont plant in Old Hickory never produced any powder that was used in the war effort. The war was over before any powder manufactured in Tennessee made its way to the front for use. Critics of the DuPonts have called the Old Hickory project both a "fraud" and "an enormous waste and extravagant expenditure of public funds not in any way justified."[46]

Though much of the old company town was sold to private individuals, DuPont insured the survival of Old Hickory five years after the government had ordered the powder plant closed by announcing plans to renew manufacturing. This time the corporate giant planned to produce "artificial silk," or rayon, a product based in cellulose. The company was immediately successful in the 1920s.

CHILD LABOR IN TENNESSEE

Child labor in Tennessee and throughout the South during the late-nineteenth and early twentieth centuries was not an occasional abuse or a passing phenomenon. Children in Tennessee, not unlike children in other predominantly agricultural areas, have always been called on by their families to share in the strenuous work around the farm. The same has been true for women. When the industrialists moved into the post-war South, bringing with them their attitudes about cheap labor, they found it quite easy to hire large numbers of both women and children. By 1880 children comprised between 25 and 30 percent of the labor force in the tobacco industry of Virginia and North Carolina.[47] It was in the southern textile industry, however, where the greatest exploitation of female and child labor was made—women and children comprised approximately two-thirds of the labor force throughout the 1880s.[48] Nearly 60 percent of the children working in southern mills were between the ages of ten and thirteen; it was not uncommon to find children under the age of ten at work in the mills.[49]

The benefit to the employer for hiring women and children was obvious. Adult employees required a greater outlay for salaries. The new machines in the mill could be operated by both women and children. When two or more members of the same family worked in a factory, even if the father was unemployed, the family wage concept earned a family income which seemed astounding to the tenant farmer family. Already accustomed to hard work on the farm, the old southern agrarian tradition was moved indoors to the factory. Once inside what was often a poorly lit and poorly ventilated factory, the child laborer answered to a supervisor who was far less congenial than his farm boss and scurried to keep pace with a machine which could be an unrelenting taskmaster.[50] The employment of children in the mills and mines of Tennessee seems to have been parallel to that of other southern states. While young boys did enter the mountain shafts to help mine coal, usually for their father or other relative, most of the working children of Tennessee during the late-nineteenth and early twentieth centuries were found in textile mills. Tennessee and the South in general were not the first to face this vexing issue. The problem had appeared in the earliest manufacturing of the northern states and when industrial expansion moved south of the Mason-Dixon line the same issue rose again. At first there was little protest to child labor. The South was poverty-stricken and seized every opportunity to get on its feet. After the ignominious defeat of war, the great morality was for all able-bodied people, young and old, to go to work. "The use of children was not avarice, but philanthropy," moralizes Broadus Mitchell in 1921, "not exploitation, but generosity and cooperation and social-mindedness."[51]

Whatever the motivations for child labor, the children suffered. Children worked alongside adults for eleven and twelve hours a day, in some cases longer, often reporting to work before daylight and leaving after sunset. There were reports of night shifts for southern factories employing children. Mill children often dropped out of school, never to return; illiteracy among mill-village children was three to four times higher than among white children outside the textile mill culture.[52]

Tennessee was one of two states, Virginia being the other, to lead the way in achieving child labor reform. The situation in the Volunteer State was somewhat different from other southern states. For one thing, the state had less textile mills than did other southern states. In 1900 the rank of southern states according to the number of cotton mill employees was North Carolina, South Carolina, Georgia, Alabama, Virginia, Tennessee, and Mississippi. Tennessee and Virginia ranked as the southern states with the lowest proportion of children employed in mills.[53] State legislators find it easier to be bold against moneyed people when those interests have less to lose by reform legislation. Another, and perhaps more important, factor is tied to the reform-mindedness of the Tennessee labor movement. The union movement not only made solid gains in the state before it did in the deep South, especially in a few trade unions in the large cities, but the unions also began to call for child labor legislation from the General Assembly. In 1893 the legislature enacted a law prohibiting the employment of children under twelve years of age in mills, factories, mines, or workshops. The employer was allowed to ask the parent of a child employed for a sworn statement of his or her age. With each passing legislative session there were more and more calls to augment this legislation with higher standards and machinery for enforcement.

When the Tennessee Federation of Labor was organized, it moved to secure from both Republican and Democratic parties a pledge for child labor reform.[54] A new child labor law was passed with little opposition in 1901 as a direct result of the demands of organized labor. Under this bill, the age limit was raised to fourteen and false swearing on the part of parents about a child's age was declared to be

Child labor was a normal feature of the textile industry in Tennessee and throughout the South; here, a looper and raveler work in the Loudon Hosiery Mills. (Courtesy— Tennessee State Library and Archives)

investigatable and punishable as perjury. Seven years later provision was made for the gradual reduction of hours that would constitute a full week's work. In 1909 the Tennessee factory inspector was given full authority to enforce all provisions pertaining to the state's factories. These laws gave Tennessee the highest standard of child labor legislation of any southern state.[55]

Meantime, there was a great stirring among humanitarian groups throughout the country for additional child labor legislation within southern states. The cause was part and parcel of a larger reform era in which Protestant ministers, women's clubs, popular magazines, and various humanitarian groups whipped up fervor not only on the child labor issue, but also on women's rights, prohibition, pure food laws, reform of marriage and divorce laws, and corruption in big business and municipal government. By 1900 Samuel Gompers and the American Federation of Labor had campaigns for child labor legislation initiated in the Carolinas, Georgia, and Alabama—the states which employed more than 90 percent of the child labor in southern textiles.

Though the individual states were implored for legislative action, the child labor issue was seen by a growing number of citizens as a national problem. The argument that child labor was a national problem, that it involved the welfare of all the states in the Union, and that it would only be solved by both a nationwide protest of its evils and a united demand for legislation, originated with a young Alabama minister named Edgar Gardner Murphy. Murphy spoke eloquently on the national scope of the problem before the National Conference on Charities and Corrections in Atlanta. The result: a few months later, in October 1903, a successful move was made toward the formation of the National Child Labor Committee. Formal organization of the national committee took place on April 15, 1904, in New York City; among the distinguished southerners on the membership roll was James H. Kirkland, chancellor of Vanderbilt University.[56] Taking their cue from Murphy, the committee did not see child labor as the product of a mill owner who was a cruel and tyrannical barbarian; instead, the cruelty was a by-product of an impersonal system. Remedy for the evil would come not simply by more laws and inspectors, but by the majority of citizens feeling a personal responsibility for the welfare of all children.

The National Child Labor Committee paid little attention to Tennessee for several years. By comparison to other southern states, Tennessee seemed somewhat progressive. The first in a series of southern conferences on child labor was called to meet in Nashville in October 1907, by a resolution of the state legislature. The meeting, however, did not receive the support of manufacturers from other southern states. Chaired by L. D. Tyson of Knoxville, the president of a large woolen mill and a prominent politico, the conference adopted a number of resolutions calling for workplace reform. A second meeting of the "Southern Conference on Woman and Child Labor," as the organization came to be identified, was held in Memphis in 1910, with Governor Malcolm Patterson presiding; Georgia was the only large industrial state represented.[57]

By 1911 events occurred which put Tennessee, especially the textile mill region of east Tennessee, under greater scrutiny. Mary Alma Jackson, a child employed by the Weis-Lesh Manufacturing Company, had a finger cut off while working in the factory. A friend helped the youngster to seek damages. The plea and defense for the

company, a cotton mill, was that since the girl was under fourteen
years of age the manufacturer could not plead "contributory negligence." On June 20, 1910, Judge S. J. Everett of the Circuit Court
decided that the state's child labor law had been irregularly passed
and was, therefore, null and void.[58] A few months later a child worker
in a Knoxville mill attempted suicide. The claim was made that the
worker revealed a suicide pact which a number of the children in the
plant had made because of the long work hours expected of them.[59]
Also in 1911 the National Child Labor Committee issued a booklet
entitled "Child Labor in Tennessee." With a text by A. J. McKelway,
the booklet contains 21 photographs taken the year before of
Tennessee children working or in group poses mainly in hosiery and
spinning mills. "Tennessee furnishes an example of a fairly good child
labor law whose enforcement has been absolutely neglected," the
booklet begins. McKelway reports:

> Only a few boys were found to be employed in the coal
> mines, after a searching investigation. . . . But in the cotton
> mills, and especially the knitting and hosiery mills, great
> numbers of children were found to be employed, and the
> pictures themselves show how small many of them are, far
> too young and small to be employed the long hours of the
> cotton mills. The woolen mills were found to be almost free
> from the employment of children under fourteen. Nor were
> children found in the phosphate mines of Tennessee, as they
> are in some other localities.[60]

The night messenger service was also one of the major concerns
of McKelway and the national committee. Investigating the night
messenger service in Tennessee's four major cities, the committee
discovered conditions identical to those in other large cities of the
North and South:

> The demoralizing nature of this service can be stated in a
> single sentence, namely, that the majority of the calls for mes-
> senger boys, after nine or ten o'clock at night, are to the resorts
> of the under-world. The boys are employed by the patrons
> and inmates of disorderly houses, are the purveyors of
> whiskey, opium and cocaine, and in this employment grow
> familiar with every form of vice, including some excesses
> mentioned in the annals of paganism. The general character of
> the work by day is totally changed in the later hours of the
> night when the forces of immorality and crime hold sway.[61]

The author proceeded to cite several cases of adolescent boys, omitting their names and the names of the messenger services, who knew the ways and means of Tennessee's big city underworld. In another issue of the *Child Labor Bulletin*, special committee agent Edward Brown lamented his discoveries in Tennessee:

> In Memphis I met a boy who at nineteen years had drifted from a night messenger to a companion of street women. At nineteen he had become a confirmed opium user. To show me how freely a night messenger circulates in the criminal groups of the underworld he brought to me a quantity of opium, which among other exhibits, is now on file in the office of the national Child Labor Committee.
>
> But usually the night messenger in the South is younger than the lad who at nineteen became a vile master and a drug fiend. In Memphis a fifteen-year-old night messenger whom I met had in his pocket a box of cocaine he was about to deliver to an inmate of a house of ill fame. "I get it for them from ten to fifteen times a night," he boasted. In delivering telegrams and notes and contraband articles to these women, the night messenger is frequently permitted to go directly to the private room of the courtesan. The stories these boys tell of the debauches they witness are of such a nature that they can neither be written or spoken, with propriety.[62]

Gradually the state legislature took reform steps which served to give more protection to women and children. In 1913 a gradual reduction of hours to 57 per week (by January 1915) was mandated for children under sixteen years of age and for women, but a 10 1/2-hour day was allowed rather than a ten-hour day.[63] In 1917, when the first federal child labor law was about to become effective, the Tennessee law was amended at several sections to meet its requirements. An eight-hour work day and six-day week, with prohibitions of night work, were provided for children under sixteen; documentary evidence was required for the issuance of an employment certificate; and canneries were added to the list of industries forbidden to offer work to children.[64] Despite the fact that Tennessee joined the ranks of states whose statutes were acceptable to federal standards by the 1920s, the vexing issue of child labor in industrial factories and mines would not easily go away.

A UNION IS BORN IN NASHVILLE

Many miles from the industrial centers of the northeast and mid-west, and hardly the center of trade union activity, the state capital of Tennessee is not a place one would expect a major union battle to be fought or for a new union to be organized. The unlikely turn of events, flavored by an interesting romantic twist, occurred in October 1914, when the delegates to the eighteenth convention of the United Garment Workers convened in Nashville. The *Nashville Tennessean* has rarely been more wrong about labor events than when it remarked in an advance story: "Apparently harmonious in all things, this gathering of toilers from the United States and Canada inaugurates its biennial convention under the most auspicious circumstances."[65]

Recognizing that unrest had developed among UGWA members in New York and Chicago, national officers carefully selected Nashville for the site of the convention. The capital city was considered to be quite convenient for the (generally native-born) delegates from the shirt and overall "labor shops" in upstate New York and the midwestern cities, but was served by rather awkward train connections from New York City. Many of the delegates would not bother to come to Nashville, union president Thomas Rickert and other officials apparently reasoned, and the convention would be much easier to control.

The delegates from New York and other eastern cities were not to be denied their say. The issue was that of representation, with New York garment workers insisting that they were not given an equal voice. The dissenters, calling themselves "progressives," were supported by the delegates from Chicago which represented 10,000 members. There were also "progressives" from Baltimore and Boston. To the dismay of UGWA leadership, the Chicago delegation had already made its plans to be in Nashville and take action. In a letter to union members signed by Frank Rosenblum, Anzuino Marimpietri, and H. Schneid, a sense of urgency was felt: "We in Chicago recognize that there is something radically wrong in the management of our international organization, and we desire to cooperate with delegates of New York and other cities who are of the same opinion. We would like to be informed of all movements along those lines so that when we meet in Nashville . . . we will be able to work together much better. . . ."[66] Before the convention opened, the delegates had arrived in Nashville and had begun huddling to prepare their own measures and strategies. The official headquarters for the union was the Tulane Hotel. The Chicago group was registered at the Duncan Hotel. The atmosphere was already tense.

The birth pangs of a new union began to be felt unmistakably when the United Garment Workers convention opened on Monday morning, October 12, 1914, in the House chanber of the State Capitol. A Protestant preacher opened the proceedings with an invocation of the spirit of the Good Samaritan and the brotherhood of all man, but, alas, his pious request apparently had little impact on the divided body of 305 delegates who had come to be seated. After the preliminaries, the first order of business was the seating of the delegates. Frank Rosenblum of the Chicago delegation and parliamentary leader of the "progressives" asked Chairman Rickert if the report of the credentials committee was complete. Rickert replied that it was not, but allowed that it was permissible for 198 of the 305 delegates, representing approved locals, to be seated. At this point the meeting adjourned.

The following day the New Yorkers sat in the gallery while their allies from Chicago took the floor to challenge the union's leadership. There were 107 delegates in all—representing cutters' and tailors' locals in New York, Boston, Rochester, Philadelphia, Baltimore, and Cincinnati—whose status had not been certified. They had been physically barred from the floor. The scene was near pandemonium. Rosenblum addressed the chair and raised a point of order, declaring that the convention was not legally organized inasmuch as there were delegates whose credentials had neither been granted nor disposed of. When Chairman Rickert ruled that the point of order was rejected, Rosenblum jumped to his feet, spun around, and addressed himself to the unseated delegates in the galleries. Calling for a true vote on his motion, the Chicagoan was reinforced with a mighty shout of acclamation from the excluded delegates.[67]

The proceedings continued with fervent determination that at least some business should be accomplished. The tension in the air had turned to hostility and open verbal warfare. One by one, leaders of the Chicago delegation stood before the hostile delegates and appealed for justice and fair play for those whose credentials had been denied. Threats of violence were shouted. Gesticulating toward the gallery, Rosenblum cried out: "These people are here to express the rights and aspirations of the workers who have elected them." One of the fieriest speeches was an appeal by an attractive, diminutive brunette from Chicago, Bessie Abramowitz.

Repeated motions by Rosenblum and his associates were declared "passed" by the gallery faction. One motion called for the removal of Chairman Rickert. A final motion gained the approval of the unseated delegates—a call for all "lawful" delegates to abandon a convention

hall which had been seized and controlled by a minority and to retreat
to the Duncan Hotel (at Fourth and Cedar, now Charlotte) and conduct
a "regular" convention. The excluded delegates and their Chicago
allies, some 130 people in all, marched out of the hall. Perhaps unknow-
ingly, the first step toward forming a new union had been made.

For the bolting garment workers, there was no turning back. They
had not been welcome or wanted by the mainline union leadership
which, in their view, did not truly represent their brothers and sisters
toiling and sweating in the garment shops back home. Now, in a rump
session, they could begin the "real work" of the United Garment
Workers. Thus they moved to establish in a quiet and congenial atmosphere their own agenda and to elect their own officers. The delegates
to the rump convention, as it was called, discovered that they actually
spoke for nearly three-fourths of the union's membership, a work force
which had been deprived of its democratic rights by the union bosses
holding forth in the capitol chamber. Now imbued with a spirit of
responsibility, the "progressives" pledged to organize a quarter of a
million garment workers and to work toward eliminating the old petty
divisions over crafts or departments in their trade.[68]

On the hill, meantime, it was business as usual. The discredited
UGWA officers declined to discuss with observers the action of the
"bolting delegations" and proceeded as though nothing out of the
ordinary had occurred. From gavel to gavel, business flowed
smoothly among the remaining delegates. The main order of business
seemed to be a successful vote to raise the annual salary of the
national president and secretary by a whopping $1500 each, with the
newsman covering the convention reporting "a marked disposition to
make the increase considerably more."[69]

Down at the Duncan Hotel there were matters to discuss which
were more pressing than officer salaries, namely, finding a capable
leader for the union. The issue was raised officially on the following
morning (Wednesday), though it had been thoroughly discussed in
informal caucus groups the night before. There was strong sentiment
for Joseph Schlossberg, leader of the New York delegation. Frank
Rosenblum had won much support for his valiant floor fight prior to
the walkout. The courageous and energetic Chicago delegate, Bessie
Abramowitz, cornered Jacob Panken of the New York delegation and
urged him to vote for a 27-year-old Eastern Jewish immigrant who
arrived in the United States in 1907 named Sidney Hillman.[70]
Hillman, though thin and slight of stature, had carried himself with a

natural dignity while working as a pants-cutter in the New York garment district and then on to Chicago to work for Hart, Schaffner and Marx. As a solid union man, Hillman had won the respect and admiration of the Chicago group. Regarded as a moderate, Hillman had remained aloof from the fracas in Nashville. After urgent telegrams from union friends, Hillman responded affirmatively to their draft; he was then nominated unanimously, with Schlossbert elected to the post of general secretary of the insurgent organization.[71]

The old guard leadership next had the unenviable task of informing the general membership of what happened in Nashville. The headline on the official paper of the UGWA proclaimed: "Convention Unanimously Decides that Delegates from Rump Convention Have No Valid Claim to Represent the United Garment Workers of America—Legal Representatives Chosen at Nashville All Seated."[72] The story of the Nashville meeting closed tersely: "The motion to adopt the report of the Committee on Credentials was carried by unanimous vote."[73] A fuller report appeared in the next two issues of the *Garment Worker*: "The efforts that were made to bring discord into the convention proved a failure, and following the departure from the hall of the bolting delegations, good feeling and unity prevailed."[74] The action of the seceding delegates was "prearranged" and dictated by "the rule or ruin policy of the New York Forward" which sought through "duplicity and dishonesty" to "gain control of the administration of the United Garment Workers."[75]

The battle continued long after the Nashville split. The secessionists had assumed the name of "New United Garment Workers," but the old leaders counseled any who would listen that the new union was an unlawful organization. Hillman, destined to become a great union leader, then turned his energies toward gaining AFL recognition for the new movement. His efforts were not successful, flying in the face of Gompers' long-standing abhorrence of "dual unionism." Mainline AFL leaders compared the action of Hillman and his associates to the secession of the southern states in 1861, when they were unwilling to abide by the decision of the majority on the issue of slavery.

Eventually, from the canyon of organizational division there may emerge the flowers of strength and solidarity. Hillman's group, having been aided by Clarence Darrow, agreed to change its name. A true founding convention was held in New York on December 26, 1914. The new constitution was to be thoroughly democratic. The founding document was adopted by delegates from 68 locals in the

U.S. and Canada, representing about 40,000 workers in the clothing trade. Article One proclaimed: "This body shall be known as the Amalgamated Clothing Workers of America," thus symbolizing the idea that various crafts, various local unions, and various national and language groups were to be brought together in common cause in one mass organization.[76]

Upon Amalgamated's fiftieth anniversary, this union, whose history had been a curious blend of combat and compatibility, had reached a high plateau in strength. The vigorous and resourceful Hillman had become an organizer of the CIO and as a New Deal figure was referred to as the "statesman of American labor." His successor, Jacob Potofsky, a Chicagoan who at age 14 began sewing pockets in trousers at five and one-half cents a pair for Hart, Schaffner, and Marx shortly after immigrating from Russia, had led the ACWA to even greater strength. As the clothing manufacturers from the North had moved into Dixie—attracted by nonunion labor, cheap electrical power and offers of free plants and tax benefits from communities eager for industry to replace a diminishing agriculture—they were dogged by a courageous union prepared to organize and

A boiler being hauled by six-mule team in Campbell County, 1900. (Courtesy—Tennessee State Library and Archives)

service the clothing workers. By 1964 the ACWA represented 97 percent of the workers in men's apparel; with 5,000 members in Mississippi, it was the strongest union in the Delta State.[77]

From 1891 until 1984 the United Garment Workers maintained their central office in New York City. In 1984 the UGW, in the only move of this kind, relocated its headquarters to Nashville.

LABOR LEGISLATION

Tennessee's constitutions of 1796 and 1834 contained little that directly affected labor. Only two articles in the bill of rights—one prohibiting the imprisonment of debtors except in the case of proven fraud and the other declaring monopolies to be "contrary to the genius of a free state"—remotely touched on the subject. An 1803 act gave the laborer one day of rest in a week; this prohibition of work on Sunday was passed on the grounds of moralism and piety and not primarily out of consideration of workers' needs.[78]

Since the Reconstruction era, Tennessee has passed its share of labor legislation. The first law which directly influenced organized labor was passed in 1875; it limited the conditions under which a worker might enter a contract.[79] The first child labor law was on the books in 1893 and, as noted, the law was stiffened to offer more protection to children as Tennessee industrialism moved into the twentieth century. Mining regulations were passed as early as 1881 which placed restrictions on slopes, safety lamps, inspection and washrooms. Before World War I a number of company abuses had been prohibited by law in Tennessee: the garnishment of wages to secure payment of debt; confiscation of a worker's possessions or certain of his tools; the misrepresentation of wages by a prospective employer; irregular paydays; false advertising for the purpose of getting labor; and to hire knowingly the employee who is under contract to someone else. The 1923 amendment of the Workmen's Compensation Law passed in 1911 was considered by labor leaders as "the greatest stride made by Tennessee during the post-war prosperity period."[80]

The Tennessee Department of Labor was created during an administrative reorganization in 1923. Prior to 1923 the state's labor legislation had been administered by a hodgepodge of agents—the state geologist of the Bureau of Agriculture, Statistics, and Mines inspected all coal mines at least once each six months; the Bureau of Labor and

Mining Statistics (established in 1891) assumed the duty of mine inspection; the state factory inspector (first authorized in 1899) and superseded by the Department of Workshop and Factory Inspection (in 1913).[81] In the original structure of the Department of Labor, four divisions were created to administer various laws: (1) Division of Mines; (2) Division of Factory Inspection; (3) Division of Fire Protection; (4) Division of Workmen's Compensation. The office of the Commissioner is filled by an appointee of the governor.[82]

THE FOUNDING OF A FEDERATION

Toward the turn of the century, with labor leaders turning their attention increasingly toward their respective state legislatures in an effort to remedy social ills, organized labor began uniting at the state level. The first state federation was established in New York in 1865 and, although a few others followed in the 1870s and 1880s, most of the permanent organizations were formed in the 1890s and early 1900s. Samuel Gompers appeared in Nashville in 1895 while traveling in the interest of the United Garment Workers and delivered an address entitled "Organized Labor, the Savior of the Republic."[83] Coincidentally, the following year labor in the state established its own organization.

Labor leaders had been none too swift in establishing their federation. Effort at organization at the state level was made in the early 1880s at a meeting in Chattanooga, but there was insufficient interest by local unions.[84] Tennessee continued to lag behind other states, though state labor leaders had been involved in the Southern Labor Congress.[85] By 1892 the parent American Federation of Labor, which constitutionally allowed and encouraged state and territorial bodies, had already issued charters to state federations in 32 states.[86] It was on September 7, 1896, that eighteen men who shared a common commitment to organized labor gathered in the state senate chamber of the Tennessee state capitol and established the Tennessee Federation of Labor.[87]

The driving force behind the establishment was a young man who worked at the old Nashville *American* as a printer and for twenty years worked as an organizer for the International Typographical Union. Nashvillian Albert E. Hill (1870-1933) was a printer, writer, unionist, civic reform leader, and state legislator. In 1892 he founded the *Journal of Labor*, which later became the *Labor Advocate*, a paper edited and published by Hill for 41 years. Hill learned about union affairs at the local level through his involvement in the Nashville Typographical Union No. 20, which he served as president for eighteen consecutive years. He was the last surviving charter member of the old Nashville Trades and Labor Council, established in 1895. As a spokesman both for the labor movement and public education, Hill was elected to the state legislature, where he became speaker of the senate (equivalent to lieutenant governor). Through the pages of the *Labor Advocate*, Hill issued a persuasive call for the founding of the Tennessee Federation of Labor [TFL].[88]

State labor federations were founded to serve two basic functions: the first was organization of workers, conducted with the cooperation of the appropriate craft or international union; the second was securing legislation favorable to the interests of organized labor. The Tennessee Federation of Labor was thus destined to become unashamedly a political agency, lobbying for legislation and working for the election of friendly officials. Though Tennessee had never been known as a state with progressive social legislation, the TFL by the mid-twenties could cite all of the state's labor legislation except early mechanics lien laws to its credit. That credit could be shared by an increased number of sympathetic legislators (sometimes union men or sympathetic farm representatives) who listened to labor's call for reform.

The Tennessee Federation of Labor promulgated a platform with the organization's basic philosophy and doctrine declared in fourteen planks. The preamble stated that the TFL "aims to secure the emancipation of the laborer from the bonds of wage slavery," but it conceded "that this object can be obtained only after years of patient effort and perfect education of the working masses."[89] The constitution called for one meeting annually. Each local union was entitled to one delegate while city central bodies were awarded three delegates each. Provision was made for at least ten committees to consider the work of the organization. The income of the Federation was derived from a per capita assessment on affiliated union membership. In the early years the tax was so low that at times the treasury was so depleted that the Federation feared to embark on new projects. The principal officers were a president and secretary-treasurer. Most of the leaders who were active in the Tennessee Federation were also connected with and active in an international union or a city central union, usually in fully paid capacities. This economically practicable arrangement assured the state body of leadership would be adequately experienced in the work world and fully conversant with the day's labor issues.[90]

Since its existence, the fortunes of the Tennessee Federation of Labor have closely paralleled the bigger picture of U.S. labor-management relations. Just as organized labor in the nation as a whole exhibited strength and optimism toward the end of World War I, so likewise did the Tennessee Federation; hence, TFL president John O'Connor of Knoxville could declare in 1919 to the convention that "the past year has been one of the most successful in the history of the Federation."[91] On the other hand, by the end of the 1920s and through the early 1930s, organized labor touched a low ebb in power and spirit, both throughout the nation and throughout Tennessee.

By the end of 1928 the Tennessee labor movement appeared positioned for great growth. The seeds of unionism had been planted across the breadth of the state and despite the categorical opposition of industrial leaders and the overall indifference about unionism by the general public, viable union locals had been established. While low wages and hideous working conditions were pervasive in some occupations, there was guarded optimism about what the future could hold for labor. What labor leaders did not know was that their fortunes would soon become much worse before they would get better.

NOTES

1. *The WPA Guide to Tennessee,* written and compiled by the Federal Writers Project of the Works Projects Administration (a reprint of the 1939 Viking Press edition; Knoxville: University of Tennessee Press, 1986), p. 81.

2. Ibid., p. 66.

3. Ibid.

4. Ibid.

5. Ibid.

6. Killebrew, a state officeholder and promoter of industrialism, published in 1873 *The Dignity and Necessity of Labor.* Claiming that "a great mass of our intelligent citizens of the South are laboring not to labor . . . wasting their time . . . emasculating their mental capacities" on already crowded professional tracts, the author counseled a solution in the industrial movement. "How much nobler and how much grander would those young men appear directing the movement of machinery, in building furnaces to smelt our ores and mills to roll our iron; in twirling the spindle and urging the shuttle."

7. Cf. Constantine G. Belissary, "Behaviour Patterns and Aspirations of the Urban Working Classes of Tennessee in the Immediate Post-Civil War Era," *Tennessee Historical Quarterly,* Vol. XIV (1955), 24-29; also, Robert Corlew, *Tennessee: A Short History,* 2nd ed. (Knoxville: University of Tennessee Press, 1981), 364-65.

8. Federal Writers Project, *Guide to Tennessee,* p. 67.

9. Ibid.

10. Corlew, *Tennessee,* p. 365. In *Tennessee: Its Resources, Capabilities, Development* (Nashville: State Department of Agriculture, 1893), Commissioner D. C. Godwin reported that the state had altogether 26 furnaces, with a total capacity of producing 12,803 tons of pig-iron per day; of these furnaces, twelve used charcoal as a fuel and fourteen used coke.

11. Corlew, *Tennessee,* p. 365.

12. Gilbert E. Govan and James W. Livingood, *The Chattanooga Country,* 1540-1976 (3rd ed.; Knoxville: University of Tennessee Press, 1972), pp. 344-50.

13. Ibid., pp. 295-96; William H. Moore, "Preoccupied Paternalism: The Roane Iron Company in Her Company Town—Rockwood, Tennessee," East Tennessee Historical Society's *Publications,* vol. 39 (1967), 56-57.

14. Moore, "Preoccupied Paternalism," 59.

15. Ibid., 60.

16. Govan and Livingood, *Chattanooga Country,* 298.

17. Quoted in Corlew, *Tennessee,* 366.

18. Govan and Livingood, *Chattanooga Country,* 351.

19. Moore, "Preoccupied Paternalism," 67.

20. Melton A. McLaurin, *Knights of Labor in the South* (Westport, Conn.: Greenwood Press, 1978), 38-39; F. Ray Marshall, *Labor in the South* (Cambridge: Harvard University Press, 1957), 21-22; Thomas R. Brooks, *Toil and Trouble,* 2nd ed. (New York: Dell Publishing Co., 1971), 57-59.

21. James Dombrowski, "Early History of Grundy County" (unpublished paper, Highlander Collection, Tennessee State Library and Archives).

22. Katherine B. Hoskins, "Miners Formed Locals in 1873, Joined Knights of Labor," feature story in *Clinton Courier-News,* March 17, 1977.

23. James L. Nicholson, *Grundy Country* (Memphis: Memphis State University Press, 1982), 66. See also William Ray Turner, "A History of Early Mining in Tracy City" in special issue of *Grundy County Herald*, Sept. 2, 1976.

24. Ibid., 67; Archie Green, *Only a Miner* (Urbana: University of Illinois Press, 1972), 212.

25. Dombrowski, "Early History of Grundy County," 5-6.

26. This depiction of early coal mining in Grundy County is based on a personal interview with William Ray Turner, Grundy County historian, Tracy City, Tennessee, November 28, 1987.

27. Dombrowski, "Early History of Grundy County," 6.

28. Ibid.

29. *Tennessean*, May 4, 1988.

30. Jack Norman, Sr., *The Nashville I Knew* (Nashville: Rutledge Hill Press, 1984), 48.

31. Ibid.

32. Quoted in Don H. Doyle, *Nashville in the New South, 1880-1930* (Knoxville: University of Tennessee Press, 1985), 188.

33. Ibid. The story of the community of Old Hickory is told well in Margaret Marie Tootle, "A History of Old Hickory, Tennessee" (M. E. thesis, George Peabody College for Teachers, 1953).

34. Doyle, *Nashville in the New South*, 189.

35. Lou Cretia Owen's *Diary*, Oct. 1, 1918-Jan. 25, 1919 (Tennessee State Library and Archives), p. 1.

36. Ibid., 3.

37. Ibid., 5.

38. Ibid., 8.

39. Ibid., 44-45.

40. Ibid., 68.

41. Ibid., 16.

42. Ibid., 96.

43. Ibid., 105.

44. Ibid., 17.

45. One critic of the DuPont empire stated: "DuPont workers were not protected by labor unions, and for a very good reason: the DuPonts did not allow unions. Nor did they allow strikes. Both were considered 'un-American' and both DuPont prohibitions were backed up by the full force of federal law (the Espionage Law of 1917 and the Violent Sedition Act of 1918) and armed troops. To keep their workers intimidated, the DuPonts hired a 1,400 man private police force trained by the former police commissioner of Washington, D. C." Gerald Colby Zilg, *DuPont: Behind the Nylon Curtain* (Englewood Cliffs, N. J.: Prentice-Hall, 1974), 163.

46. Ibid., 166.

47. McLaurin, *Knights of Labor in the South*, 15.

48. Ibid., 16.

49. C. Vann Woodward, *Origins of the New South, 1877-1913* (Baton Rouge: Louisiana State University Press, 1971), 416. A helpful summary of the southern child labor issue may be found in Henry D. Shapiro, *Appalachian On Our Mind* (Chapel Hill: University of North Carolina Press, 1978), 104-81.

50. McLaurin, *Knights of Labor in the South*, 16.

51. Broadus Mitchell, *The Rise of Cotton Mills in the South* (Gloucester, Mass.: Peter Smith, 1966 reprint of the 1921 Johns Hopkins Press edition), 95.

52. Woodward, *Origins of the New South*, 417.

53. From the U.S. Department of Labor statistics and reported in Elizabeth H. Davidson, *Child Labor legislation in the Southern Textile States* (Chapel Hill: University of North Carolina Press, 1939), 238.

54. Ibid., 242.

55. Ibid., 242-43; Child Labor Bulletin, vol. 2, no. 3 (Nov. 1913), 16-17.

56. Davidson, *Child Labor Legislation*, 122-24.

57. Ibid., 145-46.

58. A. J. McKelway, *Child Labor in Tennessee* (National Child Labor Committee, 1911), 5.

59. Davidson, *Child Labor Legislation*, 243.

60. McKelway, *Child Labor in Tennessee*, 11-12.

61. Ibid., 14.

62. Edward F. Brown, "The Demoralizing Environment of Night Messengers in South Cities," *Child Labor Bulletin*, vol. 2, no 1 (May 1913), 139.

63. Davidson, *Child Labor Legislation*, 243; *Child Labor Bulletin*, vol. 2, no. 3 (Nov. 1913), 16.

64. Davidson, *Child Labor Legislation*, 243-44.

65. From story by Rob Elder, *Tennessean* news clipping, n.d., in Eula McGill ms.

66. Quoted in Matthew Josephson, *Signey Hillman: Statesman of American Labor* (Garden City, N.Y.: Doubleday and Co., 1952), 94. A good part of the narrative is drawn from this source.

67. Ibid., 96.

68. Ibid., 97-98.

69. Elder's article in *Tennessean* news clipping.

70. Panken long after the Nashville meeting reminded Bessie Hillman of the part she played in this selection: "I remember that night in Nashville, Tennessee, thirty-two years ago, when you walked me up and down the streets of the city arguing that Sidney was the only logical person to be president of the Amalgamated. I did not know him as well as you did, but I deferred to your judgement. I am glad that I did." Quoted in Josephson, *Sidney Hillman*, 99.

71. Ibid., 98-100.

72. *The Garment Worker*, vol. 14, no. 4 (Nov. 13, 1914), 1.

73. Ibid.

74. *The Garment Worker*, vol. 14, no. 1 (Oct. 23, 1914), 1.

75. Ibid.; and *The Garment Worker*, vol. 14, no. 2 (Oct. 30, 1914), 1.

76. Josephson, *Sidney Hillman*, 107-08.

77. Myron Feinsilber, "Union Looks to Dixie," *Atlanta Journal and Constitution*, Feb. 4, 1964.

78. Federal Writers Project, *Guide to Tennessee*, 87.

79. Ibid.

80. Federal Writers Project, *Guide to Tennessee*, 88; Brown, *Development of Labor Legislation in Tennessee*, 15-26.

81. J. Fred Holly and Bevars D. Mabry, *Protective Labor Legislation and Its Administration in Tennessee* (Knoxville: University of Tennessee Press, 1955), 96.

82. Ibid.

83. Report of Gompers' visit to Nashville at a meeting presided over by Mayor Guild as well as the text of the speech are published in *The Garment Worker*, July 1895, 9-10.

84. Shirley Ayer, "Labor is the Community: An Historical Sketch of the Workingman in Memphis, Tennessee, 1827-First World War," an unpublished and undated manuscript in Memphis Labor Council Mss., Special Collections, Southern Labor Archives, Georgia State University.

85. The Southern Labor Congress, organized about 1910, gained respectable membership among fourteen southern states and worked "to bring about a closer cooperation between all the different southern states" for an education campaign which would lead to "uniform legislation" and "to discuss ways laws in the interest of working people may be enacted and those inimical to our interest defeated." *Labor Advocate*, July 30, 1915. The fourth annual convention of the SLC was held in Chattanooga (Patton Hotel in 1915) and the fifth annual convention was held in Memphis (Peabody Hotel).

86. James A. Hodges, "The Tennessee Federation of Labor, 1919-1939" (M.A. thesis, Vanderbilt University, 1959), 1.

87. Ibid.

88. Biographical information on Hill is drawn from news stories and tributes published in Nashville *Labor Advocate*, beginning with the January 26, 1933, issue.

89. Quoted in Hodges, "The Tennessee Federation of Labor," 13; by the late thirties the term "working masses" was changed to "wage earners."

90. Ibid., 14-18.

91. Quoted in ibid., 20.

3

Convict Labor and Miner Insurrection

Anderson and Grundy Miners' Campaign
Against the System

My song is founded on the truth,
In poverty we stand.
How hard the millionaire will crush
Upon the laboring man.
The miner's toiling under ground
To earn his daily bread;
To clothe his wife and children
And see that they are fed.

I am in sympathy with the miners,
As everyone should be.
In other states they work free labor,
And why not Tennessee?
The miners true and generous
In many works and ways,
We all should treat them kindly,
Their platform we should praise.

From the ballad, "Coal Creek Troubles"

Lake City is a fairly new appellation for the community which was for many years called Coal Creek. After a lake was formed behind the Tennessee Valley Authority's Norris Dam in 1936, Coal Creek renamed itself Lake City. Coal Creek was even a more appropriate name for this community in the latter part of the nineteenth century. Originally a mountain stream on whose banks the settlers once built their cabins, Coal Creek became a part of that mountainous corridor known as the Cumberland Plateau in which black mineral was discovered and mined.

A century has passed since the citizens of Anderson County were embroiled in a controversy which went beyond community borders to shake the legislative and political powers in Nashville and around the state. The Coal Creek Rebellion, as the controversy is usually referred to, was nothing less than a working class uprising against upper class management and politicians. Despite the fact that the Coal Creek story is seldom mentioned in most histories of the American labor movement (and many Tennesseans have never heard the story), it is undoubtedly the best known labor story of nineteenth-century Tennessee and one of the most dramatic and significant episodes in all American labor history.

The miners and their families, state prison inmates, coal company owners and operators, the governor and state legislators all played their roles in this intense struggle. The two years or so of Coal Creek wars had been but the climax of some 25 years of suffering and struggle. For the miners, the coal wars had been a struggle for elemental rights. Yet when the struggle had ended, the miners had been victorious in arousing public sentiment on behalf of their plight, in gaining a new measure of respect as laborers, and most of all, in ridding themselves of the yoke of unfair competition on the job market and their home state of the blight of pernicious convict lease system. By their action, the Tennessee miners, along with the workers in the mines and foundries of Virginia, Alabama, and Georgia, served notice in the 1890s that southern labor was not willing to accept the Old-South labor philosophy of the New-South leaders—not without a fierce fight anyway.[1]

THE SETTLEMENT OF COAL CREEK

In 1853 Coal Creek had one log house. By 1880 it had a population of 3000, making it a larger community than the county seat of Clinton. Farming, hunting and fishing, and cattle raising prevailed among Coal Creek residents during the early frontier years. Like the rest of east Tennessee, Anderson countians found life disrupted by the Civil War and their loyalty was divided between Jefferson Davis and Abraham Lincoln.[2]

Desultory mining on the Cumberland Plateau began in Roane County in 1814. In the 1830s east Tennessee coal was shipped by river as far away as New Orleans. By the 1850s railroads had begun to lay their lines into the mountains. Coal mining then became a major Tennessee industry.

Short-line railroads penetrated Coal Creek to the mines where the coal was loaded. The first rail car of coal was shipped out of Coal Creek in October 1867 by the Knoxville Iron Company, before the company was incorporated. By 1871 the Knoxville Iron Company had opened a mine which employed fifty men and shipped, in its first year, some 2000 tons of coal to Knoxville for rolling mill and related processes. Despite the fact that Coal Creek seemed to be just another rural Appalachian community, isolated by woods and streams, mining had turned it into an industrial boom town.[3]

The 1870s were boom years for Anderson County. By 1873 the Knoxville Iron company had leased land at Coal Creek and was shipping about ten cars a day out of the mines, each car containing ten tons of coal. That same year the Black Diamond Coal Company began operations in Coal Creek. The Coal Creek Mining and Manufacturing Company began leasing land in Anderson and some adjoining counties in 1872 to various coal mining companies or to individuals by the year. The leasing party could farm or raise cattle, with liberty to dig coal for domestic use of tenants so long as there was no interference with other tenants or agents. The earliest residents of Coal Creek came largely from Virginia and the Carolinas, but in the boom years Anderson County attracted some black as well as European immigrant miners; many experienced miners had come to the area from Wales. During 1875 more than 60,000 tons of coal were shipped from the district. In the decades 1880-1900 Anderson County led Tennessee in coal production.[4]

From the early days of working the mines, the Coal Creek miners felt the need for organization of some kind. On September 15, 1873, a group of the miners petitioned Judge O. P. Temple, presiding in Chancery Court in Clinton, for a charter to incorporate a trade organization of a benevolent and charitable character. This was granted under Tennessee law on December 3, 1873, and the organization was named the Miners, Mechanics and Laborers Benevolent Association of Tennessee. Little is known about this early union. One of its aims was "to go on in the path of progress until all who are our brother laborers among the coal mines may be benefitted thereby."[5] It was not until the 1880s that the Knights of Labor began to organize lodges in Anderson County. The period of 1903-1904 was the time of the big drive by the United Mine Workers of America for solid union organization in the

Coal Creek fields. At the time of the big Coal Creek rebellion against convict labor there was no solid union camp in the area. No one would challenge the fact, however, that the miners were solidly unified by common sentiment and the vicissitudes of life in the coal camps.

Coal interests permeated every aspect of life around Coal Creek. Some 21 commissaries or "company stores" were operated in Anderson County during the 1880s and 1890s.[6] Each company issued its own scrip enabling the miners to receive credit against their wages between paydays. Life was not easy in the coal camps. Miners and their families continually faced poverty and hunger as they eked out a meager existence.

ENTER CONVICT LABORERS

The post-Civil War South was faced with numerous problems. One vexing problem the Southern states faced was what to do with their prisoners. While Tennessee had made considerable progress in penal reform before the war, the war disrupted social and economic progress and left the state with an enormous debt. After the war there was a significant increase in the prison population, mainly among the freed blacks who were often displaced, unemployed, and ignorant of the white person's rules. Stiff penalties for petty crime were enforced rigidly against black men. Blacks, who before the war seldom composed more than five percent of the prison population, made up more than half of all inmates by 1866.[7]

Prisons were dilapidated. Overcrowding was increasing. Operational expenses were rising. Racial prejudice remained part and parcel of the Southern mind. Little wonder that the prevailing belief among both authorities and ordinary citizens was that prisoners should work to defray the expenses their keep had incurred. Hard labor on a grand scale could bring the state much needed budget relief. Tennessee was indeed ripe for a convict lease system. Some state legislators even believed that a convict lease system could bring profits for the state coffers.

Riding the wave of convict leasing legislation which swept through the post-war South and Midwest, the convict lease system began in Tennessee in 1866 when convicts were leased to a Nashville furniture firm for 43 cents a day. The company had built workshops on the penitentiary grounds, fed and clothed the men, in order for

Prison labor at the Tennessee Coal, Iron and Railroad Company's coke ovens in Tracy City in the 1890s. One of the few existing photographs of Tennessee convicts at work under the lease system. (Courtesy—William Ray Turner Private Collection)

them to build furniture for the private firm. The prisoners had no sympathy for the arrangement. Some protested vocally; others refused to work. A year later, the prisoners burned the workshops to the ground in protest over the treatment they were receiving. The protest movement over convict leasing may be dated from this act. It was destined to involve both the convicts and the free laborers. Conditions were also destined to become a lot worse before they would get better.

State officials sought new firms in a position to profit by the new lease system. Some outspoken industrialists, such as the flamboyant Nashville promoter Arthur S. Colyar, had argued for several years that convicts could be used effectively in coal mines. The result would be "cheap coal, lower taxes, and protection of city mechanics." Legislators agreed and began to look favorably toward leasing the entire prison population to coal mining operators.

In 1884, when a contract with a Memphis firm expired, a new agreement was signed with the Tennessee Coal, Iron, and Railway Company, which had extensive mining interests in Tennessee and sought to use the prisoners in the coal fields. The state contract with Tennessee Coal, Iron, and Railway Company, known to most people simply as TCI, included a five-year lease and an agreement by the company to pay the state $101,000 per year. The previous year,

Thomas C. Platt, TCI president, reported that his company was "the largest producer of bituminous coal and pig iron for the open market of any company in America." Most of the Tennessee convicts were assigned to the company's coal and iron mines in east Tennessee; some were subleased to other companies.[8]

There was some early opposition to convict leasing for labor. Before the contract with Tennessee Coal, Iron, and Railway had been signed, scores of miners, some of whom had been lured to the state by the promise of high wages, had lost their jobs and began protesting vigorously the employment of convicts in mines. Then and since, the labor movement has often agitated for an end to convict labor, but the basis of labor's protest has been a sense of unfair competition rather than of justice for the convicts. One of the earliest public critics of convict leasing was John Berrian Lindsley, a Tennessee physician, educator, and minister. His pamphlet, *On Prison Discipline and Penal Legislation*, published in 1874, along with the addresses and writings of other humanitarians, criticized southern leaders for permitting prison reform to become subservient to the desire for material gain. These voices were not heard by business and political leaders. Stronger action was needed to get their attention. Such action was forthcoming.

THE GREAT STRUGGLE BEGINS

The great struggle against prison labor in the coal mines began in the spring of 1891. Coal Creek miners had objected to prison workers as soon as they appeared in the community some fourteen years earlier, but no major strife or demonstration had occurred. By 1891, Anderson County's free miners were barely maintaining a subsistence lifestyle, although the mining industry had enjoyed tremendous growth and the owners had reaped handsome profits. Over the recent years, several grievances had risen and remained unresolved. The time had come, the men decided, to call a strike.

For one thing, miners were paid in scrip. This meant that they had to spend their wages at the company store or else have their scrip discounted in other stores. A miner who was fortunate enough to be placed at a profitable place within a mine might have been able to extract four tons of coal in a day's time. The company could pay him two dollars in scrip, redeemable at the company store for a 20 percent discount. There was one catch: at the company store nearly every item was marked up 20 percent. The miner who did not take his business to the company store was threatened with the loss of his job or the loss of a favorable working station within the mine shaft. The company's action was, of course, in violation of the laws of Tennessee, but it had no fear of legal retaliation by the near penniless miners in its employ.

A second grievance involved the Tennessee Coal Mining Company, whose mine was located in nearby Briceville in Anderson County. The company demanded that their miners agree not to employ their own checkweighman to weigh the coal and to have "implicit confidence in the integrity" of the company. The grievance was no small issue. The right of miners to select and employ their own checkweighman—a right guaranteed to them under state law—meant that they would have a representative that they could trust at the tipple where the coal was weighed and credited to the accounts of individual miners. The experience at Briceville regarding the checkweighman law was not unique—in other mines it was found that the state law could be enforced only when there was a strong union to police it.

There was a third major grievance. The company demanded that the miners sign "iron-clad" agreements before they were allowed to continue to work in the mines. Such an agreement meant that the workers would be relinquishing nearly all of their rights—the right to the checkweighman, the right to accept cash instead of scrip for salary payments, the right to cease work when they had a legitimate griev-ance—and certifying that they had "implicit confidence in the integrity" of their employers and thus pledging not to join a labor union. (Years later, the term "yellowdog contract" took the place of "iron-clad agreement.")

The miners had had enough. Not surprisingly, they refused to sign the iron-clad contract. Seeing that the Coal Creek miners were adamant in defense of their demands, the Tennessee Coal Mining Company closed its Briceville operation in April 1891. The workers' strike had been turned into a company lockout. The company announcement of July 4 must have seemed particularly ironic for any workers who may have given any thought to the meaning of Independence Day—the company would reopen the mine with con-vict laborers leased from the Tennessee Coal, Iron, and Railway Company. The prison laborers would clearly be used as strike-breakers. The next day, forty convicts arrived by rail car and were brought to the mine at Briceville where they were promptly put to work tearing down the houses of the evicted strikers and building a stockade to keep a much larger group of prisoners expected to arrive in two weeks.[9]

RELEASE OF THE PRISONERS

To see the prisoners arrive in the coal camp must have brought a sinking feeling to the miners and their families. Here had been their jobs, their means of survival, even their homes. The eviction from work and home now seemed so final. Death by starvation and the elements loomed real. The men were desperate. Something had to be done.

A meeting was called for the evening of July 14. The miners had the sympathy of nearly everyone who lived around the mountain valley. Even the merchants realized their business stood to suffer if the free workers, their major customers, were replaced by wards of the state who had no cash to spend. The miners were united in deciding to take aggressive action "for uprooting this blot and stain on the fair name of our great state."[10]

Midnight of July 14 had come. Minutes later some 300 armed miners stormed the Briceville stockade of the Tennessee Coal Mining Company intent upon eliminating "slave" labor from their count. Immediate release for the convicts was demanded. The guards and officers realized they were no match for the aroused work force, some of whom were Union or Confederate veterans now united in a common cause.[11] The convicts, along with their guards and officers, were lined up and marched to Coal Creek where they were loaded on a train for Knoxville. The miners' success was a model of affirmative action that was successful without the slightest amount of confusion or violence.

After releasing the convicts, the miners and their supporters sent a message by telegram to Governor John P. Buchanan explaining their action ("500 of the citizens of Coal Creek and vicinity [had] come together to defend [their] families from starvation, [their] property from depreciation, and [their] people from contamination from the hands of convict labor") and requesting his intervention so as to prevent bloodshed and further loss of income.[12]

A few days later Governor Buchanan, having been apprised of the urgency of the situation and warned of the potential for violence, journeyed to Briceville accompanied by a battalion of state militiamen. A large but fairly peaceful crowd was on hand to meet the governor's train. In the afternoon the governor had the opportunity to address the miners and their supporters at a place called Thistle Switch (between Coal Creek and Briceville). In his address, the governor seemed to feel sympathy for the plight of the miners. He conceded that the laws may have been unjust, but quickly added that his task was to enforce the laws and advised miners that unjust laws are redressed in a courtroom and not by insurrectionist activities.

The governor's appeal was rebutted by Eugene Merrill, the spokesman for the miners, who had been a Knights of Labor organizer in Indiana and Illinois before moving to Tennessee where he was quickly blacklisted by the mine owners for his union activities. It was a rare occasion for the union spokesman to have both the ear of the governor and a large, sympathetic audience to "amen" his grievances, so Merrill shrewdly made the most of his opportunity. He pointed out that the governor had failed to consider earlier and long-held, valid grievances by the workers against their managers. Merrill noted that for workers to sign the iron-clad contract would mean capitulation to a "modified form of slavery." Other speakers resoundingly supported the miners. "Our fathers years ago took guns and fought for liberty," exclaimed a Farmers' Alliance man, "and shall we, their sons . . . be made to acquiesce to what we think a rightful duty?"[13]

That night some of the more radical miners fired some guns in the direction of the stockade. The shots were a startling reminder that angry miners had not been pacified. The governor was spending the night in a home nearby and, hearing the sporadic gunfire, shouldered a gun in readiness to participate in the defense. The miners drifted away. The commotion soon died. The governor returned to Nashville the next day.

THE MARCH ON THE STOCKADE

Governor Buchanan, upon departure from Briceville, had ordered the militia to remain in the area in order to preserve law and order. The troops felt undermanned and unmotivated, with little desire to take a hard stand against the beleaguered miners. The consensus of community sentiment was clearly and almost unanimously on the side of the miners. After all, the prison laborers were both lawbreakers and outsiders. Though the governor had left town, the matter was far from settled.

The Virginia Mining Company near Oneida depicts Tennessee mining around turn of the century. (Courtesy—Tennessee State Library and Archives)

The second insurrection was soon to take place. A few days later (July 20, 1891) some 2000 miners from the territory surrounding Anderson County, some from across the Kentucky state border—armed with rifles, shotguns, and pistols—formed a line and began marching to the Tennessee Coal Mine. After the army of miners had reached the stockade, a three-man committee was sent to confer with Colonel Sevier, commander of the militia, carrying a proposal for a peaceful solution. The miners demanded the release of the convicts and their transportation out of Briceville. When the Colonel made a move as if to capture the three committeemen, Eugene Merrill, one of the three, waved his handkerchief and at once the 2000 miners sprang to their feet and marched in awesome demonstration to the stockade.

The display of power was humbling for Colonel Sevier. On the one side were 40 convicts, 6 guards, and 100 state militiamen. On the other side were 2000 emotionally charged miners. The Colonel needed nothing else to be impressed. Wisely he chose not to become some latter-day Davy Crockett and Alamo defender. He thus surrendered. The miners agreed not to damage company property and to safeguard the prisoners. The five-mile march to Coal Creek began. Local miners' wives handed out sandwiches and coffee to the visiting miners as they passed through. By early afternoon the entire company of convicts, guards, and militia was loaded on a train and on their way to Knoxville. The soldiers were in good spirits upon departure from Coal Creek. Upon arriving in Knoxville, the militia gave the press a statement in which they thanked the miners for the "many courtesies and kindness extended to us during our stay in camp."[14]

Meanwhile, back at Briceville, the visiting miners believed that their mission was still uncompleted. They lined up and moved on a stockade used to accommodate 125 convicts at the Knoxville Iron Company Mine, where prison laborers had been used since 1875, and placed them on another train for Knoxville. There they joined their fellow prisoners. The miners then stationed their own guards around company property in order to prevent their managers from deploying the old tactic of planting dynamite to turn community sentiment against the miners.

The second release of state convicts evoked a profoundly sympathetic response from many parts of the state. And for several reasons. First of all, the miners demonstrated courage and determination. They had also demonstrated much discipline and resourceful organization to execute the potentially volatile plan. Most of all, the miners had been successful in achieving what they had set out to achieve—the convicts had been removed from the area and no blood had been shed. Even good feeling seemed to exist among the majority of people in all parties. Newspapers in Tennessee and Kentucky carried stories of the miners' "amazing" feat.

The war was not over. Upon being informed of the second insurrection, Governor Buchanan issued an order mobilizing the full military strength of the state, 14 companies of militia (increasing the mobilized soldiers to 600 men), and prepared for armed conflict. The militia were stationed on the grounds of the University of Tennessee until the governor arrived from Nashville.

The governor arrived in Knoxville on July 22. The miners had already formed their committee to confer with him. At the meeting, the miners requested that the status quo be restored for the time being; that is, that the convict laborers be returned temporarily to the mines. The miners' requests were simple and clearly stated: first, pardon for all offenses; second, that the lease contract be rendered void and all convicts be removed from the work site; third, that the governor call a session of the Tennessee General Assembly and push

for the repeal of the convict lease law. The petition was concluded
with these words:

> It is not necessary for us to refer to the gravity of the situa-
> tion. Sufficient is it that it is so. We are neither of the school
> of the commune nor nihilist. We struggle for the right to
> earn bread by honest labor, and in principle are opposed to
> the system of labor which may be invoked to our degrada-
> tion. For us and our families we invite the sympathy of a
> common humanity.[15]

Buchanan's next move was to consult with the leasing companies.
Immediately he ran up against a major roadblock. Tennessee's coal
bosses, having tasted the fruits of convict labor profit, were unwilling
to turn back the page of history by removing the convicts from the
Tennessee coal mine or by annulling the contract between them and
the state. Besides the outright financial bonanza Tennessee Coal, Iron,
and Railway Company made off its leased convicts, the company
clearly saw the continual use of the prison laborers as a club to
hammer over the heads of free miners. As one TCI official told the
New York Times:

> One of the chief reasons which induced the company to take
> up the system was the chance it offered for overcoming strikes.
> For some years after we began the convict lease system, we
> proved that we were right in calculating that the free miners
> would be loath to enter upon strikes, when they saw that the
> company was amply provided with convict labor.[16]

With their eyes clearly focused on corporate profits, company
officials were adamant in opposition to labor reform. Closing their
eyes to the injustice done to free laborers, the state lawmakers had a
substantial interest in the system as well. Investigations authorized
by the state legislature in 1887 and 1889 brought a minority and a
majority report. While the minority in 1889 labeled the whole system
"a horror and shame upon the state," the majority pointed to the
profits accrued by the state. The following year (1890), state officials
pointed to a net profit of $771,400, which was only $176,000 short of
the entire cost of penal institutions since their inception in 1829
under Governor Sam Houston.[17]

A large meeting of Knoxville workers was convened on the Wednesday evening before the committee embarked for home. Calling the convict labor system "a sword held over the heads of our laboring people," Chancellor Henry R. Gibson added that the many pleas by the miners to the governor had not been heard "for he had corporation cotton in his ears." Gibson continued:

> In all likelihood the world has never seen so much forbearance as these miners have exercised under so great a provocation. Throughout they have conducted themselves like gentlemen and Christians. They are not fighting law or society, No, but they are fighting for their rights of manhood. The state of Tennessee is far more honored by these miners than by those who would turn the Gatling guns upon them.[18]

Despite the colorful rhetoric reminiscent of a James Otis or a Patrick Henry, the chancellor concluded his remarks with the common sense recommendation that the workers should accept the governor's proposition to allow the legislature to settle the question so that there would be no bloodshed.

Governor Buchanan and the miners' committee parted company in Knoxville, the governor returning to Nashville and the committee to Anderson County. Neither party was pleased with the situation. Buchanan believed that he had to enforce the law, even if it was unjust and its enforcement might result in bloodshed. The committeemen returned to their homes, sadly conceding they had been unsuccessful in accomplishing what all the miners and their many community supporters had desired. The governor did inform the committee, however, that he had determined to call a special session of the General Assembly to present the miners' plea.

On Saturday morning, July 25, the 150 convicts were returned to their stockades at Briceville and Coal Creek under military escort accompanied by Governor Buchanan. They were not warmly welcomed but were received in silence by a crowd in Coal Creek. Thirty-six convicts were delivered to the Tennessee Coal Mining Company and 125 prisoners were delivered to the Knoxville Iron and Mining Company. The status quo had been restored with only a faint hope for labor reform in the immediate future.

LEGISLATIVE RESPONSE

John P. Buchanan, born in 1847, was a coalition Democrat as well as the president of the Tennessee Farmers' Alliance. "Old Buck," as he was called, was elected to the governor's seat in 1890 with the labor and populist support. Prior to his election as governor, he had sat in the legislature where he had voted for the convict lease law. He had traveled to Briceville and Coal Creek and met face to face with the miners and their representatives. He had heard their plaintive cry that "The convicts must go!" He had made the miners a promise and now he had to act on it. As the governor addressed a special session of the legislature in August 1891, he recommended the repeal of the lease law at the earliest practical time and an immediate restriction of the state's prisoners to only a few mines.

The issues surrounding convict leasing received considerable discussion and debate in the legislative chambers. As discussion continued, however, it was obvious that any attempt to eliminate or even diminish the system with its evils would fail. The House threw a bone to the miners when it passed a resolution on the subject: "It is the sense of this body that the convicts in the penitentiary should never be leased again." The hypocritical-sounding resolution was received with great scorn.

As if to spite the free miners, the legislature enacted laws which would ensure perpetuation of the system. The lawmakers bestowed more power upon the governor in his use of militia to suppress all "insurrections, mobs . . . whether existing or imminent" and they gave the authority to increase the strength of the state police force. Interference with the work of a convict was made a felony punishable by five years' imprisonment. Since the newly established empowerment of the governor was effective only until the next General Assembly, the act was clearly aimed at the rebelling miners at Coal Creek. The Senate formally praised Buchanan for his "promptness, energy, and firmness" in restoring law and order at Briceville and Coal Creek.

The miners were shocked by the action of their legislature. So, too, was the entire state. The position of the legislators was not simply one of apathy or intransigence—it was a posture of selfish power and hostility. The legislators were subjected to acerbic criticism in the press. For example, the *Knoxville Journal* of September 22, 1891, described the legislators as "self-convicted of ignorance, stupidity, inability, and blind partisanship," and as being "utterly unfitted for the discharge of the responsible duties of law-makers." Senator Woodlee, a Farmers' Alliance Democrat from Grundy County, declared: "It is a disgrace to have been a member of this general assembly."

On October 28, 1891, the miners' committee, which had attempted to steer a moderate and peaceful course throughout the entire dispute, made its final report and tendered its resignation. Drawing from a poignant Old Testament story, the committee concluded with an analogy:

> As the state has so willed it, and is prepared to enforce its will with the bayonet and Gatling gun, that you peaceably give up your work, your homes and sweet memories that around you cling, and, like Hagar, be driven out with your helpless ones apparently by the power that should shelter and protect you; driven out by the dictation of the penitentiary ring which has now indeed, been proven stronger than the state, and may you as Hagar did, find a protection in a Divine Providence, for surely you can find none elsewhere; with sorrow too deep to express, we bring down the curtain on the last act in the Briceville drama by tendering to you our resignations.[19]

A THIRD INSURRECTION

Voices of moderation are effective during times of injustice for only so long. By the fall of 1891 the governor seemed weak and the state legislature seemed antagonistic. The miners were still free, but unemployed; some were destitute, many were hungry. The stage was set for another revolt. Direct action, which they described cynically as their personal "extra session," was not long in coming.

On Halloween night, following several secret meetings at the various mines, 1,500 miners disguised and armed themselves and marched defiantly to the Tennessee Coal Mining Company's stockade, and demanded the release of the convicts. The officials turned the convicts over to the militant miners and the 163 prisoners scattered over the valley, shedding their "stripes" for other clothing whenever they could. The Briceville stockade was then burned to the ground—the first violence to property in the Coal Creek wars.

Later that evening the miners liberated the 120 convicts at the Knoxville Iron Mine, though the stockade there was not destroyed due to the serious illness of the warden's wife in an adjoining house. (The guardhouse and the office, however, were set ablaze.) Local citizens helped the convicts escape by providing food and clothes.

Fellow citizens throughout the state had now observed a change in miner tactics in the coal wars. The miners, now more militant, did not want to destroy human life. On the other hand, they wanted to render it impractical and unlikely for the state to resume the old convict lease system—at least in their area. Thus, facilities were destroyed. Convicts had been commanded to flee to freedom, rather than placed on train cars for relocation by authorities. And the miners attempted to maintain person anonymity by using disguises and making tactical moves under the cover of darkness.

Many Tennesseans were sympathetic to the miners. Their attack on the stockade was compared to the storming of the Bastille in the French Revolution. When the *Nashville Banner* asked, "Shall Tennessee allow a gang of thieves, robbers, ruffians and outlaws to trample with impunity upon the law?" the *Chattanooga Republican* replied:

> They are not ruffians and they are not cut-throats. Rather call the legislature robbers. . . . Rather call the legislature inhuman because they refused to listen to the appeals of the miners; and when they asked for the right to labor and earn bread for their families, received in answer the contemptuous reply: we not only make it a crime for you to interfere with state convicts, but we send more convicts in your midst to show you that the power of the state is supreme.[20]

News of the storming of the stockade at Briceville was not long in getting to the governor. But before the governor could act, a group of miners gave him some additional news stories to consider. On Sunday night, November 2, a band of miners on horseback rode for the first time into Oliver Springs where some 200 convicts had been working at the Cumberland Mine. The miners battered down the stockade door with a sledgehammer, liberated the captives and told them to flee the county, and then laid the torch to the buildings. The convict release succeeded without a single shot being fired and without a single miner being identified.

Governor Buchanan seemed hopelessly effete to alter the situation in favor of the state officials or the leasing companies. He did offer a reward of $5000 for the arrest of the leaders of the miners and of $250 for each additional member of the miners' union who participated in attacks on a stockade. However, no one could be arrested and no legal action against the miners could be taken. The leasing companies voiced their displeasure with the governor's ineffectiveness in dealing with the militant miners; they refused to pay for the services of convicts and demanded damages from the state. Gradually and reluctantly they were concluding that their best option was to rehire free laborers to work their mines.

Many miners hoisted up their picks and shovels and returned to the mines to work once again. For several weeks following the attack on the stockade, peaceful labor-management relations seemed to reign. The relief was sweet and overdue. Committees representing the United Mine Workers of America began to talk with coal company officials. The owners agreed to allow the miners to select their own checkweighman and to desist from importing convict labor. In Briceville the company decided that "enough is enough" and refused to bring back replacement convicts.

The sense of joy and relief felt by the miners was short-lived. The destructiveness and lawlessness of miners in the third insurrection had been costly in terms of public support for the miners. People found it harder to commiserate with the miners. The governor was feeling the pinch of public criticism once again. Finally, in the middle of December, 1891, Buchanan announced that replacement convicts would be dispatched to mine stockades in Briceville, Oliver Springs, and Coal Creek, with a beefed-up military guard. The Tennessee Coal, Iron and Railway Company was all too willing to assist and implement this new policy—the company bought out some companies which had signed agreements with the miners' union, rebuilt the stockades that had been destroyed by fire, built additional new ones, and deployed the available convicts.

The work situation continued to deteriorate. The free miners still had work, but the convicts often worked full time while they worked only one or two days a week. Miners who had been active in the convict revolt were blacklisted and discharged. The best work stations in the mines were given to scabs and blacklegs. And this entire system was safeguarded by a standing army.

Dark clouds were foreboding. Once again the miners began to hold their secret meetings.

THE FINAL INSURRECTION

The final volcanic eruption occurred in Grundy County around Tracy City in August 1892. The location of this last confrontation may have seemed appropriate, for it was in Tracy City that the miners of Tennessee in 1871 were first introduced to the use of convict labor in the mines by the Tennessee Coal, Iron, and Railway Company. In July 1892, TCI announced it was cutting the free miners' work load to half time. The miners hastily moved to discuss tactics for removing the unwanted convicts. Repressed resentment of 21 years was about to explode. Miners approached the company's stockade at Oliver Springs, overcame the guards, removed the valuables, laid torch to the building, and placed the convicts on a train for Nashville. (Between Monteagle and Sewanee, prisoners uncoupled one boxcar and thirteen of them escaped.) The miners then proceeded to Inman in Marion County, where the operation was repeated, except that the stockade (positioned under a railroad bridge over which coal cars traveled) was dismantled rather than set ablaze.

The miners felt that they were finally gaining respect for them-selves—the hard way. Every other party seemed to be a loser. The leasing companies complained that they could not take advantage of convict labor so long as the state could not provide adequate assis-tance and protection for them. The press described a governor who was powerless to enforce a law against arson. The governor com-plained that he could do nothing until the stockades were rebuilt. Clearly, the convict lease system was in deep trouble.

To make a bad situation worse, the militia assigned to coal camp areas was composed of young men who were inexperienced, who did not seem to take their assignment seriously, and whose reputations were not "savory." One soldier's gun had discharged accidentally, thus killing a convict inadvertently. The unprovoked hanging of a young miner named Drummond gave birth to several local legends about the ghost of "Drummond's Trestle"; his execution demonstrated the impossibility of peace with the state in the minds of many miners.

The governor was compelled to act. Troops were sent to Grundy County, the convicts were returned, and the stockade rebuilt. Word of increased state action quickly circulated in Coal Creek. Miners from the entire surrounding area assembled in Coal Creek and there they commandeered two trains with orders to move to Oliver Springs. A small army of miners, some 3000 strong, arrived at the Oliver Springs stockade at 4:30 A.M. A committee then conferred with the warden and proposed that the company property, guards, and militia would not be harmed if the convicts were returned to Nashville. The warden realized that it was futile to resist. For the third time in a year, a carload of convicts pulled out toward Knoxville. One pledge was ignored: the stockade at Oliver Springs was again burned.

The governor ordered more troops and, acting under the recent legislation, ordered the sheriffs in the neighboring counties to furnish large forces of men for duty. Volunteers were solicited. The miners had entrenched themselves for an armed battle, but when trainloads of soldiers bearing field guns and Gatling guns arrived in Coal Creek they began to retreat. The miners were clearly outmanned and overpowered. Coal Creek was in the hands of the militia.

The state of Tennessee, with its militia and arms, had finally gained the upper hand. A rebellion that for so many months and years had been conducted with rhetoric and non-violent action had become a spell of violence and terror. At Tracy City, on April 19, 1893, the rebels staged one last, defiant battle, where the state had constructed an impressive fortress, designed with portholes from four to six inches in diameter and block houses on the corner. The miners, 150-strong, approached the stockade and opened fire. For hours the battle raged. When word reached Nashville, an emergency cannon signalled the troops into action. When several companies of militia arrived by train at the battle scene, the outnumbered miners retreated into the woods.

A NEGLECTED PERSPECTIVE

The story of the Anderson and Grundy County coal wars is not told frequently, but when it is told it is almost always recounted from the perspective of the free miners and not from the perspective of the convict laborers. Undoubtedly, racism and the mind-set of the southern mind in the late-nineteenth century shaped the attitudes and the actions of the east Tennessee miners toward the convict workers, up to two-thirds of whom were black; evidence about such attitudes is scant, however. One can only imagine how this story of convict labor in Tennessee would be told if it were chronicled from the point of view of the exploited convicts rather than from the perspective of the aroused miners.

We can know that many east Tennessee miners and their families sympathized with the convicts and did anything within their limited means to assist them. As noted earlier, miner families would take some of their much needed clothing and give them to the convicts. Store managers gave new clothing to the miners, "some because they thought they would be entered and robbed anyhow, others because they were in sympathy with the miners."[21] One survivor of the coal wars, Mollie Scoggins, in the late thirties told of her encounter with convicts over 40 years earlier:

> The convicts did not do any damage when they were turned loose though some people were afraid they would, and when one came to my door for food and picked up my little boy I was scared and just troubled. But he petted and talked to him and I thought, "He probably is a married man with small children of his own."
>
> I clothed two of the convicts myself so they could get away and so did a number of the neighbors but as the state paid a bounty of $85 a head for them, most of them were recaptured, though I don't think any citizen of Coal Creek gave them any information. An English woman that lived close to me that had just lost her husband by death gave the convict her dead husband's clothes and as she had intended to keep them it was a sacrifice on her part. But we were all ready to do anything we could to help our husbands.[22]

In contrast to the substantial sympathy held for the convicts by the miners was the harsh treatment meted the convicts by the mine officials. The work supervisors had a free rein in administering punishment. Abuse was widespread. One retired miner, I. H. Cannon of Tracy City, recalled:

> When the trouble started we had no organization. The convicts got all the work. I was a guard in the mines for a while. Convicts would be punished for not gettin' their tasks. The warden and deputy warden would do the whippin'. I never did task anyone more than six cars a day. The whipping was done with a two ply strap as wide as your three fingers, tied to a staff. The convicts were face down with their pants off. They were whipped on the hips and legs from 5 to 12 lashes. If they tried to kill a man they were whipped more.[23]

Working conditions in the convict mines would have demoralized the strongest and most stout-hearted of men. George W. Ford,

Tennessee's first commissioner of labor and inspector of factories and mines, visited the convict mines for an inspection. Ford was the right person to inspect the mines. Born in Boston, he founded the *Knoxville Independent*, a newspaper "devoted to the interests of the common people." With compassion, Ford wrote of the deplorable conditions in which convicts were compelled to work:

> A sickening stench is met with, showing the air to be so contaminated that it is a wonder human beings can exist therein; and in passing through some of the entries a person has to pass through so much mud, slush, and stagnant water that any man with a proper regard for his cattle would hesitate to keep them in such filthy quarters. . . . It is shameful to think that any class of men, whether free or convicts, are compelled or allowed to work therein.[24]

Death was not uncommon among the convicts toiling under the sting of the lash and the scourge of disease. One miner tells of visiting his brother, a guard, ". . . no telling how many a Sundays. I heared 'em beating the convicts. You could hear the strap from clear over as far as that cabin. I heard 'em holler. Yes, Lord. It was a sight to behold. I saw 'em kill 'em in the mines. The mine boss that is, for not getting their tasks. And maybe they was sick. It was shameful." One woman, Sarah Cleek, spoke freely of witnessing the disposal of the dead bodies of convicts:

> Me and a widow woman used to carry pies to the stockade and sell them to the convicts. They were treated cruelly. With my own eyes I saw where they was buried. Their thighs or shank bones were not buried deep enough or something. They used to dig there for clay to daub the coke ovens with. The bones stuck out of the ground. I could see where the coffins was buried. Nigger Hill, the convict burial ground was called. They sent them out to work sick or not.
>
> My Daddy said the warden and the doctor sent one man out to work one morning. He lay around the ovens during the day. A white man found him dead.
>
> They used to cry out to my Daddy to let 'em out. The lice and chinch bugs were eatin' 'em up.[25]

From the perspective of the convict laborer, the story of the Coal Creek mining wars is one disgraceful blight on the history of the state of Tennessee. For in the implementation of this system, the ends of the few were catered to at the expense of neglecting the needs of the many. The practical result was obvious: another system of legal slavery was reinstated, which, for the unfortunate few, was as cruel, as hopeless, and as inhumane as the monolithic system in effect before the Civil War.

EPILOGUE

By the fall of 1892 the miners of east Tennessee, while thoroughly convinced of the justice of their cause, had accepted the fact that they could not win a military war against the state of Tennessee. Their cause could only be vindicated in political and legal arenas. The gubernatorial campaign of 1892 provided a forum for the discussion of the issues emerging from convict labor leasing; the volatile events of the months preceding the election meant that the labor issue could not be ignored.

In 1892 there were three major candidates for governor of Tennessee—John B. Buchanan, Peter Turney (a Bourbon Democrat who had once served as chief justice of the State Supreme Court), and George W. Winstead (a Republican and lawyer from Dresden)—and each pledged the abolition of the convict lease system as soon as practicable. Even spokesmen for the big coal companies were now voicing opposition to the use of convicts as strike-breakers. Because of his inept handling of the chaos in Anderson County, the incumbent governor was scathingly criticized in the press, especially in east Tennessee. "The best possible definition of everything that a governor ought not to be. . . . From plague, pestilence and famine, from murder and sudden death, and above all, from such Governors, Good Lord, deliver us," the *Knoxville Tribune* of August 29, 1892, editorialized. Turney won the election polling over 126,000 votes to Winstead's total of just over 100,000 votes; Buchanan received under 30,000 votes.

When the General Assembly convened in January of the new year, outgoing Governor Buchanan urged that the lease system be abolished immediately, that the state erect a new penitentiary, and that coal fields be acquired by the state where the convicts might work. The legislature soon appointed a special joint committee to investigate the plight of the prisoners. What the committee discovered was a history of neglect. Convicts had not been given adequate clothing, night-clothing, nutrition, or health care.

On April 4, 1893, a penitentiary bill was signed by Governor Turney. The legislators had stipulated that the new penitentiary be "managed and conducted upon just, humane, and civilized principles" and be large enough to accommodate 1,500 convicts and required the state to purchase "not more than 10,000 acres" of coal lands on which prisoners could work without being in any competition with free laborers. Consequently, 9000 acres of coal lands were purchased in Morgan County and construction on Brushy Mountain State Prison, a facility intended to be modern in every way, began immediately. The prison at Petros, near Oliver Springs, was completed in 1898 at a cost in excess of $800,000. On the expansive prison grounds, state convicts mined coal solely for the state until after World War II.[26]

On January 1, 1896, the contract between the state of Tennessee and the Tennessee Coal, Iron, and Railway Company providing state prisoners upon lease for work in mines expired. "The convict lease system in Tennessee, so far as it pertains to mining," wrote E. P. Clute, state commissioner of labor, in 1896, "is a thing of the past."[27]

NOTES

There are several primary sources available to students researching the Coal Creek labor wars. Labor Commissioner Ford visited the area and his reports on the Coal Creek conflict are found in two official Tennessee manuscripts: *Special Report of the Commissioner of Labor and the Inspector of Mines to his Excellency John P. Buchanan* and *Second Annual Report of the Commissioner of Labor*. In 1937-38, James Dombrowski, an instructor at the Highlander Folk School, conducted interviews with survivors of the convict labor wars; his original interest was stirred by hearing stores told by Tracy City veterans of the convict-miners conflict. These interviews provided much of the raw material for Dombrowski's unpublished manuscript *Fire in the Hole*, a history of the people of Grundy County (the location of Highlander at the time of the interviews). A briefer unpublished manuscript by Dombrowski, "Early History of Grundy County," is located in the manuscript division of the Tennessee State Library and Archives. Some of the Dombrowski interview material is published in an article edited by Fran Ansley and Brenda Bell, "Miners' Insurrections/Convict Labor," *Southern Exposure*, 1 (no. 3 & 4; Winter, 1974), 144-59. Newspaper accounts round out the available primary sources; the *Knoxville Journal* had several reporters on the Anderson County scene whose reports are generally reliable.

By far the best secondary sources on the Coal Creek wars were written by Andrew C. Hutson, Jr. Hutson reviewed contemporary accounts and primary source material and wrote a thesis for the University of Tennessee. Two published articles were drawn from this study and these were employed heavily in this chapter. Hutson's articles are: "The Coal Miners' Insurrections of 1891 in Anderson County, Tennessee," *East Tennessee Historical Society Publications*, 7 (1935), 103-21, and "The Overthrow of the Convict Lease System in Tennessee," *East Tennessee Historical Society Publications*, 8 (1936), 82-103. These articles contain much more detail than could be reported in this study. Perhaps the best single monograph on the subject is Pete Daniel, "The Tennessee Convict War," in *Tennessee Historical Quarterly*, vol. 34, no. 3 (Fall, 1975), 273-92; the study is written in an interesting and compelling style. A detailed report with statistical listings on prison labor in Tennessee is found in Charles P. White, "Early Experiments With Prison Labor in Tennessee," *East Tennessee Historical Society Publications*, no. 12 (1940), 45-69.

Individual chapters are devoted to the Coal Creek labor wars in Philip S. Foner, *History of the Labor Movement in the U.S.* 2 (New York: International Publishers, 1955), 219-29, and Archie Green, *Only a Miner: Studies in Recorded Coal Mining Songs* (Urbana: University of Illinois Press, 1972). The latter source draws heavily on songs and folklore and includes several photographs and drawings. Robert E. Corlew, *Tennessee: A Short History*, 2d ed. (Knoxville: University of Tennessee Press, 1981) provides a short section on convict leasing in Tennessee and the gubernatorial election of 1892.

1. C. Vann Woodward, *Origins of the New South* (Baton Rouge: Louisiana State University Press, 1951), 234.

2. Historical information about Coal Creek and *Anderson County* is drawn from Katherine B. Haskins, Anderson County (Memphis: Memphis State University, 1979), 44-48. The comment about divided loyalty is drawn from Green, *Only a Miner*, 156.

3. Haskins, *Anderson County*, 44.

4. Ibid., Green, *Only a Miner*, 156.

5. From an article on early union history in Anderson County by Katherine Haskins, *Clinton Courier-News*, March 17, 1977.

6. Haskins, *Anderson County*, 45.

7. Corlew, *Tennessee*, 387.

8. Ibid., 388; Platt's statement is quoted in Green, *Only a Miner*, 211-12.

9. Hutson, "Coal Miners' Insurrections," 107.

10. Ibid., 108.

11. Green, *Only a Miner*, 159.

12. Hutson, "Coal Miners' Insurrections," 108.

13. Quoted in ibid., 110.

14. Quoted in Foner, *History of Labor Movement*, 223.

15. Quoted in Hutson, "Coal Miners' Insurrections," 116.

16. Quoted in Green, *Only a Miner*, 164.

17. Corlew, *Tennessee*, 389-90.

18. Quoted in Hutson, "Coal Miners' Insurrections," 117.

19. Quoted in Foner, *History of Labor Movement*, 224.

20. Quoted in ibid., 225.

21. A statement of W. M. Scoggins, quoted in Ansley and Bell, "Miners' Insurrections/Convict Labor," 149.

22. Quoted in ibid.

23. Quoted in ibid., 151.

24. Quoted in Green, *Only a Miner*, 168.

25. Quoted in Ansley and Bell, "Miners' Insurrections/Convict Labor," 153.

26. Information about the gubernatorial election of 1892 and the planning for the new state prison was drawn from Corlew, *Tennessee*, 391-92.

27. Quoted in Hutson, "Overthrow of Convict Lease System," 103.

". . . This generation will see here the
greatest industrial city in the United
States."

CHAPTER 4

Prelude to Depression

Revolt and Defeat for
Tennessee Textile Workers

The cool, brisk air of autumn 1928 was beginning to stir in the
southern Appalachians. To the people of Elizabethton, it seemed that
the God of all the universe had been smiling approvingly on their city.
Tucked away in the northeast corner of Tennessee, Elizabethton was
surrounded by wooded forests, clear streams and waters, and misty
mountaintops. The campaign for the United States presidency was
already underway. An air of excitement was felt everywhere in the
town. For on this day, the Republican nominee for president of the
United States had come to visit the town and to deliver an address
which would be the only campaign speech he would deliver in the
South.

Herbert Hoover's visit to Elizabethton was no fluke in campaign
strategy. The Republican candidate had come to confirm the arrival of
a New South—a South now recovered from the blight of slavery
which had been its past, a South that was now economically healthy
and "rarin'" to move forward, a South which offered abundant cheap
labor, a South ready to embrace industrialism without unionism.

For all of this image of the New South, no city could have been
more of a shining example than Elizabethton. Four years earlier the
city had been selected by a German firm as the site for building and
operating a plant to produce rayon. By October 1926 the American
Bemberg Corporation had begun manufacturing operations. Two
years later the American Glanzstoff Company, a sister company
under the same management, also began producing rayon in
Elizabethton. The twin plants represented an initial investment of
some $15 million and employed over 3,000 men and women.[1] "This

generation will see here the greatest industrial city in the United States," predicted one visiting German financier.[2]

Thousands of people turned out to hear the next president's address. Having toured the Bemberg plant and inspected the newly opened Glanzstoff facility before mounting the podium, Hoover proceeded to chronicle Southern economic development in the 1920s. "The South possesses vast resources of raw materials and electrical power, easy access to the sea, a great reserve of labor, a wealth of soil, a moderate climate," the candidate declared.[3] Elizabethton's experience was a clear example of the innumerable possibilities for the South of the future.

Herbert Hoover was elected president in November. He succeeded in winning the electoral vote of Tennessee, mainly because his opponent, Al Smith, was viewed both as a Catholic and an opponent of prohibition. Within five short months of Hoover's visit to Elizabethton, however, an unusual turn of events called into question the new president's vision of a New South enjoying the blessings of prosperity and industrialism. All of the rayon workers had walked out of Elizabethton's two magnificent mills. The strike began when a dissatisfied young female worker marched out of her work station and was followed by scores of co-workers.

Elizabethton in the spring of 1929 seemed far removed, both geographically and culturally, from the great manufacturing centers of the North and Midwest. Yet, here in the mountains of upper East Tennessee, in this remote and inauspicious region, events unfolded which would foreshadow the coming of an awful era which later would be called the Great Depression. The pattern of labor conflict at Elizabethton was foreshadowing of labor conflict not only in the Piedmont textile mills but also in plants and factories throughout the entire nation during the turbulent decade of the 1930s. Elizabethton was indeed a prelude to depression.

THE COTTON MILL CAMPAIGN

The sporadic expansion of the cotton textile industry in the South was one of the most important developments in the economic history of the post-war period. In the antebellum South, the textile industry had been small and unimportant; the Piedmont's 193,700 spindles represented only about four percent of the total national spindles.[4] In the

1880s the industry began to gain a strong foothold in the Piedmont. Southerners had long dreamed of bringing mills to the cotton fields and the cotton mill campaign began to turn that dream into reality.

The arrival of the textile mill in a southern community was seen as a godsend to the local citizens. Cotton farmers would find a convenient and ready market for their raw goods. Citizens who were struggling economically could expect steady employment. The cotton mill campaign became something of a religious revival to some southern communities, stirring hope for the future and reviving the old patriotism at the local levels. Elizabethton was typical of other southern communities which provided aggressive support to attract new industry; the town donated a large strip of land and exempted the Glanzstoff and Bemberg companies from taxation for ten years. The special privilege to industry was justified as the mills would serve as a public servant to the community.[5] "Throughout the 1930s," labor historian James Hodges points out, "the myth of the mills as public servants permeated the rhetoric of owners and served to justify their view of themselves as true stewards of the South and its workers."[6]

The chief reason the textile operators moved their spindles and looms from the North to the Carolinas and Tennessee was not the proximity to the cotton fields, but the "cheap and contented labor" offered to employers by the Chambers of Commerce of the South. Such "pure Anglo-Saxon" workers were in abundance in and around the mountain communities and could be hired to work in the mills for considerably less than their counterparts would be paid in the North. With the cost of production lower, the southern owners could maintain a competitive advantage against the older, more established textile industrialists in New England.

Reasons for the availability of cheap labor in the South in the late-nineteenth and early twentieth centuries are not difficult to pinpoint. Two contemporaries of the Piedmont and Elizabethton scene, Broadus Mitchell and George Sinclair Mitchell, writing in the midst of the textile workers' strikes, offer three plausible explanations: first, the operatives, as the managers preferred to call them, were almost entirely poor whites. The mill hands were not being drawn from other industrial jobs or from any other salaried occupations. "They came from destitution, from hopelessness, from abandonment in the country," the Mitchells observe. "It is doubtful whether Anglo-Saxon people at any time since the Norman conquest had a lower standard of life than these. Nearly all were ignorant not only of letters, but of the elements of progressive, self-reliant existence."[7] Many had been tenant farmers or sharecroppers who had eked out a new primitive existence and seized the opportunity to work in the mills and escape rural serfdom. Coming from such a background, the typical mill hand was pliant and accepting of his or her new work status.

A second reason for the availability of cheap labor in the South was rooted in the policies of the employers. The system of life in the mill village was much the same as in any other company town. Workers did not own their own homes and had to depend upon the good graces of the company for preserving health and peace in the community. Additionally, employers made clear to all workers their strong opposition to unionism. Owner opposition to the union movement went beyond mere statements and included expelling organizers from company-owned towns for trespassing and calling out troops and hastily enlisting deputy sheriffs to maintain the status quo in the mill. The mill hands knew all too well who held the cards in any labor-management power game.

A third factor which kept labor cheap in the South was linked with public opinion. The thinking people of the South, the Mitchells argued, saw the chief problem of their region as poverty, and the mills and mill villages were an important step in alleviating this problem. "Further, the South has always been less aware of the need for justice between the classes than of the appropriateness of kindliness shown by a superior to an inferior. Graceful patronage has been all that public opinion demanded."[8] Though churches have traditionally played an influential role in southern life, most pulpits offered no judgment or direction on the issue of worker exploitation, or long hours and low wages.

Another factor which enlarged the labor pool and made the South more attractive to mill owners was the near absence of protective labor legislation which had been passed in northern states. The principle of protective labor laws was barely recognized in the South in the 1920s. This meant that mill owners and operators could make heavy use of female labor and at least some use of child labor. In Tennessee a 57-hour limit was imposed on employers (by contrast, Alabama imposed no limit on hours; North Carolina and Georgia restricted the work week to 60 hours, South Carolina to 55 hours). In the individual mills, women composed anywhere from 25 percent to 50 percent of the workers.[9] About 40 percent of the work force in the Elizabethton mills was female.

Given the abundance of cheap labor, the mill owners and operators were not about to pay more for labor than absolutely necessary. The typical mill hand in the South could be employed during the period from 1894 to 1927 for a wage which was 40 percent below that in the other parts of the United States; by the 1920s, the difference was still about 25 percent.[10] This wage differential enabled the mills which were located in the South to earn profits while the New England mills barely broke even or faced deficits.

On the surface, the future looked bright for the mill operators in the South. There was a large labor pool of eager workers. Local communities welcomed the arrival of new industry with open arms.

Labor-management relations seemed relatively stable and placid compared with the turmoil experienced in northern industry. The union movement was weak and ineffective in the South and posed no threat to entrenched power. The Elizabethton experience provided clear evidence that foreign investors could build, maintain, and staff a large plant equipped with the latest, most modern equipment.

HARD TIMES AND HARD RULES

The 1930s is thought of as the depression decade, but a depression within the textile industry had begun earlier. World War I had brought an inflated demand for cotton goods which boosted production in both northern and southern textile mills. In the 1920s demand for textile goods began to drop. The industry was overbuilt and had overproduced. The industry faced the problem of declining profits, mills operating under capacity, shrinking stock and plant values. In New England, older established mills were forced to shut down operations. Though the South had become the dominant textile region, it was not going to escape the devastating effects of depression.

The list of complaints by cotton textile workers in the 1920s was substantial—low wages, heavy work loads, managerial opposition to trade unionism, long hours, arbitrary work rules, and deplorable living conditions. Most detestable was the "stretch-out," a special invention by textile managers designed to maintain a mill's competitive edge. In fact, the stretch-out was the proverbial "straw that broke the camel's back" in many of the mill strikes of 1929-1930.

The stretch-out system was the mill operators' answer to overproduction and ruinous competition. It was designed to cut labor costs drastically. Under the stretch-out, workers were given additional machines to operate without a commensurate increase in pay. Weavers were stretched from 24 to 48 looms to operate and a stretch of 76 looms per operative was common.[11] The stretch-out filled every spare moment in the work day and robbed the workers of control over the pace and the method of production. Thus, the system, as W. J. Cash points out in his *Mind of the South,* "violated the whole tradition of the South,"[12] for southern laborers had never toiled under a scientific management system with some keen-eyed supervisor holding an ever-present stopwatch. Southern mill hands saw conditions "just kept getting worse and worse." "It looked like every time you got where you could keep a job up," one female worker recalled, "they'd just add a little bit more to it. And you was always in a hole, trying to catch up. You'll think, 'Now I'll do this, and I'll be caught up.' But at the end you're just as far behind as you were to start with."[13] The stretch-out system was too much. Little wonder that many observers of the mill culture contended that the mill owner was the new master of the South, stepping in to take the place of the plantation owner.

At the heart of the textile workers' discontent was a feeling that they were not respected, that most were even despised by the managing class. As the southern mills became more isolated, physically and socially, class prejudice was heightened. Textile mill hands became known as "lint-heads" and were frequently viewed with contempt. The paternalistic system in the mill village maintained this sense of class cleavage by keeping "these less fortunate souls" dependent on the owners for the most basic of necessities. When the workers entered the mills each morning to work, their subordinate status was reinforced. At their posts, they were subject to the most arbitrary whims of the lowliest overseer or "bossman." Most jobs were simple, required little use of intelligence, were easily learned, and required constant attention. The constant state of alertness kept many workers under heavy emotional stress. Many men, women, and children who entered the mills for the daily grind resigned themselves to "second-class citizens," considering themselves as outside America's dream of success. The best they could hope for was that their own children would be able to work in a just and more humane system.

UNHAPPY DAYS IN HAPPY VALLEY

The Elizabethton rayon mills were located in an area known by the local citizenry as Happy Valley. In several ways the Elizabethton work

Females were employed as mill hands and "lint-heads" in Tennessee mills. This circa 1920 photo was made in Taubel Scott Company. (Courtesy—Tennessee State Library and Archives)

situation was different from those in the Piedmont area. There was no mill village or company store in Elizabethton. "Foreign" ownership meant the diminishing of the paternal dimension of employment. Also, the rayon industry was in somewhat better economic condition than cotton textiles.

Not many workers in Happy Valley were extraordinarily happy. Many workers in the mills were working a 56-hour week, with a weekly wage which ranged from less than $9.00 per week to about $11.00 per week. In the department where the strike began, 550 young women were employed for an average weekly wage of $8.96. Top wages in the plant averaged about 25 to 30 cents per hour, and this was comparable to wage levels prevailing in Tennessee and other southern states.[14] Compared with wages paid a New England textile worker, the gap could not be ignored, at least not by G. August Gerber, secretary of the Socialist National Campaign Committee, who held Hoover's words on Elizabethton's prosperity to more realistic criticism: "To talk of prosperity in the midst of such low wages, long hours, and sweating of labor is preposterous."[15]

Though the rayon workers did not have to cope with the paternalism of the mill village system, they did face the ordinary needs of food, clothing, and housing. A separate corporation sanctioned by the rayon company built new four- and five-room houses in Elizabethton to house the influx of workers, but proceeded to charge $27.50 to $37.50 per month for rent—a cost that many workers found excessively high for residences of shoddy construction. Housing alone could consume over half of the Bemberg-Glanzstoff employees' salary. The notion of a company village system must not have seemed totally unattractive to the Carter County mill families. When writer Sherwood Anderson visited Elizabethton with a female companion who was interested in working women's rights he was not impressed with the town. "Already the buildings have that half-decrepit worn-out look that makes so many American towns such disheartening places," he wrote. "There is a sense of cheapness, hurry, no care for the buildings in which men and women are to live and work."[16,17]

The facts with regard to hours, wages, and working conditions were, if anything, more depressing when viewed through the eyes of the mill women. Women were expected to work hard, but were also expected to be content with less pay than their male counterparts. In most mills, women were channeled into sex-typed jobs. The loom fixers were always men. The spinners were typically female. Usually the weavers were either males or females. Children of both genders were consigned to the bottom of the pyramid with the most routine, lowest-paying jobs. Under a rigid division of labor system, the mill operators adamantly opposed women moving into machine-fixing or supervisory positions.

It is difficult to imagine, as labor historian Irving Bernstein points out, which prospect was more disheartening for the mother of a large family: to start a long day in a mill that might mean working in high temperatures and amidst unswept floors, dirty toilets and water fountains made revolting by snuff chewers spitting into them or, on the other hand, ending such a day exhausted, and then beginning the cooking and household chores for the family.[18]

Many of the women in the Elizabethton rayon mills were actually quite poor mountain girls who came to town in order to draw a salary. Noting that the labor force was "shockingly young," Sherwood Anderson reported: "I saw many girls that could not have been

beyond twelve or thirteen. In these towns . . . children have two ages,
the real age and the 'mill age.' . . . These are the poorest of poor
people, from the hills, the mountain gullies. They went with weary
steps along the road. Many of the young girls were already developing goiters, that sure sign of overwork, nervous debility. They had
thin legs, stooped shoulders."[19] Yet it was from this pool of young,
hard-working women that a strike was waiting to take hold and a
union local waiting to be organized. The wait would not be long.

A "FEISTY MILL GIRL" REGISTERS PROTEST

Margaret Bowen was hardly the typical female operative in the
Glanzstoff plant. She was willing to work hard for her salary, but she
expected to be given every benefit that she was promised. Perhaps
little did she expect, when she journeyed to work on March 12, 1929,
that her spunky assertiveness would provoke a spontaneous demonstration which would be felt not only throughout the town but also
throughout the entire Piedmont textile region. In the vanguard of this
significant strike was the group that Bernstein was then to call "the
most warlike members of the human race," namely, enraged young
women.[20] The origin of the strike is traced in the words of Ms. Bowen:

> In October of last year [1928] I hired on to the Glanzstoff
> plant. . . . I was under the instruction department for two
> weeks, and after two weeks I was put in the inspection
> department. I had fifty-two girls who worked under me.
> . . . When I was hired on there I was to get sixteen dollars a
> week and a raise. The first check I got was for $10.08. . . . I
> asked the foreman what was the matter with my check. He
> said: "That is all we pay."
>
> I felt I had to have more money. When you have to pay five
> dollars a week for a room and pay board and laundry
> work you haven't much left. One day the girls asked me
> why they couldn't have a raise. I asked Mr. Burnett, the
> foreman, for a raise for the girls. He said, "No indeed, I
> will not give them a raise." I asked him if he ever intended
> to give me a raise, and he said, "No, you are making
> enough." I said I could not live on what I was getting, and
> he said I ought to have a bank account. I said, "A bank
> account on $10.08 a week?"

The first pay in February I got a raise of one cent an hour. That made it $10.64. On Friday before the 12th of March I asked the foreman again for a raise for my girls and he refused. On Tuesday morning, March 12th, while I was marking up my time he and Miss Brown, the forelady, walked in the back of my section, and Miss Brown said: "This one will do and that one will do," and picked out all my girls except five. . . .

The girls decided to strike for a raise if they could not get it any other way. My girls would not weigh any silk or work at all. There was only ten pounds of silk weighed in my section all morning. . . .

They watched me all morning. One of the girls passed me and said, "There are nine sections ready to go out if you will take your girls and walk out." Then the girls they had taken away from me were given $11.20, and another section of girls were given $12.32. . . . They did not give me any raise. We have thirty minutes for lunch. The manager came in and asked me and two other girls if we were planning on a strike. Nobody said anything. He said, "I have heard that you are going to strike at 1 o'clock." Nobody said anything. He said, "If you will stop this we will give the section girls twenty-two cents an hour." He did not say anything about the inspection girls who were doing the work. . . . While he was talking to us Miss Brown was gathering up the other section girls. When she got hold of them they decided that then was the time to strike. Out of 550 girls only 17 were left in the mill.[21]

The floodgates were open. The following morning a group of Glanzstoff strikers gathered at the plant gates, overpowered the guards, and swept through the plant summoning the remaining workers to join the walkout. A few hours later, the president of both rayon plants, his attention to the gravity of the situation having been gained by a thrown rock, proclaimed that the Glanzstoff plant was officially closed.

The strike had now begun. The plant was closed. Everything had happened so fast and, amazingly, without the aid or counsel of any labor organization. The strike was an entirely new experience, both for the mill hands and for the community as a whole. There is no doubt, as Tom Tippett points out,[22] that anti-German sentiment undergirded much of the antagonism against the company management. After all, there were monuments in Tennessee to the heroic soldiers who had died in combat to defeat the mill owners' homeland. But the grievances were real enough and had impacted deeply enough not to need xenophobic propaganda to muster worker solidarity.

What the strikers did need, however, was organization and direction. It was not coming. Counseled by Samuel C. Godfrey and William Birthright, officials of the Tennessee Federation of Labor, strike leaders called meetings to organize. Interest in a union was at a high point. Some 2000 to 3000 people attended the meetings. By Saturday, March 16, a United Textile Workers' local union had been established, despite the fact that no UTW organizer had arrived as yet on the Elizabethton scene.[23] Local 1630 of UTW enjoyed phenomenal growth. A new hope had been kindled. Sherwood Anderson witnessed the induction of 50 new members at one of the local meetings and was thoroughly impressed with the workers' enthusiasm and sense of unity. "At least there was joy in this room. Men and women, became more dignified . . . the women more beautiful." Anderson concluded that the workers "have got a realization of each other. They have got for the moment a kind of religion of brotherhood."[24] All the talk about organization of the strikers into a union must have put fear in the heart of Arthur Mothwurf, president of both rayon plants. Even before the local had been officially established, Mothwurf announced that neither company would have anything to do with a union and "we have no faith in and expect no good from an organization which has initiated its activities with riots, disorder, and considerable property damage."[25] The president announced the re-opening of the Glanzstoff plant for the coming Monday and inviting loyal workers to resume their work posts.

The attempted re-opening of Glanzstoff on Monday, March 18, was a disaster. Violence erupted when pickets turned back the few workers who sought to return to work. Rocks were thrown at passing automobiles. An enraged Mothwurf sought and gained an injunction which forbade all picketing near the mills. Within hours a company of National Guardsmen surrounded the plants. The guardsmen mounted the machine guns on the plant roofs and soldiers were commanded to escort any strike-breakers into town. In an amazing display of solidarity, the 2000 employees of the Bemberg plant refused to report on the same day. Before the day was over, worker morale, already high, was boosted further by the arrival of Elizabethton by Paul J. Aymon, president of the Tennessee Federation of Labor, and Alfred Hoffman, a representative of the UTW.

A premature settlement of the strike served only to make matters worse. Through the mediation of Charles G. Wood of the U.S. Department of Labor, a meeting was held in a Johnson City hotel on the night of March 21-22 involving Wood, Mothwurf and his assistant, Aymon, Hoffman J. Moreland, sheriff of Carter County, and Captain Frank Broyles of the Tennessee National Guard. The parties reached an agreement for a wage increase for Glanzstoff employees of two to seven cents per hour (matching the salary scale at Bemberg), rehiring the strikers without discrimination against union members, withdrawal of the injunction, and recognition by the company of shop committees to settle grievances.

The accords reached that long evening in the Johnson City hotel were apparently not reduced to a formal written document, but were accepted as a "gentlemen's agreement." Before long the chief parties were acting like anything but gentlemen. The workers met and approved the settlement, agreeing to return to work in good faith. When the local press covered the story about the settlement, the union was credited with an important role in the negotiations. A union-phobic Mothwurf immediately repudiated the story and issued his own statement denying existence of any agreement. The company president then reiterated his assertion that the company would never recognize any kind of third party. Meanwhile, the striking mill hands were drifting back to work, despite the company's failure to perform. Those workers who wanted to be both conciliatory and understanding with the company's president were asked to "buy" the argument that "he's a German and does not have a clear and complete understanding of the English language."[26]

Plant work continued, but there was an uneasy peace among both labor and management, each of which was attempting to shore up its strength for another showdown certain to come. Management refused to reinstate key union members to their old positions. A "Loyal Workers' Organization" was established and some workers claimed that they were bribed with 50 cents by their foremen to sign a pledge of loyalty to Mothwurf and the company; the foremen were given one dollar for each signature they could solicit.[27] President William Green, president of AF of L, who had been apprised of the situation in Happy

Valley, then sent his top trouble-shooter, Edward F. McGrady, to Elizabethton. McGrady, a shrewd and intelligent Irish Catholic from Boston, soon confronted Mothwurf with his finding that over 300 union members had not been rehired.

KIDNAPPING ENDS "PEACEFUL MISSION"

Edward McGrady soon learned just how much the companies' management or its sympathizers appreciated his services on behalf of the rayon workers. At midnight on April 3, Alfred Hoffman was abducted by a mob of twenty men, blindfolded, taken from his hotel by automobile, driven over the border into North Carolina and dumped with the order not to return "under the pain of death." About 2:00 A.M. that same morning, McGrady was hauled out of his hotel bed, his room ransacked, then driven to Virginia where, at the point of a loaded gun he was warned that he would be "filled with holes" if he returned. Also that same night, a third mob appeared at the home of J. B. Penix, a local unionist, but was dissuaded from an abduction by the rifle shots from his sister, a mountain woman. The Elizabethton drama was heating up.

When word of the kidnapping reached William Green, the AF of L chief fired off a blistering telegram to Governor Howard Horton. Citing the details of the kidnapping of both Hoffman and McGrady, Green reminded the governor that McGrady was in town on a "peaceful mission [and] was acting under my official orders and instructions, and there was no reason why he should be subjected to this terrifying experience and humiliation." Noting that he was sending McGrady back into Elizabethton for completing his mission, Green appealed: "in the name of the Federation of Labor I protest this outrage and I call upon you as the Governor of the state of Tennessee to bring these criminals to justice and to extend protection to the lives and persons of Mr. McGrady and Mr. Hoffman."[28]

The UTW local in Elizabethton was young and inexperienced, but McGrady and Hoffman were men of courage who would not easily be deterred from seeing that it survived against management's hostility. Or, if they were hardly courageous, then they were shrewd men who knew how to turn harassment into a good publicity stunt of their own. Either way both men appeared publicly in town the following day. Two days later, Green himself came to Elizabethton and addressed the disheartened workers near the site where Herbert Hoover had faced a much larger enthusiastic audience and praised the favorable working conditions in the New South.

A SECOND STRIKE CALL

The Glanzstoff-Bemberg management, steeling itself for an even bigger showdown, answered the quickened union zeal by discharging union members en masse. The next move was up to mill hands. Their answer: on April 15 a second strike was called which shut down both rayon plants. This strike was to continue until May 25, 1929, and eventually cost the company some half million dollars.[29] From all reports, there was considerable violence committed by both the mill hands and the management or their sympathizers. The military force ordered out by Governor Horton, some 800 state police and deputy sheriffs, arrived in town in national guard uniforms. Their presence was widely interpreted as aid from the state to the mill managers to suppress the strike. The companies had not only paid the police their salaries at a total cost of about $1000 per day (the companies hoped to be reimbursed by the state), but provided food and sleeping quarters.

Rather than quelling violence, the presence of the troops seemed to provoke it. Some homes of striking workers were dynamited. Picketers and guardsmen clashed at the picket line. Striking workers were clubbed and blinded with tear gas. In mid-May the town's main water line was blasted. Tacks were scattered on city streets in hopes of adding chaos to an already volatile situation.

Meanwhile, Governor Horton was buffeted about by strong expressions of both condemnation and support for his use of armed troops. He kept the troops in town, striving to maintain the fiction that their only purpose was not to take sides in the conflict but simply to keep the peace. The governor instigated several mediation efforts. On April 20, Horton sent Major George Berry, head of the Printing Pressmen's union, to Elizabethton to act as a mediator. Mothwurf, however, refused to mediate with Berry and in less than three weeks Berry resigned—but not without a broadside being leveled at the governor for his lack of fairness in detailing with the citizens of Carter County.

News of the Elizabethton strike continued to be closely followed and to arouse further interest in the Piedmont region. Strikes there began to pop up with startling frequency. But in Happy Valley the union fighters were beginning to wear down. Debts were accumulating. Some striking workers were going hungry.

A SETTLEMENT OF CAPITULATION

A dramatic improvement in mediation occurred in late May as a result of the intervention of an attractive 28-year-old woman, Anna Weinstock, representing the U.S. Department of Labor. Ms. Weinstock had been working on the case for three weeks under an assumed name. Neither she nor Mothwurf trusted each other, but using some leverage from New York financiers, Weinstock was able to persuade the companies' president to meet with a group of striking workers and work earnestly for a settlement. The settlement terms were: (1) former employees shall register for employment; (2) the company shall give its reason in any case of non-reinstatement; (3) a non-reinstated employee dissatisfied with the company reason may take the matter up with the new company personnel officer, E. T. Willson, who would act impartially; (4) Willson would act as sole judge in such cases; (5) the company shall not discriminate against workers on the basis of union membership provided his activities were "legitimate" and "not carried on at the plants"; and (6) management shall meet with a committee of employees to adjust grievances. The only references to a union or to the concept of collective bargaining were the weak allusions made in the working of the last two agreements.

On May 25 the strikers met and heard the terms of settlement. A chorus of boos followed their reading. The document was a settlement of capitulation and defeat. Three hours of hard talk and plain senses reasoning by Ms. Weinstock and UTW leaders followed. The mill hands knew full well that while they had been patrolling the picket line, highlanders from Buladeen, a poor and remote village in Carter County's Stoney Creek, had been taking their jobs in the mills.[30] Still, it was the UTW officials and federal mediators—not the local union workers—who were urging surrender. When a standing vote was called for, the workers began to stand silently and then to walk dejectedly from the hall. There was no sense of victory and little feeling of hope.

Could UTW Local 1630 survive? The local's sole hope of survival rested upon the good faith and fair practice of E. T. Willson, a former personnel manager who had represented employers in a textile mill strike in Passaic, New Jersey. This "impartial person," as the settlement language read, was determined to destroy the union rather than preserve it. Willson promptly started his own company union, launched a paternalistic welfare and leisure-time activities program, discriminated against union members, and blacklisted several hundred strike workers. Willson made it clear that the management did not intend to discuss employee concerns with "outside individuals or organizations," namely labor unions. Workers who disagreed were advised to find employment elsewhere.

A better program for destroying a union local in 1929 could not have been devised. In 1930 a strike call by the blacklisted mill hands was simply ignored by the mill operators; the final strike effort was thus a pathetic failure. Many of the blacklisted workers gradually left the area as the complete futility of their efforts became obvious.

The experience of the Elizabethton mill workers had been difficult and discouraging. Many had returned to their looms and spindles and the union office in Elizabethton was still open, but the outcome of several months of fierce conflict between labor and management was clear—the strike had been lost and the union had been crushed. "All that remained of the huge rayon strike," observer Tom Tippett writes, "was the few hundred unemployed ex-strikers, half-starved and disillusioned, cynical and justly bitter."[31]

"A MICROCOSM OF ALL AMERICA"

What did the Elizabethton rayon strike experience prove? First, the spontaneous strike at Happy Valley provided clear evidence that the stereotype of the southern mill hand as docile, tractable, and easily satisfied worker was largely a myth. Mill hands in Tennessee and the South possessed little or no more preference for tough working conditions and low wages than the mill hands who lived and worked in New England. Second, the hard-line stance of Glanzstoff-Bemberg against the new UTW local indicated clearly that Tennessee industrialists and southern industrialists in general believed that the South's industrial progress in the 1920s was due more to nonunionization than to any other factor. Industrial leaders in the South seemed paranoid about the union movement to their region and, in the words of one observer, showed "every intention of making a last-ditch fight against them." The non-organized status of the work force was an advantage the owners would fight to maintain.[32] Third, the

Elizabethton experience offered a clear message to the working men and women of Tennessee—the state and its political leaders were quite willing by the use of armed strength to reinforce the lard-line taken by their employers, in this case foreign managers, in order to maintain as closely as possible the status quo.

The significance of Elizabethton and the Piedmont on the eve of the Great Depression, as Irving Bernstein astutely observes, was that the experience there was "a microcosm of all America in the somber decade to follow." In this beautiful land hundreds of miles from the industrial centers of the Northeast and Midwest, the mill hands rehearsed and grappled with "the great labor issues that were to absorb the entire nation in the thirties."[33] Here were the problems of economic collapse (unemployment, poverty, and relief). Here were the issues of labor standards (low wages, long hours, working conditions, child labor, night work for women). Here, too, were the problems facing the mill owner and managers (declining demand for goods, increased competition, falling profits, worker dissatisfaction, worker violence, traditional distaste for unions and collective bargaining). Here, as well, were the fundamental issues of labor-management relations (the right to organize and bargain collectively, discrimination for union employees, the right to strike, the role of the government in labor-management disputes). Unhappily, the resolutions to these vexing issues as they emerged in Elizabethton were the same resolutions which were to be reached in depression-era conflicts at other industrial sites. Finally, the central issue, as Bernstein points out, was that of a democratic society—"whether the majority or merely a few of its members were to make its basic economic decisions."[34]

Within weeks of the first Tennessee rayon workers' strike, the war between the industrial leaders of the New South and the working men and women was fully commenced and, in fact, had already moved to the Piedmont. Elizabethton . . . Henderson . . . Gastonia . . . Marion . . . Danville. These were the battlefields where labor would fight an intermittent war against all odds and lose. Times had been tough in the 1920s and, for many, they would get even tougher in the 1930s. Elizabethton had been the curtain-raiser for these major battles between the industrialists and the workers. And yet, in retrospect, the mill hands' dismal history was unrelieved by a single union victory. The textile workers, their union, and even the American Federation of Labor, had suffered a staggering defeat. The labor movement in Tennessee had been exposed as woefully weak.

NOTES

1. James A. Hodges, "Challenge to the New South: The Great Textile Strike in Elizabethton, Tennessee, 1929," *Tennessee Historical Quarterly,* 23 (December, 1964), 344. This article is the best single monograph on the Elizabethton strike and is written by a labor historian whose major research field has been in southern textiles.

2. Quoted in ibid.

3. Quoted in ibid., and *New York Times,* Oct. 7, 1928.

4. James A. Hodges, *New Deal Labor Policy and the Southern Textile Industry, 1933-1941* (Knoxville: University of Tennessee Press, 1986), 9.

5. Tippett, *When Southern Labor Stirs,* 55.

6. Hodges, *New Deal Labor Policy,* 10.

7. Broadus Mitchell and George Sinclair Mitchell, *The Industrial Revolution of the South* (Baltimore: Johns Hopkins Press, 1930), 118.

8. Ibid., 143.

9. Hodges, *New Deal Labor Policy,* 13.

10. Ibid.

11. Mitchell and Mitchell, *Industrial Revolution of the South,* 15.

12. W. J. Cash, *The Mind of the South* (New York: Alfred A. Knopf, 1941), 345.

13. Quoted in Jacquelyn Dowd Hall et al., *Like a Family: The Making of a Southern Cotton Mill World* (Chapel Hill: University of North Carolina Press, 1987), 212.

14. Tippett, *When Southern Labor Stirs,* 56; and Hodges, "Challenge to the New South," 345.

15. *New York Times,* Oct. 7, 1928.

16. Tippett, *When Southern Labor Stirs,* pp. 56-57.

17. Sherwood Anderson, "Elizabethton, Tennessee," *Nation,* 128 (May 1, 1929), 526.

18. Irving Bernstein, *The Lean Years: A History of the American Worker, 1920-1933* (Baltimore: Penguin Books, 1960), 9-10.

19. Anderson, "Elizabethton," 526.

20. Bernstein, *The Lean Years,* 14.

21. The Bowen statement is in AFL, *Proceedings* (1929), 276, and quoted in ibid., 14-15.

22. Tippett, *When Southern Labor Stirs,* 59.

23. Hodges, "Challenge to the New South," 347.

24. Anderson, "Elizabethton," 527.

25. Quoted in Hodges, "Challenge to the New South," 348.

26. Tippett, *When Southern Labor Stirs,* 62.

27. Ibid., 63-64. Hodges states that April 22 was the date for the announcement of the birth of a "Loyal Workers Association of Bemberg" with Dr. S. C. Rhea as president ("Challenge to the New South," 353). Tippett seems to place the establishment of "Loyal Workers' Organization" before the kidnapping episode earlier in April. Tippett notes that the strikers "laughed at the way in which the signatures had been obtained. . . . I saw a number of strikers sign the petition and receive fees in Elizabethton, and I heard them make merry over the whole business at their meetings. It was plain that the 'Loyal Workers' stunt failed of its mark."

28. The entire text of the telegram is published in Tippett, *When Southern Labor Stirs,* 64-65.

29. Hodges, "Challenge to the New South," 352.

30. Hall et al., *Like a Family*, 214.

31. Tippett, *When Southern Labor Stirs*, 75.

32. This is the point made by George Fort Milton, "The South Fights the Unions," *New Republic* 59 (July 10, 1929), 202-03.

33. Bernstein, *The Lean Years*, 42.

34. Ibid.

5

Life and Death in the Coal Camps

The Saga of Davidson-Wilder and Mountaineer Heroism

Almost anytime of the year that one journeys to Monterey the visitor can expect the temperature to drop a few degrees and, especially in the summer, that change is a pleasant one. Monterey is a sleepy little town on the Cumberland Plateau, located almost halfway between Nashville and Knoxville. Going north some ten to twelve miles on State Highway 164, a traveler will link with a winding Highway 85 which takes one past the little villages of Twinton, Davidson, and Wilder.

There's not much to see in these villages now and almost no one to visit. The small bandbox of a post office is the indication that the heart of a community might still be beating. Outside the one-room frame facility is a flagpole to which a blue mailbox is fastened and a hand-lettered sign announcing: "U.S. POST OFFICE WILDER TENN.38584."

Davidson and Wilder in the early thirties were sizable and thriving mining camps. A number of mines were being worked there, though most of the mines were small. The largest mine was at Wilder and it was owned by the Nashville-based Fentress Coal and Coke Company, run by general manager W. D. Boyer and superintendent L. L. Shrivers. One former miner, Joe Welch, who dropped out of school during the sixth grade and later entered the mines at age fifteen, recalled the days when Wilder was the hub of activity: "Wilder was a big community. More people lived and worked there than in any other town in the county. There was big work there. They ran two trains out of there a day to haul the coal out, and sometimes more. The jitney came to Wilder pretty regular—that was just a small passenger train, a dinky engine and maybe two coaches."

Although one does not encounter a report of them in official labor histories, the story of those labor wars in and around Wilder are worth retelling. Perhaps because those labor stories are punctuated with intense emotions and armed violence, there remains a strong deeply felt reluctance to talk about those early days in and around Davidson and Wilder. It's almost as though the labor wars are still being fought. "There are some things I won't talk about," Joe Welch told us several times. Later it became obvious he was referring not simply to the big struggle of the early thirties, but to some of the armed violence and senseless behavior which continued to plague the area through the forties and to which he was both witness and party.

The saga of the Davidson-Wilder labor wars is rooted very much within the tradition of poverty and mountaineer folkways. Though the mountaineers had never been taught the intricacies of social ethics and etiquettes, they developed a rugged sense of independence and an intense devotion to family. Sometimes, however, the most deeply stirred emotions are suspicion, jealousy, resentment, and hate. And loyalty to family may be eclipsed by devotion to another affiliation, such as the union. The mountain people tell a story about a miner who agreed to re-enter the mine for reduced wages. This miner was visited by his married sister whose husband (and, quite naturally, she herself) had intense union loyalty. "I hear you are going back into the mine," the woman probed. "Yes, sister, I thought I'd better get back to work. I've got myself and my family to think about," the brother replied. "Well, just remember this. If you do, Bill (the sister's husband) will come over here and kill you." Then, in an afterthought, she added: "Or, if he don't kill you, I'll make him hold the baby while I do!"

The story makes for interesting retelling and should not be dismissed as merely fictional. Because the mountaineer-miners have been predisposed to rapid, clear, and, if necessary, even violent resolutions to interpersonal conflict, the gun has played a vital role in their tradition. For decades Tennessee mountain people have both lived and died by the gun. Even today in the highlands the gun remains the symbol of manhood. As in other stories of American labor conflict, the gun was all too available and readily deployed in the heat of labor wars in and around Wilder.

"THE BEST DAMN COAL COMPANY IN THE COUNTRY"

The conflict between the company and the workers cannot be fully understood apart from the context of life and ways in a coal mining company town. In most ways, Wilder was typical of the scores of other company towns throughout Appalachia. Wilder was owned "lock, stock, and barrel" by the Fentress Coal and Coke Company. The millions of tons of coal that were mined there were transported by rail over a spur line from the Tennessee Central Railroad which ran some fifteen miles through the gorge of the Obey River. Wilder was home for more than just the men who entered the mines and their families. The miners remember a Doctor Collins, company physician, and other men who worked as preacher, teacher, clerk and constable, to name a few. But the hearty male who lived in Wilder had to work for Fentress. "The Fentress Coal and Coke Company was the best damn coal company in the country," retired miner Johnny Hall declared. When Hall, who entered the mines first in 1928 at age sixteen to lay track, was asked about his assertion, "Why do you say that?" he replied tersely, "Because they was."

Mining coal in Tennessee mountains in the early years was arduous work. Joe Welch remembers working those long autumn and

A tipple operation loading cars with coal at the Consolidated Coal Company, Palmer, Tennessee. (Courtesy—Tennessee State Library and Archives)

winter days in which he never saw the light of day, entering the mine before sunrise and exiting the mine for the three-mile walk home after sundown. Welch also told of some fellow workers who had to walk or catch a ride some ten to twelve miles before arriving at the mine for work. Though almost a generation apart in age, both Welch and Hall worked as young boys to help their fathers and other older relatives during the hard times of depression. Each worked as a "chalk-eye." The "chalk-eye" got the lowest pay among the miners because he was always working for somebody else. As one miner explained: "I got a place in the mine and I'd hire a bunch of boys to work for me. I'd give them a dollar a day and maybe I'd get ten dollars a day. I worked for the company and the boys would work for me."

The single most striking fact about the miner's work in those early years, as labor historian Ronald Eller points out, was that almost all of the work was done by hand. Even though mechanical undercutting machines which helped to loosen the coal from the seam had been invented by the late-nineteenth century, these machines were slow to gain acceptance in American mines. Loading coal into the mining cars was, according to Eller, not only the most arduous and time-consuming part of the miner's job, but it was also the most dangerous.[1]

The drift mines around Overton and Fentress counties offered several advantages to both owners and workers. The drift mine could be entered easily by moving laterally across the coal seam located on a hillside above the floor or the valley. Deep vertical shafts which could develop pockets of gas and would require more machinery and more ventilation were not necessary in drift mines. And as Eller points out, mining operations could be initiated with little initial capital outlay. This low initial investment cost and the ready availability of cheap human labor contributed substantially to the overexpansion of the mining industry in the mountains.[2]

When the miner entered the mine with his helper or loader, he would swing his pick to undercut the coal seam. By making a wedge-shaped slit at the bottom of the seam the coal would become dislodged when blasted from above. Much of the pick work was done by the miner lying on his side. The undercut operation required two or three hours. The miner then drilled holes in the coal, filled the holes with black powder, and then fired them in order to bring down the undercut coal.[3] After the coal dust settled, the workers began the strenuous task of loading the coal into the mining cars, making certain to remove pieces of rock and slate from the load so as not to be penalized for delivering dirty coal. As Johnny Hall pointed out, each miner had his own check number which corresponded with his name on a list. The check number was also a payroll number. The check number was removed by the "check man" at the tipple (the place where the large rail cars were loaded by the tipping of individual mining cars, thus dumping the entire load) and the day's tonnage was credited to the proper laborers.

A miner could expend a great deal of time and energy in a mine on any given day and still not make much money, for he was paid based solely on his ability to produce. Johnny Hall remembers earning $2.50 a day to lay track into the mines. He recalls that some of the pre-1930 miners were being paid 28 cents for every ton of coal they mined and this averaged about $1.50 per day for most of the miners. According to Joe Welch, who started working in the mines in the early forties as a "chalk-eye" for 50 cents a day, the pay improved to one dollar per ton; a "chalk-eye" might be paid ten cents on that dollar.

From the earliest openings of coal mines in Tennessee in the late-nineteenth century through the depression years, young boys were employed to work the mines. These boys push heavy coal cars at the Cross Mountain Mine. (Courtesy—Tennessee State Library and Archives)

Regardless of the exact pay, the crucially important matter to the miner was that he extract coal from mother earth for the owners. As one Davidson-Wilder area miner put it:

> Used to, you'd go in the mines and take a place, a room neck, and you'd widen that out to forth feet wide, and you had that, that was your place. You set the timbers and you laid your track and pushed your car in and pushed it out. And what coal you took out of the place, why, that was your living, that was all you made. If you didn't load any, you didn't make nothing. So if you made a living, you had to get in there and work, and work hard all day. There wasn't no stopping. If you could get cars, you didn't even take time to eat. I've went many a day, the only time I took a drink of water is when I put water in my lamp. I never touched my bucket all day. But if you didn't get cars, why you'd sit there worrying you weren't going to make nothing.[4]

The hard times of the depression made it tempting for young boys to seek employment in the mines. The easiest entree into coal mining for youngsters was in working for their fathers or some other older relative. Some retired miners remembered boys as young as ten working out the mine, usually loading coal for their fathers. One recalled:

> I went to school to the sixth grade. And then I went to carrying water up there around the tip. The war broke out . . . and the foreman come in and said, "How old are you?" I said, "I'm going on 17." I was big for my age. He took me in the mines and I mashed my fingers half off on the tailchain. I was thirteen. I stayed in there from then on. I had a big old mule and I had to get somebody to help harness it. I couldn't reach up to it.[5]

WILDER AS A COMPANY TOWN

Winthrop Lane once described the strike-torn coal fields of southern West Virginia in the early twenties with his view through a train window while riding through the Guyan River Valley: "You see on either side camp after camp in which the houses are little more than shacks to keep the weather out. Some of these houses are propped up on stilts; many of them are unpainted. . . . The camps look like the temporary quarters of some construction gang at work far from civilization. Yet they are permanent residence towns."[6]

This contemporary account of first impressions of a company town in another Appalachian area could have been just as accurate as if it were written of the coal fields of the Tennessee plateau in the twenties and thirties. The company town concept was born in this country in the late-nineteenth century; it was a product both of the boom in the coal mining industry and the necessities and realities of cheap labor and mountain life.[7] No area of the personal and social life of the people of Wilder was left unaffected by the presence and power of the Fentress Coal and Coke Company.

The company houses at Davidson-Wilder were lined along the lower slopes and valley roads which led to the mine openings. Few company houses have survived the decades since the depression, but those which do give us some clue as to the living conditions of the workers. "Most of these houses were actually shacks, hurriedly thrown up along the mountainside," one miner told us. Like other mining camps, the prevalent housing plan was the "Jenny Lind," a one-story, box-like structure with three or four rooms and anchored on a post foundation. They were poorly built, well-ventilated by cracks and knot-holes, and usually unpainted. The company house was cooled by the summer breezes of the plateau and heated by a pot-bellied stove, centrally located and fired by the company coal.[8] Running water and other internal conveniences were unavailable. In Wilder only five water pumps served the entire camp. Sanitation and sewage disposal were lingering problems. As might be expected, overcrowding was a nagging problem for larger mining families. The Fentress Company reported that at the beginning of their mining operations approximately one hundred "tenement houses" had been erected and an additional seventy houses had been built by 1917.[9] Obviously, when Wilder began to boom around 1902-1905, little attention was given to the workers' comfort, to the appearance of their houses, or to community plan. The Davidson-Wilder-Twinton policy-makers had no vision— their eyes were focused exclusively on short-range monetary profits.

Other facilities were built for the community life of miners and their families. An abandoned school building with numerous class-rooms still stands in Davidson; like the old bank vault in Wilder, it contains evidence of late-night "enterprises" and activity. In Wilder a combination building for church and school was constructed at the beginning of mining operations to seat 500 people, and in 1921 Boyer Chapel, a community church equipped with factory seats for some 600 people, was constructed.[10]

At the very heart of community life in Davidson-Wilder was the company store. The miners who have retired from work in Wilder can point to the spot near the crook in the road which was the location of the company store. The store was actually a commissary which offered a wide variety of merchandise, including food, home furnishings and work supplies such as shovels, picks, drills, detonators, and blasting powder. All merchandise could be purchased with credit or company scrip. "Most folks just had scrip all the time," noted one veteran of those days. "Money, why I didn't see no money till I was 25 years old."[11]

Supplies at the company store were expensive. Some cuts of pork and beef sold for two to three times more per pound than their cost in larger towns. During the coal season the miners who could not adequately heat their houses with the bags of coal gleaned by their children from on and around the railway tracks were required to purchase their "blue diamonds" from Fentress for $1.05 per ton—triple the amount they had been paid by the company to extract that same coal out of the rugged seam of the mountain. As historian Anthony Dunbar points out, the bitter joke that the miners seemed to be paying the coal company for the privilege of working for it very nearly expressed the hard realities of the situation.[12]

True, the company store was a vital adjunct to the total mining operation. Not only did they charge for their merchandise "all the market would bear," but they, like other coal companies, discouraged competition from other independent retailers by refusing to permit outside merchants to establish operations on the approximately 10,000 acres of company land or to deliver goods and services within the company town. Little wonder that a Wilder-Davidson miner would feel "I owe my soul to the company store." One tells of preparing to shop in the company store by first going to an office and withdrawing dollars or scrip, "but you didn't dare overdraw, because if you did, you wouldn't get a penny. You were turned down. But if you made it over that, if you had money coming to you, you could get it."[13]

> Before you got that money, the company had to have their take-outs on the first of every month—house rent, your coal, light bill, doctor bill. And they held that out whether or not you made anything. The miners had to buy their powder, their fuses, and everything, to shoot that coal down with.[14]

The company store was the hub of community life. Within the store and just outside in the main street of "downtown" Wilder, the miners and various members of the Fentress management could meet and converse about the fortunes of their common enterprise as well as about any other subject that might arise. Unbeknown to pre-1932 Wilder citizens, at this location in front of the company store would be enacted a drama which would deeply impact on the future and fortunes of both Wilder management and labor.

EARLY ORGANIZING AMONG THE MINERS

Painting a dismal picture of life and work for all early Tennessee miners might be an easy thing to do. Such a picture would also be unfair. There were periods in which good times came to the miners at Wilder along with the many other American workers in this important energy industry. During World War I coal was in great demand and the industry was enjoying its greatest boom. These were in the days before the Wagner Act, but the national government seemed to be on the side of workers. The War Labor Board supported the right of defense workers to organize. As a result, when many southern miners went out of the mines on strike in 1917, the government helped pressure the mining operators into an agreement which the *Chattanooga Labor World* called "the greatest victory ever won in any union coal field in this country."[15] The need for better pay and shorter hours had been officially recognized. A year later, when the United Mine Workers of America (UMWA) started an organizing campaign throughout east Tennessee and east Kentucky, they were successful in signing a large number of mines under the new agreement. Wilder, Davidson, and Twinton were among them.[16]

The attitude of coal mine operators toward labor organization was one of unadulterated antagonism. They found no room in their social theory or political theory for the concept of collective bargaining. Both Holy Scripture and historic precedent contended that all men were obliged to obey their masters or superiors, by whatever name and title they were identified. Near the top of the list of forbidden activity in the company town was "union agitation," and, as Eller points out, most company owners would move to immediately dismiss any miners who engaged in this form of "mutiny." "Indeed, few American businessmen were more staunchly opposed to unionization than the southern coal barons."[17] Not surprisingly, then, UMWA organizers would meet secretly with interested miners, often in the wooded areas some two or three miles away from the mining camps, and there discuss the concept and advantages of union membership. Speaking of the early organization drive, one recalled:

> It would crop up from somewhere or another. You had to keep it kind of secret till you got a majority. You just signed the card and kept your mouth shut until you got enough men together. It'd be some union organizer, but he would start with the man he thought he could trust, that would work through the men. And that one, after he'd signed the card, maybe he'd work on his best friend to get him to sign a card, and just keep working that way until they got a majority of the men and then they'd call a meeting for to talk to the company and have a committee.[18]

The appeal of union organization grew stronger with the passing of each year for miners in Davidson and Wilder because of a number of factors, some of the obvious to the workers and their families and others more subtle. Even the good times of the war years were not as rosy as they seemed at first when it dawned on many miners that they were spending every penny they had earned. Most were aware that they had no viable alternative to living in the company town where there were no public facilities, no public agencies for social welfare, no public parks, and in fact, no public places except for the bed of the creek which flowed between the mountains. The laborers who had come to the mine from the farm had left behind only subsistence wages, but at least as farmers they had the opportunity to own their own houses and work their own land. The miners and their families of Davidson-Wilder knew that their company housing tenancy was conditional upon their service to the mine and that if they were dismissed for any reason they would be expelled from their houses as well. In contrast to such miserable living conditions, these men could journey to Monterey and see the homes of the mine managers which by comparison must have appeared as palatial mansions. Given the fluctuations of wages and prices in the coal industry, a number of miners constantly drifted from mine to mine seeking higher pay and better working and living conditions.

A sense of insecurity began to develop. For some it was a sense of helplessness, a sense of despair. The Tennessee miner was a slave to his company. Conditions in the mine were not going to get any better. Working hours would not get shorter. The coal dust would not make anyone any healthier. The company houses were not going to be improved or enlarged. Prices at the company store were not going to get any cheaper. The personal debts owed to the company were never going to be totally paid off. And migration to another coal camp seldom seemed practical or possible.

These conditions underlay strong emotions which needed to be vented. "The bloody mine wars that rocked the mountains every decade from 1893 to 1933 reflected the miners' overwhelming desire for greater social freedom," concludes Ronald Eller. "Although wages and working conditions were important factors in these strikes, the elimination of mine guards, overpricing at the company store, assembly and visitation restrictions, and other issues of civil liberty were almost always major areas of concern."[19] Attributing the violence of Tennessee miners to some innate characteristic of mountain people has been an easy conclusion to draw. Too easy, in fact. The violence of the miners must be more realistically seen as a response to the creeping inhumanity of an industrialism brought to the mountains rather than as a manifestation of mountain culture.[20]

Many miners quite naturally came to see organizing efforts for a union to be a realistic and constructive response to discontent over working and living conditions. At least a union provided some mechanism the miner could employ to affect his destiny. The miners of Wilder were willing to sign a contract and act in good faith as employees of Fentress Coal and Coke Company. The only question remained: Would Fentress act in good faith toward the workers and honor a contract?

THE SAGA OF WILDER BEGINS

Washington, D.C., and the intricacies of public policy of the 1920s and 1930s may have seemed light years away from the thinking and interests of miners and their families in Davidson-Wilder; but the effects of decisions made in the nation's capital, combined with changes in the national economy, did not take long to have their impact on the miners. When the war ended, so ended the coal boom. Miners saw companies try to cut corners and maintain high profits by cheating on their work agreements wherever they could. By 1921 and 1922 a depression had hit the coal industry and the unions lost many of the hard-fought gains they had won. One miner remembers that the company shut down in 1924: "We didn't come out on strike, it was just the company shut down in order to break the union."[21]

From 1924 through 1930 the Wilder mine workers labored without a contract. In order to get a job at Fentress the workers had to sign a yellowdog contract, swearing they would never join a union and never go out on strike. Already bad conditions continued to get worse. The companies were feeling the squeeze from the depressed economic conditions on the one side and from the cut-throat competition with numerous other coal operators on the other side. Their response: cut back production and cut back the miners' pay.

By 1930 the company had already cut the men's wages twice. A third cut was scheduled for 1931. A quick response from the miners was called for. They had to organize. Despite almost insurmountable odds, they succeeded in organizing a local of the United Mine Workers of America, something no other mine in District 19 had succeeded in doing. Almost immediately the workers threatened a strike. The Fentress Company took the threat seriously and the local won a contract to run through July 8, 1932, which would hold wages steady.

The contract did not cover a long period of time. The miners were soon to learn that the Fentress Company had no great enthusiasm for signing another one. The management announced that wages were going down by 20 percent and started firing active union members. Wilder's UMWA local, representing some 200 workers, ordered the men to lay down their picks; soon nearly 200 more men from Davidson Mining Company and Brier Hill Collieries in neighboring Twinton and Crawford joined the strike. The miners were not about to turn back the page of history even if only to conditions of two or three years earlier. As explained by the union president at Davidson, the company had not lived up to the contract in the first place.

> We told them that we had bummed and begged for food, had run an aid truck every week, that some miners went into the mine without breakfast or lunch, worked all day, and then at the end of the day couldn't get a dollar to buy food with because the money earned was held back to pay for house rent and other expenses. We told them that we had to issue orders on our local treasury to buy things for the miners' families to live on, and we said that under such conditions we could not take a 20% wage cut.
>
> The operators said that they had no other proposal, and they posted a notice at the mine that those who wanted to work at the wages offered could do so. Not a miner went to work, and the mine closed.[22]

The company and the workers both realized the significance of the strike. As Dunbar points out, it was the first depression-era conflict

for the United Mine Workers of America in the east Tennessee coal
fields, and yet the international had only authorized the strike after
the fact, not because it thought the locals could win.[23] The mines were
shut down for the rest of the summer of 1932 and the miners played
a waiting game, just hoping that the companies would favorably
review their plight.

By October 1932 the nation was thinking about its choice for
president between Herbert Hoover, who had attempted to lead the
country by sticking to his rigid principles through some hard times,
and a relatively unknown and untested political newcomer from New
York named Franklin Delano Roosevelt. But in Wilder that same
month the workers were evaluating the latest announcement from the
Fentress Company. Their mine shafts were going to be reopened, the
company announced, but this time it would be on a non-union basis.
"We offered them a union contract at a 20% cut in wages. They
refused," explained W. D. Boyer, the general manager. "Now we
won't have anything to do with the union. We tried it out a year and
it didn't work."[24]

The company began looking for scabs and strike-breakers. The
atmosphere in Wilder was tense. The company had its problems, at
first, finding new workers, because most people from the distant
mountain communities fell into one of two groups: the group which
was in sympathy with the striking miners, and the group which was
afraid of the striking miners. But gradually new workers trickled in
from the "hills, the hollers, and the potato patches" and a new life
began for them in mines boycotted by veterans of coal laboring.

A few days after Roosevelt had been elected president to guide the
country, on November 15 in fact, the Fentress Company had accumu-
lated enough coal to be transported to market. The train that chugged
out of Wilder that night was the first load of coal to leave Wilder since
July 8, the day that the Wilder workers walked out of the mine. On
November 16 one end of a steel railroad bridge, on the exact route that
the train had traveled, was destroyed by dynamite. A $20,000 tipple
for a mine in Davidson had been burned to the ground a few days
earlier; the incendiary action was likely a message expressing feeling
of some workers to a company announcement that their mine would
also reopen on the same basis as Wilder. Strike-breakers' barns had
been destroyed by fire and, in the light of day, two of Fentress' power
substations were dynamited with the company's own powder. The
company and the workers blamed each other for provoking the
violence and destruction in order to gain sympathy for their cause.

The striking miners were thoroughly convinced that the "High Sheriff" of Fentress County, J. M. Peavyhouse, was in complete sympathy with the company during this disturbance. It was widely rumored among the striking miners that the sheriff had deputized every non-union worker the company employed.

The strike at Wilder soon began to receive statewide attention. The *Nashville Tennessean* printed a regular slate of almost sensational headlines. The UMWA sent attorney Hal Clements to court to obstruct temporarily the Fentress Company's effort to evict strikers and the company countered by sending a petition with 250 signatures to Governor Henry H. Horton requesting intervention by troops to restore order. The governor had had enough. After the November 16 evening destruction of the railway bridge, he ordered a troop of seventeen cavalrymen from Cookeville to the Wilder area to guard railroad and company property. Less than a week later a countermove was made. A second trestle was dynamited on November 23, less than fifteen minutes after soldiers had ridden over the bridge on a rail trolley. The governor upped the ante. He sent 160 more guardsmen to the strike scene. Bloodhounds were brought in to track night prowlers. The response from the other side: two more bridges were burned on the day the additional guardsmen arrived.[25]

In listening to the veterans of the labor wars at Wilder describe the next few months, no one word can capture or describe the true situation there around the hollow. "Pandemonium" might be a start. Joe Welch remembers that as a young boy around the area "there was a lot of shooting and there was a lot of explosions. A lot of property was being destroyed, both people's property and the company's property. Scabs and strikers were being shot at. Several got killed. A lot of them got wounded." "Then," he added, "I can remember a lot of times walking into town and seeing 50-75 men carrying pistols. Some would lay their pistols on the counter while they ate or drank. I have been riding in cars that were shot at as we went by some dark corners. I've seen cars that were all shot up and had the windshield shattered with gunshot."

Convincing the miners that their co-workers were responsible for all the violence against the company would have been impossible. Some of the train trestles were dynamited after the loaded coal cars had passed over them, not before, they pointed out. Other facilities that were damaged or destroyed could only have been arranged by company managers or staff who had inside technical information. Rumors abounded.

One was that some strike-breakers were doubling as company guards for a salary of five dollars a night "and when the trouble dies down they lose their jobs. So it's up to them to keep the trouble going."[26]

Meantime, state troopers seemed impotent to bring peace and order to a town sitting on a crate of lighted dynamite. The troopers were undisciplined themselves, searching the homes of miners without warrants, consuming too much mountain-made moonshine, and indiscriminately firing their automatic weapons for no good reason and sometimes at no real target. Ostensibly, the troops had been requested to remain neutral and had been sent to Wilder to establish and maintain order. When their coming was announced, many miners, especially mothers and fathers with small children, were relieved to know armed support had been assigned. After the troops arrived, miners saw them being courted by the company, put up for the night in "fancy houses," sumptuously fed by company owners, and being enticed to protect the mining and railway company property more than to protect the lives of the miners and their families. Obviously, their presence seemed to make an already terrible situation even worse.

STIRRINGS OF OUTSIDE CONCERN AND RELIEF

What did the miners feel during the fall of 1932 and the winter of 1933? From interviews of the survivors and oral history which has been transcribed, one conclusion emerges: the working people felt deeply about the immense difficulty of their plight and about how fiercely formidable their opponent was and how that those days were but the violent climax to many years of mine injuries, hunger, and humiliation. Still, neither side was about to lay down the banner of its cause. There's no way that a complete list of all the tactics to win the battle which were dreamed up and implemented by both sides could be compiled. Some, like the company going to the county court to seek an injunction against the strikers, were legal; most, such as bribery or taking electric lights out of the homes of the 33 strike leaders, were not.

Hunger could not be called a company weapon. It directly and powerfully affected both the bodies and the minds of the miners, nonetheless. Survival itself often seemed at stake. Before the strike, the union had run an "aid truck" around the surrounding farm country, asking for donations of food for the miners and their families. The sensation of one's body starving and craving food is easily remembered:

> They run a commodity truck for a while. They'd go through the country and pick up food, you know, and deliver it to the people that didn't have no work or nothing like that. They'd get truck loads and bring it in and take it to a place, and have people come with their pokes and divide it out with them. They'd have potatoes and cabbage and all kinds of such food. Flour and lard and meal. Meat. It might do you for a week or two at a time that way.[27]

"I know sometimes that the last bit we had was cooked and put on the table and eat," another survivor recalls. "No job, no money, nothing. But somehow or another when the next mealtime came, we had something to eat."[28]

Food had to be zealously guarded lest it was stolen by other hungry people. Joe Welch remembers stories of the miners who packed their cured meats into a large pan and shoved them under the bed at night to prevent thieves from breaking into less guarded locations. Some miners would enter a hog lot, quickly slaughter a hog and remove its ham, and then run away leaving the bloody carcass on the lot. Sorghum molasses, corn meal, wild sallet, and green onions ("It weren't no steak and stuff like that") provided food "to fill up the empty places."

During the long and hard months of tension and waiting, the plight of the Wilder miners became generally known throughout middle and east Tennessee. The strikers had many sympathizers. The Fentress owners seemed to have few. Some of those sympathizers, as Dunbar points out, had previous experience with labor conflicts. But the depression years and even the decade of the 1920s with its greatly exaggerated depictions of general prosperity had formed a period quite unlike previous periods in American history. Hard times had acted as a stimulus to lead men and women of high intelligence and social consciousness to rethink political, social, and religious ideas. One of these was Myles Horton.

Myles Horton was a young man still in his twenties when he journeyed the ninety or so miles to Wilder from Monteagle, where he was educational director for the newly established Highlander Folk School. Horton had come to learn what he could find out first-hand about the Wilder situation. He was invited for a meal and a visit into the home of Byron Graham on Thanksgiving Day. Graham was the president of the local union. Horton shared with Graham and his family a simple Thanksgiving meal. The menu was mainly turnips and sweet potato pie. The meal had been provided that day by using up the last flour in the house. The following morning, Horton was arrested while waiting for a bus to leave town. The arresting officer accused him of "loafing" and of "obtaining information which he would teach in his school." After being taken to the militia headquarters, which happened to be at the mine superintendent's home, Horton was detained overnight and then released the following morning with instructions to get out of town.[29]

In Nashville, plans had been gelling in the fall of 1932 to bring humanitarian relief to the workers of Wilder before the dead of winter had closed in. Howard Kester, southern secretary of the New York-based Fellowship of Reconciliation and an advocate for the South's small civil rights movement, assembled a group of twenty people who were interested in a more activist program for Wilder. Albert Barnett, professor at Scarritt College and Methodist minister, was dispatched to Wilder to assess the possibility of peace between the Fentress Company and the Wilder union.

Barnett learned that the company officials were already claiming victory, that the strike was over, and that there was no remaining strike issue to discuss. Of more importance, however, was Barnett's discovery of the dire destitution of the miners and their families.[30] Emerging from the Barnett visit and report was the establishment of a Wilder Emergency Relief Committee, for which hundreds of cans of food were collected and distributed under the administration of Howard and Alice Kester who had taken residence in Wilder.

Other supplies were coming to Wilder from two left-wing organizations, one being the Emergency Committee for Strikers' Relief, chaired by Socialist party leader Norman Thomas, and the other being the Church Emergency Relief Committee, chaired by Dr. Alva W. Taylor, a professor of social ethics at the Vanderbilt University School of Religion and a Disciples of Christ minister. Norman Thomas was later to visit Wilder on March 5 for a first-hand examination of conditions there. While in Wilder, Thomas delivered a morale-boosting speech about the special mission of organized labor, but by then there was little power and little morale left in the workers to build on. Alva Taylor headed a church committee requested, apparently by some of the people from Highlander, to volunteer to arbitrate the strike, but the company refused the offer.

THE RISE AND FALL OF A TENNESSEE HERO

Hard times were getting harder. The company now seemed immovable and even more indifferent to the plight of its working corps. The miners' battle for their jobs had now turned into a battle for their physical survival. Workers who had strong reservations about the Socialist and other left-leaning organizations which were bringing food, clothing, and medicine from Nashville and elsewhere gradually found themselves not at all concerned about the humanitarians' political and social affiliations.

Though the striking miners could understand the strong pull on the miners to work as scabs, they fought tirelessly to keep the men from re-entering the miner. A miner who scabbed was likely to find his shed or garden raided at night or, even worse, to be shot at on his way to or from work. The bitterness and animosity were now split three ways—among the company, the union strikers, and the scabbing workers.

Talk to any survivor of the labor wars in Wilder. You'll find the man who is best known among these veterans is a man who remained firm in his resolution not to give up, a man who did not enter the mines but who chose to fight until he and his fellow miners had won back their previously won gains in a new contract. That man was Barney Graham. He was, according to Don West, the chief organizer on the Highlander staff, "the most fearless and cool-headed leader the union had ever known—indeed a dangerous man to oppression, greed, and exploitation." Graham's high moral character and the uniqueness of his historical situation had destined him to become a Tennessee hero.

Byron Graham was his real name. He came to the hollow, some say from either Kentucky or Alabama, to live and work in the mines in the 1920s. Everybody called him Barney. Johnny Hall remembers Graham as an impeccably honest man. He was a man who was fiercely on the side of the miners, who in turn trusted and respected him enough to elect him to one of the most important work stations—checkweighman. The checkweighman was the person the workers trusted to make sure the company credited them each day with all the coal they had mined. The miners said Barney was also strongly tempered; "like dynamite," one miner said of him. "Like fooling around with a gun, messing with him," another said.[31]

Integrity, intensity, commitment to the miners' cause, and strong temperament blended in the personality of Barney Graham to make him the kind of leader the Wilder miners wanted for president of their local union. The miners' chief was the kind of leader who would stand up to the company. He was also intelligent enough and articulate enough to stand up before a civic organization in Nashville or anywhere else and make a speech explaining the plight of the miners. The miners respected him. Fentress Coal and Coke respected him, too. The company also feared him as a threat to their vested interests.

Graham had left his home after sundown to buy some medicine for his wife who was suffering from pellagra. He walked down the main street past the church where Sunday night services were still in progress. Outside the company store was a group of mine officials, some of whom were wearing a deputy's badge. One was Jack "Shorty" Green, a mine guard whom one worker described as "the head thug of the strike. He never worked in the mines a day in his life and nobody knew where he was from or what he had done or anything."[32] Green was actually a Fentress County native who had most recently been an armed official in the coalfields of Illinois. Shortly after Graham had encountered the group, a heated discussion ensued. Witnesses heard "Shorty" Green cussing somebody and soon after there was a "blaze of fire." A machine gun and other kinds of guns were heard by witnesses. As the deputies told it, Graham approached them brandishing a pistol and started shouting insults. He then raised his gun, as the deputies tell it, and fired twice. Green, fearing his own life in danger, emptied his gun into Graham's body.

That was the official account, at least for the company record. The mine workers never believed a word of it. Their version of the killing of their union president was that the heinous deed was in fact an ambush by "just a regular mob." As the miners tell it, company guards were both on the ground and on top of the company store roof with a machine gun just waiting for the time that Graham would walk down the street. "And they were wanting to get shut of Barney. He was president of the local and they figured if they got shut of him, that would put us all back to work."[33] One contemporary stated:

> Barney Graham was a good man, and he was for the union. He died for the union. He wasn't afraid of anybody, and anybody'd that'd try to run over him, because he was actually one of the union leaders. He wasn't a man that got up there and talked and abused someone else. He didn't have too much too say. There's a lot of people that were afraid—the companies were afraid of him, and they hired him killed.[34]

The hearts of those miners and their wives and children who poured out of the church house and their homes that night of April 30, 1933, must have sunk low. Their friend and leader lay in the dust and gravel of main street, his body oozing blood from the ten to twelve holes which had just punctured his flesh. No union workers were allowed to approach the body as the company guards cordoned off the area where Graham lay and warned violators that they would be "riddled with shot."[35]

Evidence and common sense seem to verify the miners' version of the murder. Four of the shots, according to an examining physician, had entered Graham in the back. The *Labor Advocate* account reported that the union leader had been beaten over the head with the butt of a revolver, as though gun slugs were not enough. The "thugs" staved off union men, reported pro-union editorialist Don West, and pulled out Graham's own gun and placed it in his left hand (Graham was right-handed) and did not think to disengage the safety latch.[36]

There was no miner who was not saddened by the event. Nor was there a miner who was surprised by the event. "I was expecting it all the time," one worker recalled. "They thought if they could just get rid of him, it would be all over. He was just hard-headed; you couldn't tell him nothing. He ought to have been watching and careful."[37] Months before Graham was gunned down, the miners had heard rumors about the "gun thugs" who were in town to "get Barney Graham." Myles Horton recalled having warned Graham that he was facing danger and that people had been brought to town for the express purpose of killing him. "He was that tough kind that wouldn't quit," Horton notes, "so I went to work to try to get pressure to expose this before it happened, thinking that might bring enough pressure on the company and on public opinion that it might save his life."[38]

The night of April 30 was a long and grievous one for the already ailing widow of Barney Graham and their three children. Howard and Alice Kester stayed at the Graham home that night, trying to offer some measure of comfort and hope. Later Kester would record his recollections of this sad vigil:

> There was not a crumb of food in the house except for the groceries we had brought. Furniture was scarce and no beds were available so we spent the night in two straight back chairs. The only light available came from a cotton string wick inserted in a Coca Cola bottle partially filled with kerosene. It was an awesome and terrible night as sobs of grief came from Mrs. Graham and the children. There were

tears coming from all eyes including our own, and when morning broke neighbors began to bring in such food as they could spare from their own meagre supply.[39]

The violent death of Barney Graham in the poverty-stricken Cumberland Plateau of the 1930s set the stage for one of the most poignant, one of the most dramatic funeral services in all of Tennessee history. Graham's body had been taken to a funeral parlor in Livingston to prepare for burial. The funeral was scheduled for 2:00 P.M. on Tuesday at the Wilder cemetery. One mile out of Davidson, a most unusual procession began. Following an American flag, some 600 to 700 union men, women, and children met the body of Barney Graham and from that point all the people, usually two by two, marched down the highway through Highland Junction to Wilder, circling the spot where their fallen leader had been gunned down. This was a march for union solidarity. It was a march for labor peace. Mrs. Graham was too overtaken by both personal illness and grief to meet and march with those who mourned for their shared loss. Taken in an automobile to the grave site, she remained in the car during the services.

Nearly a thousand people crowded the village cemetery grounds for Graham's funeral. H. S. Johnson, a union miner and itinerant mountain preacher, conducted the service with the assistance of Howard Kester. Johnson, drawing upon an analogy with Jesus, declared: "Barney Graham is dead; his blood was shed so that little children might have bread. Just as Jesus was murdered by the forces of corruption 2,000 years ago, so was Barney Graham killed on Wilder Street last Sunday." Kester spoke of Graham through personal experience:

With magnificent fortitude, devotion, courage and leadership, Byron Graham was leading his fellowmen to victory . . . I knew Barney Graham intimately, I had no better friend. I loved him as a brother, not alone for his own worth, but for his place in the leadership of America's toiling millions. Those who say that Barney was a "bad man" never knew him. Byron Graham was a true son of the mountains, straight, fearless, and honorable in his dealings with men. He never hunted trouble and when possible went out of his way to avoid it. He never thought of his own comfort. When his family was in desperate need of food and clothing, I have known Barney to refuse all aid and to give it to others whom he thought needed it worse than he did. I could not keep him clothed because he gave away whatever clothing I gave him.[40]

William Turnblazer, president of United Mine Workers District 19, closed the grave site service by noting that Barney Graham would be "enshrined in the hearts of workers all over America." The UMWA reportedly provided funds for Graham's burial, but all in all, Davidson-Wilder miners did not then and still do not harbor good feelings toward the international union. There is no record of the UMWA acting in any way to prosecute "Shorty" Green and, in the words of Johnny Hall, "I'll tell you one thing—John L. Lewis sure didn't come to Barney's funeral!" When Green's trial was held in Jamestown in September 1933, the state's prosecution was anything but vigorous. The lawyer promised by the UMWA never appeared. Green was acquitted on his plea of self-defense.

What did the death of Barney Graham mean to the people in Davidson-Wilder, to the people of Tennessee, and to the people of the South and the entire nation generally? First and foremost, it meant that the ultimate power in labor-management relations in depression-era Tennessee (and in the Tennessee coal industry in particular) was still in the hands of the coal barons. It meant also that mine owners and operators were categorically unwilling to deal with working men and their families on the basis of respect and equality. It meant that the Tennesseans who either chose to mine or felt that they had no choice but to mine were almost powerless to effect meaningfully the decisions that would be made about their wages, the safety of their work, and the living conditions of their loved ones and co-workers. At Wilder it meant that the historic and heroic "strike against starvation, slavery, and poverty," to borrow the words of Howard Kester in an editorial written only days after Graham's death, was broken by the Fentress Coal and Coke Company. About Graham's "brutal treatment," Kester declared that it "appears to be one of the most dastardly crimes against labor and the rights of working men in American history." Graham died "a victim of those who live on profits and dividend derived from the sweat of other men's brows. Byron Graham is a symbol of unselfish devotion to the cause of working people. He will live not only in the hearts of the mountain people whose cabins dot the valleys and hillsides, but wherever men seek to build a society of free men."[41]

EPILOGUE

With Barney Graham's death the strike was broken, though many felt that the union had already been defeated. The long, hard, and bloody battle to preserve the only company-recognized coal miners' union south of the Ohio River had been lost. The people of Wilder became bitter and angry. Though shootings and threats flared on both sides again, the labor tension of Wilder began dissipating into an even deeper cynicism and despair. By the fall of 1933, strike leaders and supporters devoted their energies to finding new jobs for those men who were still holding out. Eventually, through the help of sympathetic and qualified assistants, such as Highlander staffers, most of the union men who wanted jobs found them. Among the projects entered by union miners was Norris Dam, the first dam in the TVA system; some of the younger men entered the manual labor camps of the Civilian Conservation Corps.

Although only twelve years old when her father died, Della Mae Graham must have been a strong and sensitive young woman. Newspapers report that she was the only mourner on a single mourner's bench at her father's funeral. There she held her composure until almost the end of the service, when the tears could not be contained any longer. At the moment the tears flowed, most of the crowd broke down with her. The week following her father's death, Della Mae Graham traveled to Washington with Howard Kester and other labor leaders to attend a labor and farm conference, to see the sites of the capitol, and to tell the story of her father—a genuine Tennessee hero. Sometime during this period of her life, she wrote a ballad about her father.

THE BALLAD OF BARNEY GRAHAM

On April the thirtieth
In 1933,
Upon the streets of Wilder
They shot him, brave and free.

They shot my darling father
He fell upon the ground;
'Twas in the back they shot him;
The blood came streaming down.

They took the pistol handles
And beat him on the head;
The hired gunmen beat him
Till he was cold and dead.

When he left home that morning
I thought he'd soon return;
But for my darling father
My heart shall ever yearn.

We carried him to the graveyard
And there we lay him down;
To sleep in death for many a year
In cold and sodden ground.

Although he left the union
He tried so hard to build,
His blood was spilled for justice
And justice guides us still.

Within the next year, Della Mae became a thirteen-year-old bride to Jess Smith, partly because she was "scared to death" to face living conditions in the mountains of Tennessee during hard times without a man to lean on. When she was fourteen she had her first child; at sixteen she had her second child. Food was scarce for everyone and illness plagued Della Mae's family. Her widowed mother, Barney Jr., and Birtha, moved in with them, and Smith became a step-father to the younger children. "It worked out good, except it's a wonder it had," she once remarked.[42] Smith mined coal until the early fifties, when he contracted black lung disease, and then moved to Dayton where he found employment in a sheet metal plant until he was killed in a car accident in 1969.

The significance of Wilder goes far beyond Barney Graham and the union he inspired and led but could not bring to victory against almost insuperable odds. However defeated and devastated the miners must have felt after Graham's death, the encounter of labor and owner forces at Wilder had an impact reaching far beyond the mountains of Fentress and Overton counties. For, as Anthony Dunbar points out, "the Wilder strike . . . was a beginning of sorts for a new radical movement in the South."[43] Myles Horton, the Kesters, and Don West had traveled to Wilder to see for themselves and share in the bitter herbs of class struggle that the miners were experiencing— the destitution, the hunger, the disease, the violence, the fear about the present and eventual despair about the future. Wilder had impacted on this group. Recalling, for example, the shooting death of Graham, Horton stated: "That just killed me. That kind of thing is a traumatic experience, I tell you. You get involved with death of people, know it's going to happen, and you can't do anything about it. Society's so cruel. If I hadn't already been a radical, that would have made me a radical right then. Didn't do anything to make me less radical, I'll tell you that."[44]

Why did Horton, West, and the Kesters come to Wilder in 1932-1933? Obviously their conscience and their ideals, informed and inspired by professors of religion and social ethics at such institutions as Union Theological Seminary and Vanderbilt School of Religion,[45] compelled them to become involved. After Wilder, this group and other dissidents would move directly into the vanguard of southern radical leadership. Their movement was a daring and prophetic one, aimed, as Dunbar describes it, at bringing forth the kingdom of God on earth. "It would reach beyond the coalfields to assail the structures of Jim Crow, take on the plantation overseers, challenge the church, expand the acceptable boundaries of southern liberalism and, as it joined the broader political current, alter state and national policy on race and rural development."[46] That movement was clearly born and deeply rooted in the experience at Wilder.

NOTES

The story told in this chapter is based on several sources, the first and foremost being the author's visit to the Davidson-Wilder area in July, 1987, for observations of the area and for brief chats with citizens who were encountered casually. On July 17, two longer interviews were conducted with two retired miners of the area who are now living in Monterey. (Joe Welch and Johnny Hall).

Highly helpful was an extensive article, with both narrative and much oral history, by Fran Ansley and Brenda Bell, "Strikes in the Coal Camps: Davidson Wilder 1932," *Southern Exposure*, Vol. 1, No. 3 and 4 (Winter, 1974), 113-36. The *Nashville Tennessean*, the *Nashville Banner*, and the *Labor Advocate* (Nashville) provided some valuable primary source material.

Three secondary sources were useful in preparing this narrative. One is Vernon F. Perry, "The Labor Struggle at Wilder, Tennessee," a Master's thesis completed for the Vanderbilt University School of Religion, 1934, and signed by Alva W. Taylor, a Vanderbilt professor who had more than simply an academic interest in the events at Wilder. A narrative of the Wilder labor strike is told in Anthony P. Dunbar, *Against the Grain: Southern Radicals and Prophets, 1929-1959* (Charlottesville: University Press of Virginia, 1981). The most useful published discussion of the work of the southern coal miners was Ronald D. Eller, *Miners, Millhands, and Mountaineers: Industrialization of the Appalachian South, 1880-1930* (Knoxville: University of Tennessee Press, 1982).

The above works will be cited in abbreviated form in the notes below.

1. Eller, *Miners, Millhands, and Mountaineers*, 175-76.
2. Ibid., 176.
3. This process is explained in ibid., 177.
4. Quoted from the oral history in Ansley and Bell, "Strikes in the Coal Camps," 115.
5. Quoted from ibid.
6. From Winthrop D. Lane, *Civil War in West Virginia* and quoted in Eller, *Miners, Millhands, and Mountaineers*, 161.
7. Eller discusses several factors that combined to render the company town concept particularly acceptable in the Southern Appalachians, "an area of scattered settlements and few organized villages and town. Good roads were sparse, and miles of rugged forest prevented the daily transportation of large numbers of employees. Pioneer coal operators in the region, therefore, had to develop their own communities to house their labor supply. The company town became a logical and expedient answer to industrial needs. It provided efficient and inexpensive housing for a large labor force, and it contained the added prospect of company control over the activities of the miners themselves." *Miners, Millhands, and Mountaineers*, 163.
8. Eller discussed the company house in ibid., 184.
9. Perry, "The Labor Struggle at Wilder," 19-20. This figure did not include company houses built since 1917 or ones built by other companies in the general area.
10. Ibid., 21.
11. Quoted in Ansley and Bell, "Strikes in the Coal Camps," 115.
12. These statistics are taken from the Kester papers and are reported in Dunbar, *Against the Grain*, 1-2, and in Perry, "The Labor Struggle at Wilder," 80-83.
13. Quoted in Ansley and Bell, "Strikes in the Coal Camps," 115.
14. Quoted in ibid.
15. Ibid., 117.

16. Ibid.

17. Eller, *Miners, Millhands, and Mountaineers*, 209.

18. Quoted in Ansley and Bell, "Strikes in the Coal Camps," 117.

19. Eller, *Miners, Millhands, and Mountaineers*, 197-98.

20. This conclusion is drawn from ibid.

21. Quoted in Ansley and Bell, "Strikes in the Coal Camps," 117.

22. Ibid., 118.

23. Dunbar, *Against the Grain*, 2.

24. *Knoxville News-Sentinel*, Dec. 2, 1932; Ansley and Bell, "Strikes in the Coal Camps," 119.

25. Newspaper reports from the *Nashville Tennessean* for November 16-26, 1932, were consulted to piece together this narrative.

26. Quoted in Ansley and Bell, "Strikes in the Coal Camps," 119.

27. Ibid., 123.

28. Ibid., 124.

29. The story of Horton's visit to Wilder is told by Anthony Dunbar, *Against the Grain*, 4.

30. Barnett also learned about the view that the Wilder strikers held toward Horton. The strikers had heard it rumored that Horton was a "red," and they wanted no "reds" in their midst. They felt much relief when reassured that Horton was not a "red" and could be trusted as a friend.

31. Quoted in Ansley and Bell, "Strikes in the Coal Camps," 127.

32. Ibid., 121.

33. Quoted in ibid., 127.

34. Quoted in ibid.

35. *Labor Advocate*, May 4, 1933.

36. "A Fallen Chief," *Labor Advocate*, May 4, 1933.

37. Quoted in Ansley and Bell, "Strikes in the Coal Camps," 128.

38. Quoted in ibid., 129.

39. This account is taken from the Kester papers and is published in Dunbar, *Against the Grain*, 9.

40. Excerpts from the funeral addresses are taken from the published account in *Labor Advocate*, May 4, 1933.

41. *Labor Advocate*, May 4, 1933.

42. Fran Ansley and Sue Thrasher, "The Ballad of Barney Graham" (an interview with Barney Graham, Jr.), *Southern Exposure* 4 (1976), 140.

43. Dunbar, *Against the Grain*, 14.

44. Quoted in Ansley and Bell, "Strikes in the Coal Camps," 129.

45. Kester and West had studied under Alva Taylor at Vanderbilt School of Religion. Myles Horton had attended Union Theological Seminary where he was trained by Reinhold Niebuhr.

46. Dunbar, *Against the Grain*, 15.

6

"... It is ... a sweeping victory for workers and the Amalgamated. We have a feeling of security that we haven't had before."

Against All Odds

The Stirring of Tennessee Labor During Depression Years

March 4, 1933. The day will remain a watershed in twentieth century American history. On that gray and overcast day in Washington, a Democratic governor from New York took the oath of office and was sworn into office as the president of the United States.

The circumstances of that inaugural could not have seemed gloomier to millions of Americans. Shortly after the famous stock market crash of October 1929, the nation plunged into a great depression. Herbert Hoover, a Republican president, insisted that recovery and prosperity lay just around the corner. Cold statistics told a different story. By the time of the presidential election in 1932, nearly one-fourth of the laboring force was unemployed. State and local machinery designed to alleviate the massive problems of depression continued to break down or prove inadequate. The gross national product had fallen to two-thirds of the 1920 total. Values had shrunk to unthinkable levels. The banking system was drowning in uncollectible notes.

Even more grim was the human side of the depression: "A host of unemployed citizens face the grim problems of existence, and an equally great number toil with little in return," the new president declared in his inaugural address. "Our great primary task is to put people to work. I am prepared under my constitutional duty to recommend the measures that a stricken nation in the midst of a stricken world may require." Tennesseans, who had voted for Hoover in 1928, overwhelmingly repudiated the incumbent and gave their electoral vote to Roosevelt. In the same election, they also turned the state house over to Hill McAlister, the Crump-backed candidate for governor.

A NEW DEAL FOR LABOR

With this inauguration was the coming of something Roosevelt had promised to give the American people—a New Deal. The "New Deal" came to represent that volatile period in recent American history which began in the middle of a deep depression and ended with the conclusion of a great world war. The period was also a time of great stirring between the industrial owners and managers and the laboring people. Labor-management relationships began to change with a shift of power.

In early 1933 times were indeed bleak for the labor movement. Nationally, the number of workers in unions had fallen to slightly less than three million, roughly the membership total in 1917. Building construction and transportation unions contained almost half of the organized labor force, and even these groups had suffered serious declines.[1] In Tennessee, organizational efforts were bearing little fruit. There was vast unemployment in the state. The Tennessee Federation of Labor was a weak organization whose annual conventions were occasions for commiserating about hard times and the poor prospects for the future.

Tennessee, along with the other southern states, was dramatically affected by the ascendancy of Franklin Roosevelt to the White House and the coming of the New Deal. Upon taking office, FDR acted swiftly to counter economic catastrophe. In rapid-fire succession, the new administration pushed through the Congress a series of bills which stabilized the banking industry and set in motion an agricultural recovery. All of this did little for industry. Only the threat of a labor-endorsed bill that arrested unemployment by reducing the work week to thirty hours spurred the president into action. On June 16, 1933—the ninety-ninth of the famous first 100 Days—President Roosevelt signed the National Industrial Recovery Act into law.

The NIRA was a godsend to the U.S. labor movement everywhere. The act stipulated that industry was to agree to codes of fair competition, thus creating conditions in which business could move forward with confidence. One small clause of the act, Section 7(a), had a sweeping impact on all the house of labor. In 7(a) workers were granted the right to organize and bargain collectively free from interference, restraint, and coercion. Furthermore, people seeking employment were not required to join company-sponsored unions. The administration of this section was by specially created boards.

A groundswell of enthusiasm swept through the workers and labor leaders in many industries. Union leaders saw a golden opportunity before them. In the coal fields the organizers for the United Mine Workers campaigned effectively with the slogan "President Roosevelt wants you to join a union." Workers in various industries soon clamored for unions to represent them and bargain with their employers for badly needed wage raises. The greatest union membership increases were, significantly, in the new industrial unions. The steel, automobile, rubber, and lumber industries experienced workers being organized by the thousands. Not surprisingly, industrial leaders were not yet ready to accept the unions' rights to what they (management) called "collective bludgeoning," and employers began to use whatever means were available to undermine union growth. Workers felt intense unrest. Their response was a series of "general strikes."

On Monday, May 27, 1935, the guillotine dropped. In a unanimous 9-0 decision in the "sick chicken" case, the Supreme Court struck down the National Industrial Recovery Act. The court had killed Roosevelt's industrial recovery program. FDR, disheartened but not defeated, called for the passage of new labor legislation. Congress soon responded by passing the National Labor Relations Act,

Bell clay pit, near Gleason, in the thirties. (Courtesy—Tennessee State Library and Archives)

commonly called the Wagner Act after its sponsor, Senator Robert Wagner. The bill was one of the most drastic legislative innovations of the decade and marked the beginning of a new era in the government-labor relationship. For many years workers did have the right to organize and bargain collectively. On the other hand, management had the equivalent right of combating labor organization and of refusing to bargain with a union. The Wagner Act stripped away this management right, requiring that companies recognize the unions chosen by the workers and bargain with the workers in good faith. The bill also established some elaborate machinery for its administration. It created the National Labor Relations Board (NLRB) to certify unions as representatives for collective bargaining when a majority of the workers voted for the union. Charges of violations of the act had to be filed with the NLRB In effect, the federal government said it would act as an impartial referee if workers wanted to join unions.

The big question that remained was whether or not the Supreme Court would uphold the constitutionality of the new labor legislation. In recent times the court had been striking down legislation which would have benefitted both organized and non-organized laborers. The legal justification for these decisions was rooted in an economic philosophy of laissez-faire and the employer's right to do business as he pleases. When it appeared that the Supreme Court would remain hopelessly out of step with the will of the other branches of government, President Roosevelt made an ill-fated move to reorganize the federal judiciary. Though the "court-packing" bill failed, an aroused public sentiment accomplished what the president had sought. In 1937 the court upheld the constitutionality of the National Labor Relations Act,[2] which in effect sealed the New Deal's partnership with organized labor and provided an historic opportunity for American labor.

Such was the setting for the Tennessee labor movement in the 1930s. As with the other southern states, the early New Deal period was a crucially important era for the Tennessee work force and its leaders. It was also a volatile period. Out of a position of relative weakness came great stirring in organization and labor activity. Against all obstacles that management could devise, the Tennessee workers were organized by the thousands and from Memphis to Bristol new union locals were continually being established. Although union membership growth was less than leaders had wanted, organized labor in Tennessee became a force to be reckoned with.

A FLURRY OF ORGANIZING

Reaction in Tennessee to the passage of the National Industrial Recovery Act was immediate. "Labor's manifest destiny" was clear and imperative, declared the *Chattanooga Labor World*, and "the labor movement must claim the field by actually occupying the field."[3] The *Knoxville Progressive Labor* interpreted section 7(a) as giving employees the right to organize and declared that labor's chief responsibility was "to organize with all the fervor and zeal and determination of a crusading army."[4]

Enthusiasm was soon kindled among the rank and file of Tennessee workers. Jake Cohen, president of the Memphis Trades and Labor Council, took the lead in explaining the new legislation and appointing committees to head the area's organizing campaign. In August 1933 some 3,000 workers met in Memphis' Gaston Park to hear Cohen discuss the organizational drive.[5] In Jellico, William Turnblazer, president of District 19, headed the organizing drive among the miners. Within the space of two weeks, Turnblazer reported, 85 percent of the miners in his district had joined the UMWA, and the miners union had been successful in almost every coal mining community in Tennessee.[6]

In Chattanooga, the formation of many new union locals and the expansion of the established locals meant that the Chattanooga Trades and Labor Council was forced to move into larger quarters. The *Labor World* reported that requests for organizers had been sent out from communities in the southeast part of the state, such as Cleveland, South Pittsburg, Chickamauga, Daisy, and Soddy. One Chattanooga organizer, T. R. Cuthbert, reported that locals were being formed for cement workers, retail clerks, upholsterers, dairy workers, furniture workers, and operating engineers.[7]

At the 1934 annual convention of the Tennessee Federation of Labor, the NIRA was endorsed in glowing terms for bringing "economic freedom" and "prosperity" to the masses. A bleak future had turned bright for Tennessee workers. The new labor law meant "labor is far along the trail to better things."[8]

LUCILLE THORNBURGH AND TENNESSEE TEXTILES

In the mid-1930s Lucille Thornburgh was "young and full of vinegar." By day she would toil for ten hours at the winding machine at Knoxville's Cherokee Spinning Company. By night she and other co-workers who had caught the union spirit would pool their money to buy gas and go door-to-door recruiting and organizing for the United Textile Workers of America Union. "If there was a heyday of the labor movement in the Knoxville area, it was during those years of the mid-thirties, and the years that followed up until the mid-40s," Thornburgh stated.[9]

Thornburgh's time as a winding machine operator was fated to be limited. Though much too intelligent and articulate to remain in an east Tennessee mill the rest of her life, her own dedication to the union cause and decisions made by UTW officials many miles away from her work site meant an early exit from the factory into a more challenging world. As a textile worker blacklisted for her union activity, she walked out of the spinning mills during the great textile strike of 1934 to become a union organizer, an officer in the Tennessee Federation of Labor, a Ruskin College scholarship student at Oxford, a staff representative of Labor's league for Human Rights, and an editor and writer for a labor newspaper. Through the eyes and the experience of Lucille Thornburgh, a valuable perspective is gained on Tennessee work life and union activities during the New Deal years.

Thornburgh remembers how difficult the depression years were for the men and women working in the mills.

> I was working at Cherokee Spinning Company, right in the middle of the depression. The working people had nothing, particularly people in the textile mills, where wages were low anyway, and in the depression, lower than ever. Everyone was looking for a way out of the depression. There was hope in the union. I first joined the union in 1933—this was the old AFL Textile Workers and my local was 1758. Up until the first Roosevelt administration there were very few unions in the South, other than the printing and building unions.

The labor movement did not get off the ground in the east Tennessee area until 1932, Thornburgh recalls. "The labor organizers had such a hard time in the late 20s and early 30s. The mill owners and mine operators were fighting the people so hard they couldn't organize." The big impetus, of course, was FDR's successful push through Congress of the NIRA, giving legal status to the existence of trade unions. Cherokee Spinning Mills was ripe for organizing.

> Conditions were terrible. Until the NRA came in, I was working 50 hours for $7.20 a week. I worked on the night

> shift, going in at 5:30 P.M. and working ten hours. You talk
> about hot. In the summer you couldn't have the windows
> open because the cotton would blow around. There were
> times you couldn't see your machine very well the lint was
> so thick. . . . We had no breaks, but did have holidays, which
> we hated because we didn't get paid.

The United Textile Workers seemed to hold out hope to Lucille
Thornburgh and the 600 other textile workers at Cherokee. In 1933-
1934 their expectations were modest compared to modern standards.

> In those days in the mills, there was no such thing as sick
> leave, vacation time or medical insurance. All we were inter-
> ested in was an eight-hour work day, decent working condi-
> tions, and some measure of job security. None of our
> workers knew or cared anything about benefits or insurance.

During her short stint at the Cherokee mills, Thornburgh soon
learned about both racial and sex discrimination in the Tennessee
industrial plant. "We were too elite at Cherokee, we wouldn't work
with blacks. The mills were snow-white," she recalls.

> I wanted to be a weaver, mainly because a weaver made $16
> per week. I also wanted to be a fixer. A fixer made $17 a
> week. I had learned to fix my own machines and I could fix
> the others. But women just weren't considered for those
> positions. I asked my supervisor about moving up to a
> machine-fixer and he told me: "You must be crazy. No
> woman will get that position." Of course, they were all
> happy I could fix my machine, because that didn't bother
> the fixer. Looking back, we know now that that was out-in-
> out sex discrimination—but it was accepted and people
> weren't conscious of it then.

The textile workers also sensed that they were frozen at one rung or
another on the company ladder and not fully respected as human
beings by the owners and managers.

> The lowest wages went to the few blacks who were hired as
> janitors at the mills. . . . We had our winding hands and the
> weaving hands and our card-room hands. We were all
> hands. We weren't employees and we were *not* textile
> workers. Our nickname was "lint heads" because you'd
> come out of that mill in the morning and you would be
> snow-white with that cotton.

Lucille Thornburgh helped to lead her co-workers into the union movement which was sweeping industrial Tennessee. "There were 600 employees at Cherokee and there were 600 union members," she recalls proudly. "Workers in east Tennessee did join in the enthusiasm of the New Deal and started challenging the employers for higher wages, shorter hours, and better working conditions." But all was not well within Tennessee textiles—nor within the textile industry in general. Speaking of textile workers in the South, Thornburgh concludes:

> The odds were against these employees and their union from the very beginning. The employers, the public, and the clergy were openly against them. The old-time craft unions didn't take much interest; "you can't organize the cotton mill workers," they said and did little to help.[10]

TEXTILE TROUBLES EVERYWHERE

Nationally, the cotton textile industry had been "sick" during the relatively prosperous 1920s,[11] as evidenced by the events at Elizabethton, Tennessee, at the close of the decade. During the early depression years this larger industry had suffered shocking losses due to overcapacity and overproduction, price cutting, and low profits. Employment in cotton textiles nationally declined 26 percent between 1929 and 1933. The working conditions at Cherokee and other east Tennessee mills were no better than those in other southern states.

The New Deal for textile and garment union leaders did not seem like a good deal at all. There was strong dissatisfaction about several features of the NRA, especially the reduced work week, a ruling (adopted July 1933) that the stretch-out did not violate the cotton textile code, and the code's inadequate enforcement machinery. The textile managers frequently ignored the NIRA's collective bargaining provisions. One observer, novelist Martha Gellhorn, who wrote reports for Harry Hopkins, found the mill owners of the South "hysterical about unions."[12] As a result, mill owners frequently refused to recognize the union or to permit it to speak for workers in a plant.

Throughout the summer of 1934 some textile workers in the South, where two-thirds of the industry's work force was located, were prepared to strike hard-line employers. In July, 40 or 42 textile locals in Alabama representing 20,000 workers called a general strike to

Rock wool, Gaither Chemical Company, Nashville, 1939. (Courtesy—Tennessee State Library and Archives)

support their demands of union recognition, a $12 per week salary, and 30-hour week.[13] Talk continued to surface about an industry-wide general strike and the experience in Alabama was an index to the union solidarity held by union ranks even in the deep South.

The time was ripe for a revolt. To the textile union leaders and their members, the NRA had turned into a colossal fraud. The modest increase in wages was more than offset by the reduction in hours of work. Owners and managers made a farce of NIRA's section 7(a). What action and language could the mill owners understand? The 500 delegates to the UTWA convention in August 1934 met to find an answer to the vital question. Answer: a general cotton-textile strike on or about September. Strikes were authorized also in silk, wool, and rayon, with dates to be determined later. Francis Gorman was elected chairman of the emergency strike committee.

On August 30 the UTWA announced that the cotton textile strike would be effective at midnight on Saturday, September 1. Gorman, the 44-year-old English-born, former union organizer, took to the NBC airwaves to explain to some one million textile workers why they must remain idle for a while. Gorman had devised a plan which would span the East from Maine to Alabama—it was a mammoth effort which would be the largest strike in American history up to that time. The "sealed orders" Gorman dispatched to the locals were merely brief, morale-boosting instructions (e.g., "We can NOT fail this time or they will drive us into slavery"). Gorman borrowed an old UMW tactic of dispatching "flying squadrons" of textile workers to carry the word of the strike from one mill to another. This tactic, notes labor historian James Hodges,

> caught the fancy of the southern workers and press. When workers left one mill shut down they would form a cavalcade of trucks and cars, race to the next mill, invade it and call for the workers still at the machines to join them in the cross-country fun. The flying squadron tactic was especially effective in the South, where mills were clustered together in large cities. . . . The arrival of the cavalcade of cars and flatbed trucks with groups of workers hanging precariously to the staked sides and shouting encouragement to workers inside was a signal in the early September heat for an exodus of even unorganized workers from their machines.[14]

Thornburgh remembers the strike vividly, especially its timing at Cherokee. "We were right on the verge of getting a contract signed when they called that strike. The strike ended the chance of an agreement. We were locked out of the plant there, just like the other workers all over the nation," she recalls. "Picket? We sure did, for about two months. I lived hard during that time, and it would have been even harder if it hadn't been for the others at home."

There can be no doubt that the mill employers faced the prospect of a strike with much confidence, having won tough skirmishes with fledgling unions in the late twenties. But in the first few days after the strike call, the ranks of the strikers was to swell to 376,000 textile workers. Surprised now by the early effectiveness and strong union solidarity in the strike, the employers then responded by importing spies and armed guards for mills and by bringing pressure on public authorities to punish and harass the strikers and families and by using the National Guard to break the strike. Little wonder that violence erupted in several work sites in the South. A union sympathizer and a deputy were killed on September 5 in Georgia and the following day six pickets were gunned down by deputy gunfire in South Carolina. Riots soon erupted in the New England states. The most forceful suppression of strike activity was by Georgia's governor Eugene Talmadge, who declared martial law and sent some 4000

National Guardsmen into practically every textile village in Georgia, arresting strikers and their families and placing them in concentration camps surrounded by barbed wire. Talmadge's actions were especially disheartening because, as a governor considered to be friendly toward organized labor in the 1920s, they were so unexpected.

Sometimes an unusual personal turn of events could have an impact on the striking workers, as illustrated by an incident at Cherokee Spinning Company. In the middle of the strike, the president of the mill, Mr. Mabry, suffered a serious heart attack and died. "The president of the UTW local wanted to call the strike off," Thornburgh recalls. "The workers felt quite bad about his sudden death and, being from the Bible belt, they felt guilt about their role in the whole thing. The union leaders said, 'Look, we've killed him. Let's go back to work.' But Franz Daniel (union organizer) reassured the workers: 'Oh, don't let what that old man's conscience did to him bother you.'"

By the third week of the general strike, the strike was falling apart, especially in the South, which was the decisive area. There was vigorous opposition to the strike from local officials in mill towns and villages throughout the area. Mills throughout the country were slowly resuming production. Labor leaders conceded that "force and hunger" were driving strikers back to their jobs. On September 21, President Roosevelt added his personal plea to a request made by a special mediation board headed by John G. Winant—the UTW should call off the strike and the employers should take back the striking workers.

The following day, the union called off the strike. The general strike ended on September 22, less than a month after it began. In one of the most ludicrous claims in labor history, UTW strike leaders claimed an "amazing victory" and "overwhelming victory" for their sacrifices. The textile workers knew better. The companies still refused to recognize the workers' union. Wages were not increased. Employers refused to rehire many strikers. Union membership began to decline. "The general textile strike," as Lucille Thornburgh put it, "was the biggest mistake the labor movement ever made." The strike experience was a crushing defeat. The UTW was left in shambles.

FROM BLACKLIST TO LABOR'S LADY LEADER

What was not lost for Thornburgh and many of her working partners in the textile mill was a faith in trade unionism. The fact that she was shut out of Cherokee and other spinning mills in the area gave her the time and motivation to devote to the union cause. "As a result of my strike activity, I was blacklisted," she explains. "All the people on our picket line were blacklisted. I was pretty good at running my winding machine, but I could not have gotten a job anywhere in a mill. For all I know, I may still be on the blacklist." In November after the general strike, Thornburgh went to work for the Tennessee Valley Authority as a file clerk, first in Knoxville, then at Wilson Dam in Sheffield, Alabama, and then back in Knoxville.

The textile strike was just the beginning of a career in organized labor for Thornburgh. Throughout the thirties she spent her free time as a volunteer in AFL organizing drives, enlisting workers in the union cause in bakeries, laundries, and a glove factory. In 1937 she was elected vice-president of the Tennessee Federation of Labor, becoming the first woman to hold office in the state organization. "I had to be right pushy. The AFL had been building trades and skilled crafts and they were not accustomed to women doing things." Her oldest sister, Mary Morgan, was also a union organizer in Knoxville for the Amalgamated Clothing and Textile Workers; Morgan worked at Knoxville's Leibowitz Shirt Factory, which was successfully organized in 1933. The two sisters lived together as close family members, but in organizing they were competitive, hiding organizing secrets from one another and playfully arguing the merits of the AFL versus the CIO.

The world of organizing brought Thornburgh into touch with fascinating people. It was a world for which she did not seem prepared. "There was no union training in those days. The AFL sent me to a union training workshop in Memphis. God knows I needed it." Some union leaders in the thirties were effective speakers and organizers because of a background in church leadership. "We had some Bible-thumping fundamentalists in our union and they make good leaders, because they were such good speakers," she recalled. "For example, Jim Barrett was an organizer who used the Bible a lot in his speeches. He could use the scriptures in an inflammatory way, getting people stirred up." Franz Daniel, an organizer who spent much time in Tennessee, "was one of the best speakers around. He was also a great guy. He was an alcoholic. He recovered and also spoke for AA." Union meetings at the local level could be as diverse and interesting as the workers who composed them.

> There was a local of marbleworkers here in Knoxville—local 173. Many were fairly ignorant and didn't know how to read. But they did hard work for low pay. Their meetings

were like religious services—they called each other "brother" and there would be a lot of preaching. A favorite sermon theme would be "We've got a lot of false prophets around us." Quite often they'd fight, but they'd close every union meeting by joining hands and singing "Bless be the tie that binds." They were very religious but they had the benefit of bottle of whiskey each Friday.

In 1941 Thornburgh joined the AFL southern organizing staff. During World War II she worked for the War Department in Washington, the Labor Department in New York City, and served as a national representative of the Labor League for Human Rights, the relief arm of the AFL. After the war she was granted a scholarship to study at Ruskin, a labor college in England. Upon returning to Knoxville in 1948 she became an associate editor and later the chief editor for the *East Tennessee Labor News*. Enhancing reader interest in a specialized newspaper was a challenge she met creatively. Thornburgh remembers writing fictitious, inflammatory anti-union letters and publishing them pseudonymously in her paper. Angry union readers would write or call her to ask why such letters were even considered for publication in the first place. "Sorry, it's tough, I know, but we labor people have got to uphold the freedom of the press and free speech," she'd reply.

As a labor activist, Thornburgh had her share of barbed attacks and accusations leveled against her. In 1946, the *Knoxville Journal* published an article, "TVA Red Cell Exposed by Knoxville Attorney," which contained an accusation by one of Thornburgh's uncles, an attorney, S. J. Thornburgh, that she had attended meetings with Communists. The union organizer was also accused of having helped organize a "Red Cell" in Knoxville. The story hit the pages of east Tennessee newspapers, leading Thornburgh to issue a categorical denial: "I am not a Communist, never have been one, and have no intention of becoming one. I did attend some meetings of the League for Industrial Democracy. . . . Some people in Knoxville thought this organization had communistic leanings, I remember. Maybe that's what my uncle is talking about."[15] Years later, in the fifties, Thornburgh was elected to the board at Highlander; but when the school's racially open policies subjected it to the suspicions of Communist influence, she was pressured by east Tennessee labor leaders to resign the board post.

As the years passed, Lucille Thornburgh never really retired from the labor movement. Instead, she broadened her social and political activities. She returned to the board at Highlander to serve as treasurer. She had a special fondness for deserving causes that barely had a chance to win. In the fifties she led a "Kefauver for President" move in Knoxville with the Democratic Women's Club. She served on the board of Tennessee Valley Energy Coalition as well as on several citizens' groups in Knoxville. She became a Unitarian in 1949 after being raised in a strict, fundamentalist Baptist tradition. The reason for her conversion: the Tennessee Valley Unitarian Church needed one more member in order to receive a charter.

Whether Baptist or Unitarian, no one could doubt Lucille Thornburgh's real religion. Since walking out of the Cherokee mill that early autumn day in 1934, her deepest devotion has been to working people and their needs and problems. Looking back on a long and eventful career of union activity, she knew that the thirties, those days of great fervor and activity, had re-shaped labor history. "The notion of a union is no longer so controversial. We don't make the news that we used to. We're accepted. And the young ones can't know the battles we went through to win acceptance and then make some gains."

"THE FIRST AND MOST IMPORTANT VICTORY IN THE SOUTH"

January and February mornings in a Tennessee mountain town mean that daylight is slow in coming. Rain or heavy fog can delay the dawning of a new day even longer. During the winter months of 1937, garment workers in LaFollette, Tennessee, marched out of their plants on strike in protest against low wages and long work hours. Working women boldly faced the intimidation of plant management and set up picket lines in the darkness of 4:00 A.M. In less than four weeks, the strike had been settled at the Atlas shirt factory, achieving what union organizer Charles E. Handy called "the first and most important victory in the South and . . . the beginning of an Amalgamated Clothing Workers drive to clean up sweat shops."[16] Despite company delaying tactics and distractions, by April the workers who had already returned to their posts at the Reade plant gave the new union an 80 percent vote of confidence. The LaFollette story involving 1000 workers not only demonstrated the fervor of Tennessee working women for the union cause, but also signaled a clear victory for the labor movement in the Volunteer State.

Life in the Reade and Atlas shirt factories (called by union organizers and workers the "big shop" and the "little shop" respectively)
was a constant pace of monotonous work routine for low pay. By 1937
the depression had a "full head of steam" and the families who had
lived in the small towns and communities of east Tennessee had felt
the crunch as much as anyone else in the state.

The 600 garment workers at the Reade shop and the 400 workers
at the Atlas shop composed a largely female work force. Most of the
workers were either young or middle-aged women and a few were
older women—but all were called "girls" by observers, by the newspaper media, and by their bosses. Many of these "girls" supported
children, with or without a father at home, on their meager salaries.
Many lived on remote plots of land, in mountain coves that were far
off the main-traveled roads. Observers in LaFollette saw them as
poorly and thinly dressed. Their shoes were thin and worn. Their
faces could look tired and their bare hands roughened with corns.[17]
Among their ranks were such delightfully southern highlander
names as Ophelia Elder, Mollie Hatmaker, Dicie Overbey, Beulah
Boshears, Gertrude Queener, Adaline Ogle, Isabel Lewallen, and
Sophie Broyles.

Work for these women was not an option—it was necessary for
survival. Eula McGill, who became a business agent assigned to
LaFollette in the forties, recalls that the women were "mostly married,
but there were a lot of women that worked in there that weren't
married. Nowadays, people don't think that much about unmarried
mothers. But I never saw as many unmarried women with children in
my life anywhere as I did up there."[18] McGill remembers one woman
who worked in the plant named Magnolia Robbins, a single parent
who was "the most courageous person I ever met up with."

> Magnolia had four girls and a boy and every one of those
> children finished high school, which is unusual for back
> then. They had jobs, one of them worked for the telephone
> company. Well, see, I didn't know she wasn't married.
> Nobody said anything about it. The war came on and we
> had to start getting birth certificates and everything. She and
> a lot of others couldn't read and write. Well, when they
> started having them time cards, they had to tie strings on her
> time cards so she would know where her time cards was.
> Now they weren't dumb. Now listen, them people, when
> you told them something they retained it because they knew

they had to because they couldn't read. They knew how to listen. It was more pleasure to be with them people; they were easy to talk to than some people that don't pay you no attention, it goes in one ear and out the other. But those people were smart; I mean they had old-fashioned natural sense; they couldn't talk good, but when you explain something to them they could understand it. And I run into people today with plenty of so called education that they don't understand a damn thing you're telling them.[27]

Whether young or old, single or married, literate or illiterate, the women toiling in the LaFollette shirt factories shared one hope and dream—that union membership would make life in general better for them immediately.

Women in the shirt factories were usually paid by the piece. Pressers were paid 20 cents a dozen for stiff collars and 15 cents a dozen for soft ones. Women were pushed to complete a dozen collars in ninety minutes, as explained to Bertha Daniel, who visited the LaFollette picket lines.

"Collars" merely signifies the kind of shirt. Pressing collars means that you use eleven pins—that you put the pleats in the yokes, fasten four buttons, and put the shirt on a collar rack. All of this is carefully inspected and returned if the least detail has been overlooked. Some pressers work ten and a half hours a day; some work twelve. Some make from $6 to $8 a week at it, others can make up to $14 of $15. It is, for the experienced hands, one of the best paid operations in the shirt factory.[20]

The Amalgamated Clothing and Textile Workers of America was barely known in Tennessee in 1937. In fact, the oldest chartered ACWA local in the South was Local 90. Later to become the Palm Beach Company, Local 90 was organized at the old Publix Shirt Corporation in Knoxville. "This company had a union plant some place in the North and the workers in Knoxville just decided they were worth as much money as those in the North," Geneva Sneed explained.[21] In mid-1936 Charles Handy moved to LaFollette to organize the garment workers for ACWA. Handy was assisted in the original drive by Elaine Wright and Zilphia Horton, wife of Myles Horton. The drive was successful. The LaFollette union may have been the second ACWA union in the South.[22]

From the day union organizers came to town, the garment workers were fully aware of their employers' distaste for trade unionism. "Honey, hit's awful," declared one shirtmaker in the Reade factory; "the boss he says that ifn' we got any religion we'll not have anything to do with the union."[23] A woman in the Atlas plant was exhorted by a fellow-worker to shun unionism. "I'm sticking to Jesus' way" was her reply, "but I told him there is going to be unions in heaven. There has got to be if there is any love."[24] When asked after the strike began, "Is the boss pleasant?" a Reade worker exclaimed, "Lord God, no! He swears and cusses at us something dreadful. He said, 'Iffen you can't make $2 a day you can get out on the sidewalk with the union.'"[25]

On January 21 nearly all of the 400 employees of Atlas Shirt Company were out on strike. Their demands: union recognition, shorter hours, and more wages. A picket line was formed around the plant and only about ten workers entered to work; they later came out. Pickets carried banners announcing "We Are Creating a New NRA." The pickets told reporters that the Atlas workers were members of a new Amalgamated Clothing Workers' local union and that they had the support of the United Mine Workers. "Our people are not organized," an Atlas official countered. "They were pulled out by the miners' union, forcing us to close up. Our girls are well paid. An experienced girl makes $2, $2.50 a day, and sometimes $3.50 a day."[26]

The strike had come quickly. Circulars which explained strike plans had been distributed by strike organizers. When the women took the plans home to their mining communities they found instant support among the miners, many of whom were husbands, brothers, or other family members. The garment workers found their bosses ridiculing the union and the strike plans. This strengthened the workers' resolve and spurred immediate action. Charlie Handy went directly to an official of UMW's District 19 to request assistance, but arrived two hours after a scheduled miners' meeting. Then, under cover in the cold darkness of the winter night, the miners with their individual lights moved from door to door throughout the coves asking for volunteers to convene in LaFollette and support the strike. Before the sun had risen the miners had formed a double line to protect their women and demonstrate a militant solidarity with all other working class people in the mountain area.[27]

The workers at the Reade plant soon followed the Atlas strikers in the walkout. The town of LaFollette had never seen anything quite like this strike effort. Despite sympathy from some influential people in town, such as ministers and American legionnaires, several of LaFollette's businessmen were successful in denying a meeting hall to the strikers. Doughnuts and coffee were dispensed from the back of a truck in the street. But the spirit of the strikers was unquenchable. "One cannot walk a picket line four hours with women like these," Bertha Daniel reported, "without undergoing a spiritual change. . . . This mass solidarity is, of course, bound to succeed. . . . There is no fear in these people today."[28]

LaFollette and New York City were hundreds of miles apart—both culturally and geographically. Yet the shockwaves that were created in LaFollette rapidly made their way to Manhattan. On February 4 the New York Shirt Makers' Union organized a large picketing demonstration on behalf of their LaFollette colleagues. About 1000 members of the New York union left their shops in the middle of the day and marched around their home office carrying signs declaring solidarity with the workers at Atlas and Reade. One sign had inscribed: "Reade Manufacturing Company is the arch employer of cheap labor in the South; an enemy of labor." For workers in New York, the development in Tennessee highlighted a sore spot among garment workers— their conviction that the garment industrialists had moved to LaFollette in order to escape unionism and to maintain sweatshop conditions that would not have been permissible in the North.

Depression-era labor conflict was often violent and the scene at LaFollette was no exception. The Reade management realized there was an inventory of shirts the women had made before the strike had gone into effect and a decision was made to ship them out to buyers. Like their sisters in textiles at Elizabethton some eight years earlier, the women garment workers proved that when they were stirred to anger, plant operations would be anything but normal. The trucks were loaded with hundreds of new shirts which were ready to be taken to the LaFollette L & N station for shipment. One of the trucks was never to make it outside the plant vicinity. Spirited women workers stormed the truck, pulled several cartons of shirts from the cargo, opened the boxes and scattered and trampled on the shirts in the muddy road around the plant. The muddy road was almost completely blanketed with fresh cloth. Deputy Sheriff Silas Cupp then brandished a pistol while guarding another load of shirts. Other truckloads were allowed to pass from the plant.[29] Before the day was over, Charlie Handy and ten others were arrested by county officers on the charge of inciting a riot. Two days later hundreds of angry miners held local deputies at bay in front of the city jail with shotguns while demanding the release of two prisoners who had just been arrested; stones were hurled through the windows and the glass in the door of the city hall.[30]

After three and a half weeks, Atlas officials had had enough. On February 17 an agreement was signed with Amalgamated which granted union recognition, a closed shop, the check-off, shorter hours, and a wage increase. The Amalgamated organizers who had journeyed to LaFollette to establish a local or to encourage the strikers—Charles Handy and his wife, Newman Jeffrey and his wife, Hilda Cobb, Alex Cohen, and Dorothy Bellanca—were all ecstatic about the union victory. Handy announced that the union workers were ready to get back to work as soon as the plant is opened by management and that the union would now turn its attention to the Reade Manufacturing Company. "Atlas did it, and we know Reade can," Handy declared.[31]

The Reade management found it more difficult to swallow the notion of a closed shop in its factory. Nevertheless, on March 13, Reade agreed to a settlement which permitted a closed shop union agreement, a return of all jobs to striking employees without discrimination, wage increases, and arbitration of any disputes. The announcement was made by the LaFollette mayor and almost immediately the striking workers and their supporters began marching triumphantly through the streets chanting "And we don't come crawling!" During the seven weeks of the strike, "not a single striker had broken ranks" at the Reade plant despite the fact that they had been forbidden in the use of the public school auditorium and other public halls and had sought shelter and meeting space on those cold winter days in the most unlikely of places.

For sheer optimism the owners at Reade were not to be topped. Still convinced that their workers did not really want to be organized, the Reade management agreed to sign a settlement only if the workers would not be asked to ratify it before April 17. Like a drowning man clinging to a string of support, the Reade owners must have reasoned that once the workers were back at their posts sewing, pressing, and pinning shirts for the rest of the country that they would throw off this strange new talk about a union and pine for the days of old. The union leaders promptly granted this request, having no doubt about how the workers would vote. The company also asked the union to agree to keep the terms of the contract secret, something the union

The Amalgamated Clothing Workers' strike against the Atlas and the Reade plants in LaFollette, Tennessee, in the winter of 1937 drew interest and support among both the United Mine Workers (who had locals in Coal Creek and Jellico), but also among shirt makers in New York City. The ACWA won both strikes. (Courtesy—Eula McGill Private Collection)

refused to do. On April 17 the workers voted four to one for the Amalgamated Clothing Workers.[32]

A union had been born in LaFollette. There were struggles ahead if it was to survive. But in the early spring of 1937, there was a new sense of family and solidarity among a thousand workers in east Tennessee. Workers in departments who hardly knew each other had survived a winter of discontent away from their machines, become friends in adversity, and were not proud to be "brothers and sisters" of unionism. Merchants and miners from Jellicoe, Coal Creek, and other mining communities who helped the strikers daily sensed that something amazingly great had taken place in LaFollette. Against owner opposition, the union movement had been strengthened. It was a victory, in the words of labor activist Alex Cohen, "felt throughout the state of Tennessee."[33]

"THE GREATEST HUMANITARIAN OF OUR TIME"

When Franklin Roosevelt entered the White House, his first priority was getting Americans relief and back to work. Early programs, such as the Federal Emergency Relief Administration (FERA) and the Civil Works Administration (CWA), provided some relief.

The Civilian Conservation Corps (CCC), designed to provide vocational relief and vocation training for unemployed young men, established 33 camps in Tennessee. By the time Governor McAlister's second term expired in 1937, over 7,000 Tennesseans had been enrolled in the program and had planted millions of pine seedlings, built fire observation towers, and developed parks.[34] By 1935 it was obvious that another approach to the economic situation would be necessary.

The new approach came with the founding of the Works Progress Administration (WPA), established in 1935 with Harry Hopkins as director. As an administrator who controlled the disbursement of $1.4 billion to get Americans back to work, as well as a close friend of the president, Hopkins was one of the most powerful men in the country. Colonel Harry S. Berry, a former commissioner of highways under Governor Howard Horton, was appointed by Governor McAlister as chief administrator of WPA for Tennessee.

Colonel Berry soon announced plans for farm-to-market roads and city road projects costing $22 million and employing 5000 men, thus benefiting every county. State work projects were about evenly divided among the three grand divisions of the state, west, middle, and east Tennessee. Other WPA projects in Tennessee included construction of schools and courthouses, establishment of more than 100 parks, and provisions for numerous playgrounds and playing fields. In Nashville, for example, WPA projects included a major $70,000 airport addition, the establishment of Percy Warner Park and the adjoining Edwin Warner Park, and a controversial $45,000 steeplechase course "similar, hardly as large, but even more beautiful than the site of the Grand National in England," to be constructed at Percy Warner Park.[35]

By the end of 1935 about 40,000 workers were on the rolls of the Tennessee WPA program. By mid-1937 Tennessee's WPA employment quota had been cut almost in half, reflecting FDR's program cuts for the national budget. But Tennessee had fared well under the WPA. In the eight years of existence, the federal program in Tennessee employed an average of about 30,000 men and women out of a total population of 2.9 million. Considering eligibility and length of employment requirements,

The New Deal established CCC camps to work outdoors in Tennessee. The "chow line" awaits the next meal. (Courtesy—Tennessee State Library and Archives)

some 100,000 Tennesseans were put to work by the federal government at one time or another during the early New Deal.[36]

Statistics do not tell the whole story, however. More than anything else, the WPA boosted the morale of Tennessee citizens and, specifically, of the labor movement in the state. Citizens had seen evidence that the government cared about the plight of the unemployed and, for those who were employed, a sense of dignity and self-respect was restored.[37] Of course no work or relief program could have met the vast need nationwide. In the Volunteer State as well as elsewhere, there were many people who could not find satisfactory work. People still suffered from lack of sufficient housing and clothing. Some still went hungry. Blacks were denied equal opportunity in the WPA programs. But at least the government had taken action on behalf of the workers. And in Tennessee as elsewhere, the most popular national figure and chief beneficiary of this good will was President Franklin D. Roosevelt. As the presidential campaign of 1936 rolled around, there was no doubt about the man organized labor would be supporting. Stanton Smith remembers well an incident during the 1936 convention of the Tennessee Federation of Labor:

William Turnblazer, Sr., like Brush Smith, was an interesting character out of the mine workers. This was my first state Federation convention, here in Chattanooga at the old Patton Hotel. Turnblazer was the district vice-president of the mine workers. He was a florid-faced firebrand. This was the convention in which Roosevelt was getting ready to run for his second term. The miners were pushing hard for an endorsement of Roosevelt. The state Federation of Labor at that time had a "no endorsement" policy in their constitution—a provision forbidding endorsement. Bill Turnblazer got up and claimed, "We are for Roosevelt, the greatest humanitarian of our time!" and then called for a convention endorsement. I remember I was watching it while he was sitting there. He would smoke cork-tipped cigarettes. Once he put the wrong end in his mouth, lit the cork tip, and took it out of his mouth and just looked at it and then threw it down. The no-endorsement rule didn't stop Turnblazer. He had the delegates with him and he just rode rough-shod over the constitution and declared, "I move the constitution be suspended. We endorse Franklin Delano Roosevelt for President of the United States."[38]

EULA MCGILL

Perhaps no man or woman pursued the union cause in Tennessee during the 1940s with more raw courage, spunk, and energy than Eula Mae McGill. Her heart, soul, and mind have been dedicated to the labor movement in the South. From 1939 to 1982 she was employed by the Amalgamated Clothing Workers of America as organizer and business agent. Born near Resaca, Georgia, on May 15, 1911, McGill's association with the union cause began years before she was formally employed with ACWA and continued years after her formal retirement.

McGill's father, Joseph Hamilton McGill (from the same branch of the family that produced journalist Ralph McGill), toiled in the ore mine near Sugar Valley, Georgia. Eula remembers riding the "little old dinky engine with a car" that pulled supplies by rail to the mine. When that mine was worked out (or "played out" as they, the miners, called it), the McGill family moved to Gadsden, Alabama, where Eula's dad worked as a carpenter in maintenance detail for Gulf State Steel Company in Gadsden. She began her education in a schoolhouse on land donated by the Dwight mills in a textile village. Eula first became aware of union activity when, at about age seven, she and her mother, Mary Rachel Suzanne McGill, would get on the street car and go to the union rallies. "My father had to work; he never was off during the times we'd have those little rallies, unless it was on Saturday or Sunday," McGill recalls. "He didn't dare go; if he was seen there, you know, he was likely to be fired, because most of the people who went were already in the unions. There were no laws in those days, no protective laws whatsoever."[39] Eula's dad joined the union and explained to her the value of union membership: "He told me . . . 'All a person has to sell is their labor, and you ought to try to get the most of it. . . . As long as anybody in this world's got more than you've got, try to get some of it. . . . If a person lives in this world without trying to make it a better place to live in, he's not living, he's just taking up space. . . . ' It stuck with me all through the years. And I agree with him."[40]

At age fourteen Eula began working in a textile mill in Gadsden. Getting hired required some devious ingenuity. If a youngster claimed to be sixteen when he or she applied for a job in the mill, the manager asked for a school permit verifying the age. The manager usually did not ask for the permit for older children, so Eula, being "big for my age," claimed to be seventeen and was hired without question. She remembers those early years of work in the mill.

> We worked 12 hours a day and ate our lunches while we worked. I didn't earn anything but I learned. The first six weeks I was a "learner," and received no pay. When the six weeks were up and I received my first week's pay, I had earned $3.10, of which ten cents was automatically taken out for ice water and a penny out of every dollar we made went to the company doctor. There was no ice water there. They didn't have fountains; it come in a spigot. After the first week I made between three and four dollars a week.[41]

McGill became personally involved with unionism in the early thirties while working in the mills. When Mollie Dowd, the executive board member of the National Women's Trade Union League, came to Birmingham to organize a chapter, McGill was one of the first women to join. While working in the mills, the energetic and outgoing McGill never missed an opportunity to preach the gospel of unionism to co-workers. Her interest and activism in the labor movement opened the door for her to travel on two occasions to the nation's capital.

*Friends and supporters of organized labor in Tennessee are addressed and encour-
aged by California's Congresswoman Helen G. Douglas, a figure who prominently
appeared in Richard Nixon's early political career. Douglas visited and spoke in
Knoxville (circa 1950). Also seated is Eula McGill (in the middle), ACWA business
agent in Tennessee, and a young Albert Gore, Sr. (Courtesy—Eula McGill Private
Collection)*

McGill's first trip to Washington was made before the general
textile strike. She, along with her boss, testified before a legislative
committee which was weighing the subject of a minimum wage; the
issue under consideration was whether the current minimum of 25
cents per hour should be raised to 40 cents per hour. McGill found
herself matching wits against big businessmen who were fighting the
wage increase. It's ironic that the people making $25 an hour were
fighting against the workers who were making 25¢ an hour," she
mused. At these hearings, McGill's boss informed legislators that
southern laborers worked under a peculiar disadvantage: "the sun
was so hot that it dulled their brains."[42]

In 1934 McGill joined other textile workers nationwide and participated in the general strike called by Francis Gorman. Her second trip

to Washington was a direct result of her activism in the National Women's Trade Union League. Joining a group of other league members, she was invited by Eleanor Roosevelt to be a White House guest for the week-long national convention in Washington. When she returned from Washington this time McGill was soon informed that she no longer had a job.

McGill's dismissal from the textile mill was a blessing for the labor movement in Alabama and Tennessee. Her interest in working people and her love for the union cause, combined with the fact it was impossible to keep her mouth closed, meant she would never be content spending all her time behind a spindle or loom. With no job and time on her hands, McGill began volunteer organizing with bakery workers, mine workers, and red-ore miners. Her arguments and techniques for enlisting new members were convincing. Her reputation as an organizer had been established. Later in 1936 she joined the staff of the Textile Workers' Organizing Committee (TWOC) as a salaried organizer, a post she kept until 1939. In 1939 McGill began a long and illustrious career with Amalgamated.

In the early months of work for ACWA McGill found herself traveling throughout Alabama, Georgia, South Carolina, Kentucky and east Tennessee. In 1941 she helped get the first union contract with Cluett-Peabody in Atlanta. She returned to Knoxville and worked in the Hall Tate campaign and then moved to the Palm Beach shop, where she remained until 1943. McGill was working in Roanoke, Alabama, in a Palm Beach Shop when Gladys Dickinson, vice president and southern director of organizing at ACUA, assigned her to LaFollette. In this mountain town Eula McGill was destined to devote three tumultuous years servicing the garment workers as their union business agent.

As it turned out, McGill's first job at LaFollette was to rescue the young ACWA local from the encroachment of John L. Lewis and the United Mine Workers. As she tells it, the mine organizers "were trying to get the people in the two shirt factories that we had organized in LaFollette to join their union, and of course using the mine workers' name, the United Mine Workers, to attract them to this. And they couldn't make any success. They couldn't get anywhere with the people. They wouldn't join."[43]

By 1943 the old Atlas and Reade plants had been acquired by different companies and had become the Southeastern Shirt Corporation and the Imperial Shirt Corporation respectively.

Amalgamated union people found relations with the new management pleasant by comparison with the stormy days of 1937-1938. The garment workers in these two factories felt no real need to abandon the union that had first brought labor organization to their mountain city. Their working conditions had been improved by the union contract and a good salary had been secured. Some shirtmakers were making $40 to $45 per week, as McGill recalls (McGill's own salary during those years as ACWA business agent was $35 per week).[44] The workers had a union hall which would accommodate 1000 people. The hall was a center of community life for the garment workers and their families. One night a week was "family night," a time when the kitchen facilities were heavily taxed. The single women came to the union hall in the evening for visiting and recreation.

The relative calm in labor-management relations in LaFollette did not discourage outside labor elements, especially UMW activists, from attempting by whatever means available to disrupt worker solidarity. The presence of outsiders kept the situation tense. As for the miners and some of the "riffraff" they had organized, their reasoning was that they were merely reclaiming the union locals they had helped to organize and which belonged to them in the first place. McGill contends that she was sent to LaFollette because her union felt that a woman would be safer there than a man; nonetheless, as she points out, "I didn't depend on that. I carried a gun with me and I was careful not to go out except to the union hall, the restaurant, and to my hotel at night."[45] Sporadic violence had already broken out before McGill arrived. Organizers Ed Blair and Franz Daniel had been roughed up by thugs. On another occasion, Daniel was shot in the chest, but the bullet lodged in a "coal breast pocket" which had been lined with either a Bible or a thick wallet.[46] On another occasion the outsiders broke into the union office. McGill remembers advising the men in the shirt factories to "stay clear" of the labor wars in town "because they would be victims of violence." And as for the women workers' response to threats of violence and harassment:

> They held their heads up and went on, until they started shooting in their houses and beating up their husbands and threatening. The pressure got a little bad after they finally put a picket line out and wouldn't let the people into work, and that's how they finally got one of the shops. They never did get the other. But they came. We was having a meeting over at the hall, and they came up. We had the door locked.

There were seventy-five or a hundred guys and one or two
women, and the people who knew them said they worked
in Jellico. They were not workers from our plants. None of
the workers from our plant was involved in this. And they
were trying to get the door open, and they couldn't get it
open. They kept trying. Frankly, we had clubs inside the
hall to protect ourselves. And every time they'd stick their
finger through the crack one of the girls would hit their
fingers, and they yelled. A cop was standing outside, the
policemen, watching all this. And they yelled back to him
and said, "They've got clubs in there." And he came up and
asked me to open the door. We opened the door, and he
stepped back and let them in. Then them women beat the
tar out of them.[47]

The intruders tried to retaliate, "but they couldn't fight. Them
women was terrors. They were trying to get me. Some of the women
took me back of the hall and made me stay there. They knew they
were after me."[48]

McGill's adversary through the LaFollette strike was Silas
Huddleston, a miner from Caryville, Tennessee, and a local president
and staff member for United Construction Workers. The pressure
exerted first by intimidation and then by outright physical violence
was the longest and most trying labor experience in McGill's career.
"And it was quite embarrassing," she recalls, "coming from a so-
called union. That's what I told Silas. . . . I said, 'We have a hard
enough time to organize without two unions having to fight each
other.' That's the way I felt about it. . . . I'm still proud that we did not
attack another union. We did not attack any of their members. We just
merely tried to protect ourselves."[49] The loss of one shop was due in
part, McGill is convinced, to the local management "playing footsie
with this other union . . . they knew it would be a weaker union."[50]

Sometimes the pressures of work life resulted in incidents which
became humorous only in retrospect. McGill once had to intervene for
a worker named Elise Huddleston.

The plant manager over at the big shop was Litoff. People
didn't like him. He thought he had to fight the union. He
would pass me and wouldn't speak. Funny thing, because
later he called me and asked for a job; I got to like him. I was
told to come to the plant and there was Elise in an office
with Cooper, the owner's son and the plant manager. The

manager was crying. I said, "I see you crying." The story was that him and her got into an argument, she got up and was going to walk out. Mr. Litoff went to meet her, thinking she had reconsidered and decided to come back to work and when she got to him, well, it was pretty embarrassing for this poor soul. She hit him over the head with an umbrella. Made him cry. She didn't have good sense. Donald fired her and I had to go to the little shop to get her a job. I said, "Now, Elise, let me tell you something. This is your last chance. You worked over here and you got fired and you worked over there and got fired, and now I've talked to the manager about bringing you back. Now there's nothing else I can do for you if you don't do it right." That poor girl had to work—she was her sole support.[51]

From 1946-1952 McGill covered mainly the territory in middle and west Tennessee and western Kentucky. Garment shops were organized and serviced in such cities as Dickson, Martin, Bruceton, Livingston, and at Huntingdon where she maintained headquarters for many months. Whether dealing with management, the press, or even a union member who got out of line, the straightforward and salty-tongued union woman was a sharp and tough-minded communicator. No one ever accused McGill of being open-minded, ladylike, or delicate in her speech, and her propensity to express an opinion on any subject often kept her at odds with others. The stories of those years are numerous. McGill could be a tough colleague. On one occasion, she and colleague Buster Smith had such a sharp disagreement while traveling on a west Tennessee highway that the two stopped and exited their car and fought it out physically alongside the road. Whether or not the fight resolved the differences between the two high-strung unionists, it at least provided some relief from tension. On another occasion, McGill physically manhandled Hansel Lassiter, an attorney for the Siegal Company, and the fight ended by the lawyer running past the railroad tracks.[52]

One story in particular McGill loves to tell. The ACWA was working diligently to organize a Dickson garment factory, but did not have much success. Finally, the union was voted in. Shortly thereafter a strike was called. McGill and Mary Morgan traveled to nearby Bruceton to ask the recently organized garment workers there to come out of their plant in sympathy with their Dickson brothers and sisters. When picket lines effectively dissuaded truckers from making

Eula McGill, business agent for ACWA, addresses a union rally audience in west Tennessee, circa late forties. (Courtesy—McGill Private Collection)

deliveries on the plant grounds, the townspeople and farming community confronted McGill and Morgan and demanded they leave town. A mob of some 150 men, as McGill tells it, approached the home of a Methodist minister where the two women were staying, and at 7:00 A.M. demanded their immediate departure from Bruceton. No threats were made and no violence occurred. That afternoon a story appeared in the *Commercial Appeal* reporting that the people of Bruceton had run the two union women from town.[53]

McGill spent thirty additional years working for Amalgamated in other southern states after leaving Tennessee. It was only natural that upon her official retirement that she would set up an office in her hometown, maintain strong and active ties with the labor movement, and devote time to new causes and organizations, such as the League of Women Voters. But the old struggles and labor wars as an indefatigable union organizer and business agent are the ones she has cherished most. For the fiery labor activist, both the organizer and the business agent had its own special challenges and rewards. Noting that it made no real difference which of the two assignments she was given, McGill added:

> Sometimes I feel that a business agent is more rewarding, to see some good you're doing. When you're organizing sometimes you feel like, well, you're out here to get these people out on a limb, and you have to fight. You worry yourself to death, afraid that something'll happen and you're not going to be able to protect him. And they don't follow your advice a lot of times. And when they talk union, they're going to talk union, and you try to advise them how to do it so that the boss won't catch them off-guard so we can protect them with whatever the law can protect them with. [Laughter.] And you worry constantly about it, that maybe somebody is in there talking and they don't know how to protect themselves. And if they get fired, you worry yourself to death. I know when I first started organizing, when anybody got fired I tried to get them back in there. I had no relief or nothing. I used to spend most of my paycheck keeping people up who get fired, families, they had no income. Organizing is a heart-breaking job in a lot of respects. You feel sometimes that you're back with your head against a stone wall. But all in all, you know that it has to be done, that you have to keep at it. If you don't, well, you can slip backward a heck of a lot faster than you can go forward. If you don't keep up the battle, why you'll slip backward.[54]

"AN ORGANIZATION FLAME IN TENNESSEE"

The decade of the thirties was in some ways both the worst of times and the best of times for the labor movement in Tennessee. Industrial workers faced the critically hard days of full depression. They both sacrificed and suffered deprivation. Industrial workers also saw a great stirring of organized labor in their state. Against the odds of management antagonism and intimidation, they had seen new locals being formed and favorable contracts won. Despite remarkable success, there was even greater hope for the future because the strong arm of the law was finally on their side. "In the wake of" the Roosevelt administration's "history-making decisions," President R. S. McCann exhorted the delegates to the 1937 annual TFL convention meeting in Jackson: "I hope that an organization flame will be kindled in Tennessee and that it will flare and engulf the entire state. . . . No stone should be left unturned to take advantage of this opportunity to strengthen the labor movement and extend the protecting wing of organized labor over the workers of Tennessee."[55]

NOTES

1. Sanford Cohen, *Labor in the United States*, 3rd ed. (Columbus: Charles E. Merrill, 1970), 102.

2. In *National Labor Relations Board v. Jones* and *Laughlin Steel Corporation*, 301 U.S. 1.

3. Chattanooga *Labor World*, June 2, 1933; quoted in John Dean Minton, "The New Deal in Tennessee, 1932-1938," (Ph.D. dissertation, Vanderbilt University, 1959), 203.

4. Knoxville *Progressive Labor*, June 22, 1933; quoted in Minton, "New Deal in Tennessee," 204.

5. Minton, "New Deal in Tennessee," 204.

6. Ibid.; Chattanooga *Labor World*, June 9, 23, 30, 1933.

7. Minton, "New Deal in Tennessee"; Chattanooga *Labor World*, July 7, 28, and Sept. 1, 15, 1955.

8. *Book of Laws of the Tennessee Federation of Labor Together With the Proceedings of the 37th Annual Convention* (hereafter cited as TFL, *Proceedings of the Annual Convention*), 14, 23, 38.

9. Personal interview with Lucille Thornburgh, Knoxville, Tennessee, Dec. 18, 1987; see also Lois Reagan Thomas, "Knoxville Labor Then and Now," *Knoxville News-Sentinel*, Sept. 1, 1985. The statements from Ms. Thornburgh in this section are taken from the Dec. 18, 1987, interview unless otherwise noted. Features on Ms. Thornburgh appeared in *Knoxville Journal*, Nov. 29, 1984, and *Knoxville News-Sentinel*, Dec. 9, 1970.

10. Lucille Thornburgh, "United Textile Workers Has Made Tremendous Progress," *East Tennessee Labor News*, Aug. 25, 1966; *Textile Challenger*, October 1966.

11. Irving Bernstein discusses this point in *Turbulent Years: A History of the American Worker, 1933-1941* (Boston: Houghton Mifflin Company, 1970), 298-317.

12. Ibid., 303.

13. Ibid., 305-06; F. Ray Marshall, *Labor in the South* (Cambridge: Harvard University Press, 1967 167.

14. James Hodges, *New Deal Labor Policy and the Southern Textile Industry, 1933-1941* (Knoxville: University of Tennessee Press, 1986), 105. The human side of the southern cotton textile world and the general strike is vividly portrayed in Jacquelyn Dowd Hall et al., *Like a Family: The Making of a Southern Cotton Mill World* (Chapel Hill: University of North Carolina Press, 1987).

15. *Knoxville News-Sentinel*, Feb. 16, 1947.

16. *Knoxville News-Sentinel*, Feb. 18, 1937.

17. Bertha Daniel, "The Epic of LaFollette, Tennessee," *The Advance* (March 1937): 13.

18. Personal interview with Eula McGill, Birmingham, Alabama, May 26, 1987.

19. Ibid.

20. Daniel, "Epic of LaFollette," 13.

21. Personal interview with Geneva Sneed, Knoxville, Tennessee, Dec. 18, 1987.

22. *Knoxville News-Sentinel*, Sept. 1, 1985.

23. Daniel, "Epic of LaFollette," 13.

24. Ibid.

25. Ibid.

26. *Knoxville News-Sentinel*, Jan. 22, 1937.

27. Daniel, "Epic of LaFollette," 13.

28. Ibid., 28.

29. Pictures of the scattered shirts on the road and of the deputy sheriff holding a gun in front of a group of workers are published in *Knoxville News-Sentinel*, Feb. 10, 1937.

30. *Knoxville Journal*, Feb. 12, 1937.

31. *Knoxville Journal*, Feb. 19, 1937.

32. *The Advance* (April 1937 and May 1937).

33. Ibid.

34. Robert E. Corlew, *Tennessee: A Short History*, 2nd ed. (Knoxville: University of Tennessee Press, 1981), 470.

35. James A. Burran, "The W.P.A. in Nashville, 1935-1943," *Tennessee Historical Quarterly* 34:3 (Fall 1975), 300.

36. Ibid., 305; Minton, "New Deal in Tennessee," 370-71.

37. The author's "Harry L. Hopkins: Spokesman for Franklin D. Roosevelt in Depression and War" (Ph.D. dissertation, Wayne State University, 1970) reports this idea as a main theme in all the Hopkins' speeches and defense of the W.P.A. to the press.

38. Personal interview with Stanton Smith, Chattanooga, Tennessee, April 10, 1987; see also Resolution No. 19 in T.F.L., *Proceedings of the 39th Annual Convention*, 41.

39. Jacquelyn Hall, "Oral History Interview with Eula McGill," Atlanta, Georgia, February 1976, p. 18. Used by permission of Ms. McGill.

40. Ibid., 20-21.

41. Personal interview with author; see feature stories on Eula McGill in *Birmingham News*, June 17, 1982, and *Atlanta Journal and Constitution*, Feb. 9, 1964.

42. McGill interview.

43. Hall, "Oral History Interview with Eula McGill," 92.

44. Personal interview.

45. Ibid.

46. McGill states that it was a thick wallet which stopped the bullet from piercing Daniel's body. Lucille Thornburgh relates that a Bible stopped the bullet. Geneva Sneed told the *Knoxville News-Sentinel* that "that union's birth was not without violence, mainly because the miners union opposed it. We had a couple of people shot in that. Ed Blair was beat up and Franz Daniel was shot. He had a Bible in his pocket and it stopped the bullet." September 1, 1985.

47. Hall, "Oral History Interview with Eula McGill," 97.

48. Ibid., 98.

49. Ibid., 101.

50. Ibid., 102.

51. Personal interview.

52. James Neeley is the source of both stories. Personal interview, December 7, 1987.

53. Personal interview.

54. Hall, "Oral History Interview with Eula McGill," 109.

55. TFL, *Proceedings of the 40th Annual Convention*, 23.

7

CIO Blues

The Struggle of Tennessee's Industrial Workers

The 1930s was the most important decade for the modern labor movement in the United States. Working people, many of them unemployed, had elected a president who was friendly to organized labor. The passage of the NIRA and its successor, the Wagner Act, was seen by millions of workers as a green light, if not an outright government invitation, to join a labor union. While union membership surged, labor leaders contemplated the potential for organizing the large mass production industries, such as automobile, steel, rubber, and textile. The stage was set for the most serious schism in the history of the American labor movement.

The movement to organize the masses of industrial workers was led by the chief of the Mine Workers. John Llewellyn Lewis was a miner and the son of a miner, born of Welsh parentage in 1880 in a small Iowa community. An avid reader and adventurer in the western United States, Lewis' rise to power began in a miners' local in Panama, Illinois. By 1920 he was president of the United Mine Workers, the largest single union within the AFL with a membership of 500,000. When Lewis was unable to convince the AFL leadership to finance and support big organizing campaigns in the non-union industries, he announced in November 1935 the creation of the CIO— the Committee for Industrial Organization—composed of several AFL leaders of AFL unions who would join him in the campaign for industrial unionism. As a fervid orator, Lewis' bitter words of attack on his former AFL colleagues hastened the breach. In 1936 the various CIO unions were expelled from the Federation and in 1938 the CIO held its first constitutional convention and subsequently became the Congress of Industrial Organizations.

Lewis' dramatic move was a well-calculated gamble. The CIO began a remarkably successful series of organizing campaigns, leading to signed agreements, often after strike activity, with major corporations in the auto, steel, rubber, glass, meatpacking, and other mass production industries. The unions that remained within the AFL also enjoyed substantial gains in membership during the mid- and late thirties. Meantime, the great debate over industrial unionism was being rehashed in Tennessee. By early 1936 the relative merits of industrial unionism versus craft unionism had been discussed at a meeting of the Nashville Trades and Labor Council.[1] During that same year, the annual convention of the Tennessee Federation of Labor became a forum for a "fiery word battle between advocates of craft and industrial unions," with William Turnblazer, president of UMW's District 19, leading the charge for industrial unionism.[2]

When the AFL executive council suspended from its organization those unions that held membership in the old CIO, repercussions were felt at the state and local levels. For example, AFL President William Green telegraphed the Chattanooga Central Labor Union that "all CIO affiliates should be dis-associated," but the Chattanooga CLU president, Joe Dobbs, had accepted employment with the CIO and was director of textile organizing activities in Chattanooga. The squeeze was on. Dobbs attempted to delay the matter pending further investigation. The Chattanooga labor movement was divided. By the time of the next meeting, President Green had dispatched George Googe to preside over a new local election and to insure that CIO delegates were barred from TFL activities.[3]

By early 1938 the *CIO News* reported that a city council had been established in Nashville which included ten local unions with a membership of 7000 workers. The Tennessee Industrial Union Council held its first state convention in Knoxville in May 1940; a constitution was drafted and William Turnblazer was elected president. By 1940 four councils had been established in Tennessee, one in each of the four largest cities; there were some 50 locals in the state CIO organization with a membership of approximately 20,000 workers.[4]

THE CIO SOUTHERN RECEPTION

Southern CIO leaders did not expect their message of unionism to be received in their region with open minds and open arms, but many were not prepared for the degree of hatred, hostility, and irrationality they faced below the Mason-Dixon line. Throughout the South, the CIO, tainted by charges of race-mixing and communism, was viewed as a dangerously radical and subversive movement. At virtually all CIO organizing activities, taunting, angry shouts and threats awaited the organizers. Sheriffs and other local officials of various southern communities were freely quoted with one clear message: "We don't want CIO organizers in our town to stir up trouble!" The Textile Workers' Organizing Committee found itself under attack from all sectors of the southern community, according to James Hodges, who quotes from one journalist:

> In tackling cotton, the CIO is incurring the active opposition of all combined interests of southern capital, for southland is Cottonland in field and factory. Industrialist, banker, utility magnate, plantation owner, merchant, newspaper publisher—all . . . aim to halt the CIO tenant union in the cotton field, and textile union in the cotton factory.[5]

The employers had many weapons at their disposal to halt or slow down the CIO movement in the late 1930s—company unions, collusion with local government officials to deprive organizers of their civil rights and liberties, discriminatory discharges, threats, evictions from mill-owned houses, labor spies, and disruption of union meetings. Plant owners were known to seduce the influence of local pulpits, so that any susceptible evangelist could preach against the CIO, meaning "Christ is out." CIO organizers have alleged that the preachers were bribed, but proof is not available. Union organizers were frequently flogged by company officials, non-union workers, or angry citizens. Between 1936 and 1939, nineteen southern union organizers and workers were killed.[6]

Perhaps no weapon against the CIO was any more effective than the charge of communist influence. The battle between AFL and CIO leaders was so intense that otherwise reputable AFL leaders resorted to making irresponsible allegations that the CIO was using communist tactics or of being aided and abetted by communist organizations. The charges stung and stuck. The CIO in the South never fully escaped the taint of these charges.[7]

BOSS CRUMP AND THE UNIONS

The battle against the emerging Congress of Industrial Organizations was never more heated or more intense anywhere in the

South than in Memphis. "We aren't going to have any CIO nigger unions in Memphis," Edward Hull Crump declared defiantly. "They can do what they want in Detroit, Chicago, and New York City, but we aren't going to have it in Memphis."[8] Crump's opposition to the CIO's brand of unionism was no secret—not in Memphis and not throughout Tennessee. Because of this one politician and his big city machine, industrial unionism enjoyed few early successes in the Bluff City.

The political machine which totally ruled Memphis during the depression years was largely the creation of one powerful figure, Edward H. Crump. Migrating from Holly Springs, Mississippi, the eighteen-year-old Crump came to Memphis in 1893 to seek his fortune in business. What Crump could not leave behind in Mississippi, as Roger Biles points out, were the deeply ingrained values and mores of the southern white planter class—his mother's family had owned a plantation and slaves in North Carolina and his father, a former Confederate soldier, maintained modest holdings in Holly Springs.[9] Crump soon married into a socially prominent family, accessed handsome funds to gain control of a carriage and saddlery firm for which he worked, and quickly established himself as a successful businessman in the river city. "The Red Snapper," as he was called in those early years, soon made a successful foray into politics.

Crump pursued the mayor's office on a city reform platform. Memphians' displeasure over high tax rates, but inadequate fire and police protection, poor garbage collection, and muddy streets presented Crump a noble cause. In 1909 he was elected mayor of the city under the new commission government, an office he was to hold until 1916, when he was forced by his enemies to resign from office for his failure to enforce Tennessee's prohibition law. In the following years, however, Crump's every move only increased his grasp on political power both in Memphis because he controlled votes in the state's most populous county, and also throughout Tennessee. He soon had assembled one of the most efficient urban political machines in the nation—a machine which reached its peak in the 1930s and continued to remain strong until the election of 1948.

Like all big city bosses, such as Frank Hague or Richard Daley, Crump's power base rested solely upon patronage. An estimated 20,000 county and municipal workers felt indebted to Boss Crump for their jobs. This strong force, combined with thousands of blacks who responded gratefully to Crump's unabashed paternalism, translated into ballots cast for the boss or his anointed candidates. How efficiently the machine ran!

Crump's greatest weakness, perhaps, was his unwillingness to tolerate challenges to his authority and to his views. Despite his own scrupulous integrity (no hint of scandal ever touched his machine), Crump found it impossible to restrain completely the activities and emotions of his people at the lower levels of the organization. He also made little if any effort to restrain a vivid and blunt expression of his own views and emotions. "Notoriously thin-skinned," according to Biles, Crump's vitriol was reserved especially for such antagonists as CIO leaders and opposing newspaper editors. Speaking of three *Nashville Tennessean* editors, for example, who sardonically referred to Memphis as "Crumptown," the wounded city chief responded:

> This trio of mangy bubonic rats are conscienceless liars . . .
> cowards at heart yellow to the core. . . . There is not one of
> them who, singly or together, would meet us on the street
> . . . and say all the things to our faces that they have said in
> their scurrilous newspaper behind our backs. The honey-
> moon of this lying, corroding crowd of murderers of
> character is over. Their swill barrel is empty.[10]

Playing the role of a country gentleman scorned, Crump felt obligated to answer in kind by falling back on some favorite epithets: "an insipid ass"; "low, filthy scoundrel, pervert, degenerate"; "silly, sissy"; and "a mangy, bubonic rat."

Whatever else his opponents may not have liked, no one could deny that Crump was in favor of Memphis. Memphians saw the leader as one of them, unified in the belief that a truly great and prosperous city was rooted in tranquil race relations (meaning, of course, a quiescent acceptance of racial segregation), freedom from state sales or income taxes, inexpensive power and transportation costs, and a cheap and docile labor pool to attract industry. Overall, Ed Crump was a unique combination of urban progressivism and the Bourbon tradition. The assumption of most Crump partisans, most certainly, was that boss rule and a closed society was a fair price to pay for an admittedly clean, efficient, and benevolent city government.[11]

Crump seemed to have a love-hate relationship with the Memphis labor movement. On the one hand, during Crump's mayoral terms the forces of Memphis organized labor prospered. The Memphis Trades and Labor Council, an affiliate of the AFL composed of some two dozen unions, maintained an active organization from 1900 to

1920. Publicly, the mayor supported the council and took an interest in labor affairs; several union leaders, such as Robert Tillman of the local printer's union, were brought into the machine. The image projected by the Chamber of Commerce of Memphis was that of a progressive, non-union city which was remarkably free from labor-management strife. This was the image which Crump sought to maintain for his beloved city.

There were limits, on the other hand, to Crump's tolerance of unionization. The Trades and Labor Council tested those limits and was rebuked when it decided to organize municipal employees. Early in 1936, a group of Memphis city firemen formed a local union of the International Firefighters Association. Mayor Watkins Overton called R. S. McCann, the council's president, an "agitator" simply out "to make trouble" and the police and fire commissioner fired fifteen firemen (including five officers) reputed to be leading the organizing movement. The anti-machine *Press-Scimitar*, led by editor Edward J. Meeman, immediately joined the battle on behalf of the firefighters. The paper ran editorial after editorial pleading the cause of the charter members of the new union and reporting on the destitute condition of their families. Crump was only exacerbated. The boss's rejoinder to editor Meeman was typically Crumpian: "I realize you do not like a bone in my body and came here from Knoxville with the very great desire to try and smear me, but you have failed."[12] By May 1936, when the TFL convened in Chattanooga, McCann, also president of the Federation, reported "the fifteen firemen are still out of work, but they are clinging to their charter and don't consider the fight lost."[13]

Firefighters were not the only city employees to incur the wrath of the Crump machine. In March of that same year, the Board of Education, controlled by Crump and Watkins Overton appointees, adopted a resolution which outlawed the Memphis Teachers Association, an affiliate of the American Federation of Teachers. Though the teachers' local had been organized eighteen years earlier and seemingly presented no cog in the efficient city machine, Crump leaders were increasingly intolerant of unionism within their boundaries. Both school teachers and school custodians were ordered to relinquish their union membership or face dismissal at the end of the spring semester. The school board adopted a resolution requiring all teachers to sign a "yellowdog" contract. The teachers capitulated. The machine had steamrolled to another victory over organized labor.[14]

The image of a city boss who kept the union movement on a leash was all too appealing to several firms who recoiled at the thought of industrial unionism. Firestone was one of the companies locating in Memphis because, in large part, the company had assurances that the nascent CIO would not gain a foothold in the city. Once in Memphis, Firestone required that all job applicants provide proof of birth in Shelby County, thus diminishing the possibility of "outside agitators" among the work force. Firestone encouraged its workers to vote the "right way" and provided company transportation to the polls on election day.[15]

The sources of Crump's antipathy toward the CIO, according to Biles, were fairly easy to trace. Supposedly it was not trade unionism per se which Crump and the Memphis business community opposed, but it was the dangerously irresponsible and radical CIO which roused their concern. The rumors of communist influence took their toll in the Bluff City, but an even greater factor was race—nearly 40 percent of the city's population in 1930 was black and the CIO was unashamedly integrated at all levels of organization. The CIO was clearly a threat to Crump's deeply entrenched southern caste system and style of paternalism.[16] Conditions were right for a war between the city of Memphis and the CIO. The period of calm would not be a long one.

Despite some successes in contract negotiations by women garment workers in the CIO-affiliated ILGWU, only a modest number of Memphis workers were benefiting from new agreements. The CIO had not as yet penetrated the large firms, particularly Ford and Firestone—two firms that Crump, Mayor Watkins, and Police Chief Will Lee had walled off from union organizers. Ford and Firestone were powder kegs waiting to explode. In August 1937 a Ford assembly line worker who was overly enthusiastic in his expression of appreciation for the CIO's organizing drive elsewhere in the automobile industry was rewarded for his union zeal by a dozen office employees who blackjacked and beat him. A few days later he was beaten again for having made derogatory remarks about management's plan to establish a company union. After an extended absence to recover from injuries, he returned to work in time to be summarily dismissed in person.[17]

Crump could read the handwriting on the wall. He knew that if the CIO pressed the issue, his city officials would have an all-out fight on their hands. Despite the fact that Memphis hourly workers were paid less than their northern counterparts, the work force seemed content and docile. Crump's chief fear was that a successful CIO drive in his fair city would make Memphis less attractive for industrial expansion. His hope that the CIO would avoid Memphis like the plague was shattered when CIO organizers began arriving and organizing among garment workers, grocery clerks, and auto workers. No case was more celebrated than that of Norman Smith.

The CIO-affiliated United Auto Workers, fresh off organizing successes in Detroit and other cities in the Midwest, wanted to spread the gospel of unionism into the South and Memphis. In early September, they dispatched Norman Smith, veteran UAW organizer and former auto worker, who immediately announced to Memphians his intention of organizing the local Ford plant. The Ford management had already made clear its opposition to its employees joining a union. Ben McCullough, a union leader in the plant, had twice been ganged and beaten by thugs. On September 8, shortly after Smith's arrival, a group of Ford employees conducted an anti-union rally; speakers expressed determination to shut the door on the CIO and hinted that violence might be necessary if other means failed.

Ten days later the city administration entered the fight—on the side of the company. Mayor Overton took the lead in anti-CIO statements, defending the city's position:

> Imported CIO agitators, communists and highly paid professional organizers are not wanted in Memphis. They will not be tolerated. Their tools are violence, threats, sit-down strikes, destruction. They demand the American worker to submit or starve. They seek strife and conflict. They care nothing for Memphis—only to use us if they could. The City Government favors fair wages and right working conditions for the laboring man. We will oppose CIO violence, threats, and un-American policies from start to finish. Let them go elsewhere, if anyone wants them. We don't, and won't tolerate them.[18]

Also making anti-CIO statements were William Jasspon, president of the city's Chamber of Commerce, and Cliff Davis, Commissioner of Public Safety, who endorsed the mayor's stand and added: "We know Norman Smith and his whereabouts and will take care of that situation very soon."

The pledge to "take care of that situation" was kept "very soon." Three days later, in fact. While leaving a cafe, a gang of a dozen or so assailants attacked Smith and, in the presence of several bystanders, knocked him down and beat him with empty beer bottles and pieces of wire cable. Reportedly, no words were spoken; the assailants left in an automobile waiting nearby. The same evening, Charles Phillips, a local Ford employee who had been assisting Smith in organizing, was beaten. The following day the mayor released another statement that the presence of CIO organizers in Memphis would not be tolerated. Though there were detailed descriptions of the thugs, the police failed to make any arrests.

The CIO and Smith were not intimidated. They announced that Smith would continue his work and that additional UAW organizers would be dispatched to Memphis. Critics of the Crump city administration, including the American Civil Liberties Union, expressed dismay and indignation that local officials were so lackadaisical in law enforcement. Some charged police complicity in the attacks on CIO organizers, but concrete evidence was not marshalled. At the very least, most interested Memphians were convinced that the Crump people acted directly or indirectly as party to the persecution.

Meanwhile, Norman Smith had begun a series of radio broadcasts to present to local citizens the good news of unionism. On October 5, while traveling from his hotel to the radio station, the unionist was halted, drug from his car, and beaten with a pistol butt and a hammer by six assailants. During the attack, a gun was held on another UAW organizer, Harry Elder. The assailants concentrated all their efforts on Smith, likely unaware of Elder's affiliation. Later, while Smith was rushed to the hospital for emergency care, the shaken but unharmed Elder delivered Smith's pro-labor broadcast as scheduled.

The second attack on Smith, like the first, occurred openly on a public street and in the presence of witnesses. Memphis police were furnished with descriptions and license plate numbers. No arrests were ever announced and, according to union people, there were no visible attempts to apprehend the persons responsible. The second assault was enough for the UAW. The controversial organizer was recalled to the union's national headquarters, thus signaling the union's inability to penetrate the Ford fortress. The UAW in Memphis had been defeated. An uneasy peace followed.[19]

Ed Crump was never beyond deploying political power for a cheap shot at his antagonists. Having fallen out with Watkins Overton over an issue, Crump told fellow Memphians that he was running for mayor in 1939 as a proxy candidate for U.S. Congressman Walter Chandler, who wanted to stay in Washington in order to cast a decisive vote on a bill to prepare for war. Crump promised to serve one day and step down so the city council could name Chandler mayor. The city boss ran unopposed, but his vote tally was impressive. On New Year's Day at 12:15 A.M. he took the oath of office on the platform of a train bound for the Sugar Bowl game in New Orleans. Crump performed one official act as mayor before resigning—a rescinding of an invitation extended by his predecessor to the CIO's American Newspaper Guild to hold its 1940 convention in Memphis. "I know the people of Memphis are against all CIO activities and you will not be welcome," Crump tersely declared.[20]

Attending the unusual inauguration event was Paul Coppock, the reporter from the *Commercial Appeal* assigned to cover the story. Coppock had a special interest in Crump's action. Coppock was a charter member and secretary-treasurer of the Newspaper Guild of Memphis. As a newspaperman, Coppock reports, Crump had "attacked me by name" at the inaugural party, and in an earlier face-to-face situation "had demanded that I resign from the guild":

> There I was, a few months after the San Francisco (national CIO) convention, face to face with a demand from the most powerful man in Tennessee politics that I get out of the guild. I had felt the full thunderstorm of the Crump wrath before this incident, and would feel it again later. But this was different. It was more like an evangelist wrestling for the soul of a sinner. Crump could be persuasive in direct confrontation—most persuasive. . . . There was tenseness and there were firm words, without abusive language, but with total conviction that I was foolishly misguided unless I did what he said. . . . He was simply sure that he knew more about Communists and labor unions than I did and that I must accept his guidance. He considered himself a friend of union labor.[21]

The official message telling the president of the CIO that the guild convention was unwelcome in Memphis had been written in advance. After serving for mayor for about thirty minutes, Edward Crump spoke to New Year's Eve celebrants, handed his resignation to the city attorney, entered the coach, and departed for the football game.[22]

Meantime, the uneasy peace which followed the departure of the UAW from the city was interrupted in 1940 when the United Rubber Workers set its sites on the Memphis Firestone plant, the largest unorganized tire and rubber factory in the country. Firestone had located

in Memphis in 1937, in large part because of low wages as well as
Crump's unequivocal position on unionism. Crump had agreed to
keep the plant outside the city limits, thus allowing the plant to be
beyond the jurisdiction of the Trades and Labor Council and permitting lower tax rates. Given the size of the Firestone work force, both
the AFL and the CIO were interested in the tire plant. The issue of race
soon became a divisive factor among organizers. The AFL's proposed
remedy was the creation of two racially separate locals, as well as two
separate seniority systems. Though the CIO could agree to separate
seniority systems, the leadership insisted on one local. Given the fact
of 1940 Memphis and southern custom, the position was a strange
and unusual one indeed![23]

When organizer George Bass arrived in Memphis to begin the
URW campaign, he found that his reception was no warmer than the
one accorded Norman Smith. First, some 25 men, many of whom
were supervisors at Firestone, came to Bass' hotel room and threatened to throw him into the nearby Mississippi River. The hotel manager was embarrassed by the incident and forced Bass to evacuate his
room. Bass was later assaulted by a Firestone employee, but an
unsympathetic judge refused to consider the incident as a disturbance
of the peace. Mayor Chandler served Bass a personal judgment and
warning: "Foreign labor agitators who seek to stir up strife and
trouble are not welcome here." As if to prove the validity of the
mayor's declaration, a gang confronted Bass while in his car, over-
turning his vehicle, but the organizer escaped to face more persecution. On August 29, 1940, while distributing union literature in front
of the Firestone plant, more than a score of plant supervisors
assaulted Bass with pipes and chains while several hundred workers
looked on. Finally, a sympathetic worker drove his automobile
through the throng and, like a Good Samaritan, carried the victim to
a nearby hospital, thus literally saving his life.[24]

In order to stave off CIO gains at Firestone, local officials began to
push the more friendly AFL as the agent to be given exclusive right of
employee representation. The battle for recognition at Firestone
heated between the AFL's Rubber Workers Local 22456 and the CIO's
United Rubber Workers of America. In the 1941 election, the Crump
henchmen appealed to racial fears and prejudice to create votes
against the CIO; the AFL won the NLRB election by a 1,008 to 805
margin. The CIO had failed again.

All hope was not lost for the CIO, however. The NLRB later discovered that Firestone's black workers, composing 40 percent of the plant's work force, had been threatened with reprisal and even firing if they did not vote for the AFL. Knowing of the AFL's racial policies on separate unions and separate seniority systems, many of the plant's black employees simply sat out the election. Once apprised of these unfair labor practices, the NLRB ordered a new election. In 1942 the CIO-affiliated United Rubber Workers finally won an election at Firestone in Memphis. Crump was in a huff. He did not relent graciously. Summoning R. H. Routon, the president of the new CIO local, to his insurance office, having him chauffeured in a police squad car, Boss Crump delivered his "We aren't going to have any CIO nigger unions in Memphis" soliloquy.[25] Crump never relented graciously when it came to a union victory inside his beloved city domain.

Despite the great strides of the New Deal's "labor on the march" of the 1930s, and despite great stirring among workers, very little had changed in Memphis' labor movement. The city's workers had to wait another ten years for major breakthroughs by the CIO, as Biles points out.[26] Until the mid-thirties, the labor movement in Memphis had been largely parallel to the movement in the rest of the nation. One man's public actions and public words altered the flow of Tennessee labor history.

Union people throughout the Memphis area and Tennessee were not about to forget the irascible city boss. Though his personal antagonism toward unionism continued through the mid-forties, Crump's influence began to decline. In the 1946 campaign, CIO forces lost mightily in their first effort to defeat Crump candidates Kenneth McKellar for U.S. Senate and James McCord for governor; but they learned much about election tactics and stoked a flaming desire to deliver a knockout blow to Crump in the next general election. Two years later, black Memphians joined the heavily white labor precinct of Frayser, populated by CIO Firestone rubber workers, Ford's UAW auto workers, and various AFL locals, and voted 55 percent for Estes Kefauver; Gordon Browning also defeated Crumpite Jim McCord.[27]

BIRTH OF THE UNION AT ALCOA

While the CIO struggled to gain a foothold among industrial workers in west Tennessee during the thirties, the story of industrial workers in the eastern part of the state moved to a much more successful conclusion. If one is looking for a drama where the predictable early struggles laid the groundwork for the largest and one of the most successful unions not only in Tennessee but throughout the South, one need only look at the experience of the steelworkers in Alcoa. The early struggle to establish a union, company resistance, discord and contention created by competition among the AFL, CIO, and the UMW, and eventual strength and harmony among union members are all woven into the Alcoa story.

The origins of the Aluminum Company of America can be traced to its organization in 1888 as the Pittsburg Reduction Company. Like other northern-based companies, the lure of the South was made enticing by tax exemptions and tacit commitments against certain kinds of labor legislation, and other incentives. By 1914 ALCOA had purchased some 700 acres in Maryville, fifteen miles south of Knoxville, and began construction of the smelting plant and about 150 houses for company employees. By 1920 a sheet mill was in operation; the Alcoa townsite had a population of 3,358, and 3,672 workers were on the ALCOA payroll of over three million dollars.[28]

During the early years of the company's venture into east Tennessee, Alcoa was a company town in the traditional mode. The city was divided into four sections, each named after a prominent local personality. In the early years four-room houses rented for $7.50 to $9.00 per month and three-room houses for $ .50 per month—each equipped with "running water, electric lights and a toilet in the house."[29] The company lured new employees with the promise of short hours, fair wages, and excellent working conditions.

From the outset ALCOA intended to employ black workers. A recruitment campaign was waged in the deep South—particularly Georgia, Alabama, and Mississippi—to enlist blacks to toil in the hot potrooms of the smelting or reduction process. During plant construction days, black workers lived in barracks and temporary tar paper shacks. Later they lived in company housing in Hall, their segregated section of the city. When the company began production the black population in the city was little less than the white population; there were also 130 Hispanics. Twenty years later, with the gearing up for war production, the white population had increased significantly while the black population had dropped.[30]

The first attempt to establish a local union at ALCOA was short-lived. Plans were drafted for the new union in 1920 to be affiliated

The original ALCOA plant, 1922. (Courtesy—Tennessee State Library and Archives)

with the AFL. The move toward this early union was enhanced by "back-breaking" working conditions and a wage scale which was below what workers earned for the same work in the company's northern plants. Lamar Taylor, later to be president of the local, offers a recollection:

> In the fall of 1920, every lineman and electrician were laid off except the foreman. I was transferred to the Sheet Mill, now known as the West Plant. I had worked about three weeks when one morning I was called to the office of the Electrical Superintendent, who said to me, "Taylor, I am firing you for belonging to the Union." I told the superintendent that we had sent the Union Charter back, but he said that made no difference. I will never forget that morning, how my wife cried when I told her that I had been fired for belonging to the Union. It was just before Christmas.[31]

Other workers who were union members or prospects were also fired on the spot.

After working for eighteen months with a communications company in the Knoxville area, Taylor was one of the first to be called back to ALCOA in order to install the electric boilers in the steam plant. "We worked long hours. We would work outside all day, go home, eat supper, hurry back and work inside, sometimes until the wee hours in the morning," Taylor recalled. "I was making 62 1/2 cents per hour.

One week we worked 100 hours and drew $62.50, exactly as many dollars as I drew cents per hour."[32]

Given the general decline of the labor movement in the country during the 1920s, the union drive in Alcoa was delayed some thirteen years after the demise of the first local. In December 1933 interested aluminum workers began meeting in a variety of Maryville locations to discuss the merits of organization. With the impetus of the New Deal, the workers knew that unionization was on the upswing. Out of these meetings Aluminum Workers Local 19104 was formed; the membership elected Fred Wetmore as the first president and Lamar Taylor as the first vice president.[33] With this small beginning, amidst weakness and insecurity among its members, a milestone was reached—the union's formation, as labor historian Sammy Pinkston points out, "was a big step forward for organized labor in the entire South, in that it was one of the first successful unions in the region."[34]

Local union organization was one thing. Union recognition by the company was another, as the ALCOA workers knew full well. Like other large corporations of the twenties and early thirties, ALCOA opposed the union movement in principle and rejected the concept of collective bargaining. Local 19104 had the power of a strike, with an almost unanimous vote to use the extreme weapon if necessary. The union's list of ten demands was largely rejected by company officials. On Friday evening, August 10, 1934, President Wetmore returned from unsuccessful negotiations to call a meeting of the union employees. That night at the 10:00 change of shifts a picket line was put up around the plant, thus heralding the first union strike at Alcoa. The strike lasted for 26 days with Local 19104 failing to achieve many of its demands. Though ALCOA had shut down operations during the period and hired special police, "this was probably the most peaceful major strike up to that time in the South. Not a blow was struck on either side during the twenty-six days."[35] By 1936 the Aluminum Company of America had reached its first agreement not simply with all its employees, as in the past, but with the Aluminum Workers' Union, thus signaling its acceptance of the principle of collective bargaining. After sixteen years of operation in east Tennessee, the industrial giant finally recognized officially the concept of "union."

ALCOA found the union to be an unrelenting partner. When workers in 1937 realized they were making eighteen cents per hour less than their brothers earned at the ALCOA plant in New

Kensington, Pennsylvania—wages were 63 cents per hour in Pennsylvania compared with 45 cents per hour in Tennessee—union members voted overwhelmingly to strike. AFL representative Francis J. Dillon was able to suspend the strike call in order to extend negotiations, but negotiations broke down over squabbles about comparative costs of living in the two communities. When the company walked away from the negotiating table, union leader Wetmore called to strike at the fabricating plant on May 18.[36]

The aluminum workers prepared for a long strike. After all, they were backed by the AFL and union strike relief of about seven dollars per week. The company had another idea. It began recruiting policemen from surrounding counties to reinforce Blount County officials and the Alcoa police force. On July 6, while Wetmore was in South Pittsburg conferring with company officials, E. M. Chandler, superintendent of the fabricating plant, announced that the plant would resume operations the next day at 1:00 P.M. The Alcoa city manager and the police force, fully aligned with the company, ordered their force to the picket lines.

Tension soon mounted on the picket line. With Wetmore out of town, the task of leadership for the union fell to Vice President Taylor. "I called a meeting at the union hall that morning of some 30 to 40 men and told them that we did not want any trouble, that if a few men did go in the plant the company could not run the plant because the rollers were all good solid union men and would not enter," Taylor recalled.[37]

The meeting was hardly over until trouble started. Tension had been mounting at the picket line as the hour for reopening the plant had grown closer. As workers in large vehicles were transported through the plant gates, bedlam broke loose. A school bus loaded with workers passed unscathed through the line, but the sight of strikebreakers and nonunion men taking their jobs raised the pulse rate of the striking workers. Huddling around two trucks filled with workers, the strikers obstructed the plant entrance. The increased hostility soon led to gunfire. The police apparently started firing first at the pickets, who began scattering frantically in an effort to get out of harm's way. Some strikers were caught in a crossfire, according to some reports, between police gunfire inside the gate and police gunfire outside the gate. Pickets grabbed sticks and clubs they had carried to the strike scene.

When the firing of 200 or more shots had ceased, and those crouching behind cars or lying behind fence rows were able to stand

and walk again, 21 people had been shot in what the *Knoxville Journal*
called "the bloody labor battle at Alcoa." Arching the gate to the
sheet mill which was to have been reopened was a large "SAFETY
FIRST" sign. Two men died as a result of the battle. One was a
special deputy. The other was a 27-year-old union worker, Henson
Click, who was to become the first martyr for the labor movement in
the aluminum industry. "He wanted to die as he lived, a union man,"
declared his widow.[38]

The gunfire and bloodshed, accompanied by the company's
reopening of the plant, settled the issue for the union employees. The
strike was completely broken. Large numbers of workers, the exact
count disputed by the company and union, returned to their jobs.
Fearing more disorder, ALCOA officials phoned Governor Gordon
Browning and requested the National Guard; four companies of
guardsmen began arriving that night. There was no more violence.
The strike was over. ALCOA had won.

Little remained for union officials to do. Three days later Wetmore
filed a complaint in Atlanta with the NLRB charging that ALCOA had
interfered with the workers' rights under the Wagner Act. Soon a federal
mediator was dispatched to Alcoa with a proposal for both sides, but the
company would not accept any settlement and maintained its position
that there was nothing to mediate. When AFL representative Francis
Dillon arrived on the scene and criticized local union leaders who
pushed for an immediate end to unequal regional pay scales, Wetmore
resigned his post. The 300 National Guardsmen had all departed the
area by July 15. Alcoa seemed to be a place of "business as usual."

All was not well within the aluminum workers' local. They had
seen an outside union man come in, take charge, and ask Wetmore to
resign. "The union had lost all faith in the American Federation of
Labor, but we never gave up," Lamar Taylor recalls. "We were determined to stay organized one way or another."[39]

THE CIO COMES TO ALCOA

By calling off the 1937 strike, discrediting its local president, and
refusing to pay the hospital bills of union workers injured in the strike
effort, the American Federation of Labor had thoroughly discredited
itself. Some union members had visited New Kensington,

Pennsylvania, where they witnessed the CIO "growing by leaps and bounds." One member, John Whitley, brought back a bucket full of CIO buttons for distribution; this, according to Lamar Taylor, "seemed to be the handwriting on the wall."[40]

The CIO was not a shoo-in for the aluminum workers. The company-backed Aluminum Employees Association had gained the confidence of a larger group of ALCOA employees. The AEA's strongest period of influence was 1937 to 1939, once claiming a membership of 2000 workers. Association leaders contended that dues should not be placed into the coffers of any outside organization and that ill-advised strikes should never be called.[41]

Meantime, the opportunist CIO was gaining momentum among workers. It had picked up the tab on the hospital bills which the AFL had refused to pay. Within days after the ill-fated strike, a CIO local was established with Fred Wetmore installed as local leader. CIO leaders clearly and persuasively stated their objectives for the new union: (1) union policies controlled by the membership; (2) economic equality for southern aluminum workers; (3) a guaranteed wage for production workers; (4) paid vacations and a seniority system.[42] The CIO's chief selling point over the Employees' Association was that no local union was any stronger than the international organization which supported it. New members of Local 9, the new Alcoa local, were required to pay a two-dollar initiation fee and maintain one dollar per month dues. Local 9 also endorsed some ambitious educational, social, and work-related goals.

The opposition to the CIO's Local 9 would not die without a fight. ALCOA management, quite naturally, favored the Aluminum Employees Association. There also remained some sentiment for the AFL, whose local leaders made claims linking the CIO and John L. Lewis with Fascism and Communism. The showdown for representation rights would be held in a democratic election of all the workers. The NLRB set the election for December 1938. The informal campaigning began with all its charges and countercharges.

The CIO finished second to the Aluminum Employees Association by over 300 votes (1,296 to 961); the AFL gained 708 votes. Since there was no majority, a run-off election was held. This time the CIO won a narrow victory, but the results were a matter of dispute. Further dispute followed a third election in June 1939. A fourth election seemed necessary. Meantime, the AFL scrambled to unite all Local 9 opponents under its banner, proclaiming the well-worn slogan: "United we stand, divided we fall." United or not, the opposition to CIO fell to defeat in the final employees' election on August 31. Efforts to defeat and discredit Local 9 had failed and ALCOA management had no choice but to recognize the CIO as the sole representative agent of their workers. The struggle had seemed long and hard for those who had worked so hard for a CIO victory among aluminum workers. Attention was then turned to negotiation of a working agreement, culminating in a contract satisfactory to the workers which was signed on November 11, 1939.[43]

The years following this foundational contract were eventful and prosperous for both the company and the union. Preparation and involvement in war in the 1940s increased enormously the demand for aluminum, when 90 percent of ALCOA's output was put to military use. Production increased by about 600 percent and $300 million was expended for expansion. The North Fabricating Plant at Alcoa was constructed in 1940-1941; it covered over 65 acres and was the largest plant under one roof in the world. The work force swelled to 12,000.[44] Despite the fact that southern workers continued to clamor for equal pay with their northern counterparts, aluminum workers were proud of the fact that at that time ALCOA was the only aluminum plant in which female employees received the same pay scale as males.[45]

The Aluminum Workers made a momentous step at their annual convention at Hot Springs, Arkansas, in June 1944 when they voted to unite with the United Steelworkers. Steelworker President Philip Murray was also president of the CIO; the move, therefore, seemed natural and beneficial to both unions. Local 9 became Local 309 in the United Steelworkers of America. Months later an effort to put the word aluminum into the name of the organization failed. Not all of the workers approved of the merger; still others harbored reservations about the CIO. Seeing a great door of opportunity, the United Mineworkers came to Alcoa and initiated a campaign to represent the aluminum workers. The mineworkers were tenacious in their challenge, eventually forcing a NLRB election in May 1945. The CIO won overwhelmingly against the UMW and the AFL. The election was a vote of confidence for the CIO for the progress which had been made since 1939. Local 309 was now positioned to move into a new era of strong and cordial membership relations.[46]

Labor-management relations at ALCOA in 1945-1946 were volatile. By 1945 Local 309 had become the largest local union in the South and it was ready to flex its muscles. Disputes flared up over such matters as the dues check-off and seniority privileges. Two major strikes were called and, while short-lived, thousands of employees were affected. In January 1946, 7,500 ALCOA workers joined steelworkers nationwide to participate in what was then the biggest strike in American history. Altogether 750,000 United Steelworkers were involved in a strike effort that President Harry Truman and special negotiators had attempted feverishly to avoid. The strike shut down 1,200 plants in some 30 states nationwide; the reduction plant in Alcoa remained open. The main issue was wages. In mid-February President Truman relaxed price controls, permitting the industry to raise its prices and offer modest wage increases. The strike ended on February 16.

In less than three months, the union had called another strike to protest the reduction of working hours in the potrooms. An agreement was reached five weeks later, but leaders of Local 309— including Gordon Ballew, Joe Cummings, and Howard Strevel— began speaking out against the "wildcat" strike tactic and reasoned that the membership should rely on the grievance procedure for future disputes. The contract signed in 1947 between ALCOA and Local 309 established new machinery for the parties to employ when an agreement could not be reached. The workers received a number of highly favorable concessions from the company. Indeed, the new labor-management relationship at ALCOA seemed strike-proof.[47]

The decades of the fifties and sixties were times of union membership growth and maturity. One of the union's chief objectives was reached in 1953 when the ALCOA aluminum workers were granted a 10 1/2-cent per hour wage increase, thus eliminating the geographical wage differential. Local 309 made contributions to Tennessee's CIO legislative program and USWA's District 35 strike fund. Leonard Evans and Howard Strevel, both 309 members, each served as president of the state CIO convention; Evans later served as a founding officer in the merged AFL-CIO state labor council as well as a state commissioner of labor. A union commercial retail store was operated from 1957 to 1967 in order to pass savings on consumer goods to the workers and their families. Financial support was given to strike efforts at other east Tennessee industries. Local members were urged to become active politically and to buy only union-made consumer products. During these decades of prosperity, ALCOA and the union were successful in resolving most of their major disputes

through the collective bargaining process. As the largest local industrial union in the South, as well as the largest local in District 35 of
the United Steelworkers, Local 309 set the standard for amiable
labor-management relations in the South.[48]

By the mid-1980s the Aluminum Company of America in Alcoa
was manufacturing aluminum for almost every conceivable use from
computer parts and soft drink cans to automobiles. The plant
employed 3,900 men and women, almost 3000 of them represented by
the USWA. The amenities enjoyed by the 6,780 residents of Alcoa—
effective city planning, recreation facilities, good schools—were the
positive by-products of the old company town.[49]

The general pattern of good labor relations was broken by the
company, according to the union, when aluminum workers joined a
nationwide June 1986 walkout which also involved members of the
Aluminum, Brick, and Glass Workers; 15,000 workers struck ALCOA
nationwide. In Alcoa, the company hired new security guards and
outfitted them in military-type uniforms. Striking workers were
appalled. Soon the name "Rambo-guards" was the widespread label
for the company security men. By talking about "Rambo-guards" to
the media, the union won a public relations victory. The company was
put on the defensive. The new guards had just been hired and they
may have looked military, ALCOA management conceded, "but
they're not armed . . . it's something new and different and because of
that it may be bothering them (the strikers) somewhat."[50] The month-
long strike was ended when workers agreed to a three-year contract
that cut benefits by $.95 per hour; the average benefits package was
brought to $10.05 per hour.

Despite the benefits cut, and despite the Rambo-guards experience, most ALCOA workers felt that they were fortunate to be among
the highest paid industrial workers in the South and to belong to a
union which effectively represented their needs and interests to the
company. The CIO venture into east Tennessee some two generations
earlier had survived during the hard times of depression and war and
had thrived during days of prosperity. "This is a great place to live,"
declared one worker, Duane Giddy, a native of Michigan who
migrated to east Tennessee to find work. "Anybody who thinks times
are rough here ought to try Saginaw Valley," Giddy continued,
speaking of the 1986 strike against ALCOA. Giddy doubted the strike
would affect trade at his used car lot down the street from the plant.
Most of the ALCOA workers buy new automobiles, he noted.[51]

THE MOST DRAFTABLE UNION LEADER

Few people shared more deeply the ups and downs of CIO fortune in east and middle Tennessee than Howard Strevel. Born in Knoxville on September 13, 1916, Strevel and his six brothers and three sisters soon learned the meaning of hard work. After completing the eighth grade, young Strevel dropped out of school to take a job at Knoxville Fertilizer Company in order to relieve the financial strain on his father, a furniture worker. His work as a dolomite roller was hard and pay for ten hours a day of toil and sweat was fifteen cents per hour. Strevel later went to work at the Standard Knitting Mills where he was first introduced to unionism. Strevel remembers the impact of the International Ladies Garment Workers Union on both the management and the workers:

> The ILGWU tried to organize our plant. The organizers gave out handbills telling about the union. The workers got interested in the union right away. When this happened, the company gave the employees a week's vacation with pay. I got to thinking: "If the company would do this just for us receiving those hand-bills that were handed out, what would the company do if we all joined the union!" A lot of workers signed cards. A local was started. The union workers soon took a notion that they would call a strike. Now the head of the local was a preacher, but when he got out of the pulpit he didn't know much about anything.[52]

Strevel stayed out on strike against the mill for eight weeks. He was among the fortunate ones who were called back to work. Convinced that his status as a mill hand was not secure, Strevel approached his uncle about the possibility of landing a job at ALCOA. Strevel was soon hired as an aluminum worker and immediately joined the union. It was not long until Strevel started serving his union in a series of offices, all of which he was drafted for by his union brothers. ("Every union job I got was unsolicited!" Strevel claims.)

While Strevel worked in the pot room at ALCOA, he impressed his co-workers as a man who was not intimidated by management and who had no reluctance to confront management with a problem. The young steelworker had earned the nickname "The Greaser" (upon leaving Tennessee for Alabama, his co-workers and union brothers gave him a gift-wrapped oil can as a farewell present) for his uncanny ability to smooth over labor-management rifts. At a meeting he did not attend he was elected committeeman. Later he was elected chairman of the grievance committee. Next he was drafted to serve as treasurer of his local. Strevel recalls that he was not at that election meeting either:

> Back in those days there weren't a lot of people seeking the office. The meetings were held on Saturday nights. The way I became treasurer is that I was nominated at a meeting and I was not there to decline. So when I heard about the nomination, I called the chief officer to decline. "You can't decline," he told me. "There were only two men nominated. The other man was there and he declined and that left you!"[53]

During the forties in Alcoa, Strevel moved up the ladder of union leadership in the CIO. He defeated Horace Brock by thirteen votes to become the president of his local; in the next election he ran unopposed. Strevel recalls grooming Leonard Evans for union leadership, asking him to serve as vice president and promising Evans he would later resign during the term so that he could move up to the presidency; Strevel resigned ten months later. Strevel then served as president of the Knoxville Industrial Union Council and president of the Tennessee CIO Council. The state's top CIO position came to Strevel unsolicited in 1950. During a conference of CIO leaders in Memphis at the Chelsea Hotel, M. C. Weston, the "logical choice" of the group, declined to run. Again, Strevel was drafted.[54] But his tenure in office was slated to be a brief one. The vice president of the international Steelworkers asked "The Greaser" to move to Birmingham to handle problems related to wages and promotion among steelworkers there. Strevel transferred his local union membership to Local 1013 in Fairfield where he remained a member until his retirement.

During the mid- and late forties, Strevel strengthened his ties with CIO union leaders throughout Tennessee. He traveled to union meetings with Paul Christopher; the two were good friends. He traveled with Matt Lynch and others to Washington to sit down with Estes Kefauver and discuss the possibility of repealing Taft-Hartley. He had experienced strikes at ALCOA and offered counsel to union officials about other Tennessee CIO grievances and strike strategy. Among all the labor battles in Tennessee in which he was involved, no conflict was as fierce or explosive, even in a literal sense, than the Steelworkers' strike against Vultee Consolidated in the cold winter of 1947-1948. It was a strike that Strevel had helped to call.

"A MARVELOUS DEMONSTRATION IN
NON-UNION TERRITORY"

That the CIO unions still struggled to survive under a cloud of suspicion in Tennessee is no better illustrated than by the fierce battle that raged between the United Steelworkers and Vultee Consolidated in Nashville. The Vultee Corporation, also known as the Nashville Corporation, employed approximately 2000 workers to manufacture stoves, refrigerators, and motor buses. The plant was a hotbed of controversy, not only between the employees and management but also between the employees.

One strike issue was pay. The Steelworkers called for a general 30 cent per hour wage increase and were turned down by the management. The salary for production workers at Vultee was 50 cents per hour in 1940. The company claimed it had raised the pay to a maximum of $1.73 per hour and the CIO countered by claiming that "no one in the plant made *that* maximum."[55]

A more volatile issue centered on exactly which union represented the workers at Vultee. To the general public, the whole conflict was a part of a running feud between the United Steelworkers and the International Association of Machinists. Though the company had recognized the Machinists in earlier elections, on August 20, 1947, the CIO and the Steelworkers had won an election among Vultee employees by a 2-1 margin. The victory was not readily acknowledged. Claiming that the Steelworkers had failed to comply with all the provisions of the recently passed Taft-Hartley bill by refusing to sign non-Communist statements or file certain financial reports, the National Labor Relations Board refused to certify the victorious union.[56] This left an opening for the IAM which claimed that by default it was the only legitimate bargaining agent of the Vultee work force. IAM representatives began to charge, in the words of Guy Matlock, IAM public relations official, that the CIO does not begin groundwork organization but instead "raids the unions which are already set up and working well with its philosophy of 'rule or ruin.'"[57] Indeed there was no love lost between the IAM and the CIO. The battle was soon to spill over into almost every court in Davidson County (U.S. District Court, Chancery Court, and General Sessions Court) and into the Nashville streets.

On November 10, 1947, the Steelworkers began their strike against Vultee. The vast majority of workers honored the picket line the first

day of the strike effort; only about 25-30 people reported for work.
State law officials were ready to pounce on any would-be trouble-
makers from the ranks of the union workers from day one. It was
obvious from the start of the strike that the chief antagonist of the
striking workers would be Lynn Bomar, the state's Commissioner of
Safety who had at his command the entire Tennessee Highway Patrol
force. On November 11, the second day of the strike, Commissioner
Bomar arrested Milton Clay ("M. C.") Weston, Steelworker representative, for telling strikers: "Watch your Political Action dollars and we
can clear up a situation like this." It was some two months later before
Judge Elmer Davies ruled that Weston's rights to free speech and
assembly had been abrogated by Bomar.[58]

Throughout the strike the scene around the picket line was always
tense. As the strike continued, workers began to break ranks with the
strike call and return to their jobs. Governor Jim McCord had no reluctance to grant permission to Commissioner Bomar to continue using
highway patrolmen to keep "law and order" along the picket line. A
veterans' committee, representing 84 veterans who worked at the
plant and crossed the picket line, adopted an open letter to the governor thanking him for his involvement and saying it would obey all
laws. The open letter charged the CIO with instituting "a wave of ter-
rorism in Nashville in its brazen attempt to circumvent the law [Taft-
Hartley] and force its demands upon the Nashville Corporation."[59]

In the early days of the strike, the Steelworkers pressed their claim
as the only legitimate union representing the Vultee workers. The CIO
union petitioned the NLRB for certification and was rejected. Matlock,
an IAM spokesman, gloated: "This leaves the CIO out in the cold!"
Arnold Campo, international representative for the USWA, countered
that the rejection was expected and would have no bearing on the
strike. The CIO statement was issued to the press because "it is possible that someone may attempt to ballyhoo this meaningless ruling
as a 'victory.'" The CIO continued to employ its two major arguments
for legitimacy: first, its 2-1 victory in the August 20 election; second,
"when we shut down the Vultee plant and kept it shut," the CIO
proved it represented the workers.[60]

Meantime hostilities were rising on the picket line. A court injunction by Chancellor William Wade moved Steelworker pickets some
sixty feet away from the gates leading to the plant and off plant property. Union attorneys argued in vain that for all practical purposes the

injunction prevented the union from picketing the huge plant. Shortly after the injunction, some 23 strikers were found in contempt of the court order.[61] In early December, three cars belonging to workers who had crossed picket lines to enter the plant were burned. Howard Strevel, who left his post in east Tennessee and traveled to Nashville on weekends to assist in the strike effort, remembers that M. C. Weston was a special target of Bomar's persecution:

> The situation was explosive. Lynn Bomar's people would come down there to the plant site and have a tommy gun under their arms and walk up and down the picket line and cuss and call the workers "a bunch of damn commies" and then threaten them, just trying to get something started. I think they wanted to kill somebody. They arrested M. C. Weston. He was driving a Buick Roadmaster and had $500 in his pocket and they arrested him for vagrancy. They got Weston in the back seat of a patrol car and cussed him and called him a communist. The whole police force was hostile.[62]

By mid-December, the CIO had received some publicity of its own against the safety commissioner by filing a suit against him, a move which made the front page of the *Nashville Tennessean*. A day later, the NLRB dismissed charges against the CIO and the Steelworkers' local union and both began to proclaim jubilantly that their strike was legal. At the work site, following a decision by attorney Robert Denham of the NLRB not to go to federal court to obtain a strike-breaking injunction against the steelworkers, the strikers promptly put up a banner announcing the strike and asking workers not to cross the picket line. Though a county permit allowed the union to put up a sign near the intersection of Vultee and McGavock Pike, the Tennessee Highway Patrolmen promptly tore it down. More assault and battery charges and arrests were made. Governor McCord then huddled with top state leaders to discuss how much the Tennessee National Guard could be used to protect those workers who wanted to cross picket lines.[63]

The winter of 1947-1948 was one of the coldest on record in Nashville history. In January, Nashville papers headlined the dropping of the mercury below freezing and reported the plight of poor people who were trying to stay warm. The story receiving daily coverage in Nashville newspapers, however, was the steelworker strike at the Nashville Corporation. While the weather kept getting colder from mid-December throughout January, the labor war at Vultee kept getting hotter. Telephone cables of the Southern Bell Telephone and Telegraph Company which led to the plant were cut, apparently with an ax. Roofing nails were strewn on McGavock Pike leading to Donelson. Two strikers were followed to Central State Hospital grounds by state highway patrolmen and, according to strike director Philip Clowes, were arrested on "flimsy causes" and beaten "without cause."[64]

The introduction by the strikers of a new weapon focused attention upon the intensity and recklessness of the strike effort. Between Christmas and New Year's Day, 24 sticks of dynamite were discovered at the Nashville Corporation's power station. The company made available to the press a letter from Charles Cox, president of Local 4057, which read:

> Dear Sir and Brother:
> Monday is THE DAY—Monday, December 29, 1947.
> Do you want to get our strike over in a hurry and win the 30¢ per hour wage increase? . . .
> Monday is the day to shut down the Nashville Corporation plant completely!
> Strike the knockout blow—Land the winning punch.[65]

Drawing a connection between the letter's message and the discovery of dynamite was all but unavoidable in the public's mind. The union could only fall back on the logic that if it had planned to destroy the company's power plant by dynamite that it certainly would not have announced it in an open letter to all striking workers. In their final official act of the year, Lee Sanders, president of Nashville Trades and Labor Council (AFL) and O. B. Fuson, a member of the executive board, issued a statement denying any connection with the strike: "The deplorable tactics being employed are definitely in opposition to the ethics of the American Federation of Labor."[66]

A month later, two men were charged with entering the plant with 24 sticks of dynamite and 50 feet on the fuse wire attached to a blasting cap. Eight other workers were arrested; a 25-page indictment contained seven counts and cited 36 alleged overt acts of conspiracy ". . . to take human life of the class of individuals who continued to work after November 10."[67] The company reported that approximately 1,500 employees were on the job. Several of them had their automobiles mysteriously destroyed by fire and many others had tires deflated by roofing nails. Many of the strike supporters had been frightened and repulsed by union tactics and weapons. One such person was CIO official Paul Christopher. Christopher had accompanied another CIO activist from east Tennessee in an automobile to meet a Vultee strike leader in Rockwood. At Rockwood the young activist opened the trunk and pulled out the sticks of dynamite he was delivering for the strike effort. The driver then opened the glove compartment and retrieved the caps for the dynamite. "Christopher's eyes got real big. He didn't know there was any dynamite in the car," the young unionist recalled; "then he chewed me out to no end for what I had done and said he wanted no part of it."[68]

As the Vultee strike wore on, production at the plant moved toward normal, according to plant manager W. B. Lawrence. Philip Clowes could only counter that any production had to be "gold-plated production" because of the high costs involved with the reduced work force. Legal authorities squared off against each other—District Attorney J. Carlton Loser began an investigation of any possible link between the CIO and the dynamiting and a young attorney named Ben West was solicited to council strikers on their legal rights and was able to reduce the bond for one worker who had been arrested. But as the bitter cold weather lingered, and as the headlines announced the death by exposure to cold of unfortunate citizens and the assassination of Mohandas Gandhi, the resistance of the strikers began to wear down. Less than 400 workers out of approximately 2,000 employees had kept the faith through the end of January 1948.[69]

The handwriting for the CIO at Nashville's Vultee plant was clearly on the wall. In mid-February, the waters of the Cumberland River around Nashville rose ten feet above flood stage as though to pronounce a continuing curse of mother nature upon the strike effort; and as the FBI was called into the strike for the second time to investigate dynamite blasts which damaged a railroad spur line, the strikers' resolve weakened. The long cold days of trying to stay warm on the picket line, the harassment of the safety commissioner and the highway patrol, the defection among their ranks, an antagonistic state government and general public, a divided labor movement, the ups and downs of court judges—all had taken their toll!

On February 22, nearly 450 striking steelworkers gathered in the union hall to consider continuing their fight or capitulating to hard realities. It was a question they had thought about many times over the past 104 days. This time, by a 5-1 vote, the workers voted to end the strike. The battle had been lost. There was nothing that the steelworkers could show for their sacrifice. Vultee officials said the company was not obligated to return all 450 remaining employees to their jobs and that it would continue to recognize the IAM whose contract with the corporation had expired eleven days earlier.

The experience of the United Steelworkers at Nashville Corporation had proven that the CIO's presence was widely felt in the Volunteer State but that there was a major limitation to the power it could exert against an alliance of big industrial leadership and a hostile state government. The defeat was a bitter experience for those who faced a cold winter wind carrying a picket sign in one hand and a coffee mug in the other and fortified only by a union relief check. Still the valiant effort by the steelworkers was not lost by Philip Clowes: "This was a marvelous demonstration for them to put on so long in non-union territory."[70]

NOTES

1. John Dean Minton, "The New Deal in Tennessee, 1932-38" (Ph.D. diss., Vanderbilt, 1959), 224; *Nashville Labor Advocate*, Feb. 20, 1936.
2. Ibid., 225; *Chattanooga Labor World*, May 8, 1936.
3. Story told in ibid., 225-227, and based on *Chattanooga Labor World*, April 30 and May 14, 1937.
4. Ibid., 227-28; unfortunately, many valuable records and documents belonging to the state CIO organization were destroyed by a fire at the Exchange Building in Nashville, November 1954.
5. James Hodges, *New Deal Labor Policy and the Southern Cotton Textile Industry, 1933-1941* (Knoxville: University of Tennessee Press, 1986), 157.
6. Ibid., 158-59; in her personal history of CIO organization efforts in the South, Lucy Randolph Mason devoted some twenty pages to chronicle physical intimidation of CIO organizations between 1937 and 1940. *To Win These Rights* (New York: Harper, 1952), 39-59.
7. Cf. Hodges, *New Deal Labor Policy*, 159.
8. Quoted in David M. Tucker, *Memphis Since Crump* (Knoxville: University of Tennessee Press, 1980), 55.
9. Roger Biles, *Memphis in the Great Depression* (Knoxville: University of Tennessee Press, 1986), 31-32.
10. Quoted in ibid.
11. An interesting reassessment of Crump's role in Tennessee politics may be found in William R. Majors, "A Re-Examination of V. O. Key's Southern Politics in State and Nation: The Case of Tennessee," East Tennessee Historical Quarterly's *Publications*, no. 49 (1977), 117-35. Majors contends that Crump did not have a statewide organization and while he had influence with the governor's office, his power over the entire state has been exaggerated.
12. Quoted in Roger Biles, "Ed Crump Versus the Unions: The Labor Movement in Memphis During the 1930s," *Labor History* 25 (Fall 1984), 539.
13. T.F.L., *Proceedings of the 39th Annual Convention*, 22.
14. Story told in Biles, "Crump Versus the Unions," 539, and T.F.L., *Proceedings of the 39th Annual Convention*, 22-23.
15. Biles, "Crump Versus the Unions," 540.
16. Ibid., 541.
17. Story told in ibid., 543.
18. Quoted in ibid., 544.
19. Story told in ibid., 543-46, and in an address delivered at Highlander entitled "People's Rights in Memphis," by Joe Gelders and Laurent Frantz, Highlander Folk School Collection, Tennessee State Library and Archives.
20. Ibid., 544.
21. Paul Coppock, *Memphis Memoirs* (Memphis: Memphis State University Press, 1980), 246-49.
22. Ibid.
23. Earl Green, Jr., "Labor in the South: A Case Study of Memphis—The 1968 Sanitation Strike and Its Effect on an Urban Community" (Ph.D. diss., New York University, 1980), 67-68.

24.   The incidents related here are reported in Biles, "Crump Versus the Unions," 546-47; Tucker, *Memphis Since Crump*, 54-55; and *Commercial Appeal*, Aug. 30, 1940.

25.   Tucker, *Memphis Since Crump*, 55.

26.   Biles, "Crump Versus the Union," 551.

27.   Tucker, *Memphis Since Crump*, 58.

28.   Russell D. Parker, "Alcoa, Tennessee: The Early Years, 1919-1939," East Tennessee Historical Society *Publications*, no. 48 (1976), 86-87.

29.   Ibid., 88.

30.   Ibid., 88-89.

31.   Lamar Taylor, "History of the Alcoa Aluminum Workers Union: Some of the Funny, the Sad and the Most Rewarding Things that Happened in the First Ten Years, as Related by a Past President" (unpublished manuscript, 1971), 4.

32.   Ibid.

33.   *The History of Local 309: United Steelworkers of America, AFL-CIO, Alcoa, Tennessee, 1933-1977*, based on research of Sammy E. Pinkston and compiled by Craig Billingsley (Alcoa: Local Union 309, 1976), 13.

34.   Ibid.

35.   Ibid., 15.

36.   Ibid., 18-19.

37.   Taylor, "History of the Alcoa Aluminum Workers Union," 19.

38.   Quoted in Pinkston, *History of Local 309*, 23; a report on the strike violence may be found in Taylor, "History of the Alcoa Aluminum Workers Union," 18-23; the *Knoxville Journal* and *Knoxville News-Sentinel*, July 8, 1937; Parker, "Alcoa, Tennessee," 100-01.

39.   Taylor, "History of the Alcoa Aluminum Workers Union," 22.

40.   Ibid., 23.

41.   Pinkston, *History of Local 309*, 28.

42.   Ibid., 31.

43.   Ibid., 32-35.

44.   Russell D. Parker, "Alcoa, Tennessee: The Years of Change, 1940-1960," East Tennessee Historical Society's *Publications*, no. 49 (1977), 99.

45.   Pinkston, History of Local 309, 39.

46.   Ibid., 42-43.

47.   Ibid., 44-50.

48.   Ibid., 56-64.

49.   *Maryville Daily Times*, June 3, 1986.

50.   *Knoxville Journal*, June 3, 1986.

51.   *Maryville Daily Times*, June 3, 1986.

52.   Howard Strevel, personal interview, Birmingham, Alabama, August 14, 1987.

53.   Ibid.

54.   Ibid.

55.   *Nashville Tennessean*, Dec. 18, 1947.

56.   *Nashvi'le Tennessean*, Nov. 15, 1947.

57.   *Nashville Tennessean*, Nov. 19, 1947.

58.   *Nashville Tennessean*, Jan. 20, 1947.

59.   *Nashville Tennessean*, Nov. 15 and 19, 1947.

60. *Nashville Tennessean,* Nov. 20, 1947.
61. *Nashville Tennessean,* Nov. 26, 1947.
62. Strevel interview.
63. *Nashville Tennessean,* Dec. 13 and 16, 1947.
64. *Nashville Tennessean,* Dec. 23, 1947.
65. *Nashville Tennessean,* Dec. 30, 1947.
66. *Nashville Tennessean,* Dec. 31, 1947.
67. *Nashville Tennessean,* Jan. 28, 1948.
68. The union activist who told this story to the author requested anonymity.
69. *Nashville Tennessean,* Jan. 28 and 31, 1948.
70. *Nashville Tennessean,* Feb. 23, 1948.

8

"Monteagle is a focal point for the new labor forces gathering in the South. . . ."

In the Eye of the Storm

The Story of a "Radical Hillbilly" and a Southern Workers' School

Few enterprises could have begun in less auspicious circumstances than did the Highlander Folk School. The idea for a folk school originated in the fertile imagination and untempered idealism of a young Tennessean who could offer no concrete assurances that his nontraditional concept would take hold. Apart from the fervent desires and strong commitment of the founders, there was no encouraging sign that the project would succeed. The founders had no real cash, but, providentially, a 40-acre mountain farm with a two-story frame house was donated to the cause; school operations began soon thereafter. The site of the school was in Grundy County, situated in the southern tip of the Cumberland Mountains, at that time one of the eleven poorest counties in the United States.

The year of Highlander's founding was 1932, a watershed year in American politics. Depressed economic conditions prevailed throughout the country. Wage earning men and women were talking about jobs—how to get them and how to keep them—and how to make the mortgage or rent payments and how to buy groceries. A labor movement which had enjoyed some organizing and negotiating successes in previous decades now appeared to be both immobile and impotent. Few things had seemed stable or secure since 1929. Among Grundy countians, the depression had begun much earlier.

Few noticed the start of operations for Highlander Folk School in November 1932. And few would have given the new adult education center any real chance for more than limited success and effectiveness. In the following three decades or so the school would be subjected to some of the most intense criticism and vicious gossip ever heaped on a private institution in Tennessee. Highlander could never rid itself of controversy—persecution was inevitable. Eventually, the school's charter was revoked by the state for irregularities in its operation as a nonprofit organization.

The goal of the founders of Highlander Folk School was to provide an adult education center which would "prepare rural and industrial leaders for a new social order." Regardless of one's view of the social order, the goal of providing adult training was reached and more. The impact of the center was felt far beyond Grundy County and the southeast section of Tennessee. The school's leadership chose not only to operate in the toughest of times but also to confront the stormiest of issues which were facing their immediate area and the region at large. The school became a meeting place for liberals from all over the South but also, more importantly, it became the leading training center for southern labor and civil rights leaders for nearly three decades. Highlander's list of alumni and supporters includes Dr. Martin Luther King, Jr., Andrew Young, Eleanor Roosevelt, Woody Guthrie, Pete Seeger, Reinhold Niebuhr, and Rosa Parks.

To Myles Horton, co-founder of the center, Highlander was more of an idea than a training center. Both the idea and the program survived both the taints of charges in the McCarthy era of its being a "communist training school" and the forced termination of its residence in Grundy County. After a brief stay and eviction at a second home in Knoxville, the school relocated and settled at another mountain site, this time twenty miles northeast of Knoxville.

The rise and influence of Highlander Folk School under the direction and leadership of an activist who once described himself as a "radical hillbilly" has not been neglected by either historians or educators. In fact, Highlanders' fortunes have been more completely chronicled than any other development in Tennessee labor history.[1] Though the Highlander experience may be approached from several perspectives, the emphasis here is on the school's role in the story of Tennessee labor and in the civil rights movement up through its forced closing in 1961.

A CREATIVE IDEA FROM OZONE

A place named Ozone would hardly seem like an ideal location to develop a down-to-earth idea. And yet, in the summer of 1927 between his junior and senior years at Cumberland University, Myles Horton spent weeks in Ozone, Tennessee, thinking and dreaming about an idea for a new school. Horton was on the payroll of the Presbyterian Church in the U.S.A. for three months that year and had been assigned to the small Cumberland Plateau community in order to organize daily vacation Bible schools. While living among the people of Ozone the young church worker saw stark poverty and human need. Times were hard and the Great Depression had not even officially arrived. Horton could never get away from the early impressions and encounters he felt and experienced that summer.

Horton felt a pull to stay in Ozone. He had spent many hours in public meetings and in private conversations with the people of the community and he had developed a great empathy for them. He concluded that the people understood the nature of their problems and that they could discover the answers to their problems. The help they needed, if any, was for a facilitator to get them talking, to listen to their ideas, to raise questions, to sharpen issues, and to keep listening and trusting their judgment. The young church worker had learned a great deal from field experience, but he felt he had much more to learn. That fall he was back in college.[2]

Horton, who was born in Savannah, Tennessee, in 1905, graduated from Cumberland in 1928. The following year he traveled to New York City and enrolled in Union Theological Seminary. At Union he met and studied under Reinhold Niebuhr, the prolific theologian who was just beginning his distinguished career. One classmate who lived in the same dormitory with Horton was a theology student named Dietrich Bonhoeffer, but the Tennessean was almost singularly unimpressed with the young German.[3]

Horton was fascinated with Niebuhr's critique of capitalism, but was most heartened by his interest and commitment to working people. Months had passed since Horton's summer in Ozone, but he could not forget the people living there. Horton had kept his dream of a mountain school for mountain people alive and Niebuhr encouraged his student to follow that dream. The student visited institutions, conducted interviews, and read extensively in his search for a model of the kind of school he envisioned. His pursuit of the "Ozone Project," as he called it, became a magnificent obsession. In 1930-1931 he studied at the University of Chicago in order to learn from the experiences of Jane Addams' Hull House. Acting on the counsel of a Chicago cleric, Horton traveled to Denmark later in 1931 where he observed firsthand the operation of Danish folk schools. The Danish folk schools were free from government control and, functioning with wide variety in curriculum, they were not bound to the typical restrictions of grading, ranking, and examinations. Horton had now found an acceptable model for his own project. In early 1932 he returned to New York and to his friend and professor, Reinhold Niebuhr, where together plans were laid to implement the Southern Mountain School project.[4]

Horton continued to launch his project on faith. His immediate needs were staggering—a staff, operating funds, and a place to locate the school. One by one, the building blocks began to fall into place. Former Union classmates James Dombrowski, from Tampa, and John Thompson, a Tennessean, agreed to join Horton on the staff. By chance Horton was introduced to Don West, a native Georgian who had just completed his work at Vanderbilt. Horton and West soon discovered that they had much in common—both had been to Denmark and both were interested in establishing a folk school. Quite naturally, the two young men joined forces. Their high hopes were soon reinforced by almost unbelievable good fortunes when they met Lillian Wyckoff Johnson, a teacher and college administrator who had a special interest in cooperative communities. Dr. Johnson owned a house and land upon Monteagle mountain in the Summerfield community, two miles from Monteagle.

Timing could not have been better for Horton and West. Dr. Johnson had been talking about retirement and donating her home to someone who would continue her work. The two young men sat down with Johnson and carefully explained their hopes and plans for a community residential school. Though some of the ideas for the school went against the grain of Johnson's educational philosophy, she respected their ideals and their zeal for the project. She gave them a year's probationary lease, beginning in the fall; the lease was later extended indefinitely.[5]

Confidently Horton and West moved into the spacious house. Though their treasury was small and there was no guarantee that people would respond generously to their appeals for financial contributions, the two moved to ready the house as a community center and to implement their program. Horton and West also needed to settle on a name. "Folk" had a positive political and anthropological connotation. And an Appalachian was also known as a highlander. The Highlander Folk School was thus created in November 1932.[6]

" . . . GETTING INFORMATION, GOING BACK, AND TEACHING IT"

Grundy County was hardly an ideal place for initiating a project in cooperative adult education. It was a place, as Frank Adams points out, "where the right to work and the right to live had been a constant struggle."[7] Before the discovery of coal in the mid-nineteenth century, the few Grundy countians eked out a pioneer existence. Rail was laid through the area after the mining operations began and the timber industry soon followed. Grundy County was a booming community in the 1870s and 1880s, but the mine workers felt abused by the owners when hapless convicts were leased to take their jobs and prevent or break strikes. By the 1930s many of the mines were worked out and abandoned as desolate slag heaps and the once-rich timber- land had been cut over. Grundy County's relief rate in the thirties was nearly five times higher than Tennessee's relief average. By 1938 nearly eighty percent of Grundy's population of 2,250 families were on relief, placing it among the poorest counties in the entire nation.[8]

Horton was fully aware that the workers of Grundy were not the only Tennesseans struggling just to work and eat, but he had not expected to be drawn so quickly into the labor wars of another com- munity. Circumstances in a somber Tennessee mining village named Wilder changed that. The strike by miners at Wilder had continued for some time when representatives for the workers traveled to Highlander in order to solicit Horton's help. Learning that the situation among the Wilder miners was becoming desperate, Horton decided to travel the one hundred miles to Wilder to see conditions firsthand.[9]

Horton's fact-finding mission uncovered some deplorable reali- ties. The Fentress Coal and Coke Company owned the town and treated the miners as virtual slaves. The workers' debts were piling up. Food supplies were dwindling. When the miners struck, the com- pany shut off the electricity feeding the houses and removed doors from the houses. When the Red Cross responded to the situation, it handed out flour and other food supplies to the strike-breakers rather than to the strikers and their families. Horton met Barney Graham, the tough mountain man who was directing the strike, and through the union leader and other strikers was impressed by the miners' morale and will to win against all odds.

Here was a concrete opportunity afforded Horton and Highlander to get involved in the plight of Tennessee working men and their families. Horton began writing letters to leading newspapers in the state in order to call attention to the plight of the strikers. John Thompson, who had just joined Highlander, remembers teaming with Horton and traveling over mountain roads in order to deliver food supplies which had been donated by "a little group of Socialists in

Nashville."[10] "I will never forget the long line of gaunt, haggard, brave people who lined up to receive the scant rations we handed out to last them a week," Thompson recalls. "Each family got a pound of dried beans, a half-pound of coffee, two tins of canned milk (if they had a baby), half a pound of sugar. Those rations saved many lives, but meanwhile many babies had died of starvation."[11]

Horton's efforts on behalf of the striking miners and their families were not at all appreciated by the Fentress Coal and Coke Company. Horton and Thompson were informed that if their relief efforts were continued that they would have trouble getting out of Wilder alive. Horton persuaded Norman Thomas to come to Wilder and address a mass meeting of some 700 strikers and their supporters. Despite the notoriety of the Socialist, it was a song written and sung by Uncle Ed Davis, one of the Wilder strikers, which was the hit of the day. "We had Ed sing the song again and the audience cheered and ate it up," Thompson remembers. "It was their song; it was their life."[12]

Not surprisingly, Horton was arrested in Wilder. It was his first arrest. "You can't arrest me—you've got to have a charge," Horton tactfully told the National Guardsmen as bayonets were punched and pressed against his midsection. The guardsmen then huddled for a discussion, after which one returned to the articulate mountaineer whom they considered to be a "mystery teacher"[13] and an intruder, and announced: "You're arrested for coming over here and getting information and going back and teaching it!"[14] With a chuckle Horton has often told people that the Wilder arrest was the only time that the charge against him was precisely accurate. The Grundy countian was held for eight hours and then released.

The Wilder story moved swiftly to a sad ending. Horton, Thompson, and others had evidence that union leader Graham was a target for assassination but they could not convince the authorities to provide protection. The company started evicting strikers from their rented homes. Graham was gunned down in the main street. The local union had lost its most defiant and courageous leader. The strike was soon broken.

The Wilder strike experience had impacted heavily upon Horton, Thompson, and other Highlander staff members and students. As they returned to their own community, the miners' words in song, in pleas, and in prayers continued to haunt them. Now they saw more clearly the intense class consciousness that existed among both southern owners and their workers. If workers were to organize and exert their collective strength, they first had to be taught all about the issues which were at stake in this classic struggle. Labor education now took on new urgency.

THE "PERCOLATOR" SYSTEM IN LABOR EDUCATION

Education was the main mission of the Highlander Folk School, but education there did not always follow traditional patterns. Horton's aim was to develop leaders in the labor force and in the community, but he believed that the men and women who would develop as true leaders would emerge naturally from the ranks when they were given the opportunity to develop their potential. One term used by Horton to describe his philosophy was the "percolator" system rather than the "drip" system of education—ideas begin perking from the rank and file rather than dripping down from some authority figure at the top.[15]

The Highlander approach respected the people's experience and valued their input. Education and training at Highlander began at the precise point where the workers clashed with fellow employees or management. "The only way that you can learn anything is to tie it into something that you previously know. That's what learning is. That's what labor education has to be," Horton once stated.[16]

> At Highlander, we took people who were already doing something in their own community, in their unions. They were emerging leaders, people who were just beginning to do something and have a leadership role. . . . When they came to the school they would bring specific problems with them, situations that they wanted to deal with. We would take those students' problems and have them discuss them. They would talk about their situations and how they dealt with them and exchange ideas. It was peer learning; they would learn from each other. Then we'd learn from history and other things, but it was always related to that specific thing. It wasn't subject-oriented like at most schools, it was situation-oriented, problem-oriented.[17]

Some of the guest college professors and writers who wanted to visit and lecture at Highlander were ineffective in teaching situations, Horton noted, because they had trouble understanding that "workers weren't containers into which they poured their ideas."[18]

In the first year of operation, the Highlander staff offered regular classes, attended by 20 to 25 students, in psychology, cultural geography, revolutionary literature, and contemporary social and economic issues. There was also a seminar in social reform. Much of the class discussion was based on "actual labor situations in the Southern industrial area" with firsthand experience and information contributed by both students and teachers.[19]

The Highlander educational program had developed into three separate phases by 1936. A residential program which lasted six weeks was designed for union members who showed promise of becoming local leaders or organizers. Most of the students came from the mine and textile union locals; a few farm organizations were represented. While Highlander's students were taught how to become better workers and how to deal more effectively with their employers, they were not taught to adjust to exploitation, as Frank Adams points out.[20] Neither were they taught to be quiescent union members. Highlander encouraged activism at all strategic levels of interaction with society.

A second phase of Highlander's program focused on community life in the immediate Grundy County area. Highlander in the thirties was the social and cultural center for all interested workers in Summerfield, Monteagle, Tracy City, and other Grundy communities.

Early labor education in the South. A teacher from the Highlander Folk School in Monteagle convenes a class for miners outdoors. (Courtesy—Highlander Folk School Collection, Tennessee State Library and Archives)

The Highlander library was well stocked with several thousand books donated by educators and friends of the school and its doors were open to all workers. Free music lessons were offered to workers and their children. Despite admonitions from the local religiously devout that "dancin' is sinnin'," the staff organized square dances and folk dances. Zilphia Johnson, a music major from the College of the Ozarks who was later to become Mrs. Myles Horton, taught and directed hymns, labor songs, and mountain ballads. An outdoor stage was built. Plays written and produced by the staff and students at Highlander were staged for the general public. Highlander and pleasurable experiences seemed to go together naturally.[21]

A third phase of the Highlander practice of adult education was its extension program away from the Summerfield community. This program was never static; it remained flexible in order to respond to requests for services to help in actual social situations. Highlander students experienced firsthand involvement with social conflict in general and with the southern labor movement particularly. Highlander students assisted in union organization drives. They traveled to strike scenes and assisted and encouraged strikers, even offering informal classes and teaching songs on the picket line. Students were involved in the mundane tasks of local union administration as well, such as running errands, handling grievances, or operating a mimeograph machine. Highlander teachers took their educational program on the road. Regular classes were offered in such subject matter as parliamentary law, steward training, political action, and legislative procedures. It was not unusual for a teacher to travel to the work site and then sit down on the ground or along a fence row with a dozen or so of men still wearing their work clothes and begin a session by asking about their work problems. A three- to ten-day institute might be offered to unions located further away from the Grundy County center.[22]

"DAISY, COME OUT"

Highlander's extension services, perhaps the most diversified and creative phase of its overall labor education program, was not without its risks to student welfare. With the flurry of labor organizing and strike activity of the early New Deal period, the school and its students were thrust into the eye of the storm. Everyone soon learned the meaning of perils and persecution. When students were assigned to a strike scene, they usually boarded in homes of the striking workers—quite often, homes that were hit with gunshot from local citizens who entertained a different opinion about the strike effort. Even at home the Highlander classroom instruction was considered by the Grundy Board of Education to be little less than seditious. From early on in the life of the school, Horton and West were barred from teaching and conducting meetings in county school buildings.[23]

Highlander's involvement in a 1935 strike by hosiery workers at the Richmond Hosiery Mills in Daisy, Tennessee, illustrates both the almost tragic and almost comical dimensions of the school's extension program. Staff and students from the school journeyed to the small southeast Tennessee community to support the strike effort. Once in town and taking residence in the homes of the strikers, they joined the picket line where they helped make protest signs and led songs. The sense of solidarity was strengthened.

The creative genius of the Highlander folk was not to be stymied. A Washington's Day parade was organized to call local attention to the strike issues. Preceded by the nearby Soddy school band, the parade marchers wended their way through the town waving banners which read "Americans, fight for freedom, 1776-1935" and "Washington took a chance, why not you?" The holiday spirit was free and festive.

As the marchers reached the mill gates, the gaiety of spirit turned to panic. A volley of machine gun shots was fired from the front windows of the mill directly into the procession. Among the four people wounded in the violent outburst was Wellesley College graduate Hilda Hulbert, Highlander's librarian. Hulbert remembered hearing Horton hollering, "Don't shoot. A woman's been shot!" before she was taken to a hospital and later released. Though the strikers scattered immediately, they were rallied moments later at the gate when Zilphia Horton began leading them in "We Shall Not Be Moved."[24]

For years following the Daisy incident, the Highlander staff continued to pass along a story about one of the workers in the Daisy mill that day who felt more dramatically than anyone else the message of a parade banner. Coincidentally, the mill hand's name was Daisy. Described as "not very bright," Daisy was determined not to miss the parade. But when the parade came into view and a banner proclaiming "Spring is Here! Daisy, come out!" caught the worker's eye, a shocked Daisy exclaimed, "They've come after me!" and fainted.[25]

ORGANIZING AT HOME AND ON THE ROAD

Early in the Highlander's existence, Myles Horton concluded that before labor education could be a reality and before labor leaders could exert power in the work place, one prerequisite had to be met—labor unions had to be organized. Thus, beginning in 1935, union organization in the South became a major priority of the school. The emphasis in organization had to begin first at home. Wherever Grundy countians joined hands in solidarity to enhance the quality of their work life or raise their standard of living, the Highlander Folk School was in some way involved in that effort. The federal government's relief program provided a stimulus for the school's most extensive involvement with the working men of its own county.

Shortly after the Works Progress Administration initiated relief among Grundy citizens, numerous grievances emerged among workers in the various county locals. There were complaints about safety regulations violated, capricious discharges, favoritism in promotions, and anti-unionist tactics. Such grievances, however, were minor when compared with the workers' dissatisfaction with their salary scale. The average wage rate in the county was the lowest in the southeastern United States; in a region where the highest rate reached $75 per month, the average WPA employee in Grundy County earned a meager $19.20 a month.[26] Highlander assisted with the organization of these laborers into locals of the Hod Carriers, Building and Common Laborers' Union (AFL). The majority of the Grundy WPA workers remained unorganized, however, in part because they could not afford to pay the necessary initiation fees and dues. The secretary of a Tracy City local (848) penned an appeal to his legislator for assistance in reclassifying the county's agricultural status. Referring to the intent of President Roosevelt's security wage program, the unionist asserted: "We know of no dietician or economist who would claim $19.20 a month a security wage for a family and are at a loss to know how Mr. Hopkins arrives at such a figure."[27]

To counter the effects of poverty on union organization, Highlander endorsed the Workers' Alliance, which charged no mandatory membership fees. Still, conditions went from bad to worse. Local 848 contacted both the Washington office of the WPA and Colonel Harry Berry of the Tennessee WPA concerning Grundy County's alleged misclassification as an agricultural rather than an industrial district. The WPA union leaders contended that fifteen cents an hour for work on county projects was not the prevailing wage in Grundy. The appeals were to no avail—the national office deferred the matter to the state office and Colonel Berry turned a deaf ear to the union's pleas. The Grundy relief quota of 1,200 government jobs was cut almost in half, thus adding hundreds more to the ranks of unemployed. A summer drought which reduced the yield of family gardens seemed to deepen the sense of a demonic plague upon the mountain people of Grundy.[28]

In the first year of organization, the WPA union workers had gained precious little for their efforts. Using a work stoppage, Local 891 in Palmer succeeded in winning a wage adjustment from fifteen to twenty cents an hour for skilled workers on a gymnasium project.[29] A major strike attempt in March 1937 to gain union recognition, a new county WPA administrator, and assurance of grievance adjustments was unsuccessful and quickly abandoned. Local 930 in Laager tried sending a telegram to the president in Warm Springs on behalf of all Grundy WPA workers, but the appeal went unanswered. A petition with over two hundred names of Grundians supporting the WPA unions was sent to Harry Hopkins, the program's national director, requesting once again that the county be reclassified. Again, no answer.[30]

Highway building over Tennessee mountains involved use of hand tools and mules. This crew in Grundy is constructing Highway 56. (Courtesy—Tennessee State Library and Archives)

During these hard times the WPA workers began talking about political action. By the spring of 1938, Highlander had taken the lead in organizing Labor's Political Conference of Grundy County. Ten of the eleven Grundy County local unions, including the four locals of the WPA workers, elected to align with the conference. Planning for the next election soon began. All the untiring work and planning soon paid off handsomely for the labor activists. In the Democratic primary in August, all but one of the labor conference's candidates were elected. The local labor vote had elected the sheriff, the superintendent of schools, the county register, and two road commissioners.[31] Union strength and solidarity had reached a new peak in Grundy County by the fall of 1938.

The intoxicating taste of political power was short-lived. The ax began to fall. Leaders in the union lost their jobs on the WPA projects; one local lost its president, vice president, and job steward in one fell swoop. Colonel Berry threatened to close the county's entire WPA operation unless the road commissioners resigned their position, justifying his hard line against Grundy's sons of toil by contending that their roads were built "with the hammer and sickle rather than with pick and shovel."[32]

When Colonel Berry shut down all WPA farm-to-market road projects in Grundy County in January 1939, approximately 700 men were suddenly unemployed. Berry's action sparked both a dramatic increase in union membership among the six locals of the Hod Carriers and Workers' Alliance as well as public protests in the streets of Tracy City. Union leaders succeeded in arranging for some food supplies to be trucked into the county from Chattanooga, but the supply was quickly exhausted. When the county WPA officials issued work cards to only about half of the previously dismissed workers, in what was perceived to be a thinly veiled move to split the union ranks, many of the workers had been pushed enough. Approximately 150 workers seized the WPA office in Tracy City and announced their intention to occupy the headquarters until relief work resumed. Highlander stepped into the strike situation by donating supplies and offering assistance. Workers paraded through the streets of Tracy City in protest. Finally, the workers and their supporters caught the eye of federal officials; a representative was dispatched to Grundy County to investigate the allegations of discrimination against the union workers. Remarkably, a settlement was soon reached, giving workers the right to remain in unions and to have their grievances settled equitably. Most union workers were issued new work orders, but the amount of relief work steadily declined until the WPA terminated all operations later in 1939.[33]

Highlander's interest in organizing southern labor was not limited to the Grundy County area. In 1937 Horton took a leave of absence from Highlander to work in a CIO campaign. As one of thirty persons recruited by the Textile Workers' Organizing Committee (TWOC), Horton worked in an organizing drive in the South. The educator and his staff had gained a great deal of understanding and insight into the problems and lives of miners and mountaineers through working and living among Grundy citizens. But the textile industry had been growing as an economic force in the South; and, if Highlander was to establish and maintain an effective labor education role among textile workers, Horton and the faculty reasoned, the staff of the school needed to become directly involved in the lives of the textile workers.[34]

With a clear sense of mission, Highlander faculty members fanned out in different directions from Monteagle Mountain. Most of them joined the southern textile movement. Horton went out as a full-time organizer in the South for TWOC. Dombrowski also left for TWOC, agreeing to take an assignment in Atlanta to edit the union's newspaper. Zilphia Horton traveled north to join a former Highlander student who was leading a strike in LaFollette among the Amalgamated Clothing Workers. Elizabeth Hawes was placed in charge of the TWOC headquarters in Greenville, South Carolina. The remainder of the staff packed the recreation equipment, mimeograph machine, and part of the school's library and headed northeast to LaFollette where a six-week summer school was conducted.[35] The following year, Mary Lawrance, daughter of a Reading, Pennsylvania, physician and a Duke University graduate, came to Highlander and moved directly into the extension program. Lawrance believed that it was better to take education to the workers than to bring workers to education. Believing also that many union members were leery of education, she contended that the regular union meetings presented a better opportunity for teaching than did specially scheduled classes. In 1940 Lawrance was sent to Alcoa to stir up interest in unionism and begin labor education among the aluminum workers. Besides her position at Highlander, Lawrance also served two years as Tennessee CIO education director; her education programs were presented for unions in urban centers such as New Orleans, Atlanta, St. Louis, Louisville, and Knoxville.[36]

LEARNING AND LAUGHING AT LUMBERTON

When the 1937 CIO campaign began, one of the first assignments given by Horton by TWOC officials in Atlanta was organization among workers at the H. B. Jennings cotton mill in Lumberton, North Carolina. Within three weeks of Horton's arrival in town, about 175 Jennings mill hands struck to protest a production stretch-out; in other words, they were ordered to complete almost twice as much work in the same time. A company overseer had already been convicted of violating the Child Labor Act by permitting a fifteen-year-old female to work a twelve-hour night shift; for ten nights of work, according to testimony, she was paid $28.05. The townspeople had been tense ever since the company first learned about the organizing drive.[37]

H. B. Jennings soon took the offensive. The striking workers were denied credit at the company store. Strikebreakers were brought in to work under the protection of the unit of the National Guard which was housed in the same hotel in which Horton was registered. At one point strikers passed the factory gates and rushed the mill, demanding that their jobs be returned to them and ejecting strike-breakers through windows and doorways. Horton was arrested along with nineteen other union people for blocking a road leading into the plant grounds, and, on another occasion, was detained for inciting a riot when a union meeting became heated.[38]

The morale of the strikers remained high, thanks to some ingenious tactics and moves by the young organizer and educator from Tennessee. Seeing North Carolina highway patrolmen armed with machine guns and hearing the commander talking about breaking up the strike effort, Horton swung into action. He rushed to the picket line where a vigil had been kept throughout the night. He asked the strike leaders to send the workers home, but to return themselves to the picket line with a big American flag, their prettiest daughters, and some people who could sing and play stringed instruments. Horton's tactic was disarming.[39] Years later he recalled the incident:

> We'd have a picket line, wouldn't let anybody get anywhere near that mill, real militant picket line, and tough, you know, and the time the troops got there, we'd send practically everybody home, we'd have—we'd keep all the gals around, we'd get some pretty women, and we'd get some guys who played instruments—guitar player—and by the time they got there, there'd be just a few women sitting

around, and fellows sitting there picking a guitar, and me sitting under a tree listening to the music, you know, and there'd be nothing going on. And then when they'd drive up with their—they drove up with their masks on, you know, getting ready for warfare with their guns in the cars, and these girls would go over and say, "Hey, Buddy," you know, "how're you doing? You're nice looking, what've you got there?" And they'd start hiding the stuff, they were so embarrassed. We'd pull stuff like that. And then the troops would go back and they'd say, "No, we couldn't—nothing's happening down there."[40]

The strikers regarded the tactic as a delightful diversion in an otherwise grim situation. Horton also spoofed the patrolmen by using his hotel telephone, which he knew to be tapped, to speed the officers on pointless nighttime expeditions. Calling union friends to make bogus appeals for more manpower to bar scabs from the mill, his friends would offer, "Yes, we'll bring them into East Lumberton on back roads at 3:00 A.M." At 2:30 A.M. the highway patrol would speed away to await and sidetrack phantom truckloads of union sympathizers.[41]

The strike continued through summer. Scab laborers enabled the owners to keep the mill in operation. Striking workers were beginning to feel the pangs of hunger. Welfare assistance was not easily available. Late in July, the company used a newspaper advertisement to invite the strikers to return to their jobs. Horton urged them to accept this offer despite the charge from some workers that they had been sold out. The union maintained its membership. Within a matter of weeks, an agreement was reached between the union and the company for an NLRB election to determine if the mill hands wanted the union to represent them as their sole bargaining agent in matters pertaining to hours, wages, and working conditions. The union won handily. Elsewhere in the South, the TWOC registered steady progress.[42]

By the late thirties and early forties the Highlander Folk School and the southern labor movement seemed permanently joined. Myles Horton and other staff members had been involved in a variety of labor-management conflict experiences. At home in Grundy the staff and students had worked to organize the laborers, but only to see the unions gain few material rewards; they had encouraged political action at the local level, but only to see gains at the polls reversed by political power at the state level. Federal assistance to Grundians brought temporary relief, but few enduring gains to the mountain working men and their families. "In the final analysis," as Michael Price points out, "mountain poverty was simply too extensive to eradicate with stop-gap measures," and "in effect, Highlander's inability to bring lasting progressive change to Grundy County was the failure of the New Deal."[43]

Highlander's role with the CIO organization drive, on the other hand, met with modest successes. The school's staff became known as crackpot and indefatigable organizers. Highlander Folk School became the premier labor education center in the South and thousands of workers at the Summerfield campus or on the road were influenced through its classes in labor history, steward training, parliamentary law, economics, public speaking, journalism, union problems, and other subject matter which underscored and advanced union solidarity. Students departed from Highlander classes with some new skills and new information and, consequently, with a sense of confidence about their identity and importance both as laborers and human beings. Little wonder, then, that influential labor leaders such as Paul Christopher, a CIO regional director, endorsed the school's program and urged its continuation.[44]

"COMMUNIST STOOGES" AND EARLY PERSECUTION

As Highlander's reputation became entrenched among the ranks of labor, so grew the suspicion and resentment among politically conservative elements in Tennessee and the South. Given the school's umbilical link with unionism in a region that was often intolerant of labor organization, and given also the openly and avowed Socialist leanings of the staff members, strong attack and even persecution were to be expected. Actually, charges leveled against the school generally contended that the institution was a communist training camp, un-American, and subversive.

The attacks on Highlander began early. As early as 1933 a union official with the Knoxville Central Labor Union reportedly accused three Highlander staff members of being atheists and Communists; under interrogation, the accuser insisted he had characterized only Zilla Hawes, and not Franz Daniel or Jack Coope, of being a Communist and an atheist.[45] Highlander's critics and attackers did not aim their poisoned arrows from any single corner. Conservative newspapers, mine and textile mill owners, state and county WPA officials, and the American Legion were among the more vocal and persistent foes. Even the noted acrobatic evangelist Billy Sunday took his own potshot in a 1935 sermon in Chattanooga when, in sermonizing on "red and labor organizers," he referred to Highlander as the "communist organization . . . out there on the mountain."[46]

Suspicion about Highlander spread throughout Tennessee when one major newspaper, the *Nashville Tennessean*, encouraged by the *Chattanooga News*, began "exposing" the school. In October 1939 the *Nashville Tennessean* published a series of six front-page articles under four column headlines charging the school with being "a center, if not the center, for the spreading of Communist doctrine in thirteen Southern states." The expose was written by a reporter-detective dispatched to the Summerfield campus by Silliman Evans, president and publisher of the Nashville daily. By posing as a Texas college professor suffering with a stomachache, using an assumed name and by claiming to have been sent by a relative who had once spoken at the school, John McDougal Burns somehow managed to gain entrance to the school grounds—"a feat matched by only five hundred other visitors during 1939," Horton has been quick to point out.[47] Finding copies of the *Daily Worker* among many other papers in the library and discovering that one of the teachers, James Dombrowski, had visited Russia as a young man, and that the school's secretary had once taught at Commonwealth, the newspaper leveled some frightful charges: Highlander's leaders were using Grundy County as a "laboratory" to spread communist doctrine in Tennessee; the school's leaders are connected with Moscow; "it's faculty spreads Communism, approves this red doctrine, and sends its alumni into labor organizations" where they continue to spread its teaching over a wide area"; the school "has kept in close contact with Commonwealth College . . . which is widely known for its communistic teachings and life."[48] The *Chattanooga News* applauded its sister newspaper for the expose: "We nominate the *Nashville Tennessean* for the next Pulitzer award to the newspaper which has given the greatest public service during the year."[49]

Meantime, despite categorical denials by Highlander officials of a connection with any faction or party, democratic or authoritarian, the intensity of the storm against the school increased significantly on its own turf. In early 1940 a group of fearful, witch-hunting Grundy residents banded together to form the Grundy County Crusaders. The vigilante force was of one mind and shared a single mission—to rid their county of the Highlander Folk School. The leader of the

Crusaders, C. H. Kilby, an official with a coal company and sometime preacher, harbored avid antipathy for unionism, communism, and Highlander; he apparently considered all three to be one and the same. In the early months the Crusaders stumped the county, warning their fellow citizens of the imminent danger lurking at their doorstep. The red-hunting crusaders held a public meeting at the Tracy City School gymnasium in which they asked the folk school to leave the area. The crusaders claimed that their county had progressed until Highlander moved in, "but since the establishment of this school, Grundy County has received a tremendous amount of undesired and unfavorable publicity through their activities."[50] A march involving two to three hundred people was planned to protest Highlander's presence. Soon there was talk of "bombing the place."[51]

Reaction was immediate. Friends of Highlander rushed to the school's defense. Some Tennessee unions threatened retaliation should the Grundy County Crusaders make a violent move against the school. "The CIO and Tennessee State Industrial Council have endorsed the Highlander Folk School," Paul Christopher cautioned in a telegram to the Crusaders' head, "and will defend it against any Fifth Columnist attack such as the Tracy City Citizen's [Committee] is reported to be instigating."[52] James Dombrowski had been reminding critics that Highlander had the "confidence" of a "great number of men in Washington who give it support" and whose contributions would benefit all of Grundy County.[53] The march was canceled. A violent move on the facility and personnel was not attempted.

Highlander remained at its founding location near Monteagle for the time being, but Horton and his staff had felt the sting of verbal attack and bad press—financial support dropped dramatically. To counter a dire situation, the national Highlander Folk School Committee was established in Washington. A fund-raising benefit was scheduled for December 1940, and the list of sponsors, according to one writer, "read like a Who's Who of the New Deal and organized labor."[54] The list of sponsors included Cordell Hull, Justice Hugo Black, Sidney Hillman, Harold Ickes, and one of Highlander's staunchest supporters, Eleanor Roosevelt.

With this impressive demonstration of support by such a respected list of national figures, Highlander's fortunes enjoyed a reversal. Opposition to the school cooled considerably. FDR's re-election to an unprecedented third term underscored the validity of the labor movement nationally. With the deepening concern of Americans with another war in Europe, Tennesseans had other matters on their

Students and supporters of Highlander Folk School were frequently privileged to meet and listen to distinguished guests. Here, in an outdoor meeting, Myles Horton introduces Eleanor Roosevelt. (Courtesy—Highlander Folk School Collection, Tennessee State Library Archives)

minds. Still, Highlander's reputation was clearly and firmly established in the minds of Tennesseans and southerners in general. A number of labor activists continued to be troubled by Highlander leanings. The school's link with the leftist Southern Conference for Human Welfare, for example, led to one unfortunate development—at the Tennessee CIO convention in 1941, Franz Daniel, long considered a friend of Highlander and its leading staff, announced that he and his wife, organizer Elizabeth Hawes, were severing their ties with the school because its staff members were "Communist stooges." The loss of this respected couple's endorsement and support could only impair the school's credibility.[55]

Later in the forties the marriage between Highlander and the southern labor movement seemed to be more troubled. True enough, the school continued its active role in labor education, attracting workers from even more geographically distant points than ever before. The Grundy County school still attracted attention from the national media. "Nowhere else in America today, with all the good city-bound labor schools, is there any place like this backwoods Southern school, which brings together the city industrial worker and the farmer in a continuous, active program," noted a writer for the *Nation* magazine. "Monteagle is a focal point for the new labor forces gathering in the South," the writer continued.[56] By the late forties the CIO had fully imbibed the red-scare spirit of the Cold War and had moved to expel members of the Communist party. Because Highlander had adamantly refused to sever its working relationship with the Mine, Mill, and Smelter Workers, one of the last militant unions in the South, the CIO canceled its usual workers' training institute at Highlander.[57]

By 1950 it was obvious that fundamental differences between Highlander's ideology and that of the labor movement in general were not going to be reconciled. Labor's rank and file saw the school leaning too far leftward. From Horton's perspective, the labor forces were complacent and reactionary. Perhaps the adult training center which started in 1932 had completed its mission of direct involvement in the organized labor movement in Tennessee and the South. Highlander was on the verge of a new direction.

"WE SHALL OVERCOME"

"We are at our best at Highlander when we are pioneering," Myles Horton observed in 1953,[58] and for the next eighteen years the Monteagle school which had taken a lead in one swelling social movement, southern unionism, was now in the forefront of another swelling social movement—the campaign to end racial segregation in the South.

One of the early goals which Horton held for a folk school in the South, even before Highlander was founded, was to bring black and white students together. Such a notion was a radical one for whites in the thirties. But it was also a radical notion for blacks. "We made a statement at the very beginning: 'Highlander is open to blacks.' The first announcement of Highlander said it. So we had a principle established," Horton recollected. "But we had no takers. Neither blacks nor whites would come on that basis, but our position was clear. We were open."[59] Horton sought assistance in bringing black students to the

Highlander classes were often taught outdoors. Addressing students and guests is Eleanor Roosevelt. (Courtesy—Highlander Folk School Collection, Tennessee State Library and Archives)

Highlander campus, but to no avail; black leaders expressed interest in his educational project, but could not recommend suitable black candidates who had a desire to enroll in the school. What Highlander was offering to blacks was a new concept; additionally, it was a dangerous idea and "there wasn't any reason for them sticking their necks out."[60] This failure to attract blacks as students on any significant scale continued until 1944.[61]

Horton and his staff were not content to allow Highlander to flow with the southern current in terms of race and education. Horton remembers the feeling of being "bothered" by the fact that black students did not come to Monteagle for adult education, but, he adds, "it didn't bother us as much as it would have if we hadn't established the principle, because we knew that eventually it would help us in working through it."[62]

Horton knew that if he was to play a significant role in promoting racial harmony and progress that he would have to take the initiative.

214

TOIL, TURMOIL, AND TRIUMPH

He invited Dr. J. Harman Daves, a professor at segregated Knoxville College, to come to Highlander to teach a course. Resident students were interested in discussing the role of blacks in the labor force. Dr. Daves and wife thus became, in 1933, the first black people to stay overnight and eat at Highlander, thus violating a state prohibition against blacks and whites eating together or staying overnight under the same roof. The Jim Crow law was never respected at Highlander.[63] The Highlander staff also made a conscious effort when on the road to organize blacks and include all working people, regardless of race or gender, in all their labor activities. "The union is for everyone!" was their simple message. In labor education classes, instructors used available opportunities to point out both the history and psychology of racism as well as the practical costs and damage of discrimination. Horton worked to build a little network of black labor leaders and college professors to teach classes and lead discussions on issues related to race and labor.[64]

Additionally, Highlander staff members either joined or established their own organization whose avowed purpose was to combat racism. Horton and Dombrowski joined other southern liberals to call the All-Southern Conference for Civil and Trade Union Rights which was scheduled to meet in Chattanooga in April 1935; the conference setting got pushed around by fidgety officials until it finally landed at Highlander, but was among the first attempts in the thirties to organize a southern coalition of black and white political, religious, and labor groups.[65] The much more successful Southern Conference for Human Welfare, initially convening in Birmingham and attracting over 1,200 delegates in November 1938 enjoyed the enthusiastic support of the Highlanders. In 1942, Jim Dombrowski resigned at Highlander to become the conference's executive secretary.[66] It seemed that everything which was touched by a Highlander staff member received the bliss of controversy and the Southern Conference for Human Welfare was certainly no exception.

By 1940 Highlander's position on racial segregation was clearly established in the community, the state, and among southern labor leaders. Put simply, racial segregation was not tolerated at the school or in any phase of the school's projects or services. That same year Highlander informed all the southern unions that it served that it would no longer hold labor education programs for unions which discriminated against blacks. Four years later, Paul Christopher, by then regional director for the CIO and a board member at Highlander, organized a Highlander workshop for the United Auto Workers which brought to the campus forty unionists, black and white, from all over the South.[67] The visitors knew that the problems of labor-management relations, of grievance handling, of collective bargaining, and of understanding co-workers knew no racial boundaries. Together black and white workers could discuss issues and learn from one another. And, leaving the classroom with renewed solidarity, together they could play games, sing songs, cook meals, and wash dishes. After broadcasting word through the Tennessee CIO that the workshop was an integrated one, the staff urged that all other unions follow this pattern. "Actually we just took one statement and parleyed that into a statewide mandate on it . . . we made it almost impossible for them not to bring blacks," Horton remembered.[68]

Once Highlander had made this courageous policy on race clear and had affirmed it in daily practice, less heralded, yet meaningful events began occurring. More and more blacks began to make use of the school's facilities. Three black men and one black woman joined the Highlander's board of directors during the forties. Increasing attention was given to the issue of race and labor relations in the school's classes and workshops. Black workers returned to their homes and their work sites with renewed pride and confidence, at times bursting with an enthusiasm to share with their co-workers some of the ideas and experiences gained at Highlander.[69]

Monteagle in the forties and fifties was not always one glorious, idyllic oasis in a desert of prejudice and discrimination. Established traditions were not forgotten. Old customs died tough. The integrated workshops and campus lifestyle sparked sporadic racial incidents, simply because new thought patterns require time for acceptance and words which give rise to insults come easily. Through it all, Highlander was a laboratory in interpersonal relations. Horton and his staff would insist on an immediate and full resolution of conflict between two parties who felt estrangement. Horton also believed that song and dance could soothe the feelings of hard times and spawn solidarity and group determination in ways that no other communication medium could. Zilphia Horton was uniquely gifted in uniting working people from all backgrounds through her own musical compositions and performances and through her ability to involve ordinary folk in musical experiences. She also had the uncanny ability to adapt familiar tunes and melodies to contemporary situations.[70]

Perhaps the most striking example of Zilphia Horton's gift for musical adaptation is found in a song which she, along with folk singers Pete Seeger and Frank Hamilton, modified for workers. As the civil rights movement gained momentum, the song became a great anthem for American blacks and people everywhere who joined hands and hearts in the battle for a full and just equality. Myles Horton has told the story about "We Shall Overcome":

> There was a strike of tobacco workers, working in the tobacco plant in Charleston, South Carolina, and we always encouraged students to bring songs that they had written or used on a picket line. . . . And that song was a kind of rough-hewn song that they'd gotten from a black hymnal; the blacks had sung it, and the white people had picked it up—they had tried to make a strike song out of it. And it was a song that Zilphia said it wasn't singable, it was too hard to sing. So she sat down at the piano like she always did with people like that, and they worked out the music so it'd be simpler. She used to say there was singable songs, and then there was songs like "The Star-Spangled Banner," which nobody should sing. You know, she thought songs should be easy to sing. So that was revised, and that became a very popular song that week. People liked it after they had simplified it a little bit.
>
> For ten years it was just a Highlander song, and then the labor movement started using it a little bit more, and then it died down, and just kind of stayed in the Highlander domain. And then Guy Carawan, who is in charge of music here now, taught that song, which is a black peoples' song, to a lot of his people in SNCC, and later on did it for the Southern Christian Leadership Conference, and it kind of— the song came back to the people where it originated from, and then it became a popular song again in the civil rights movement, and now as you know it's sung around the world. It's everywhere. . . . I don't know of any song of that kind that is so widespread.[71]

THE VOLUNTEER STATE VERSUS THE
HIGHLANDER FOLK SCHOOL

Given Highlander's clear and established policy on racial integration, the announcement of the Supreme Court decision in the case of

Brown v. Board of Education on May 17, 1954, which called for an end to segregated public classrooms, was fully welcomed by the staff as an opportunity for even more activism in race relations. In fact, the Highlander staff had already conducted workshops the previous year on "The Supreme Court Decisions and the Public Schools" which were designed to involve informed workers in the drive to desegregate public schools. Following the *Brown* decision, the Highlander staff conducted two major workshops aimed at promoting a better under-standing among white and black southerners of race relations in their home communities. Then the staff began to search for ways to press for the rapid desegregation of public institutions. Funds were raised, more workshops were conducted, and literature was distributed. Still, opposition among southern whites to the court decision was formidable and the Highlander staff believed that the civil rights movement needed some spark to ignite involvement.[72] The spark was not long in coming.

On December 1, 1955, Rosa Parks refused to yield her bus seat to a white passenger. She was thus arrested for violating a Montgomery, Alabama, ordinance and the arrest set off the historic Montgomery bus boycott. Fatigue from a long day of tedious work does not fully account for her act of civil disobedience. Only weeks before her refusal to heed the instructions of the bus driver, Parks had attended one of Highlander's desegregation workshops. Parks, a seamstress in a local department store, had already developed an intense interest in civil rights and racial justice; years earlier she had joined a local chapter of the NAACP. Her visit in Monteagle had been an exhila-rating experience of, in her own words, "a unified society . . . of differing races and backgrounds meeting together in workshops and living together in peace and harmony."[73] Parks felt that she gained at Highlander the "strength to persevere in my work for freedom, not just for blacks but all oppressed people."[74] Parks found that the price paid for moral courage was high; her rent was raised and she lost her job as a seamstress. She eventually moved to Detroit.

Highlander played no direct role in the Montgomery bus boycott, but the sudden stirring in southern race relations kept Highlander in the suspicious eye of both government agencies and white segrega-tionists. Then, on Labor Day weekend of 1957, Highlander staged an event which gave white supremacists all the ammunition they needed to wound the school and embarrass the civil rights movement.

The occasion was the celebration of Highlander's twenty-fifth anniversary. About 180 people, mostly southerners, gathered on the campus to renew friendships, reminisce about earlier times, and discuss race relations in the role of Highlander in effecting a more harmonious South. Civil rights was the chief subject of public discussion, but the entire weekend was planned as an occasion of celebration and joy; square dances were held and Peter Seeger led the visitors in group singing.[75]

The anniversary celebration was keynoted by two speakers: Aubrey Williams, a former president of the Southern Conference for Human Welfare and editor of *Southern Farm and Home*, and Martin Luther King, Jr., head of the Montgomery Improvement Association. King used his time to commend Highlander for producing southern leadership: "For twenty-five years you have stood with dauntless courage and fearless determination. . . . You have given the South some of its most responsible leaders in this great period of transition."[76] King spoke of a new era in race relations for the South and urged his listeners to remain "maladjusted" to the physical violence, discrimination and economic exploitation found in the nation and to work for a new day.[77]

The celebration was a public gathering and Edwin Friend, an undercover agent acting under orders of Georgia governor Marvin Griffin, was freely admitted. Friend took copious notes on all he saw and heard, mingled with the crowd, and snapped photographs of blacks and whites visiting, eating, and dancing together. One photograph of Friend's collection was destined to gain wide circulation and much exposure. The famous photo captured Dr. King seated near Myles Horton and Abner Berry, a known member of the Communist party. Some 250,000 copies of the photograph were distributed throughout the South, most with Governor Griffin's stated purpose "to identify the leaders and participants of this Communist training school." A glossy brochure financed by the state of Georgia and entitled "Highlander Folk School-Communist Training School, Monteagle, Tennessee" contained a broadside which began: "During Labor Day Weekend, 1957, there assembled at Highlander the leaders of every race incident in the South."[78] The picture would not go away. Years later billboards in cities throughout the South posted a bigger-than-life photographic enlargement with an arrow pointing to King and bold lettering that bluntly made a disturbing connection: "MARTIN LUTHER KING AT COMMUNIST TRAINING SCHOOL."

Monteagle was now on the map of millions of Americans. Paradoxically, while the Georgia governor assailed Highlander and schemed to close it, the anniversary celebration turned into the school's high water mark for national interest and attention. As in years past, Highlander's most eloquent defenders came from outside the South. *Time* magazine noted the occasion. In an editorial, the *Christian Century* deplored the "undercover" and "infiltrating" activities at a "well publicized, entirely open meeting." "All this would be sad and sordid enough if it stayed south near wherever paranoid minds nurture such deceit," the editorial continued. "What makes it more disturbing, though, is the evidence of a 'sovereign state' sending its secret police outside the state, and then using public funds to spread something very near libel."[79] Weeks later the *New York Times* published a statement released by Highlander which condemned the "irresponsible demagoguery" which equates leadership in desegregation drives with communism. The statement was signed by Eleanor Roosevelt, Reinhold Niebuhr, Monsignor John O'Grady, and Lloyd K. Garrison, the latter a former law school dean at the University of Wisconsin.[80] Horton considered taking legal action against the Georgia governor, but concluded that the likelihood of a fair trial in a Georgia courtroom was not great and that the school's best course of action against the smear campaign was to continue its educational program in mutual good faith with all people who sought its services.[81]

One continuing point of interfacing with the civil rights movement of the fifties was Highlander's Citizenship Education Program. The program was designed to teach blacks who lived and worked on the South Carolina sea islands the fundamentals of reading and American government. One of the goals was to help the adults read the part of the state constitution they would have to read in order to register successfully to vote. The program was administered through Septima Poinsette Clark, one of Highlander's students who was dismissed by the Charleston school board after she had been actively urging blacks to vote. After her dismissal, Clark came to Highlander to serve as director of education; from this position, and funded through a grant from the Schwartzhaupt Foundation, Clark and Highlander teamed for this novel experiment. King's Southern Christian Leadership Conference eventually absorbed this project and opened its own citizenship training center in Georgia.[82]

Meantime, segregationist voices of concern about the real purpose and direction of Highlander were growing louder and louder. Bruce Bennett, the attorney general for Arkansas, was the next to fire his salvo against the school. The Arkansas official had established his reputation throughout the South by his vigorous legal maneuvers to block the desegregation of Little Rock's Central High School. Demonstrating magnanimous concern for the orthodoxy of his sister state, Bennett journeyed to Nashville to deliver a message of urgency to the Tennessee General Assembly. The Arkansas traveler's remedy was clearly stated—the Highlander Folk School should be thoroughly investigated with officials having the full power to subpoena, impound records, and take necessary action. The verdict Bennett had in mind was already determined well before any investigation; he recommended to the legislature that the folk school be closed immediately and conceded that he would do it personally if it were located in his own bailiwick.[83] The legislators listened. Despite a *Nashville Tennessean* editorial which criticized Bennett and reasoned that "if there is anything Tennessee does not need at this point, it is the distinction of reviving McCarthyism,"[84] a House Joint resolution was passed authorizing hearings in Tracy City and Nashville concerning the school. At Tracy City the most damaging evidence mustered against the operation was a litany of rather innocuous recollections and rumors passed along by Grundy residents. The investigating committee acknowledged that it uncovered no finding in fact about alleged communism at Highlander but recommended that the school be closed due to imperfections in the charter's language and certain alleged financial irregularities. The investigators were also quite exercised about the fact that no witness other than Horton himself had ever seen an American flag fly over the school ground. They were convinced, too, that Highlander was not really a school since it did not "carry on the usual activities as one would normally associate with school activities."[85]

A concerned public opinion needed a dramatic incident, something with heavy moral overtones, to crystallize and confirm its fears about Highlander. Circuit Attorney General Albert Sloan soon moved to provide an incident. Under his direction, and on the evening of July 31, 1959, state agents raided the Monteagle school in search of whiskey. (Grundy County was dry and the possession or sale of whiskey was illegal.) The county and state officers, most in plain clothing, found no alcohol in the main building, nor in any other school building. They did, however, find a small quantity of liquor in Horton's private home at the edge of the campus. The fact that Horton's home was a private dwelling not covered by the search warrant or that Horton himself was in Europe at the time did not deter the enthusiastic officials. At the time of the raid, Septima Clark, then aged 61, was conducting a desegregation workshop. She was arrested and charged with illegal possession and sale of whiskey and with resisting arrest. Ironically, the veteran teacher had been a "teetotaler" all her life; the other charge was based on her request to phone a lawyer. Three other Highlander personnel were arrested on charges of public drunkenness and taken to the county jail at Altamont to spend the night. A padlock was placed on the main building.[86]

Highlander's fight for survival began in a trial room at the county courthouse in the small mountain town at Altamont, some 25 to 30 miles from the campus, in early November 1959. A. B. Sloan brought the state's charges against Highlander. Before Judge Chester Chattin, who had sworn in twelve jurors, all of whom admitted that they believed in segregation and did not want an integrated school in Grundy County, the 18th Judicial Circuit Attorney leveled three charges: (1) Highlander had conducted integrated adult workshop meetings in violation of Tennessee laws; (2) Highlander had peddled beer and whiskey without a license; (3) Highlander had been operated for the personal profit of the school's director, Myles Horton. The prosecutor recommended that Highlander's property be confiscated and disposed of by the state.[87]

Highlander and Horton were not left without an eloquent defense. Their attorney was Cecil Branstetter of Nashville, for years the legal advisor for the state labor council and friend of Charles Houk and Stanton Smith. Branstetter, assisted by Nashville attorney George Barrett, conducted a brilliant defense. The defense team paraded before the jury a distinguished array of educators and ministers who had visited Highlander on various occasions and could attest to the nature and quality of the program. Two or three of the defense witnesses had been college presidents. Sloan worked to minimize their testimony and kept injecting the issue of race at Highlander into the proceedings, once referring to Clark as "September" Clark, "a big ramrod out at Highlander." A photograph made on campus showing a white woman and black man in near embrace was one of the prosecution's exhibits, though the scene depicted was of a folk dance.[88]

Throughout the proceedings Horton maintained his good sense of humor which had been a saving grace in numerous other stressful situations. At times during testimony, facetiousness slipped into his words. The controversial educator felt certain that the court would find him guilty as charged, but he was confident that Highlander would not really be defeated for one important reason—in Horton's mind Highlander was not a place but an idea, and an idea could not be put out of business by confiscating property. The judge gave Branstetter thirty days in which to file a brief and the state ten days to answer.[89]

On February 17, 1960, Judge Chattin found that Highlander was guilty as charged on all three counts and ordered the school's charter revoked and its property confiscated and liquidated. The school appealed to the Tennessee Supreme Court, which threw out the violation on practicing racial integration but upheld the judge's ruling. Racial integration, then, could not be an issue when the case was appealed to the U.S. Supreme Court which, in October 1961, denied the school a hearing. The legal existence of Highlander Folk School in Monteagle had been terminated. Two months later the announcement of an auction on the Summerfield grounds had enticed over a thousand people to the property. In an almost circus-like atmosphere the state auctioned the school's equipment, 5,000-volume library, and furniture. The following summer, fourteen school buildings and nine residences, which included Horton's private home, and 175 acres of land and a private lake, were auctioned off by the state for $43,700. The old house originally donated to the project by Lillian Johnson was included in the sale, but mysteriously burned to the ground before new occupants could move in. Not one penny of compensation was ever paid to Horton or Highlander Folk School for the seizure of the property. The school's staunchest and most vocal enemies could at long last breathe a sigh of relief—Highlander Folk School had been closed![90]

EPILOGUE

Fully aware of the fate which awaited Highlander in Grundy County by the hands of state officials, Horton made a move to secure the Highlander idea even before all appeals to save the school for Monteagle had been exhausted. Horton and four colleagues sought and rather routinely received in August 1961 a new charter for operation under the name "Highlander Research and Education Center." The prospect of a new Highlander propagating the old ideology and still practicing racial integration, now in another part of Tennessee, predictably baffled the general public and exasperated its angry opponents. The center's headquarters was moved to an aging, two-story mansion in a racially mixed neighborhood in Knoxville. During most of the sixties the Highlander faculty continued to support the civil rights movement, though some leaders in the movement concluded the center's program lacked direction and that its involvement was no longer significant. The Poor People's Campaign of 1968 fired up the old zeal among faculty and students, but activity on the civil rights battlefront was never to be as intense again. Highlander directors learned that much of the controversy and even persecution which surrounded the school in Monteagle eventually made its way to Knoxville.[91]

Highlander moved in 1972 to a 104-acre farm near the town of New Market, Tennessee, twenty-five miles northeast of Knoxville. Horton resigned as president in 1970. Dissension and deep divisions among the staff over administrative decisions then followed. By the mid-seventies, everything about Highlander seemed to be in steady decline—student enrollment, demand for services, enthusiasm for programs, and measurable achievements. In the midst of this malaise, the staff was unwilling to pronounce a slow death had come upon Highlander. Believing that the problems of Appalachian people were as real and complex as at any time in the school's history, the staff turned again to its roots within the mountain culture. Focusing on Appalachian issues, approximately two hundred residence conferences and workshops were conducted on such subjects as land mineral ownership, welfare rights, strip mining, occupational and environmental-health hazards, and tax and public school reform. The center also expanded its research services.[92]

As attention has been paid to preserving the heritage of the institution, several grandiose terms and labels have been attached to Highlander—"pioneer," "extraordinary," "unique," and "on the cutting edge of social change in the South," to name a few. Often lost in the retelling of the Highlander story is all but scant mention of the internal dissension, loose institutional practices, and administrative negligence which not infrequently plagued the school. And however the motives of the school's foes may be adjudged, the charges of which the Monteagle school was convicted, however trivial in retrospect, were based on valid evidence. Nonetheless, "the history of the Highlander Folk School is in many ways the history of dissent and reform in Appalachia and the American South since the onset of the

Great Depression," concludes John Glen, the definitive historian of the school's first three decades. Highlander played "a crucial role" in the southern labor movement of the 1930s and 1940s and in the civil rights movement during the 1950s and 1960s "because it did one thing better than any other institution in the region: educate industrial workers, farmers, blacks, and the poor to focus on their grievances and nurture the seeds of their discontent."[93]

In his formal retirement from Highlander's leadership, Myles Horton had time to travel and speak for social and economic justice. He also had time to reflect on a long, eventful life:

> I've had a lot of satisfaction spending my life working for a truly democratic society. I've always known that in working for a more democratic society that I was working with theoretical possibilities. I spent my life the way I wanted to. I've done what I wanted to do. Of course, I've had plenty of opposition, but at the same time I have never given up hope. What has always meant a great deal to me is that all kinds of former students from here will tell me that the direction of their lives has been changed by being at Highlander. Helping people to understand and realize their potential and helping people to gain control of their lives and then re-direct their lives—well, that is certainly one of life's most satisfying experiences.[94]

NOTES

1. A number of sources were used and consulted in the construction of the narrative in this chapter. First and foremost among published materials is John M. Glen, *Highlander: No Ordinary School*, 1932-1962 (Lexington: University Press of Kentucky, 1988); Glen's volume, based on numerous interviews and private manuscript collections, is the definitive volume on the first thirty years of Highlander's turbulent history. Other sources drawn from in this study include the following: Thomas Bledsoe, *Or We'll All Hang Separately: The Highlander Idea* (Boston: Beacon Press, 1969); Frank Adams, "Highlander Folk School: Getting Information, Going Back and Teaching It," *Harvard Educational Review*, vol. 42, no. 4 (November 1972), 497-520, and *Unearthing Seeds of Fire: The Idea of Highlander* (Winston-Salem, N.C.: John F. Blair, 1975); Anthony P. Dunbar, *Against the Grain: Southern Radicals and Prophets, 1929-1959* (Charlottesville, Va.: University Press of Virginia, 1981); Hulan Glyn Thomas, "The Highlander Folk School: The Depression Years," *Tennessee Historical Quarterly*, vol. 23 (December 1964), 358-71; and Michael E. Price, "The New Deal in Tennessee: The Highlander Folk School and Worker Response in Grundy County," *Tennessee Historical Quarterly*, vol. 43 (Summer 1984), 99-120. Horton is interviewed by Mary Frederickson in "The Spark that Ignites," *Southern Exposure*, 4 (Spring/Summer 1976), 153-56. An interview with Bill Moyers broadcast on PBS on June 5 and June 11, 1981, has been reproduced as "The Adventures of a Radical Hillbilly: An Interview with Myles Horton," *Appalachian Journal*, vol. 9, no. 4 (Summer 1982), 248-85. The above sources will be cited in abbreviated form hereafter in these notes.

A chief source of information for this chapter was the special manuscript collection titled "Highlander Folk School Collection" at the Tennessee State Library and Archives. The collection contains over 4,200 items, including addresses and speeches.

A more recent primary source arrived with the publication of Myles Horton, with Judith Kohl and Herbert Kohl, *The Long Haul: An Autobiography* (New York: Doubleday, 1990). "Were I to choose America's most influential and inspiring educator," Studs Terkel is quoted on the front dust jacket cover, "it would be Myles Horton of Highlander."

An outstanding recent publication which offers detailed discussion about the connection of various affiliations and institutions and the southern civil rights movement is John Egerton's award-winning volume, *Speak Now Against the Day: The Generation Before the Civil Rights Movement* (New York: Alfred A. Knopf, 1994). Egerton discusses the impact of both Horton and a number of other figures with Highlander Folk School connections on liberal socio-political causes. Specific discussion of HFS is found on pages 158-62. Egerton, one of the South's finest writers, has provided an account of the ordeal by trial of Highlander and Horton in "The Trial of Highlander Folk School," *Shades of Gray: Dispatches From the Modern South* (Baton Rouge: Louisiana State University Press, 1991), pp. 58-76.

The author has also had informal conversations about Horton and Highlander with Nashville attorney Cecil Branstetter and author John Glen while the three of us conducted a panel on this subject for the Southern Festival of Books, October 1989.

A final major source of information was the author's personal interview with Myles Horton, April 10, 1987, on the Highlander campus in New Market, Tennessee (hereafter referred to as Horton interview).

2. Adams, *Unearthing Seeds of Fire*,1-4; Glen, *Highlander*, 6-8.

3. Bonhoeffer, the widely acclaimed theologian who was placed in a German concentration camp and later executed by the Nazis for his role in a plot to assassinate Adolph Hitler, was one of several famous people whom Horton encountered. "Most of the famous people that I had the privilege of knowing were not famous people when I knew them and I did not know at the time that they would later be famous," Horton pointed out. About Bonhoeffer, Horton recollected: "I knew him during the academic year of 1930 at Union, but I did not know him well. I felt rebuffed by him because he was better educated and tended to look with contempt on some of our radical activities. Later, when he found out that although I was a southerner I shared his views regarding the black church, he became more friendly. Of course, I followed his development with interest and admiration and have been affected by his life." Horton interview.

4. Adams, *Unearthing Seeds of Fire*, 11-24; Glen, *Highlander*, 9-14.

5. Adams, *Unearthing Seeds of Fire*, 26-27; Glen, *Highlander*, 16-17.

6. Adams, *Unearthing Seeds of Fire*, 27-28; Glen, *Highlander*, 17-20.

7. Adams, "Highlander Folk School," 503.

8. Ibid., 503-04; Price, "The New Deal in Tennessee," 100.

9. Glen, *Highlander*, 22-25; Adams, *Unearthing Seeds of Fire*, 30-35. The story of Wilder is told in a separate chapter in this volume.

10. From Thompson's account in American Folksongs of Protest and quoted in Bledsoe, *Or We'll All Hang Separately*, 174.

11. Ibid.

12. Quoted in ibid., 175.

13. A headline for the *Chattanooga Times* on Nov. 29, 1932, reads: "Mystery Teacher Slaps Guardsmen; Describes Drinking of Soldiers at Wilder." The story begins: "Mystery surrounds the location of the 'Highlander Folk School' and the exact identity of its director, Myles Horton, who was arrested by National Guardsmen after visiting the mine strike area near Wilder last week and later arrested."

14. Horton interview.

15. Kermit Eby, "The 'Drip' Theory in Labor Unions," *Antioch Review* 13 (Spring 1953), 97.

16. Frederickson, "The Spark That Ignites," 153.

17. Ibid.

18. Ibid.

19. Based on a report by Horton in 1932 and quoted in Adams, "Highlander Folk School," 506.

20. Ibid.

21. Thomas, "The Highlander Folk School," 362; Adams, *Unearthing Seeds of Fire*, 40-41.

22. Adams, *Unearthing Seeds of Fire*, 40-43; "Story of a Southern People's School," 3.

23. Adams, *Unearthing Seeds of Fire*, 43.

24. Ibid.; Glen, *Highlander*, 34-35.

25. "Story of a Southern People's School," 2; Adams, *Unearthing Seeds of Fire*, 43.

26. Price, "New Deal in Tennessee," 113.

27. Quoted in ibid.

28. Ibid., 113-14.

29. Ibid.

30. Ibid., 115.

31. Ibid., 117; Thomas, "The Highlander Folk School," 363.

32. Quoted in Price, "New Deal in Tennessee," 118.

33. Ibid., 118-19; Adams, *Unearthing Seeds of Fire*, 47-53; Glen, *Highlander*, 50-52.

34. Adams, *Unearthing Seeds of Fire*, 54.

35. Ibid., 54-55; Dunbar, *Against the Grain*, 145; "Story of a Southern People's School," 2.

36. Glen, *Highlander*, 77-86; Adams, *Unearthing Seeds of Fire*, 82-83; "Story of a Southern People's School," 3.

37. Glen, *Highlander*, 73; Adams, *Unearthing Seeds of Fire*, 55-56.

38. Dunbar, *Against the Grain*, 147.

39. Adams, *Unearthing Seeds of Fire*, 58-59.

40. Quoted in Moyers, "Adventures of a Radical Hillbilly," 263.

41. This incident is told in Adams, *Unearthing Seeds of Fire*, 60.

42. The best source for the story of Horton's work in Lumberton is Adams, *Unearthing Seeds of Fire*, 54-71; see also Moyers, "Adventures of a Radical Hillbilly," 263-66.

43. Price, "New Deal in Tennessee," 120.

44. Joseph Yates Garrison, a biographer and student of Paul Christopher, has written of the friendship between Horton and Christopher. Garrison concludes that "of all the friends Christopher made during his tenure in the labor movement, none was closer to him than Myles Horton." The two became close friends during the 1937 TWOC drive. Christopher offered technical advice to the young organizer, beginning with the organizing effort in McCall, South Carolina. Later, Horton solicited Christopher's support for Highlander. Christopher lectured on the TWOC organizing drive and the stretch-out at the school's 1938 winter session. The same sessions also featured Lucy Mason as a lecturer and included a CIO training program entitled "Let Southern Labor Speak." Christopher continued to teach a number of courses at Highlander and also served on the school's executive council. See Garrison, "Paul Revere Christopher: Southern Labor Leader, 1910-1974" (Ph.D. diss., Georgia State University, 1976), 188-96.

45. Bledsoe, *Or We'll All Hang Separately*, 65.

46. *Chattanooga Times*, May 4, 1935.

47. Quoted in Bledsoe, *Or We'll All Hang Separately*, 65.

48. One of Burns' articles is quoted verbatim in ibid., 69-75; see *Nashville Tennessean*, series of six articles beginning with the October 15, 1939, issue.

49. *Chattanooga News-Free Press*, October 17, 1939.

50. *Chattanooga News-Free Press*, November 13, 1940.

51. Thomas, "The Highlander Folk School," 368.

52. Quoted in ibid.

53. *Chattanooga News-Free Press*, November 13, 1940.

54. Thomas, "The Highlander Folk School," 368.

55. Dunbar, *Against the Grain*, 213.

56. Alden Stevens, "Small-Town America," *Nation* (June 29, 1946), 784.

57. Adams, *Unearthing Seeds of Fire*, 86.

58. Quoted in Glen, *Highlander*, 129.

59. Frederickson, "The Spark That Ignites," 155.

60. Ibid.

61. Such is the conclusion of Frank Adams in *Unearthing Seeds of Fire*, 91.

62. Frederickson, "The Spark That Ignites," 155.

63. Adams, *Unearthing Seeds of Fire*, 91.

64. Ibid.

65. Ibid., 93-97.

66. For a history of the brief life of this voluntary organization, containing a separate chapter (2) on the Birmingham convention of 1938, see Thomas A. Krueger, *And Promises to Keep: The Southern Conference for Human Welfare, 1938-1948* (Nashville: Vanderbilt University Press, 1967).

67. Adams, *Unearthing Seeds of Fire*, 100.

68. Frederickson, "The Spark That Ignites," 155.

69. Adams, *Unearthing Seeds of Fire*, 122.

70. See chapter 5, "A Singing Army," in ibid., 72-88; Glen, *Highlander*, 54.

71. Quoted in Moyers, "Adventures of a Radical Hillbilly," 268-69.

72. Glen, *Highlander*, 129-36.

73. Quoted in Adams, *Unearthing Seeds of Fire*, 122.

74. Ibid.

75. Ibid.; Glen, *Highlander*, 142.

76. Martin Luther King, Jr., "The Look to the Future," address presented at the 25th anniversary, Sept. 2, 1957, Highlander Folk School Collection, Tennessee State Library and Archives.

77. Ibid.

78. Quoted in Dunbar, *Against the Grain*, 251; cf. Adams, *Unearthing Seeds of Fire*, 123-35, and Glen, *Highlander*, 181-82.

79. "Georgia Invades Ohio," *Christian Century*, October 30, 1957.

80. "Leaders Defend School in South," *New York Times*, December 22, 1957; cf. Glen, Highlander, 183.

81. Glen, *Highlander*, 183-84.

82. See more detailed treatment of the Citizenship Education Program in ibid., 155-72, and Adams, *Unearthing Seeds of Fire*, 110-20.

83. Glen, *Highlander*, 185-86; Dunbar, *Against the Grain*, 252-54; Adams, *Unearthing Seeds of Fire*, 127-30.

84. *Nashville Tennessean*, January 29, 1959.

85. Quoted in Adams, *Unearthing Seeds of Fire*, 131; cf. Glen, *Highlander*, 187-93.

86. Glen, *Highlander*, 193-94.

87. Ibid., 194-209; Adams, *Unearthing Seeds of Fire*, 134-41; Dunbar, *Against the Grain*, 252-53.

88. Ibid.; cf. David Jarrard, "Folk School Focus of Free-Speech Battle," *Nashville Tennessean*, August 6, 1987; *Concern*, vol. 15, no. 6 (November 1959), 6-7.

89. Glen, *Highlander*, 194-209.

90. Ibid.

91. Glen, *Highlander*, 210-17.

92. Ibid., 218-19.

93. Ibid., 220. A concise summary of Glen's study may be found in his article, "The Highlander Folk School: Fostering Individual Growth and Social Change," *Chronicle of Higher Education*, June 15, 1988, p. B5. Journalistic overviews of the school after more than fifty years may be found in the *Knoxville News-Sentinel*, April 24, 1983, and Tom Eblen, "'Folk School' Spurs Change in the South for 52 Years," *Atlanta Journal*, June 30, 1984.

94. Horton interview.

9

"... there ain't no such thing in this country as a damn 'right to work' ... you go tell your government they owe you a job because you have a right to work and find out what happens."

Political Stirring

The Political Awakening and Early Struggle
for Tennessee Labor

Nineteen forty-seven was a pivotal year for the Tennessee labor movement. Riding the crest of strong anti-labor sentiment in the country, Congress easily passed the Labor-Management Relations Act on June 23 over President Harry Truman's veto. The bill, more commonly known as the Taft-Hartley Act of 1947, has served as one of the three basic statutes providing the foundation for a complex structure of rules, regulations, and decisions governing organized labor. (The Wagner Act of 1935 and Landrum Griffin Act of 1959 were the other two.)

If the Wagner Act had seemed like a godsend to unions, the Taft-Hartley Act seemed like a "slave labor act." In the dozen years since the enactment of Wagner, many members of Congress became convinced that the balance of power in labor-management relations had been too heavily weighted in favor of labor. Unions had been growing in membership and power—from 3.6 million members in 1935 to 14 million in 1947.[1] The year prior to Taft-Hartley's passage, strikes had been called in the automobile industry, led by U.A.W.'s new leader Walter Reuther, and in the steel, electrical, and meat-packing industries. The Wage Stabilization Board, established by Truman to work out agreements in such disputes, seemed more and more ineffective in satisfying worker demands. Labor seemed to have been building its own power throughout the war and Congress was prepared to go on the counter-offensive.

In the months prior to the passage of Taft-Hartley, various states had been active in passing laws which consisted almost entirely of an array of union limitations. Business and agricultural interests grew increasingly uncomfortable with the show of union strength and had appealed to their state legislatures where their voices of concern received a favorable reception. Union leaders began to realize that while their eye had been focused on the legislative activity of the U.S. Congress, the emerging new enemy of organized labor was its opposition in the state legislatures. Labor had been forewarned. At the convention of the Congress of Industrial Organizations in November 1946, the union's counsel, Lee Pressman, sounded the tocsin:

> Let's not make the mistake of solely concentrating our attention on Congress, because our enemies are not resting with Congress. There will be plenty of fights in Congress, but at the same time let us mobilize our forces in the various States to carry on the fight before the State Legislatures.[2]

In early 1947 Tennessee joined some 27 other states which enacted laws that year which dealt with the conduct and organization of unions. Bills outlawing the union shop had already been passed in Florida, Arkansas, Nebraska, Arizona, and South Dakota. The Tennessee General Assembly, still dominated by rural legislators despite some impressive urban and industrial growth in the previous decade, waited no longer—on February 21 it passed Tennessee's own version of a "right to work" law. Section 50-208 reads:

> It shall be unlawful for any person, firm, corporation, or association of any kind to deny or attempt to deny employment to any person by reason of such person's membership in, affiliation with, resignation from, or refusal to join or affiliate with any labor union or employee organization of any kind.

The intent of the law was plain. The shop floors of every Tennessee industry had to be open to union and non-union workers alike. The closed union shop was illegal, even if the majority of workers in a plant elected to have a union shop.

With the spate of state "right to work" laws that had been passed by early 1947, labor leaders nationwide raised a major question— were such state statutes compatible with federal law? That question was soon to be answered with the passage of Taft-Hartley. While the Wagner Act established the principle that employees should be protected in their rights to organize into a union and to bargain collectively, the Taft-Hartley Act established the principle that employers and non-union employees needed protection against unfair union practices. Taft-Hartley was a complex piece of legislation. The bill contained numerous provisions, but none had quite the impact of section 14(b) which permitted the states to prohibit the closed union shop. Under the new law the union shop was permissible upon the condition of employer-employee accords. On the other hand, the congressional stamp of approval was granted to all state "right to work" laws ex post facto. By 1948 thirteen states had prohibited the union shop, and several others made the closed shop conditional upon the voted approval of a stipulated majority of the workers covered by the contract.[3]

Labor leaders and activists in Tennessee were both embarrassed and angry over the anti-labor legislation. John L. Hand, president of the Tennessee Federation of Labor, told the delegates to the 1947 annual convention meeting in Johnson City in early May, that he had done his part to halt the state legislature from making a move against organized labor. "Just as soon as the vicious anti-closed shop bill was introduced," Hand reported, he "immediately made arrangements for the largest mass meeting of organized labor that had ever been held in the state to protest passage of this bill."[4] The protest brought together an assembly of working men, "the largest to gather on Capitol Hill in a generation,"[5] to be addressed by George Googe, southern representative of the AFL, and Robert Tillman, president of the Memphis Typographical Union.

The protest by labor on Capitol Hill was too little too late. In retrospect, some labor leaders felt that the membership in Tennessee in 1947 had been "asleep politically" and ill-equipped for a major legislative battle.[6] In 1947 the ranks of Tennessee organized labor were still small, despite the fact that at the annual convention the United Mine Workers were readmitted to the Federation. From that convention, a strong presidential appeal went out to the members "for more organizing of the workers in the small towns and urban areas where most of this anti-labor legislation originates." Labor was convinced it could be vocal enough to be heard.

Nothing prior to 1947 had impacted on the labor movement quite as fiercely as the state's compulsory open shop law. "It was the passage of Taft-Hartley, the state's 'right to work' law, and the election of 1948," Stanton Smith recalls, "that provoked a great surge in political activity among organized labor in Tennessee."[7] The state government in Tennessee had thrown down the gauntlet and labor leaders were willing to pick it up and do battle.

REHEARSAL FOR THE REPEAL BATTLE

Before the watershed election of 1948, Tennessee labor leaders had already gained some experience in political activity. Bleak prospects for new political gains in the forties motivated the executive board of the Congress of Industrial Organizations (CIO) to establish the Political Action Committee (PAC) on July 7, 1943. Sidney Hillman, president of the Amalgamated Clothing Workers, was appointed director and chairman of the new organization. Within a few months the national CIO convention had budgeted $700,000 for operating costs, thus enabling state PACs to be established in most southern states.[8]

Nine southern states (excluding Arkansas and Texas) were placed in a PAC regional organization which was directed by George S. Mitchell. His tenure as regional director was brief. Mitchell left the position shortly after the 1944 election and the post was filled for about a year by Paul Christopher. The post deserved an intelligent and capable person who could communicate with all kinds of people. Such a person was found in Daniel A. Powell.

Born in 1911 in Wilson, North Carolina, Powell had gained valuable experience in communication skills as a reporter and a correspondent for various newspapers. He began working with PAC in the South by the end of 1945 and was named PAC southern director in July 1946. "I would say Dan Powell was one of the best friends I ever had," Stanton Smith reminisced. "Dan had a very fertile brain which was full of highly constructive ideas and innovations."[9] One brainchild of Powell's was the "Program for Progress," which he sold to all the State Federations while serving as regional director.

Labor has long been in politics. In the late 1820s and 1830s some sixty labor parties operating in fifteen states—which constituted the beginnings of a labor movement in this country—were soon working for free public schools.[10] Labor's involvement in politics has spawned more criticism of labor than any other issue. Labor leaders have constantly found themselves having to defend their unions' involvement in the political process. But organized labor learned quite early "that the effectiveness of lobbying was in direct proportion to the political power and the political organization at the grassroots level."[11] Nobody was better equipped by training or commitment to the movement to defend labor's political behavior than Dan Powell. "The experience of the labor movement for nearly 150 years has proved that it cannot divorce itself from politics," Powell concluded.[12]

The post-war years were years of transition for Tennessee workers. As outgoing Governor Prentice Cooper noted in 1945, Tennessee had become an industrial state. "Tennessee's actively at work industrial population has increased from about 325,000 in 1940 to more than 500,000 in 1944," he reported. Labor leaders countered that in the face of industrial growth the legislature still considered Tennessee to be predominantly agricultural. Other states, they noted, had coped with the challenge of taking care of both kinds of workers, but Tennessee had not.[13]

A solid front by the entire force of Tennessee labor played a major role in removing a long-standing blight in the state's political system. In the 73rd General Assembly session, the most important piece of legislation considered was the repeal of the poll tax as a prerequisite for voting. The *Legislative Report* for 1943 asserted proudly: "Labor can justly lay claim to a major portion of the credit for repealing the poll tax."[14]

In the mid-forties the CIO's Political Action Committee survived a decline in influence. PAC-endorsed candidates suffered massive defeats in the off-year general election; the Republicans won a conservative majority in Congress. Some large unions drastically reduced their contributions to PAC. Budget cutbacks meant reducing the office staff. Adding to its difficulties of 1946, PAC's director, Sidney Hillman, had died unexpectedly in July of that year.[15]

The Taft-Hartley Act of the following year stimulated the political arm of organized labor like a fresh shot of adrenaline. The CIO's program revived completely. New political life was pumped also into the AFL, which established Labor's League for Political Education (LLPE) with Joseph D. Keenan, secretary for the International Brotherhood of Electrical Workers, as director. By the time of the 1948 election, LLPE units had been established in most southern states and city federations. In 1954, when LLPE expanded its program to include regional directors to plan and supervise field activities, Charles Houk, secretary-treasurer of the Tennessee Federation of Labor, was appointed LLPE southern director.[16] The appointment of Houk, a pipefitter and steamfitter out of Local 538 in Johnson City, was seen as "a significant step toward increasing the efficiency of LLPE in the important elections of 1954."[17] Houk continued to discharge his duties as secretary-treasurer of the TFL as a spare-time activity, which was the basis on which the secretary worked prior to 1948; President Stanton Smith was at the time named by the Executive Council as legislative representative.[18] Houk found time in 1954 to travel to southern Illinois and work in the Paul Douglas campaign.[19]

When the AFL and CIO merged at the national level in December 1955, it was only natural to merge PAC and LLPE. The new organization was called the Committee on Political Education (COPE). National COPE established a field staff of nine directors. In Tennessee during the early years of the merger, the COPE committee was composed of a 21-member executive board, plus a number of others, including a representative from each of the five central labor councils, the chairman of each local or congressional district COPE, AFL-CIO regional directors and representatives of the Building Trades Council. Officially, the state COPE could result in some 65 members, but the total was reduced by fifteen or so since the same individual could occupy two positions within the structure.[20]

LABOR AND A NON-COMMITTAL GOVERNOR

January 17, 1949, was a significant day in Tennessee gubernatorial history—the day Gordon W. Browning was inaugurated and thus became the state's only governor to return to the chief executive's office after a hiatus of a dozen years. The old war horse from Huntingdon, who had been a popular field artillery officer in World War I and had served in Europe as captain during World War II, was first inaugurated Tennessee governor on January 15, 1937. Browning was supported by the Crump machine in his first victory, but abandoned by Crump for Prentice Cooper at the next election time. Browning's victory in 1948, along with Estes Kefauver's victory for the U.S. Senate that same election, broke the back of the Crump machine.

Governor Browning had several strong legislative interests. Administrative reorganization was an early interest. Public education was another. Election law reform was still another one. Unfortunately for the Tennessee labor movement, organized labor's agenda was not a high priority with Governor Browning in either of his administrations. "In the tradition of rural Southerners," Browning biographer William R. Majors points out, Browning "viewed labor organizations with disdain and was repelled by the increasing activities of unions in Tennessee."[21]

One major decision made by Browning which brought visibility and credit to the labor movement involved the selection of a person to fill a U.S. Senate seat vacated upon the death of Senator Nathan Bachman. Browning was besieged with all kinds of advice and even considered resigning his governor's seat so that his lieutenant governor could appoint him to the choice position. Eventually, Browning selected Major George L. Berry for the vacated seat. Berry was a devoted New Dealer and a labor leader who had a rags-to-riches career as a printer and had advanced to the presidency of the Printers' Union. Berry was respected in the labor community. President Roosevelt hailed Browning's selection, but Berry became a disappointment as a political leader.[22]

During Browning's second administration, the governor received considerable correspondence in the form of letters and telegrams on the "open shop" issue. A sample telegram would read: "Working conditions under the existing anti-closed shop law have been satisfactory at the place where I work, and I am opposed to repeal or change of any kind."[23] But the rhetoric and arguments of the union shop opponents could and often did become strident and extreme. "I think the majority of our people, including the so-called wage earners themselves, would not want to be hampered with the closed shop (which is) thoroughly selfish, un-Christian, and even brutal," declared Fred Peoples in a letter to Browning. Claiming the unionism is "dangerous" to the country and has brought the nation "slavery of workers," Peoples continued to tell the governor:

> The fact is, the finest institutions in America are run without unions at all. They have a superior type of worker, and a far better American citizen. . . . They don't want to be handicapped and trampled down and dictated to by selfish, overlording union bosses. You do not build citizenship with any such methods. We must at all costs protect any individual worker's right to deal directly with his employer.[24]

Browning was willing to meet with labor leaders. He attempted to project an image of neutrality on labor's concerns. Stanton Smith remembers interviewing Browning: "We began to bring up all of our legislative matters. Soon we got around to the question of the repeal of the open shop law. Browning said, 'I wish you wouldn't ask me about that matter because I won't make any commitment to you that I won't make public. I'd rather you wouldn't ask.' The implication of what he said was that 'I'm for you but don't put me on record and when the time rolls around, then I'll help you.' Well, when the time rolled around, he didn't help us."[25]

"Far Hills," a Georgian home on ten acres on Curtiswood Lane in Nashville, became the Governor's Mansion in 1949. Gordon

Browning was the first governor to live there. His residence there, however, was destined to be limited. For Browning was something of an anachronism—he failed to understand and respond creatively to the rapid social and economic changes that were sweeping through Tennessee in the late forties and early fifties. Organized labor was growing and Browning was both perplexed and fearful of its power. Browning was fated to make one major decision which would seal labor's opposition to his leadership.

It was the spring of 1950. In March the workers of the American Enka Corporation's plant near Morristown had gone out on strike when their demands for a wage increase and other benefits were not met. The ranks of the striking employees were held intact for several weeks. By late May, however, some of the workers joined with nonunion members and returned to work. This spurred violence. The Hamblen County sheriff charged that "professional agitators" were on the scene and appealed to Browning for assistance. The governor moved swiftly, sending in the highway patrol and alerting the National Guard. Two days later there was more violence. In this situation, Browning could have consulted his commissioner of labor, Lee Case. Instead, he called out the National Guard to the strike scene. Pickets were arrested and newspapers reported that some of the pickets were roughly handled.[26]

Browning was only being neutral in the labor conflict—or so he told inquirers. But he was not being neutral in placing blame for the violence, which was squarely placed on the shoulders of the union. Commissioner Case was placed in an untenable position of having to defend his Chief Executive but, in retrospect, believed that Browning had simply listened to the wrong advice, overreacted, and made the wrong tactical move by sending in the state troops.[27]

Browning had returned to the governor's office in 1949 with labor's support. This support came largely by default because during the decade prior to the 1948 election labor in Tennessee had made little, if any, progress in getting progressive labor legislation for industrial and craft workers of the state. The "open shop" law had just been passed and that seemed like a repressive law to labor.[28] But the Morristown incident turned labor's support almost completely around. Many members of the AFL, the CIO, and other unions broke with the governor. The independent railroad brotherhoods, however, remained with Browning in 1950. When the primary election of 1950 rolled around, labor made no decisive endorsement, but many in the labor movement voted for Clifford Allen. After serving several terms in the state senate, Allen had gained a reputation as something of a vociferous maverick. He solidly endorsed all of labor's positions, including making a pledge to repeal the anti-union shop, advocated free textbooks for public school students, and had gained solid respect in the black community of Nashville. Allen did not seek labor's endorsement. "He asked us just to be neutral, thinking he would get our vote," Stanton Smith recalls.[29]

Allen's candidacy was not taken seriously at first, but in the end he had tallied an impressive number of votes, many coming from organized labor. In the general election, the Republican party failed to have a candidate for the governor's race, a first-time phenomenon for the Tennessee Republican party. Browning handily defeated independent candidate John R. Neal, but he had already lost the confidence of a labor movement which would bide its time until a governor more attuned to its needs could be elected. The wait would only be two years.

YOUNG GOVERNOR AND A NEW ERA

On March 1, 1952, Gordon Browning announced that he would be a candidate to succeed himself as governor. A young Dickson lawyer had announced some eighteen months earlier his intention to seek the same nomination. Only 32 years old, Frank G. Clement, associated with his father, Robert S. Clement, had no previous experience as a legislator or administrator. A graduate of the law school at Vanderbilt University, Clement had experienced brief stints of service with the F.B.I., with the army near the close of World War II, and with the Tennessee Railroad and Public Utilities Commission as counsel.

Clement was a handsome man whose oratorical ability had been hailed from Bristol to Memphis. Public speaking was a talent that he cultivated. He was also a deeply religious man; his facility in quoting the Scriptures and in adapting them to his political rhetoric gave his campaign rallies the strong flavor of a religious revival. During the preceding two years, Clement had been at work around the state building his own political machine by establishing ties, earning awards and recognition, and making speeches. The end result was that the young lawyer was able to overcome his greatest handicap— the lack of name recognition.[30]

Frank G. Clement holds young son of IUE member at the Tennessee State CIO Convention in Memphis in 1954. On far left is Leonard Evans and on far right is Matt Lynch. (Courtesy—Maud Lynch Private Collection)

The Democratic primary of 1952 was a lively contest. Based on his impressive showing in the gubernatorial primary in 1950, Clifford Allen entered the fray. Allen had a core of support among organized workers in middle Tennessee; he was pro-labor on all issues affecting organized labor. Although some labor leaders considered Frank Clement to be too young and inexperienced, the movement officially endorsed him for governor. Clement was very young and very ambitious, Stanton Smith recalls:

> My own feeling about Frank was favorable, although I didn't know him well. Matt Lynch knew him and favorably supported him. So I said, "Well, on the basis of statements Frank was making he was either going to be the most liberal governor we ever had or the biggest hypocrite we ever had, I didn't know which!" So I went along with the endorsement. Frank was pledged to the repeal of the open shop and this was something organized labor sought fervently.[31]

The primary election campaign seemed to present to Tennessee voters the choice between a 63-year-old exhausted, outdated, machine-type incumbent and an intelligent, youthful, exuberant new-comer. Given Browning's action in Morristown, there was no way that labor would deliver to him its bloc of votes. The result was a decisive, though not overwhelming, victory for Clement. Clement polled 302,491 votes to Browning's 245,166.[32]

Meantime, another friend of labor was elected to the United States Senate from Tennessee. In the same primary election, Congressman Albert Gore, hitherto having represented the fourth congressional district (the district which once sent Cordell Hull to Washington), challenged and defeated 83-year-old Senator Kenneth McKellar. Gore needed no other campaign issue than the age issue to win the support of fellow Democrats. Both Clement and Gore won easily in the general election. At the national level, the Democratic ticket of Adlai Stevenson of Illinois and John Sparkman of Alabama failed by less than 2,500 votes out of nearly 900,000 votes cast to win the electoral vote in Tennessee. The Volunteer State, for only the second time in a quarter century, had voted Republican in a presidential election and joined the nation's majority in placing Dwight Eisenhower and Richard Nixon in power.

LABOR'S NUMBER ONE OBJECTIVE

The Tennessee labor movement had one overriding legislative objective from the late forties through the early sixties—the repeal of the state's "right to work" law. No other issue consumed as much of the movement's time and energy. Labor leaders during those years took on the challenge as a kind of divine mission to which they were called. The effort was a mighty one, involving every legal method of persuasion and lobbying known to labor.

As though coming into a boxing ring to fight against the interests of big business, Tennessee labor seemed lethargic when the bell rang to start the match. Before the fight to repeal the law was begun, labor had already been struck a deft public relations blow by company owners and managers. The opponents of labor called the anti-labor bill by the name "Right to Work," but, as Stanton Smith pointed out, "we never called this bill the 'Right to Work' law because the title was such a terrible misnomer. Labor leaders always referred to the act as the anti-union shop bill or the compulsory open shop bill," thus providing something of a public relations slant for their own cause. "Of course, that was a real public relations strike that the right-to-work people made when they got that name for their bill. The name was appealing, so we never would use it," Smith continued.[33] Eula McGill put it more bluntly: "I used to tell people I tried to organize that, hell there ain't no such thing in this country as a damn 'right to work.' If you're unemployed and need a job in this country, you go tell your government they owe you a job because you have a right to work and find out what happens."[34] Matt Lynch was fond of telling audiences that "the only constitution that guarantees the citizen a right to work is in Russia."[35]

In the late forties several labor organizations were sending lobbyists to Capitol Hill, thus creating the question in the mind of many legislators as to who exactly was speaking for labor. Tennessee labor leaders wanted to increase their clout in the General Assembly and perceived the need to coordinate their political activities and lobbying. The outgrowth of their concerns led to the establishment of the Tennessee Joint Labor Legislative Council with headquarters in Nashville. The Legislative Council was composed of those independent unions sending lobbyists to Nashville, primarily the state Federation of Labor, the state Industrial Union Council of the CIO, the Railroad Brotherhoods, and the United Mine Workers. The activities of the council with each session of the General Assembly were published in the biennial *Legislative Report of the Tennessee Joint Legislative Council.*

Prior to Clement's election there had been bills introduced in the legislature to repeal the "open shop" law. The bills never reached the calendar. Labor had had a hand in its own failure by not being united on the kind of bill to be introduced. Some labor leaders wanted a bill to repeal the Tennessee law, and others called for an amending bill. Those who wanted an amending bill believed it would have a much better chance of passage in the Assembly; those who advocated total repeal argued that a principle was involved and that labor needed to feel the satisfaction of repealing a law that never should have been placed on the statute books in the first place.[36] Some of the issues became confused when committee hearings were conducted—hearings attended not only by representatives from labor but also from the Tennessee Businessmen's Association, the Tennessee Manufacturers' Association, and Nashville Chamber of Commerce.[37]

Though Frank Clement was uncomfortable with the "right to work" issue,[38] labor embraced the young lawyer even before he took office as the knight in shining armor who would rescue the union shop from the throes of business reactionaries. In the weeks between the primary and the general election, business groups began to court the man most likely to be governor, seeking a commitment from him to modify his support of a bill to amend the compulsory open shop law. As labor legislative representatives told the story, these business people

> were met with rebuff without exception. Governor Clement told them that he believed the law should be amended; that it was part of his platform; that he had made his public commitment; that he had given his promise and intended to pass the bill if he could. Labor's opposition knew, therefore, that for the first time they were in for a real battle in the legislature. They had plenty of warning.[39]

Governor Clement's good intentions toward organized labor did not translate into victory on the union shop issue. The failure to pass a bill reversing the 1947 General Assembly action was due in part to the increased lobbying activity by representatives of business and manufacturing community. But it was due in larger measure to the fact that "right to work" was a popular and democratic-sounding concept to the majority of Tennesseans who were cool to the idea of reversing a legislative decision in order to serve the interests of "power-hungry" unions.

The sheer force of Clement's power and personality might have been enough to repeal or amend the bill if the governor had had no other agenda for which to fight. Like a gunman on the streets in an intense battle, Clement only had so many bullets in his revolver to fire before he needed to take time to reload. Stanton Smith remembers hammering out the proposal for an amending bill which would square with the provisions of Taft-Hartley, thus "permitting a union shop if the employer and the union were in agreement and at the election of the employees."[40]

> But Clement in his first term was very young—just 32. He got all of his own legislation through and labor's proposals were still sitting there on his desk. I was getting more and more agitated about this and I thought this was absurd. Clement was playing all of his cards and winning rounds with the legislature and I said to myself and others, "The governor's not going to have any cards left to play when he gets around to us," which turned out to be the case. We

didn't die, but we sure came close. . . . Finally, my assistant and I just went to the governor and said, "We want this thing brought up." But it was too late. I knew what had happened. Clement had played all of his cards. He used up all his chips. So we got beat.[41]

Labor could be both understanding and forgiving. For despite Clement's failure to push successfully labor's proposed amending bill on "right to work" or to enact a Safe Train Crew bill which labor sought, the union leadership remained solidly behind the governor in his quest for re-election. "We are convinced that Governor Clement did not confine his efforts towards passage of labor's two main bills to the spoken word," legislative representatives concluded. "We were present on several occasions when the Governor told members of his cabinet and his legislative leaders of his intense interest and his personal stake in the enactment of these two labor bills."[42] Two years later these same representatives for labor reached an even more positive conclusion: "In our judgment Governor Clement did all that labor can expect of any governor to pass the union shop amendment."[43]

MISSION IMPOSSIBLE

In the gubernatorial campaign of 1954, Frank Clement did not repeat his pledge of two years earlier to "pass" the union shop bill. He did promise, however, to make it an administrative measure and to give it his full support. Clement's support was open and early. A few days after taking the oath of office on January 11, 1955, the governor addressed in person a joint convention of the House and Senate of the General Assembly. Included in his message were perhaps the strongest statements in labor's behalf ever made declared publicly by a Tennessee governor:

> The promotion of industrial peace and the welfare of both management and labor is a legitimate concern and responsibility of government.
>
> I have full confidence in both management and labor. While temporary disagreements may sometimes arise, I believe each group may rightfully have ultimate confidence in the other. Certainly each is dependent upon the other for its existence.

I believe that these two collective partners have an inalienable right to negotiate mutually acceptable contracts, provided these contracts are otherwise legal under the Federal law.

The existing Tennessee statute regulating such contracts is at variance with the Federal labor policy and contains an obstruction which unreasonably restricts the right of contract and free collective bargaining and denies to the laborers of Tennessee the rights which even the Taft-Hartley Act permits.

Believing that this impediment should be removed, I shall submit for your consideration and recommend for your passage, an amendment which would legalize the union shop in Tennessee. I sincerely hope you will study it before you act— and I believe that your study will convince you—as study and reason convinced me, that the opponents of this particular measure have overstated their case. It is sound in principle, just in its effect and complementary of the public interest. I sincerely hope you will give it favorable action.

The governor then added extemporaneously the following concerning the union shop bill:

There has been something said—about two years ago—that perhaps I recommend it but was not interested in it. I can assure you I shall not insult you, nor prostitute my own honor, by recommending to you any measure in which I am not interested and in which I do not believe and which I do not hope that you will pass. And if anyone has a doubt about any measure I submit for your consideration, please come to see me before you come to the conclusion from unfair and unjust propaganda that I have submitted something in which I do not believe. I think this is a good measure and a step forward and in the interest of industrial peace and for the benefit of all Tennesseans.[44]

With the opening of the 79th General Assembly, labor increased its efforts to sway the lawmakers. By then all efforts to repeal the "right to work" law were ceased. Fighting for a principle had its face-saving value, but if labor was going to achieve its most important objective it had to become totally pragmatic. Many state legislators were ignorant of labor law technicalities and needed clear information.

Clement's return to the governorship and the seating of a new legislature had renewed hope among labor leaders. But when the battle lines were drawn, labor found that the 1955 General Assembly "achieved the dubious distinction of being one of the worst legislatures in the history of our state. Without any doubt, it was the most anti-labor of any session in the memory of most of the labor legislative representatives."[45] Labor representatives portrayed themselves to rank-and-file members as diminutive David up against Goliath of the business community. Supposedly, there were 63 anti-labor lobbyists on Capitol Hill. "The would-be assassins of organized labor in Tennessee" pulled "all stops" to defeat labor's legislative program, they complained. "The members were given a choice of everything from $3,000 parties in swanky 'nite spots,' the costliest of liquors, and even debasing sex exhibitions."[46]

Even still, the "right to work" amendment bill was almost passed despite a largely non-sympathetic legislature. In the legislative proceedings of the fifties, any well-known lobbyist was permitted to walk on the floor of the House or Senate. Stanton Smith remembers a rule which barred everybody from the floor except members of the legislature. The rule was pretty much ignored until the floor was overwhelmed with lobbyists; then it was invoked. Smith would take his seat right beside a senator on the floor and, given the parliamentary expertise he had developed while in the teachers' union, would be consulted on parliamentary procedure.[47] Smith remembers how the speaker's ignorance about parliamentary procedure contributed to defeat of labor's big bill in the 1953 legislature:

> We came very close; as a matter of fact, we had the votes in the Senate for passing. Pete Haynes was the Speaker of the Senate. I will never forget this day. They debated on the issue for a while and somebody moved the previous question, seconded it, and voted on it, and didn't get the necessary two-thirds. Now the effect of the previous question was to merely close debate and bring about a vote on the issue. But the failure of the motion to reconsider merely lets the debate go on. Just says we're not going to close the debate, we're going to argue about it some more. But Pete Haynes, when the vote closed debate failed, he said the vote debate failed, bring up the next bill. And none of our legislators were smart enough to catch that, so they went on to the next bill and we were done. We had the votes to pass it that day. Years later, I told Pete Haynes about that, he said, "Did I do that?" "You sure did, Pete."[48]

The failure of the amending bill put Clement in a defensive posture with a labor movement which was holding him accountable for its defeat. To the many labor people who criticized Clement on this issue, the governor's standard answer posed several valid points. First, Clement noted, the union shop bill was "one of my main recommendations" in the message delivered in person to the legislature. Second, the labor bill was "introduced, sponsored, and vigorously supported by the speakers and floor leaders." Third, no decision was made about the bill without consulting appointed representatives of organized labor in the state. And finally, all of the Clement administration team had convinced labor's legislative representatives that it had acted in good faith and had done all that it could to steer the bill through the legislature. Clement added:

> Whether or not things turn out as we desire, all of us must admit that in this democracy of ours a member of the legislature has a right to vote in accord with what he thinks is proper; and I do not feel I can be condemned when the bills did not pass, in view of the facts set out above which represent the truth.[49]

Energy and effort expended on ridding the state of the despised "right to work" law reached its climax in the mid-fifties. By the early sixties, many Tennesseans, if they had any opinion on the subject (and many did not), were inclined to believe that an open shop law was not a significant factor one way or another in influencing the location of industry and opening up new job opportunities in Tennessee.[50]

The campaign for repeal or amendment did not officially end; rather it seemed to run out of steam with each passing year. There were still newspaper editorials and commentary. Letters continued to be written to the newspapers. Opinions and arguments favoring the union shop were garnered from whatever authoritative source was available. For example, the state labor council newsletter published an opinion by Reinhold Niebuhr, prominent Protestant theologian, speaking out against "right to work" laws; Niebuhr noted that the real purpose of such laws is to weaken labor and that its supporters "are either stupid or dishonest in their pretensions."[51] One speech prepared by Matt Lynch some twelve years after the Tennessee statute was passed was delivered in one form or another before several groups and organizations and on radio talk shows around the state. In his conclusion, Lynch spoke of the long-range effects of the law as he saw them: lower wages and less economic freedom for Tennessee workers; weakening rather than strengthening of individual workers; negative value to the general public; and "a premium has been placed on irresponsible labor leadership."[52]

Tennessee labor in the late eighties was still talking about "right to work" laws, but the movement never came quite as close again to getting passed an amendment bill as it came in Clement's second term. The quest for repeal had seemed, indeed, a mission impossible. The laboring force in the state had grown considerably. But labor leaders had learned through this battle the limits of their power. Once they had resigned themselves to the reality of Tennessee sharing indefinitely a part of the bloc of a dozen or so "right to work" states (mostly in the South), they found deserved satisfaction in the fact that the General Assembly had not since 1947 passed a single major piece of anti-labor legislation.

Throughout the fifties Frank Clement remained a powerful politician. The Dickson native was the first person to serve three successive two-year terms and the first to serve a four-year term. During the eight years in which Clement could not serve as governor, the office was filled in a kind of leap frog arrangement by his friend and commissioner of agriculture, Buford Ellington. The Clement years constituted a new era for Tennessee. With the sales tax increased, state services were expanded, teachers' pay was raised, and educational facilities were improved. Tennesseans began to hear about "racial integration," "constitutional reform," and "reapportionment"—catchwords of the fifties and early sixties.

Despite solid accomplishments and national recognition in other areas, labor leaders in the sixties did not know quite what to do with Clement when he sought re-election. Browning had been a major disappointment to labor, and labor had embraced Clement. Clement in turn had not been able to deliver on his major promise to labor, and the once-again disappointed labor leaders began naturally to turn to Rudy Olgiati, mayor of Chattanooga and acknowledged card-holding union man.

The *Nashville Tennessean* was the key factor in the election of 1962, as Charles Houk has analyzed it. According to Houk, he and Olgiati visited the *Tennessean* editorial offices to discuss an endorsement for Olgiati. Houk felt that Silliman Evans and John Siegenthaler had made a commitment not to endorse any candidate unless it was the Chattanooga mayor. "Later the *Tennessean* came out and endorsed Bill Farris. Farris took votes away from Rudy, who was the most honest politician I've ever known. We felt like the *Tennessean* had more to do with the election outcome than anything else."[53] Matt Lynch, who by 1962 was secretary of the state council, continued to support Clement despite an impressive if not unanimous labor endorsement for Olgiati. The contention and strong division which was to remain within the movement for nearly twenty years was now fully underway.[54]

LABOR'S INFLUENCE IN RETROSPECT

How does one evaluate the impact of organized labor on the politics of a state? The answer, of course, is very carefully. The labor force of Tennessee, like other states, is a disparate mixture of working groups. The leadership of the unions has not always been united. Other dynamics, such as the race issue, have been factors determining its political strength. Clearly, labor support or labor activism in Tennessee has not always been decisive, but it was never to be despised by prudent public officials. Since the late forties the laboring people of the state constituted a formidable bloc whenever it could be delivered to any one candidate.

Evaluating the impact of PAC and COPE on state politics is not easy. In the South as a whole, as Dan Powell points out, labor's political defeats have outnumbered its victories—a fact which should not be surprising since labor-endorsed candidates were usually liberals running in a conservative region.[55] In a listing of memorable defeats of PAC and COPE candidates of high caliber, Powell cites three Tennesseans:

1. Ross Bass (U.S. Senate, 1966)
2. George Grider (U.S. Rep., 1966)
3. Albert Gore (U.S. Senate, 1970)

Arguing that Estes Kefauver's nomination for United States Senator from Tennessee in the 1948 Democratic primary would not have been achieved without the support of PAC, Powell cites other PAC and COPE Tennessee victories which are "pleasant to remember":[56]

1. Gordon Browning (Governor, 1948)
2. Frank Clement (Governor, 1952, 1954)

3. Albert Gore (U.S. Senate, 1952, 1958, 1964)
4. Ross Bass (U.S. Rep. and U.S. Senate, 1954, 1964)
5. Richard Fulton (U.S. Rep., 1962)
6. George Grider (U.S. Rep., 1964)
7. William Anderson (U.S. Rep., 1968)
8. Harold Ford (U.S. Rep., 1974)
9. Ray Blanton (Governor, 1974)

If one were to go into the eighties, additional names could be added to either list.

James Neeley and Al Gore, Jr., (1984). (Courtesy—Tennessee State Labor Council)

Though Tennessee working men and women helped elect Bill Clinton and native son Al Gore, Jr., to the White House, working Tennesseans shared what seemed to be the mean mood of the rest of the nation and, in the off-year election of 1994, sent home incumbent Senator James Sasser and helped place Republicans in power in Congress. Two new Republican senators, Bill Frist and Fred Thompson, were easily elected, as was gubernatorial candidate Donald Sundquist over his Democratic challenger Nashville mayor Phil Bredesen. Whether the new Republican congressional leadership would heed the concerns of labor remained an issue for debate.

Labor in Tennessee has not always been successful, but the experience of the forties and fifties taught it the political ropes as well as the limits of power in a state traditionally dominated by agricultural interests. These were lessons that would not be lost by future labor leaders.

NOTES

1. Sanford Cohen, *Labor in the United States*, 3d ed. (Columbus: Charles E. Merrill, 1970), 490.

2. *New York Times*, Feb. 23, 1947.

3. Cohen, *Labor in the United States*, 488-89. Cohen points out: "The union limitation laws were spotty in a geographical sense. The highly industrialized states of Illinois and Ohio enacted practically no legislation dealing with unions, while many of the agricultural states, where unionism was almost non-existent, pushed through some of the more severe anti-union measures. In the South especially, the quantity of labor union legislation that appeared was impressive. The areas where unions had only tenuous footholds were bracing themselves in anticipation of future organizational drives."

4. T.F.L., *Proceedings of the 49th Annual Convention*, 19.

5. Ibid., 28.

6. Charles Houk interview, Johnson City, Tennessee, December 17, 1987; also from a statement in a 1949 *Nashville Tennessean* news clipping among Stanton Smith ms. (otherwise n. d.).

7. Personal interview with Stanton Smith, April 10, 1987.

8. Daniel A. Powell, "PAC to COPE: Thirty-Two Years of Southern Labor in Politics," in Gary M. Fink and Merl E. Reed, *Essays in Southern Labor History* (Westport, Conn.: Greenwood Press, 1977), 244.

9. Interview with Stanton Smith, Chattanooga, Tennessee, Dec. 19, 1987.

10. Daniel A. Powell, "Labor and Politics," *High School Journal*, vol. 50, no. 8 (May 1967), 417.

11. Ibid.

12. Ibid.

13. *Legislative Report of the Tennessee Joint Labor Legislative Council*, 1945, pp. 2-3.

14. *Legislative Report of the Tennessee Joint Labor Legislative Council*, 1943.

15. Powell, "PAC to COPE," 244-45.

16. Ibid., 245.

17. Memo from Tennessee Federation of Labor, dated for release on Nov. 30, 1953, Tennessee State Labor Council Mss.

18. Ibid.

19. Houk interview.

20. *Chattanooga Times*, March 14, 1962.

21. William R. Majors, *The End of Arcadia: Gordon Browning and Tennessee Politics* (Memphis: Memphis State University Press, 1982), 192.

22. Robert E. Corlew, *Tennessee: A Short History*, 2d ed. (Knoxville: University of Tennessee Press, 1981), 482.

23. William M. Terry to Gordon Browning, January 16, 1951, Browning Mss.

24. Fred Peoples to Gordon Browning, January 25, 1951, Browning Mss.

25. Smith interview.

26. Majors, *End of Arcadia*, 192-93.

27. Ibid.

28. *Legislative Report of the Tennessee Joint Labor Legislative Council*, 1951, p. 8.

29. Smith interview.

30. The story of Clement's entry into gubernatorial politics in Tennessee is told in Lee S. Greene, *Lead Me On: Frank Goad Clement and Tennessee Politics* (Knoxville: University of Tennessee Press, 1982), 42-84; Majors, *End of Arcadia*, 204-05; Corlew, *Tennessee*, 493-99.

31. Smith interview.

32. Corlew, *Tennessee*, 498.

33. Smith interview.

34. McGill interview, August 14, 1987.

35. Address, "The Tennessee Open Shop Law," n. d., Tennessee State Labor Council Mss.

36. *Legislative Report*, 1951, p. 12.

37. Ibid.

38. Greene, *Lead Me On*, 53.

39. *Legislative Report*, 1953, p. 6.

40. Smith interview.

41. Ibid.

42. *Legislative Report*, 1953, p. 6.

43. *Legislative Report*, 1955, p. 5.

44. Published in a memorandum circulated by the Tennessee Federation of Labor (n.d.), Tennessee State Labor Council Ms., and in *Legislative Report*, 1955, pp. 6-7.

45. *Legislative Report*, 1955, p. 9.

46. Ibid., 15.

47. On one occasion members of the House got into such a parliamentary tangle that it could not be resolved satisfactorily. Legislators knew that Stanton Smith was proficient in parliamentary procedure, an expertise he developed as head of the teachers' union. The floor leaders called a recess of both Houses and huddled around Smith, who gave them parliamentary direction which saved the moment. Smith interview.

48. Smith interview.

49. Letter from Clement to Naomi Houser in Knoxville, d. Feb. 24, 1955. Attached to the letter from the governor is a note from Lucille Thornburgh to Charles Houk: "Charlie, all our people are getting this same answer back from the governor." Tennessee State Labor Council Ms.

50. An editorial in the *Nashville Tennessean*, Dec. 8, 1960, quotes an independent survey which cites the factors determining industry location. Unionization was not a major factor one way or another according to the study. The editorial was circulated by labor leaders who were informing the public that the open shop was not a drawing card for outside industry to come to Tennessee.

51. Newsletter of the Tennessee State Labor Council, Dec. 20, 1957. Niebuhr goes on to say that "though the democratic arrangements of some unions leave much to be desired, unions on the whole are freer of irresponsible power than is management."

52. Address, "The Tennessee Open Shop Law." Lynch received numerous letters of congratulations on the speech from state labor leaders. Tennessee State Labor Council Ms.

53. Houk interview.

54. Lee S. Greene, Clement's biographer, reconstructs the endorsement hassle: "The State Labor Council had a campaign fund of some $50,000 (no mean sum in those days). Matt Lynch continued to support Clement, while Steve Para and Charles Houk backed Olgiati, and on March 17, labor's Committee on Political Education urged the

statewide convention of COPE (the political arm of the AFL-CIO) to endorse Olgiati. Para claimed the vote was unanimous, but even the *Tennessean* reported that this was a spurious last-minute unanimity. Actually, according to the *Tennessean*, the vote was about 27 to 16 in Olgiati's favor.

"When the statewide convention of COPE met in April, it did in fact endorse Olgiati, but the vote was anything but unanimous. The vote, taken by voice alone, was ruled by Chairman Steve Para to be two-thirds in the affirmative, but the *Banner* and the *Tennessean* agreed that the 'no' shouts were about as loud as the 'ayes.' These tactics, familiar enough to all students of legislative activities, had been agreed upon by COPE's executive board less than an hour before the convention was to open. Neither Clement nor Farris made any attempt to stop the steamroller, for the endorsement of COPE was admittedly weak, leaving the candidates about where they were before." *Lead Me On* (Knoxville: University of Tennessee Press, 1982), 282. See also *Nashville Banner*, March 17, 1962; *Nashville Tennessean*, March 15, 18, and 20, 1962; *Chattanooga Times*, March 14, 1962.

55. Powell, "PAC to COPE," 252.

56. Ibid., 253-54.

10

"... The Tennessee labor movement has been known throughout its entire history as a movement of integrity and that integrity goes pretty deep and pretty far."

The Emergence of a Voice

Tennessee's Labor Leadership
in Modern Times

The strengths and weaknesses of the Tennessee labor movement are in large part reflections of the strengths and weaknesses of those leaders who have directed the movement since the end of World War II. These leaders have been shaped in attitude and action by work experience as diverse as the Piedmont textile mills and public classroom teaching. Among the many in union administration who have been devoted to the cause of trade unionism in Tennessee, there are four men whose dedication and achievements to the movement have earned for them special mention: Paul Christopher, Stanton Smith, Matthew Lynch, and James Neeley.

PAUL CHRISTOPHER: FROM PIEDMONT MILL HAND TO TENNESSEE CIO CHIEF

By almost any standard, Paul Christopher should have been a lifetime mill worker. Born on Valentine's Day in 1910 in Easley, South Carolina, and patriotically named Paul Revere, Christopher was fully nurtured in the social and political environment of the Piedmont mill culture. His parents, Clarence and Mary Christopher, worked in the mills; Clarence Christopher was a union man, holding membership in the United Textile Workers of America. Christopher began working in the mills as a teenager; by the time he was 20 he had worked in six different mills in the Greenville, South Carolina, area.[1]

On the other hand, Christopher possessed some traits that were not desired in mill workers. He was intelligent. He was thoughtful.

He was amiable. He was ambitious. He also was understanding and sympathetic of his fellow workers. It did not take young Paul long to comprehend the system of cotton textile manufacturing that he had observed in the South, a system which involved cleaning and combing raw cotton and then spinning and weaving the material into a finished fabric. Neither did it take long for the young mill hand to perceive the paternalistic attitude of the mill managers and the subservient and docile attitudes of the mill workers.

Christopher saw these attitudes working in a kind of symbiotic relationship, each reinforcing the other, with unrelenting benefit to the mill owners and perpetual disadvantage to the mill hands. He plainly saw that as long as the mill managers could contract with workers on an individual basis rather than a collective basis that management could exercise almost complete control over both the mill operations and the mill workers. The mill hands would thus be mired in the lowest levels of pay with no mechanism for escaping their plight.

Christopher aspired to completing a college education and thus enrolled in Clemson Agricultural College. Times were hard for him in early 1932, so he dropped out of Clemson after three semesters of study and returned to work in the Piedmont mills. That same year he married Mary Elizabeth Lybrand and by the fall he was working at the Cleveland Cloth Mill in Shelby, North Carolina. At this point in his life, biographer Joseph Yates Garrison points out, he met a number of union people and came to the conclusion that the main hope of the Piedmont mill hands lay in the textile union.[2]

The cause of southern textile unionism did not have much going for it in the late twenties and early thirties. The major roadblock to unionizing the Piedmont workers was the strong resistance by the mill executives. Mill executives wanted to believe that the white, unskilled laboring force in the Piedmont was abundant, docile, easily tractable, and eager to labor for low wages. Only a small percentage of the textile workers, about four percent, was organized during this period. Those workers who did dare to become affiliated with the union risked an immediate loss of employment; once discharged, their names often made their ways to a blacklist available to other employers. Union organizers had it even rougher as they were often subjected to violent harassment and persecution.[3]

Despite these obstacles, Christopher was fully committed to the cause of textile unionism in the South. He saw the enactment of the National Industrial Recovery Act, and especially Section 7(a), as a godsend to the struggling United Textile Workers of America. Disillusionment soon set in. The textile mill executives frequently denied the rights to workers given granted them in 7(a); old problems in the textile industry persisted and were not being solved by the federal government. The great general textile strike of 1934 seemed an almost inevitable consequence of intransigence by industrial leadership.

The general strike of 1934 provided an intensive training ground for Christopher. He formed a "flying squadron" from among his union associates and with whirlwind speed they visited 27 different mills around Shelby, North Carolina; by the end of the first day these mills were all shut down. Soon, Christopher was named the strike coordinator for all of western North Carolina.

Despite the enthusiasm and energy of Christopher and other union leaders, the general strike of 1934 was a dismal failure. The barriers of management resistance and worker culture of mill and village seemed insuperable. Immediately after the strike, those UTWA organizers who remained with the union were cut back from a full salary to only three weeks' pay per month. (Christopher was not to return to his full-time salary of $30 a week until January 1937.)[4] Old problems persisted. Mill hands who had had their civil rights violated were likely to be unwilling to testify for fear they would be blacklisted. As Garrison notes, "Stretchouts, wage reductions, and occasional massive discharges continued in Christopher's region despite all his efforts to bargain collectively with management, cooperate with it, and foster support for the mill hands from government agencies."[5]

Christopher often seemed spinning on a fast treadmill, bogged down in busy work servicing mills, hearing complaints, addressing small union meetings, and entering mill villages to find converts to the union cause. Through all of this, the young organizer kept the faith against all odds. He was heartened when, early in March 1937, Sidney Hillman of the Garment Workers met with representatives of the CIO and the UTWA to create a Textile Workers Organizing Committee (TWOC) charged with the task of executing a massive organizing campaign among textile workers. Christopher's training, temperament, and energy rendered him highly qualified to be approved by Hillman to continue working in the Piedmont under TWOC.

The Textile Workers' Organizing Committee was well planned, but like the general strike which preceded it, the program faced worker fears about losing a job, poverty and destitution among the mill hands and their families, and the overall shaky state of the economy. Christopher was disconsolate. All of this, not to mention that management antagonism and anti-union propaganda continued unabated. True, the TWOC experienced modest success, especially outside the South, in signing up textile workers; by the end of 1937 over half of the textile workers were under contract. Yet, in the southern mills some 45,000 to 50,000 were unemployed and, as Garrison states, "it is one of the cruelest ironies of American trade union history that the Roosevelt Recession and the TWOC organizing drive occurred simultaneously."[6] The zeal and punch of the strike leader who had directed the flying squadrons was gone. Christopher resigned his directorship with TWOC effective September 7, 1940.[7]

That decision made in despondency was a turning point which would soon bring Christopher to Tennessee. Only in the preceding April (1940), William Turnblazer, CIO regional director for Tennessee, had called for the establishment of a Tennessee State Industrial Union Council to coordinate the activities of CIO unions in Tennessee. Upon hearing of his resignation from TWOC, Myles Horton recommended that Turnblazer hire Christopher as council secretary. Christopher had maintained strong reservations and criticism of the AFL for its failure to support industrial unionism in the South, but he had deep respect for the philosophy and programs of the CIO. He was quick to accept the new offer. By early October 1940 Christopher was working for the CIO in Tennessee.

The little coal mining town of Jellico, near the Kentucky state border, was the site where Paul Christopher resumed his career work as a trade unionist in Tennessee. The state Industrial Union Council (IUC) director, William Turnblazer, had already established headquarters there. In March of the following year Christopher moved his office to Knoxville where he assumed full responsibility for the operation of his office.

Christopher's view of Tennessee of the early forties was that of a state filled with workers who deeply needed the kind of wages and job security which could come through membership in a trade union.[8] This was a challenge ideally tailored for the man with his deep devotion and many skills. For the next six years, Christopher set out to organize Tennessee workers and to serve as a consultant to union locals on matters involving political action, fund raising, public relations, and local issues. The special need for organizing the state's miners is discussed by Garrison:

No workers in the state were more in need of union assistance than were the miners. In East Tennessee, workers
mined bituminous coal, zinc, copper, magnesium, limestone, and sandstone. In Middle Tennessee, they extracted
phosphorous and calcium limestone. West Tennessee
miners dug clay. Unlike Pennsylvania, Ohio, and West
Virginia, Tennessee had few "captive mines," so its miners
had not benefitted from the unionization of the nation's
steel and chemical workers. Most Tennessee mines were
independently owned, small, labor intensive operations.
They were always the first and hardest hit by recession, and
the miners suffered greater job and wage insecurity than
almost any other group of industrial workers.

Since the major consumers of Tennessee coal were the
electrical utilities, especially the Tennessee Valley Authority,
Christopher realized that to organize coal miners, one first
had to organize TVA employees. Over the next few years, he
assumed an increasingly active role in the CIO's program of
unionizing TVA.[9]

Christopher maintained his strong desire to organize textile workers,
as Garrison points out, and he made a strong effort to organize
Tennessee garment and leather workers, canners, meat packers, pulp
and paper workers, and copper and aluminum refiners.[10]

As secretary-treasurer of the Tennessee Industrial Union Council,
Christopher spent as much time out in the field among the workers in
organizing and problem solving as his schedule would permit.
Increasingly, administrative work made inroads into the time spent
among the rank-and-file members and less time was available for
field work. "At heart, Christopher remained a labor activist,"
Garrison notes, "happiest when he was in the midst of a group of
picketers, or at the collective bargaining table, thrashing out a contract
with management."[11]

Anti-union violence was by no means a relic of the past in the
South, as Christopher was to learn dramatically within the first year
of his tenure in Tennessee. In September 1941, after conducting a
union meeting, two union representatives who had been organizing
workers in Harriman were kidnapped, beaten, and tarred.
Christopher was infuriated. Relentlessly he pursued a just and legal
resolution of the incident by collecting evidence, seeking the assistance of the American Civil Liberties Union, and soliciting the aid of
Governor Prentice Cooper and the state attorney general. Rumors that

the local sheriff's deputies were involved in the incident were not corroborated. No one ever came to trial for the incident.[12]

Though a young man in his early thirties, Christopher had sufficiently impressed his CIO associates and the state membership with his commitment and resourcefulness after only the first fifteen to eighteen months on the job. He had traveled the length of the state and formed strong working relationships with local leaders. These efforts were rewarded in May 1942 when he was appointed CIO Regional Director for Tennessee.

On December 7, 1941, Japanese forces attacked the American base in Pearl Harbor. For months, like other politically astute citizens, Christopher had closely monitored American policies as they pertained to the war in Europe. Despite reservations about American involvement in the war, Pearl Harbor was an event that crystallized his support for the U.S. war effort. In the months ahead, Christopher would coordinate CIO contribution to the war effort. A number of Tennessee manufacturers signed contracts with the federal government to produce service uniforms and clothing as well as other war material and supplies. In August 1942 Christopher accepted an appointment to the National War Labor Board where he conferred with representatives of labor, management, and the public sector for determining NWLB policies on wages and job security. He also served

Campaigning for the AFL in Oak Ridge, 1945. (Courtesy—Tennessee State Labor Council)

on the Area Appeals Panel (Region 8) of the War Power Commission.[13]

That same year, along with various union representatives, AFL and CIO organizations in Tennessee, Christopher had a role in creating the Tennessee Federated Labor Committee for Political Action. The committee lobbied with the General Assembly for pro-labor bills and against anti-labor legislation. Through the committee Christopher and his lobbyist colleagues pursued a varied and ambitious legislative course for labor, including the fight for a 40-cent per hour minimum wage, a standard eight-hour workday, a child labor bill, unemployment compensation, and elimination of the poll tax. Some consciousness about laboring people's needs was raised, but otherwise all of the lobbying efforts failed.[14]

Christopher's encounters with the state legislature whetted his appetite for more political involvement. The following year, under the leadership of CIO president Philip Murray, the CIO Political Action Committee (PAC) was formed. The first order of business was to mobilize the workers into a force at the polls; Christopher led the voter registration drive in Tennessee. As the 1944 presidential election drew closer he stepped up his campaigning for Franklin Roosevelt. In the January after the election he was named the Southeastern Director of the CIO-PAC, replacing George Mitchell. In April 1946 he asked Tennessee members to assist in establishing a state CIO-Political Action Committee. As director of both the Southeastern region of CIO-PAC as well as the Tennessee CIO-PAC, Christopher was strategically positioned to push his agenda on labor politics. In July 1946 he was replaced as Southeastern director by Daniel A. Powell in order to help lead a massive CIO organization drive which was dubbed "Operation Dixie."

The late forties and early fifties were years of frenzied organizing activity for Christopher. Under Van Bitner, director of the Southern Organizing Drive, some early successes were enjoyed in recruiting members into the CIO unions. The drive was moderately successful in smaller Tennessee plants and less successful in large industrial plants. Christopher continued his political activity in the face of the realization that CIO unions in Tennessee would never represent more than a small percentage of the work of the state. As the months passed, "Operation Dixie" experienced fewer and fewer successes.

By 1952 Christopher was at the point of being totally burned out. He had few tangible results to show for this almost indefatigable work. His wife had been seriously ill. Christopher began entertaining an opportunity to remove himself to Alaska and there organize workers. The thought of an escape may have been more alluring than the appeal of fresh challenge, for all the causes for which he had so fervently fought had suddenly opened.

After the house of labor was united by the big merger of 1956, Christopher's span of power and influence was greatly expanded by his being named AFL-CIO director for Tennessee and Kentucky. The years ahead were years of additional administrative work, public relations for the union cause, counseling of younger men and women who could benefit from his bitter and challenging experiences of the earlier years, and the deepening of professional and personal relationships which had been initiated earlier. By the time he came to this position, however, Christopher had already gained widespread respect and admiration for his career in the CIO. He had also assured his place in both southern as well as Tennessee labor history.

STANTON SMITH: ELDER STATESMAN OF TENNESSEE LABOR

Few people fit the general public's stereotype of a labor leader less than Stanton Smith. Had it not been for his capacity for leadership and the happenstance of depression-era circumstances, he was destined to complete an entire career with distinction teaching high school math in the public classrooms of Chattanooga. Fortunately for Tennessee labor, his friends will argue, Smith's vast talents and energies were not confined to the classroom.

To whatever degree the cause of organized labor was advanced or the image of labor in the state of Tennessee was enhanced during the decade of the fifties may be credited in large measure to Stanton Smith. From 1949 to 1960 he served as president of the Tennessee Federation of Labor and the Tennessee AFL-CIO. Even his critics conceded that Smith is bright, intelligent, and also articulate. But most of all he is thoroughly a gentleman. While several fellow unionists faulted his left-leaning political and social philosophy, friends and foes alike concurred that his character is beyond reproach. Smith dealt honestly and fairly with friends and critics alike. He was not easily threatened by harsh and unfair criticism, of which anyone in a position of such a controversial office would expect. Under his firm leadership, the Tennessee labor movement was accorded increased visibility and credibility.

Smith's schooling in labor education was in the practical experience of involvement with the American Federation of Teachers. Smith
entered the classroom Chattanooga school system in 1930, earning a
salary of $125.00 per month for ten months. The city of Chattanooga
had worked out an extra month's salary in order to "tide the teachers
over" through the summer vacation. As the depression deepened into
1931, the city cut off the extra, tenth month. "That was easy to do,"
Smith recalls, "but that was a ten percent cut right there."[15]

> Then the next year—and this was what precipitated the for-
> mation of the teachers' union—they were going to cut all
> the city employees' salary by ten percent, including the
> teachers' salaries which had already been cut by ten per-
> cent. So we were going to get a second ten percent cut while
> everybody else was only going to get one. The teachers
> didn't think that was quite fair, so they decided to organize.

As Smith and his fellow teachers compared their plight to that of
local firemen and policemen, they had further reason for grievance.
Noting that the firemen and policemen had a salary law which gave
them around $1,900 per year, compared with $800 or $850 for
teachers, Smith argued that teachers must convince the legislature to
receive their salaries by provision of state law. Additionally, the city
was talking about sending all non-resident teachers home. "I never
quite understood what they meant by that," Smith quipped; "I guess
that if you were not born here you were not a resident teacher. And
that scared a lot of people."

There was talk of organization among the Chattanooga principals
before Stanton and Nancy Smith joined the movement.

> Me, with my propensity for popping off, I spoke up in the
> early meetings, so I got elected chairman, and we went on
> from there. We worked in the movement. Nancy and I had
> a big organizing concern. We had about 1100 teachers in the
> two school systems at that time. We had about 900 of them
> in the union. At that time the American Federation of
> Teachers had only about 5,000 members nationwide. So we
> had almost 20% of the members.

Smith was vice president of the American Federation of Teachers for
nine years, serving from 1937-1946.

One of Smith's achievements as a leader of Chattanooga teachers was, in 1935, pointing the state legislature toward a successful passage of a teachers' tenure law. For too long, Tennessee teachers had labored in the classroom without uniform standards of either work evaluation or salary. The campaign for a teachers' tenure bill required a great deal of work.

> We did a careful analysis of the entire situation in preparing for that legislature. We did an analysis of the salary for base pay. The average salary was something like $850.00 a year. There was no rhyme or reason for the salaries that were paid. So we secured passage of a tenure law, which had been unheard of in Tennessee at that time. This gave to teachers their much needed protection after a crucial probationary period as well as objective standards and uniformity in teacher salaries.

Smith's goals for the teachers were not achieved without delays and further entanglements. The city of Chattanooga and Hamilton County refused to abide by the new law and the teachers' union was forced to file suit. The case went to the state Supreme Court where the teachers lost on a technicality related to dual city and county school systems. As a direct result of this experience, Smith worked inside of the Tennessee Education Association to "agitate" for another statewide teachers' tenure law. The first one that was adopted by the TEA was sabotaged by an education administrator and did not become law. Later the state did adopt a statewide teachers' tenure law. The entire movement originated with Smith and the teachers in Chattanooga. "Those were exciting years," Smith recalls. "That's when I was learning more and more about the labor movement."

The public school teachers in Memphis of the 1930s had a fledgling union, Smith recalls, but it was forced out of existence by Ed Crump. "Ed Crump was quite a political boss—he controlled everything. Because he was unhappy about the way that the teacher acted in an elections, the union there soon went out of existence." Smith traveled to Memphis in 1939 in an effort to re-organize the teachers there, but was unable to overcome the obstacles he encountered there.

By 1942 the United States had entered the war in Europe. The preparedness policies of Franklin Roosevelt had turned into the policies of combat involvement abroad and mobilization at home. In 1942, Smith stopped teaching and went to work for the labor movement.

By the end of 1941 Nancy was pregnant and we discovered it was twins, and that would make three children. I knew she could not go back to work for a while, so I had to get a job where I could earn a living. So I went to work for the International Ladies Garment Workers Union, in the Southeastern region, under John Martin, who was regional director for that region. I was assistant director and the director of education for that region. But this was during World War II in 1942; the war was getting up a pretty good head of steam for us, so I spent most of my time servicing four big locals here—one in Knoxville, the Appalachian knitting mills, the Signal knitting mills, in Chattanooga, the Gardiner Waring knitting mills, down in Florence, Alabama—all of which were engaged in war production. So I was doing grievance settlements, contract negotiations, and handling the kind of business for those locals and also for a local in Atlanta.

The late forties were exciting times for organized labor. Congress had passed the Taft-Hartley Act in 1947. The election of 1948 brought to focus a number of issues relevant to labor and, as Smith put it, "that election saw a great surge of political activity" on the part of the labor movement. "The CIO had been active in political issues. In fact, they were much more active politically as a whole in Tennessee than the AFL; however," Smith recalls, "the Chattanooga AFL group was very active politically and also quite successful politically. We had organized what was called Labor's Political Conference and we supported Estes Kefauver the first time he ran for the state senate—the only late race he ever lost. In 1951 our whole ticket, including the mayor, was elected for the city commission. So we had quite a bit of political success here locally."

Smith's performance in both the Chattanooga AFL local and in the ILGWU was both noticed and appreciated. The young labor leader all along had been involved in the Chattanooga Central Labor Council, building ties and relationships among other labor leaders and gaining respect for his leadership abilities. Nineteen forty-five was a watershed year for Smith. He was invited to take on the job as a full-time employee of the Tennessee Federation of Labor and the Chattanooga Central Labor Union. It was a dual job with one salary.

The State Federation had built up a rather substantial treasury in those days, $25,000 or so, and wasn't doing anything, had no full-time officers. And so, George Googe, who was the regional director for the AFL located in Atlanta, prevailed upon the state Federation to set up an organizing program in the state under which the state would pay half of the salary and expenses of an organizer to be located in each of the four major cities—Knoxville, Nashville, Memphis, and Chattanooga. I was the one that did it in Chattanooga. At the same time I was the secretary-treasurer of the Central Labor Union. It was not a paid office, either, but that put me on full-time, so I worked here full-time from 1945 to 1956, when we moved to Nashville.

Smith was elected president of the Tennessee Federation of Labor in 1949.

The year before Smith was elected TFL president, state leaders created and filled their first full-time office. Charles Houk was elected secretary-treasurer. But the biggest move of all during the fifties was the decision of state labor leaders to follow the lead of the national organizations and merge the Tennessee Federation of Labor (TFL) with the Tennessee State Industrial Union Council (TSIUC).

When we merged in 1956 we were actually the second state to merge—after the official merge of the AFL-CIO. As a matter of fact we worked out a merger agreement and the constitutional government for this newly merged organization before any other state. Arkansas picked up on what we were doing and the leaders there scheduled their convention ahead of ours. So Arkansas became the first state to merge, and we were the second state to merge—but we were the first state to work out a viable plan and Arkansas used our constitution as a model.

The merger, both nationally and at state levels, was not without its critics in Tennessee. Newspapers, such as the *Chattanooga News-Free Press*, kept up an attack upon "labor bosses" for their concentration of power. In an editorial praising Barry Goldwater for his attack on "labor bossism," the *News-Free Press* offered: "In nearly every election in Chattanooga there is a 'Stanton Smith Ticket' handpicked by the local AFL political labor boss."[16] Seeing an increase in union power as a threat to freedom, the paper editorialized that the South has a greater love of freedom "because of a rich tradition handed down from Anglo-Saxon heritage."[17]

The purpose of the merger was indeed to enhance the power of laboring forces in the state that would come from a unified labor movement. But if that power were already inordinate, as critics contended, it was news to Stanton Smith. Speaking before the Tennessee Federation of Labor in Memphis, October 1955, he called the 1955 Tennessee legislative session "the most anti-labor in history. All you had to do was mention the word 'labor' and legislators would start shouting 'no.'"[18] The 450 delegates to this fifty-seventh convention of the TFL met in the midst of a strike at the Serbin Company in Fayetteville—a strike which E. T. Kehrer of Atlanta, southeastern regional director for ILGWU called "one of the biggest, greatest, and most important labor struggles in the United States." The conflict was between a garment industry which "seeks the lowest possible wage level it can find" with the ILGWU which helped bring the pro-union garment firm to Fayetteville in order to show that the AFL is interested in building southern industry.[19]

The 1955 meeting was also addressed by Governor Frank Clement, who defended his administration against labor criticism by contending that 19 bills favoring labor had been passed since he became governor, and by Senator Albert Gore, who emphasized the importance of international trade.[20] It was Smith himself who made what may have been the most important announcement in stating that the AFL-CIO merger "is all but an accomplished fact":

> There is every reason to believe that by the end of the first week in December, we will no longer be a divided labor movement, but united in one great movement, seeking to advance the cause of all labor and, indeed, the general welfare of all people.[21]

Throughout the fall of 1955 Smith led the way in making plans for the merger of the two state organizations. At that time, he recalls, the AFL had about 60,000 members and the CIO had about 40,000 members. The merger agreement and new constitution were hammered out by a joint committee and then submitted to the conventions of both organizations for ratification. George Meany, who had moved to the presidency after the death of William Green in November 1952, was earnestly requested by Smith to address the merger convention. "We believe this will be the first state central bodies to merge and for this reason we sincerely hope you can take time from a busy schedule to help us mark this significant occasion," Smith appealed.[22] Meany congratulated Smith and other officers for their "initiative and efforts which they have given in bringing about this amalgamation,"[23] but when the time came for the convention Meany was unable to attend.

In the early months of the merger of competing union affiliations (June, 1956), the Tennessee AFL-CIO was served by the following members of the Executive Committee (from left around the table): E. B. Hester, Fred Comer, Charles Houk, Dan Powell, Paul Christopher, Matthew Lynch, Stanton Smith, Leonard Evans, Forrest Dickinson, Ruth Vaughn, and Earl Burnette (one member remains unidentified). (Courtesy—Southern Labor Archives, Special Collections Department, Georgia State University)

The first convention of the newly merged Tennessee AFL-CIO was an auspicious occasion. Meeting in Chattanooga's Memorial Auditorium on April 7, 1956, special recognition was given to Mayor Rudy Olgiati, the first union member to be elected mayor of Chattanooga who held a union card. Andrew J. Biemiller, director of the AFL-CIO's Department of Legislation, spoke to the new central body on "The New Emphasis on State Legislation" and attacked the "right to work" law.[24]

Speaking in the slot that could have been reserved for Meany was a long-standing labor organizer whose fiery oratory had been inflamed by the labor wars and persecution by opponents of labor in Tennessee. A native of Missouri, Franz Daniel entered the labor movement through the Amalgamated Clothing Workers Union; he came to Tennessee as an organizer in 1933 and spent most of the next 23 years organizing in the South and as field assistant to Walter Reuther, then president of the CIO.

Daniel began his oration by invoking the names of Brush Smith, Joe Dobbs, Clare Killiam, Tom Cuthbert, and John Martin, "who have

contributed so much to the labor movement of Tennessee and who
have held the standard high during the past years." Then, in the best
tradition of political convention rhetoric, Daniel proclaimed:

> The Tennessee labor movement has been known
> throughout its entire long history as a movement of
> integrity and that integrity goes pretty deep and pretty far.
> It has maintained its principles. It has maintained those
> principles in the face of intense opposition, intelligent oppo-
> sition and ruthless opposition. There has never been any
> taint of corruption in the Tennessee labor movement nor,
> my friends, will there ever be that evil which hurts the
> movement in other places. There has never been a taint of
> Communism in the Tennessee labor movement, nor has
> there been a taint of Fascism.[25]

When Daniel touched on the themes of communism and racism,
he touched some nerves that were sensitive to a number of the council
members. Labor everywhere in the United States has been criticized
as communist-led and communist-influenced by those who felt
threatened or confused by the labor movement. Tennessee was no
exception. As a progressive leader of a state organization, Stanton
Smith was particularly vulnerable both to attacks outside the movement and to attacks from within by fanatic union members. For
example, while Smith was still living in Chattanooga and serving as
executive secretary of the Central Labor Council, he was nominated to
serve on the Chattanooga Electric Power Board. At a meeting of the
city commission, Smith's appointment was opposed by Attorney
Charles Coleman, who referred to the young labor leader as "communist" and "socialist." Speaking to fellow Chattanoogans in the
audience, one of whom was a silent Raulston Schoolfield, Coleman
claimed that "you couldn't look over Stanton Smith if you were trying
to make up a list of Socialists and Communists in this community."[26]
Commissioner Olgiati was instrumental in getting Smith elected to
the board with only one dissenting vote. The following day, the
Chattanooga Times leveled criticism on the "issue of tagging or
smearing another person because he does not agree with you."[27]

The accusation of being a communist was something Smith had to
face from time to time during his tenure as the state's top labor leader.
Most of the time he ignored the charges, claiming to follow the admo-
nition of a wise man: "Never explain—your friends don't need it, and

your enemies won't believe you anyway." On one occasion, at least, Smith felt the charges could not be ignored. In the race for U.S. Senate in 1954, Representative Pat Sutton, along with the apparently eager assistance of the *Chattanooga News-Free Press*, attempted to link Smith with the Communist movement by revealing his participation in the Southern Conference for Human Welfare some fifteen years earlier. Sutton's aim was to injure his opponent, a candidate supported by the Tennessee Federation of Labor.

In a statement published originally in the *Chattanooga Times* and then widely circulated to TFL unions, Smith declared "it is time to speak out and put the lie to such misrepresentations."

> I have a reputation, of which I am proud, of fighting Communists where it counts—in the labor movement and in other organizations which they try to infiltrate for the purpose of promoting the Communist Party line. . . . My first and most enlightening experience in fighting Communists was in the American Federation of Teachers during the period from 1935 to 1941. . . . I was Vice President and member of National Executive Council of the American Federation of Teachers from 1937 to 1946. I am proud to say I took a leading part in bringing about the expulsion of the three Communist-controlled locals.
>
> Since then no other AFL union has had a serious Communist problem and the CIO has taken corrective measures to clean up the situation formerly existing in its ranks. Today it can be said without fear of successful contradiction that the AFL and the CIO are among the strongest bulwarks against Communism in the United States.[28]

Smith reminded his accusers that he had fought for a resolution by the conference in 1940 which condemned Communist aggression in Finland and that he resigned from the conference when certain officers acted without authority of the membership and threw support to an organization seeking "to keep America from aiding the democratic forces in Europe."[29] In almost uncharacteristic aggressiveness, Smith concluded his statement by noting that his conference affiliation had never been a secret of his past. "The only thing secret is the process of tortured reasoning by which Mr. Sutton and the afternoon newspaper think they can win elections by destroying—or attempting to destroy—the reputations of those who oppose them."[30]

The mid-fifties were years of questioning and unrest over the country's race issue. The Supreme Court decision in the *Brown v. Board of Education* case had far-reaching implications, even for the labor movement. In no other area of leadership did Stanton Smith steer the labor movement with vision and courage than he did on the race issue. Given the independent and autonomous nature of local labor unions, Smith's role in the area of race relations was only advisory; but he did not shrink from offering his considered opinions and seeking to persuade affiliate unions to take a just and progressive stand. When, for example, the Brown decision was handed down, the Chattanooga Central Labor Union advised its local affiliates to "reserve Judgment" on the school integration issue until various questions it raised were clarified. Smith, along with C. A. Brown, wrote union affiliates that the central council would seek ways to comply with the Supreme Court. "All citizens have a duty to abide by the law of the land," Smith urged publicly.[31]

Smith's statements on race seem safely moderate by standards of recent times. In the mid-fifties, however, such statements challenged the strongholds of southern segregationist thinking. Several locals were critical of Smith's support for city school boards which had decided to integrate black and white students in public schools. One local took action. The Chattanooga Printing Pressmen and Assistants Union (Local 165, AFL) adopted a resolution demanding Smith's "retirement from all positions of leadership." The reason: Smith had shown by word and by deed that he favored integration "and has tried to use his position of leadership to impose his theories of social equality with the intentions of bringing about a social order that will, in turn, bring forth a harvest of blood for our children."[32] Despite the resolution, Smith's vision of racial justice was ratified later that month in Memphis at the Tennessee Federation of Labor convention. With the hostile Chattanooga pressmen in Local 165 abstaining, Smith was re-elected president by acclamation. Only Arthur A. Canada, a member of the pressmen's group, voted no; Canada was president of the Tennessee Society to Maintain Segregation.[33]

In early 1960 events were taking place in Washington which would spell a premature end to Smith's career in Tennessee and the opening of new opportunities to serve the union movement at the national level. At a national conference, the AFL-CIO membership ratified a proposal for a specially created position of Coordinator of State and Local Central Bodies. There were many possible candidates for the position, but George Meany turned to Smith for the appointment.[34]

Deciding to leave Tennessee was not easy for Smith. Tennessee was his home. But he had given the State Labor Council eleven years of strong leadership and felt rejuvenated by the honor of a new challenge. "I will leave the State Labor Council with considerable regret," Smith wrote Tom McGrath, secretary of Nashville's Central Labor Council, "but with the knowledge that its affairs will be in capable hands."[35] Smith had good feelings about his home state. "There is no reason that Tennessee should not have the finest labor movement in the South. Certainly the challenge to do a good job is more insistent today than it has ever been."[36]

The last fifteen years of an illustrious and interesting career in labor leadership for Stanton and Nancy Smith were spent in the nation's capital. They were years of close interaction with the nation's most powerful labor leaders.

> I worked with them on different things. Of course George Meany was the big guy, and he is an interesting person. He developed and grew in his outlook; we saw this over the years. He became a staunch civil rights advocate. I remember one speech he made in Washington (I think it may have been a press conference). He said, "Yes, when I was a business agent in the Plumbers' Union in the Bronx, we discriminated. But we discriminated against everybody. The only worker that could get in was the son of a member." But he was strong, and it was just a matter of growth for the man and we saw this. I worked with Lane Kirkland. Lane was there most of the time as Meany's administrative assistant.

In mid-1974, Smith retired. He had no pension until he moved to Washington and in just under fifteen years had not earned much for a retirement fund. Living in Washington seemed impractical. Owning a piece of property on the side of a mountain in Chattanooga, he and his wife left Washington and returned to their hometown and built a house. Though retired, the concerns and interests of organized labor were still in his blood.

MATT LYNCH: "LABOR'S TALL MAN ON THE HILL"

It was September 17, 1979. The place was Nashville's new Hyatt Regency Hotel. The scene was one of the most poignant ones in all of Tennessee labor history. Matthew Simpson Lynch stood before several hundred of his brothers and sisters in the state's AFL-CIO Council, his eyes filled with tears and his voice quavering with deep emotion, and announced that he was not seeking re-election to the presidency of the Tennessee State Labor Council. The decision to step down was made rather quickly and not without a great deal of pain, although thoughts and plans for retirement had long been entertained by the ailing leader. In effect, Matt Lynch was saying good-bye to the people he had served so diligently and to the union cause he had loved so dearly.

Lynch's decision to step down from the council's top executive position marked the end of an era in Tennessee labor history—a point which was not missed by the *Nashville Banner*, which devoted the top headline and most of the front page to two stories and a picture of the unexpected convention development. From 1946, when he took over the leadership of the old CIO organization in the state, until his retirement in 1979, no state labor leader was better known or stirred for himself more personal respect or antagonism than Matthew Lynch. To survey his life is to sample the whole spectrum of union activity in twentieth-century American life—as mill worker, union organizer, labor lobbyist, and union administrator.

Lynch was born on September 30, 1912, in Chattanooga and was reared in a labor household. Union fever ran in his blood. His grandfather was an early organizer of the shoe workers in New England; his father, Francis M. Lynch, was a delegate and fiery orator to the Chattanooga Central Labor Union in the early thirties. Lynch was only a teenager when he started working in a hosiery mill and joined the American Federation of Hosiery Workers. As a youngster, he attended Notre Dame Academy where he participated in sports and other extracurricular activities. After spending time working in the Davenport Hosiery Mill, Lynch soon realized the importance of completing more education. While working in the mill by day, he enrolled and began attending classes at night at the Chattanooga College of Law. At Davenport was the beginning of a pattern of tension and strife with management for the young unionist. For a mill hand to stir up union enthusiasm by day and then pursue a degree in law was something new for a mill manager. "The supervisor at Davenport did not like Matt," Maud Lynch remembers; "he was far too controversial for them."[37] Despite his interest in working people and his zeal for the hosiery workers' union, the tall and slender college student still found time to play basketball on Davenport's company team and to test his skill in amateur boxing, competing once in the area's Golden Gloves tournament.

Upon completing his studies at the Chattanooga College of Law on June 1, 1934, the young graduate made a momentous decision which continued both to puzzle his friends and fellow mill hands and to fascinate journalists. Shunning the prestige and security of the life of a practicing attorney, Lynch chose the tough adventure and challenges of a career in union organizing. "Economically, you can't figure it," he told *Tennessean* journalist Max York. "The wages didn't amount to much for an organizer. And in those days, there was a pretty good chance you'd get hell knocked out of you."[38]

Small wonder that Lynch survived his days as a union organizer. Once, in Loudon County while on an organizing mission, he stepped out of a lighted doorway and heard gunfire; a bullet passed between his legs and splattered in the ground behind him. Another day he was driving around a mountain road when a barrage of rifle bullets punctured his car. Lynch ducked his head, floorboarded the accelerator, and escaped the ambush unharmed. The young unionist was not easily intimidated.

The most celebrated incident involving Lynch occurred in the mountain town of Rockwood and it had nothing to do with organizing. In early 1936 the workers at Rockwood Hosiery Mills had gone out on strike in order to better wages and working conditions in their Roane County plant. The strike stirred strong animosities in the area among mill owners and their sympathizers. Strikers were arrested and thrown in jail, according to the union, "upon the slightest provocation," and "armed thugs" patrolled the property of the Rockwood mills.[39] A 23-year-old Lynch journeyed to Rockwood to offer counsel and support for the workers. Lynch knew about a hostility of mill owners toward organizing and union activity, but he was not prepared for the kind of reception he got in the county. As he tells the story,

> I was walking with some of the workers out on this country road next to the mill. I saw two cars drive up and block off the road on both sides of me. I didn't have sense enough to be scared. They shoved me into one of the cars. There were three men. Another car followed us. When we got out on the edge of town, they blindfolded me with a towel and put me on the floorboard. They drove around for a while and finally they stopped. We were at a cabin up in the mountains. They beat me but the towel blindfold helped me. They kept hitting me about the head. The towel softened the blows. One guy who was kicking me must have worn out his right shoe.[40]

Lynch was kept in the cabin overnight, beaten again, and warned never to return to Roane County. He was then dropped on a country road by the kidnappers. At the time the mountains in Roane seemed impenetrable, and young Lynch thought he would never return to town alive. Later officers arrested a deputy sheriff, the son of a police chief, a cab driver and a mill foreman in connection with the case. The court freed them.[41] The Rockwood incident gained newspaper coverage in middle and east Tennessee and it was very much on the mind of TFL delegates when they gathered in Lynch's hometown of Chattanooga in May for their 39th annual convention. The first resolution passed by the delegates that year, presented by William Turnblazer, made reference to recent "shocking kidnappings," such as the kidnapping of the son of American hero Charles Lindberg four years earlier and of AFL representative Edward McGrady in Elizabethton. Then Turnblazer referred to Lynch as "a young law student and a citizen of Hamilton County, who was trying to advance the interest of his fellow workers in that particular locality," cited the facts of the kidnapping incident, and requested that Governor Hill McAlister offer a substantial reward for the arrest and conviction of those responsible for kidnapping this "young, upright, honorable citizen."[42]

The following year, Lynch was assigned to Griffith, Georgia, some 40 miles south of Atlanta, where he assumed the task of organizing the hosiery workers in Dovedown Mill. American women were wearing "full-fashion hose," with a seam and special knit, and Dovedown Mill produced them. While in a drugstore with a friend in Griffith, the tall, slender organizer spotted a beautiful young women. Immediately he wanted to meet her and he successfully implored his friend to arrange a blind date. As it turned out, Virginia Maud Purdy was an instructor in English at the local high school and the daughter of a local attorney. Maud Lynch recalls vividly the story of their courtship:

> From that blind date we continued our courtship. I thought that he was a fascinating man and had a brilliant mind. He had a great dedication to the labor movement—more than any person I've ever known. Of course, at that time my family and I knew almost nothing about organized labor. People would tell my dad, "Did you know your daughter is dating a man who works for the CIO?" What disturbed dad was not Matt's working for the union, but that he had never gone into the practice of law. My family knew that textile owners were fighting labor; it was repression all the time. We knew what Governor Talmadge did to the textile

workers during the general strike. My daddy despised
Gene Talmadge, not just for his behavior in the strike—he
despised him for everything.[43]

Matt and Maud Lynch were married in 1939 and moved to
Tennessee, living in hotels in Nashville and Knoxville for the first year
of marriage. In 1940 they moved to Chattanooga where they would
live for the next twelve years. But Lynch was away from home a great
deal of the time, traveling throughout east and middle Tennessee as a
UTWA organizer. Toward the end of World War II, he was drafted into
military service and was able to receive an assignment in the Navy as
a radar technician on the U.S. Waukesha stationed in the North
Pacific; he did visit Okinawa but did not see combat duty. Upon
returning from the service, Lynch had a bout with tuberculosis and
spent time convalescing in a Chattanooga sanatorium; he was destined to suffer from weak lungs for the rest of his life.

Despite the distractions of military service and poor health, Matt
Lynch was still respected by Tennessee working people as one of the
most dedicated and effective labor organizers and administrators in
the state. Those qualities were rewarded when in 1946 Lynch was
named executive director of the Tennessee Industrial Union Council.
The new position meant an increasing proportion of time needed to
be spent on lobbying and public relations; less time remained for
organizing. In 1952 Lynch moved to Nashville in order to be close to
the halls of legislative power; there he opened an office on Church
Street, near Printers' Alley. Later the office was destroyed by fire and
with the blaze several years of valuable CIO records were consumed.

When Tennessee's CIO and AFL organizations merged in 1956
Lynch became the secretary-treasurer on the new administrative
staff. The labor administrator studied the practical arts of state and
local politics and continued building for himself a strong support
among local labor leaders and officers. He became a personal friend
of Frank Clement and Buford Ellington, maintaining his staunch
support for Clement especially—a commitment which later became
a divisive factor in the ranks of labor when Clement ran for re-election in 1962. In the fall of 1959, an editorial in the *Nashville Tennessean*
commended Lynch as "a dedicated professional labor leader and an
astute politician."[44]

Lynch was elected president of the Tennessee State Labor Council in
1963, succeeding Steve Para, a railroad unionist, who had served only
one term after Stanton Smith had resigned to go to Washington. The

council's 1963 election was hard-fought, with Para and his supporters leveling charges that Lynch had not worked effectively as a lobbyist against Clement legislation which was detrimental to labor and had betrayed the movement by sticking with Clement rather than Olgiati.[45] Despite the charges, Lynch had amassed great support within the council and was able to maintain his office for the next fourteen years.

During the sixties and seventies no man or woman spoke more effectively or authoritatively for Tennessee labor than Matthew Lynch. This was an era in which there was a great deal of change and increased sophistication in labor-management relations. As labor's chief administrator, Lynch visited several hundred of the state's union locals. According to his friends, he often put in 80-hour work weeks, arriving at his office around 10:00 A.M. and working until 2:00 A.M. His chief objective was an ambitious one—to raise the council membership from about 91,000 when he became president toward the half million mark. Lynch understood the strength in numbers when it came to power at the polls.

The arena Lynch seemed to enjoy most was the legislative halls and chamber. When the legislature was in session, the labor chief did not get home for days, keeping quarters in the Hermitage Hotel near the Capitol. When columnist Max York dubbed Lynch "Labor's Tall Man on the Hill," the labor leader shared part of his philosophy about labor relations and lobbying:

> The goon squads and the tear gas are pretty much a thing of the past now, and only a few signs of the feudal system remain . . . however, opposition to unions is as intense as ever. It's just more sophisticated. Now they offer a man sugar in one hand and a cocklebur in the other . . . I never saw a politician—even one running for constable—who didn't think he was presidential timber. All politicians have monumental egos. . . . There are some things you have to learn about lobbying. Don't threaten them, or this ego will flare and they'll hump their backs and fight back. But don't give in too easily, and don't beg.[46]

Being neutral about Matt Lynch was difficult, if not impossible, for other labor leaders. Friends, such as Geneva Sneed of ACTWU described him as fiercely dedicated, astute, intelligent, and indefatigable, and as a shrewd behind-the-scenes fighter. Those who got in his way found they had a formidable opponent; yet, "he is quick to defend what he believes are rules of fair play."[47] Enemies, of which he understandably had a large share, accused him of spending too much time promoting himself and his own private agenda and not being attuned to the needs and wishes of the council membership. Observers and insiders may have exaggerated the differences between Lynch and his supporters and Stanton Smith and his supporters. Those differences, according to Smith, were not personal, but related primarily to fundamental differences in practical political philosophy and strategies.[48]

Through the mid- and late seventies Lynch's health and energy declined dramatically. The steady, hard pace of earlier years or the long hours at the state office could no longer be maintained; a portable oxygen supply was on hand at all times. Lynch's critics concluded that as long as the ailing chief was in office, the welfare of the council would also decline. Lynch had planned to run for one more term in office, having listened to friends who told him that "given his long term service to the Tennessee labor movement, he deserved one more term."[49] A majority of the membership, especially in the Steelworkers and Machinists, felt the retirement should not be delayed. After Jim Neeley's election one unionist commented: "It isn't a case of a young man whipping an old guy. Lynch has let things slide. And Neeley is the sort of man who gets things done."[50]

The labor career of Matthew Lynch may have seemed to end abruptly on an anti-climactic note. In the final analysis, however, Lynch withdrew his name from nomination because of his love for the council, the cause of labor in his home state, and his desire to maintain unity within the ranks of union membership. And the causes he championed, though sometimes in failure, were issues vital to Tennessee's working people—repeal of the state's poll tax, simplified voter registration, higher minimum wages, and repeal of the open shop law. At 66 years of age, looking older than his years but still standing tall, the veteran labor warrior recounted the cost in his farewell address to the delegates.

> I went to jail more than sixty times. I was beaten—a scared
> kid left lying on the side of a mountain. People would spit
> at you. But we built a labor movement of free people in a
> free society. It has all been worth it.[51]

In September 1981, almost two years exactly from the day he stepped down from his leadership in the Tennessee State Labor Council, Matt Lynch died in Nashville.

JAMES NEELEY: FROM BUNDLING DUTY TO BOARD POWER

In August 1960 the nation was considering a choice for its president. The choice was between a man who had served as vice president under Dwight Eisenhower for eight years and a young, Catholic senator from Massachusetts. That same month, in Huntingdon, Tennessee, an eighteen-year-old high school graduate began employment as a bundle boy or expediter carrying shirt parts to the workers in the Publix Shirt factory. As a young worker, he was impressed early with the value of union membership. There were never any second thoughts about joining the Amalgamated Clothing Workers Union. Thus began a career in labor service that would take James G. Neeley from the factory floor to the board rooms of labor power in Tennessee in less than fifteen years.

Neeley's interest in union activities and his commitment to union principles grew during his early months of work at Publix. Looking back on his days in the "rag industry," as he calls it, he dolefully tells people, "You're looking at an antique. With so much of the garment industry work being done overseas, the U.S. garment worker may well be a thing of the past."[52]

On August 20, 1962, exactly two years after he began working at Publix, Neeley went out of the plant and joined the staff of ACWA as an organizer. By the mid-sixties, he was a business agent for the union, serving companies in west Tennessee. From those years Neeley vividly recalls an incident in which, as a young union business agent, he was hauled off to jail in Martin, "simply because I enforced a contract on a visitation right. The employer denied me the right to enter the plant and I went on in anyway because the contract specified that I was entitled to go in."

> The moral of the story is that I ended up in New York in union headquarters for a series of meetings with international union leaders. The executive vice president, Hymie Blumberg, called Dave Wechsler and the president of Martin, Mr. McQueen, out of Philadelphia, into his office where he berated them to no end. He chewed them out and strongly advised them never again to have one of his representatives arrested for enforcing a contract for which he himself had been a signatory. (Blumberg had negotiated the original contract.) The end of that conversation was that

Mr. McQueen announced that his company was going to expand and build another plant and that it would be a union plant. That's what took the pressure off being arrested.

By the early seventies Neeley had become general board manager of the West Central Tennessee Joint Board of ACTWA which had jurisdiction over west Tennessee and parts of Kentucky. The garment industry had strong roots in Tennessee and Neeley's role was an important one especially during times of labor-management conflict.

I remember a large strike in Ramer, Tennessee. It was a tough strike, but we got it settled. The plant was struck over the failure of the company to pay an arbitration ruling of $1.16. We didn't strike over the amount of money, but over the principle. It was a tough strike, but we got it settled.

Union members picket downtown Nashville's Castner Knott in support of Farah workers on strike. Leading the Church Street demonstration, from left to right, circa 1968, were Jim Neeley, "Miss Farah," and Matt Lynch. (Courtesy—James Neeley Private Collection)

Neeley remembers an especially bitter strike against G and G Manufacturing in Halls, Tennessee. In that strike, saboteurs set fire to the plant, causing considerable damage. Union workers were blamed for the sabotage, but the charge did not stick. The strike Neeley called was the climax of some six months of negotiations with G and G over 24 arbitration cases in which the company was bound to award a substantial amount of back pay. The company stubbornly refused to pay the arbitration awards. Neeley remembers being in a quandary.

> I called Jack Shankman in New York. (Shankman is president of the union; he was secretary-treasurer then.) I told him that the company would not pay the arbitration awards, that there had been six months to pass, and that I wanted the right to strike. Jack told me right there on the phone, "Strike the bastards!"

The strike was not an easy one. It cost the union some $250,000. During the course of the five months, Neeley was called to New York twice where Shankman told him he was going to have to shut down such an expensive strike. "I told him the hard stories of what was going on down there in Tennessee and what the company was trying to do to the people," Neeley appealed. During the months of the strike, no union worker lost any pay. Auto loan notes were met. Other payments were made. Workers had money for food. On his second visit to New York to see Shankman, Neeley's people had already spent $200,000. Shankman and the international officers were caught between the financial drain on the one side and the union principle on the other. "The union principle won out in this strike as well."

As state union leader, Neeley demanded commitment from his people. And he got it. As general board manager of ACTWU in the early seventies there were some 3,100 ACTWU members in the western part of Tennessee. One of Neeley's "proudest moments" during those days was his ability to inspire a strike in a garment plant that no one in management thought could be struck. At Huntingdon's Publix operation local workers could not get a contract. As a result, they faced substantial cuts in their pension and insurance programs—two sensitive areas to most union members. Neeley recalls the details vividly:

> At 12:01 midnight I go down to the plant and pull the workers out on strike. Nobody thought this would happen. No one had given any credibility to the possibility of a

strike—but the night shift walked out with me. The next morning the plant manager and a group of foremen were going to St. Louis to see a professional football game. I had gotten a call saying that a settlement had been reached at 3:00 in the morning. So I go to the plant manager and tell him that the strike is about to be called off. I'll never forget what he said to me: "Are you going to call these guys back to work or do you want me to?" I said: "I'll call them." I was proud of this because it happened right at my doorstep and it was something that nobody believed could happen.

Neeley's rise to the head of the state labor council leadership might not have been likely at such an early age had he not served as one of Tennessee's commissioners of labor. "I figure I became Commissioner of Labor by mere accident," Neeley remarks, "and by being at the right place at the right time."

As a leader in one of Tennessee's most important unions, Neeley was approached by Ray Blanton seeking Amalgamated's support for the 1974 gubernatorial race. Blanton's voting record in Congress had earned for him a place on the Garment Workers' honor roll, thus a union endorsement was easily gained. Blanton, a west Tennessee contractor and Hardin County native, won the primary over fellow Democrats Jake Butcher, Franklin Haney, Hudley Crockett and others. Blanton was then pitted in the general election against a young, able, east Tennessee native named Lamar Alexander. Alexander's time had not arrived. Blanton won by more than 100,000 votes.

The task of forming a cabinet was handled by Blanton in a prudent manner. The governor-elect appointed a blue-ribbon committee of leading citizens across the state to make recommendations for cabinet appointments. Neeley remembers all major groups being represented on the committee—all groups except labor, that is. There was a woman, a member of the farm bureau, a lawyer, a county official, and others, but no member of labor's camp was appointed.

Blanton's work with the special committee was being done, coincidentally, in the Continental Inn in which Neeley was staying. Finding the new governor free for a moment, Neeley approached him boldly and said, "Govern'r, you've got a diversified group in that conference room. You've tried to cover the whole area of interests in Tennessee, but you have neglected to appoint a labor person and I think we deserve a place at that table." Blanton agreed to take the matter under consideration. The next morning a member of the governor's staff phoned Neeley, asking him to submit a copy of his resume and not to reveal the fact that he would be asked by the governor to serve on the committee. Serving on the committee was a highlight for Neeley's young career; experience helping to select the 21 most powerful people in Tennessee was a "heady" experience.

Committee work involved the glamour of submitting nominations to the governor as well as the busy work of checking backgrounds and experience. The labor commissioner was one of the last positions to be considered. Neeley's recommendation was crucially important. "I had gone to the committee and recommended Don Corn of the United Auto Workers for the commissioner's post," he states, but the UAW had caucused and was recommending Jerry Roberts for the position. The committee felt uncomfortable recommending Corn for the commissioner's office. The position was open and there was no apparent candidate to step in. Almost out of the blue, Ray Blanton asked Neeley if he would be willing to serve. As Neeley tells it:

> My answer to the governor was: "Governor, you know better than I whether I have been an asset or a liability to you while I've served on this blue-ribbon committee and I have no idea how many calls you may have gotten from people about appointing a labor person to your committee. But if you think that I can be an asset to you and not a liability, then I'll consider serving. Irrespective, I'm a team man. I'm not going to just take my bat and go home. I'll play the same way you do." I left and went home with the expectation of taking a plane the next morning for New York to work with contract negotiations. Before I had arrived home, Blanton had already called my wife and asked me to call him upon arriving home. (It was a two-hour drive from Nashville.) He asked me to return to Nashville and meet him for a press conference the following day at 12:00. He didn't say "I'm going to appoint you Commissioner of Labor" or nothing, but I knew what he was talking about.

The commissioner's post provided Neeley with four years of interesting and challenging experiences, although he admits that the ACTWU international leaders regretted losing him to government work. As a young commissioner, assured of a position within his own union if government service did not work out, Neeley was determined to be an activist administrator. Within ten days after he was sworn into office, Neeley enacted a new wage scale for state construction which was slightly under the prevailing union wage; the old wage scale had been "cut to the bone" under the Winfield Dunn administration. Soon, Neeley had moved to create the first mine rescue team in Tennessee. The new commissioner was one of the creators and founders of the Tennessee Safety Congress.

Several giant steps in labor legislation were made by Neeley and sympathetic legislators in Tennessee during the late seventies. One sensitive bill, which manufacturers fought tenaciously, was the expansion of a limited list of "occupational diseases" to a full coverage of all diseases caused by or growing out of a worker's job employment. The seventeenth vote for passage was cast by a manufacturer, state senator Carl Koella, who, as Neeley recalls, was interested in a judgeship being dangled in front of him while that bill was being considered. The other piece of major legislation was the removal of the three-year cap on medical benefits, thus making benefits payable for lifetime. "No bill that we fought for lost," Neeley boasted. "There was even a bill to consolidate various departments and put Labor in with the Department of Commerce. I fought it and we remained separate."

Neeley considered his work as Commissioner of Labor as a brief and separate unit of his life and career. There were tugs both from associates and the newly elected Lamar Alexander to remain in the post. Alexander proposed first to keep Neeley on board for six months. He next proposed that Neeley stay at his post for a full year.

> That was probably the source of my first problem with Lamar Alexander, the fact that I turned him down. A lot of people contacted me about the Department of Labor, because it had been such a high profile department. We had a good perception about us. We were clean. We could walk with our head high.

Especially remembered by Neeley was the high degree of esprit de corps among his 208 department employees. "It was just like a family. They trusted me. They followed me. We were 100 percent in everything that we did and it showed up on all the reports and brought the department a lot of credibility."

When Neeley left state government, he fully expected to resume his work with Amalgamated and remain within full-time service the rest of his career. Thus, he returned to Amalgamated in January 1979. But forces within the Tennessee AFL-CIO were already moving to draft him into a larger arena of labor service. One of these forces was a persistent and burgeoning feeling that Matt Lynch's health problems had rendered him highly incapacitated and another was the desire by large union delegations on the state council to appoint another person as Tennessee's top labor leader. Still another force was the reputation Neeley had established for himself at Amalgamated and in the Labor Department. Neeley recalls what happened from his side of events:

> It was still in my waning days in the Department of Labor. Dan Powell from the COPE office came to see me. "Jim," he said, "you are soon going to be the next president of the Tennessee AFL-CIO." I said, "Dan Powell, you've always had some of the craziest ideas, but now you're crazier than ever." But Dan was sincere and I knew that he must have known something that I did not know. Months later I got a call from the Steelworkers, wanting to know if I would come to a special meeting. I agreed to attend. It was a closed door meeting. There were some 78,000 workers represented by votes on the council. These people wanted me to accept the presidency of the state labor council. Bruce Thrasher reported that he had a block of some 15,000 votes which he wanted to deliver to me. There was also IBEW, then CWA— it was right on down the line. I kept up with the vote tally and knew that it was impressive. The union spokesmen said, "If it's not going to be you to take over for us, then it's going to be somebody else. You're the first one we're coming to."

In a way, Neeley was not surprised by the purpose of the meeting. He had witnessed the increasing divisiveness within the state labor movement. He had heard openly aired criticism. He knew there was division in the ranks. He had heard the talk by some unions about developing their own independent legislative and political program. He knew that Matt Lynch was a sick man and believed that, although he had enjoyed an "illustrious career," he had "gotten to the point where he could just not function." These were ominous days for labor leadership in Tennessee.

There were reasons enough for Neeley not to run for president of the State Labor Council. Lynch had been a strong contender. Other people had attempted to defeat him and were unsuccessful. Lynch would be a formidable opponent. He had a strong band of ardent supporters who would stop of nothing legal to keep the leader with over thirty years seniority in office. John Siegenthaler, publisher of the

Tennessean, phoned Neeley in Jackson where Mrs. Neeley was having major surgery just to warn him that he could not win the office and asking him to work for labor unity. By then, Neeley's resolve had become firm: "I told him, 'John, I know that I've got the votes to win. But I want you to know that I am not getting into this election to defeat Matt Lynch. I am running to serve the Tennessee AFL-CIO.'"

A delicate and sensitive task faced the Neeley camp. How was Matt Lynch to be replaced in a way that enabled him to maintain the dignity and respect he deserved and avoid a bitterly fought election which might destroy the State Labor Council? The answer was for Neeley to persuade Lynch to resign rather than to run for re-election. That would be no easy task, Neeley felt. Only on the evening before the conference convened was an agreement hammered out. Neeley remembers:

> I was willing to grant to Matt at his request the things that he wanted done, provided that he made an announcement at the opening of the convention as soon as it was called to order. We wanted him to take the prerogative of the chair and make his personal announcement. Matt agreed to do that. So on Monday morning of the convention, Matt announced that he was going to retire from labor leadership and that he would not be seeking re-election. He made his usual talk to the delegates and then he departed in good stead. He left with his credibility. I tried to be very kind and generous to him in my remarks when I was elected by acclamation. Just as we promised, we elected him president emeritus. Matt also wanted his car, the personal things in his office, and to stay on the payroll for the next six months. I had gotten together with Steel, IBEW, the Machinists, and CWA and we agreed to do this for Matt.

For Matthew Lynch to stand before the State Labor Council and address the delegates for the final time was a sad experience. It was a tearful Lynch who surrendered his position. "It's hard to walk away from something you've done for 30 or 40 years," he said.[53] Later, the council sponsored one of the biggest retirement parties ever for Lynch; some 500 people attended the gala event in Nashville's Hyatt Regency Hotel. Some of the bitterness remained with the delegates as the transition in power occurred. "This distinguished man deserved to be honored," Neeley offered, "but I never did see the benefits of strewing the laborers' blood all over the parking lot when you don't have to." A good many state officials agreed. A resolution from Metro

Eddie Bryan and James Neeley. (Courtesy—Tennessee State Labor Council)

Government of Nashville and Davidson County honored Lynch for "his undying dedication to the improvement of the quality of life for the working class of America" and on January 24, 1980, Tennessee House Joint Resolution No. 435 honored the retired president for his long-term service; later, the main campus on Nashville State Technical Institute was named the Matt Lynch Campus.

For Neeley, the 1979 convention was a landmark in his career. He had not sought the office, but neither would he shun the summons to serve. More than any personal achievement, it was an opportunity to draw together the 100,000-member council in the strength of unity and to restore the faith in state labor leadership, both among rank-and-file union members and in the general public. As Neeley took the gavel for the first time, he immediately pledged to join the fight to help Democrats retain control of the state legislature the following year and he promised an active lobbying effort on behalf of Tennessee labor. Neeley was now labor's voice. And that voice was being heard.

Neeley's tenure was destined to be a lengthy one, at least by the standards of typical elective office. By the mid-nineties he was antici-pating retirement from office that would occur only after the turn of the century. The legislative accomplishment of which he felt the greatest pride was the Reform Act of Workers Compensation (1992) which raised a maximum benefit in workers' compensation to 100 percent of the state's average weekly wage. "The Reform Act helped the higher income union laborer, and I expect the benefit to reach over

$600 a week," Neeley commented in 1995. "When I first started my involvement with the legislature in the mid-seventies, the maximum benefit was $65 a week. All this in twenty years. During this same time frame we have protected important areas—such as the state's maternity leave, the provisions of the Occupational Safety and Health Act, and the state's unemployment compensation—against those who would politically harm those programs."

What is Neeley's greatest failure and disappointment? In his own words: "We have not achieved any meaningful legislative recognition and success in helping public employees. We've passed a firefighter's check-off, but on most other legislative proposals we have encountered such major opposition from mayors and municipal leagues. They are afraid of collective bargaining. They don't want a third party having any impact. This will always be a difficult legislative problem."

The recognition of Tennessee as a state with a climate friendly to both labor and management, the maintenance of strong local unions in the state, the Labor Council's education and referral program in drugs and alcohol (as well as his membership on the board of Cumberland Heights Treatment Center), the Tennessee Center for Labor-Management Relations—all were areas in which Neeley has taken special pride in the nineties.

Why, after so many years, has James Neeley continued to allow his name to be placed in nomination for president of the Tennessee Labor Council? "There is a certain satisfaction in protecting workers," Neeley replied. "You fight for something of value to the workers. You go all out for it, and you know when you win and when you lose. Representing workers and fighting for their rights brings much gratification. If it ever comes to where I don't enjoy it, then I'm getting out."

NOTES

1. Biographical information about Paul Christopher is drawn from Joseph Yates Garrison, "Paul Revere Christopher: Southern Labor Leader, 1910-1974" (Ph.D. diss., Georgia State University, 1976).

2. Ibid., 22.

3. Mitchell tells of isolated cases of kidnapping, tarring and feathering, and even flogging as part of the entire resistance to textile unionism. *Textile Unionism and the South* (Chapel Hill: University of North Carolina Press, 1932), 84.

4. James A. Hodges, *New Deal Labor Policy and the Southern Cotton Textile Industry, 1933-1941* (Knoxville: University of Tennessee Press, 1986), 129.

5. Garrison, "Christopher," 52.

6. Ibid., 78.

7. Ibid., 128.

8. Ibid., 138.

9. Ibid.

10. Ibid., 139.

11. Ibid., 14.

12. The incident is reported in ibid., 141-42.

13. Ibid., 145.

14. Ibid., 150-51.

15. Personal interview with Stanton Smith by the author, April 19, 1987, Chattanooga, Tennessee. All quotes from Stanton Smith in this section, unless otherwise stated, are drawn from this initial interview or from subsequent personal interviews.

16. *Chattanooga News-Free Press*, Oct. 25, 1955.

17. Ibid., Dec. 3, 1955.

18. *Chattanooga Times*, Oct. 25, 1955.

19. *Chattanooga News-Free Press*, Oct. 25, 1955.

20. *Memphis Press-Scimitar*, Oct. 25, 1955.

21. *Chattanooga News-Free Press*, Oct. 25, 1955.

22. Stanton Smith and Leonard Evans to George Meany, Jan. 11, 1956, Stanton Smith Mss., Southern Labor Archives.

23. George Meany to Stanton Smith, Jan. 23, 1956, Stanton Smith Mss., Southern Labor Archives.

24. *Summary of Proceedings, First Convention, Tennessee State Labor Council, AFL-CIO,* Chattanooga, April 7, 1956.

25. Ibid., 75.

26. *Chattanooga Times*, Aug. 23, 1950.

27. *Chattanooga Times*, Aug. 24, 1950.

28. *Chattanooga Times*, Aug. 1, 1954, and memorandum from the Tennessee Federation of Labor, n.d., Smith Mss., Southern Labor Archives, Special Collections, Georgia State University.

29. Ibid.

30. Ibid.

31. *Chattanooga Times*, Aug. 18, 1955.

32. *Chattanooga News-Free Press*, Oct. 5, 1955.

33. *Chattanooga Times*, Oct. 27, 1955.

34. Letter/Memo from George Meany to all state and local bodies, Feb. 26, 1960, Smith Mss., Southern Labor Archives.

35. Stanton Smith to Tom McGrath, March 15, 1960, Smith Mss., Southern Labor Archives.

36. Ibid.

37. Personal interview with Mrs. Matt Lynch, Nashville, Tennessee, March 1, 1988.

38. Max York, "Labor's Tall Man on the Hill," *Nashville Tennessean Magazine*, July 1, 1962, p. 9.

39. T.F.L., *Proceedings of the 39th Annual Convention*, 42.

40. Quoted in York, "Labor's Tall Man on the Hill," 8.

41. Ibid.

42. T.F.L., *Proceedings of the 39th Annual Convention*, 33.

43. Maud Lynch interview, March 1, 1988.

44. *Nashville Tennessean*, Oct. 23, 1959.

45. Strong charges were leveled against Lynch as labor's spokesman to the state legislators in two documents which gained circulation among the council's membership. One is an eleven-page (legal size) memorandum entitled "Report of a President" by Steve A. Para; the other is a 24-page pamphlet containing a number of newspaper articles and concluding: "Lynch's ties to Governor Clement for the past 11 years have been highly advantageous and glorifying for Lynch personally but 140,000 Tennessee AFL-CIO members have not fared so well." The pamphlet is published innocuously enough by "The Committee for an Effective Tennessee Labor Movement." Both mss. from Tennessee State Labor Council Mss., Southern Labor Archives, Georgia State University (Special Collections).

46. Quoted in York, "Labor's Tall Man on the Hill," 9, 15.

47. Ibid.; personal interview with Geneva Sneed, Knoxville, Tennessee, Dec. 18, 1987.

48. Personal interview with Stanton Smith, Chattanooga, Tennessee, Dec. 19, 1987.

49. Geneva Sneed interview, Dec. 18, 1987.

50. *Nashville Banner*, Sept. 17, 1979.

51. Ibid. Two stories in the *Banner* that day on Lynch and the unexpected development were written by George Barker. Additional information about Lynch was drawn from a feature by Ken Renner in the *Nashville Banner*, Sept. 29, 1977, and bits of recollection by present labor leaders.

52. Personal interview with James Neeley by the author, Nashville, Tennessee, Aug. 20, 1987. All quotes from Neeley in this section, unless otherwise stated, are drawn from this initial interview or from subsequent follow-up interviews, the most recent of which was May 1, 1995.

53. *Nashville Tennessean*, Sept. 18, 1979.

11

"The Unionists paid a price for this hard-fought victory, but at least they protected the principles of the trade union movement. . ."

Scenes and Personalities in Turmoil and Triumph

Tennessee Labor Movement in
Modern Times

The story is told that a west Tennessee landowner was conversing with his last tenant farmer, an ecstatic black man who was departing for Chicago to "shake the money tree." Underscoring his new liberation to his former employer, the man declared: "I'm not reckonin' on ever again sayin' 'Giddup' to a mule—unless it's settin' in my lap."[1] The anecdote is symbolic of the important shifts that were taking place in the Volunteer State in the modern era.

By the mid-twentieth century, the nature of the Tennessee work force and the kind of jobs that workers held changed dramatically from what they had been one hundred years earlier. Since territorial days, Tennesseans had worked close to the soil to find meaning in toil and earn their living. Even though significant industrial progress was made in the decades after the Civil War and the state's readmission to the Union, Tennessee's economy rested predominantly on an agricultural base.

The Second World War was an important time in the life of the United States for many reasons, and it was also a dividing line in the economy of Tennessee. After World War II, the state's economy began moving to a much broader industrial manufacturing base. Farming continued in the state, to be sure, but it was revolutionized by technological improvements in agricultural equipment and methods. The mule, that obstinate symbol of independent, small farming for so many years, had all but vanished from fields and hillsides of Tennessee as it was rapidly replaced by modern gas-powered trucks and tractors. A new day had dawned!

Not only had work horses and mules become outdated and unnecessary, but Tennessee farms no longer needed large numbers of men and boys to cultivate the fields and harvest the crops. The number of farms dropped along with the amount of farm acreage. The amount of farms had reached a high of 252,657 in 1920, but began declining gradually in the 1920s and by the late 1970s had dropped to a little more than 100,000.[2] Despite the decrease in farms and farm acreage, productivity had increased enormously due to such advancements as superior seeds, animal feeds, improved fertilizers, selective breeding, and mechanized farm equipment.

In the early fifties cotton was still king among Tennessee farmers. By the 1960s, however, cotton began to decline in importance and was replaced by tobacco as the chief money crop. The many and varied uses of the soybean soon propelled that crop to the first position among the Volunteer State's farmers by 1972. Throughout the seventies and eighties, the soybean, which had been virtually unheard of a generation or so earlier, continued to be produced abundantly by Tennessee farmers. Raising livestock and processing dairy and poultry products continued to bring the state's farmers about half of their income.[3]

Tennessee workers, their children, and those who migrated to the state moved and settled into the urban centers of the state. The rural counties declined and the urban counties increased in population. This population shift went hand-in-hand with the rise in industrialism in the decade of 1955 to 1965. In 1960, the state's urban population surpassed its rural population for the first time.[4] By 1970 Tennessee was just under 60 percent urban.

The shift in black population is significant. At mid-century black families pulled up rural roots and headed to the cities. In some cases they headed for the large cities of the North and Midwest, such as Detroit and Chicago, and in many cases they headed for cities such as Memphis, Nashville, Knoxville, or Chattanooga. The chance to move to the big city and find an industrial job was like a new lease on life for many blacks.

The doors of industrial plants were open to black men and women, many of whom were unskilled and untrained for other kinds of jobs. The farm held no more appeal for most black Tennesseans: 64.1 percent of Tennessee's black population was in cities in 1950; 80.1 percent in 1970. Memphis had the highest percentage of black population, followed by Nashville and Chattanooga.[5]

Tennessee at mid-century became famously appealing to businessmen and investors who were seeking sites to build industrial plants. The economic environment was irresistibly attractive to some. In the late fifties and early sixties, new industrial plants began springing up all over the populated areas of the state, beckoning Tennesseans to take on new jobs with set wages and hours and promising a better life. Prior to the 1980s, the state's greatest industrial gains were made in the decade 1955 to 1965. During this period, Tennessee enjoyed a 28 percent gain in manufacturing jobs, thus leading most southern states in industrial growth.[6] Suddenly, it dawned on Tennesseans that they were no longer a part of a rural state of country folks living in country ways. A new day had dawned indeed!

A MERGER IN TENNESSEE

The biggest move made by Tennessee's labor leaders in the 1950s was their decision to follow the lead of the national labor organizations and merge the Tennessee Federation of Labor (TFL) with the Tennessee State Industrial Union Council (TSIUC). The merger was intended to present a united labor movement to the general public, to end competition between the umbrella organizations, and to strengthen the position of organized labor in the state (especially in seeking its political objectives).

State labor leaders demonstrated a high degree of progressive thinking and unity in their decision to create a single trade union central body for their state affiliates. In fact, they worked out a merger agreement and the constitution to govern the new body before any state had moved as far.

The agreement for the merger of the TFL and the TSIUC was made by the respective executive boards on December 17, 1955, and was adopted and amended by the separate conventions of the two organizations on April 6, 1956.[7] To the total membership of this new body the AFL brought approximately 60,000 members and the CIO brought approximately 40,000 members.

The first convention of the newly merged Tennessee AFL-CIO was held in Chattanooga's Memorial Auditorium on April 7, 1956. The occasion was an auspicious one. Stanton Smith, who had served as president of the TFL, was installed as president of the new body. Although George Meany had been invited but was unable to attend this first convention, the delegates were addressed by Chattanooga Mayor Rudy Olgiati, a union member and friend of labor who would later seek the Democratic nomination for governor, Andrew J.

Biemiller, director of the AFL-CIO's Department of Legislation, and Franz Daniel, a fiery orator and long-time organizer in Tennessee with the Amalgamated Clothing Workers Union.

Not everyone in the state welcomed the idea of the two labor bodies merging. Some newspaper editorials decried the "concentration of power" of labor forces as well as "labor bosses." In the fifties there was great concern about communism, which the more extreme critics attempted to link with the labor movement.

City central bodies naturally found it expedient to follow the lead of the national and state organizations. The first area merger was successfully made in Knoxville, where talk of merger began in 1956. This merger united the old Knoxville Central Labor Union, founded in 1889, with the Knoxville Area Industrial Council, founded in the mid-1930s, thus forming what is today the Knoxville-Oak Ridge Central Labor Council, AFL-CIO. The first regular meeting of the new Knoxville body was March 25, 1957, at which Paul Christopher administered the oath of office to President Fred Comer and the other officers.[8]

LABOR'S BEST FRIEND IN TENNESSEE

A full generation has now arrived on the American scene since the passing of one of Tennessee's truly great legislators and statesmen. The death of Senator Estes Kefauver on August 10, 1963, brought an end to a special era in senatorial statesmanship. Adlai Stevenson chose typically apt words to describe the man born in Madisonville, Tennessee: "a modest gentleman, a colorful political figure, a tireless public servant and an implacable foe of privilege and monopoly . . . a gallant champion."[9]

As a young Chattanooga lawyer, Kefauver joined a group of civic activists called "The Volunteers," who set out to reform Hamilton County's antiquated judicial system; the group later elected him president. In 1938, he made his first run for elective office, campaigning for the state senate with courageous stands against the state's poll tax and against the constitutional prohibition on a state income tax. Kefauver was defeated in that election by 307 votes, his first and last ever election lost in Tennessee.

There seems to be nothing in Kefauver's upbringing or his education at the University of Tennessee and Yale University School of Law that would have led him to identify with organized labor. Much of what Kefauver learned and felt about the labor movement was rooted

Stanton Smith, Estes Kefauver, and Charles Houk. (Courtesy—Charles Houk Private Collection)

in his experiences and associations in those early years in Chattanooga, a heavily industrialized city by the early twentieth century. The young Kefauver learned of how many Chattanooga industrial fortunes were built on a combination of low wages and poor working conditions. While unionism waned in the 1920s in Chattanooga, as in other places, it revived under the policies of Franklin D. Roosevelt. "By the time Kefauver came into direct contact with the labor movement there, the city had some fifty different unions with about 10,000 members," Charles Fontenay, one of Kefauver's biographers, points out. "Labor was developing into a powerful political force in Chattanooga, and at every step it met the bitter resistance of entrenched management."[10]

Chattanooga labor officials harbored their suspicions about the young and rising lawyer in their city. One of them, Stanton Smith, who later would become a close, personal friend of the Kefauvers, relates an incident which became an eye-opening experience for the young man destined to be a U.S. senator:

Back in the middle 30s Kefauver had come out of Yale Law
School and went to work for a law firm here that did mostly
corporate practice. There were some labor struggles that
had been going on in the 30s. Kefauver made a speech to
one of the civic clubs here in Chattanooga [Sons of the
American Revolution] where he sort of lambasted the action
of the union in one of the strikes that was going on here.
This intensified the doubts that the city's labor leaders had
about him, even though he was the attorney for the
Chattanooga News which was a pro-labor paper.

In the next issue of the *Labor World*, which is out of publication now but was published every week at that time as the
news organ of the Central Labor Union, the editor, Tommy
Cuthbert, who later became city commissioner and was a
printer by trade, wrote a scathing editorial about Kefauver.
The blast was called "Estes Kickover."

The upshot of it all was that Kefauver went to see Cuthbert
at the *Labor World* office. Kefauver told him, "I read your
editorial and I got to thinking about it and maybe I don't
know everything I ought to know about that particular
labor situation and I thought it might do me some good to
get to meet some of you fellows in the labor movement and
see what I can learn."

So Kefauver sat down and talked with Cuthbert about the
strike situation in question and the editor told him some of
the facts of life with respect to labor negotiations and
disputes. Kefauver had a chance to hear about some of the
economic, political, and human problems which led to the
beginning and growth of a labor movement. At the end of
the discussion, Kefauver said to Cuthbert, "Well, I guess
that I was wrong in the remarks that I made."[11]

After a stint in state government as Governor Prentice Cooper's
Commissioner of Finance and Taxation, Kefauver was easily elected
as the Democratic nominee for the third district to the U.S. House of
Representatives. Thus began a distinguished career in Washington
politics by a young man who cherished deeply rooted values of
integrity, straightforwardness, and sincere concern for the welfare of
the working people, both black and white, of this nation.

Organized labor, both in Tennessee and in the nation at large, was
convinced that it had a true friend and supporter in Senator Estes
Kefauver. The high view of the Tennessee senator, however, was not

held because he always voted labor's agenda; for example, as a congressman in 1943 Kefauver voted for the Smith-Connally Act, requiring a thirty-day notice before a strike against a war contractor and authorizing the government to seize strike-bound plants.

The litmus test for Kefauver, as well as for other congressmen in the view of labor leaders, was his vote on the Taft-Hartley Act. Though Kefauver held high respect for the bill's Senate sponsor, Ohio Senator Robert Taft, he could not reconcile himself to some of the provisions of the bill, mainly the outlawing of closed (union) shop contracts. In standing against Taft-Hartley, Kefauver was one of only twelve southern Democrats out of the 112 in the House of Representatives who votes against passage of the anti-union bill.[12]

In 1948 Kefauver challenged incumbent Tom Stewart for his Senate seat. Labor's endorsement and support for the young congressman was spurred by his vote against Taft-Hartley as well as by the fact that Stewart was running as "Crump's man." Kefauver's impressive victory, along with that of Gordon Browning for governor, dealt a solid defeat to the Crump machine which had long dominated Tennessee politics. It was a defeat from which the Crump forces never fully recovered.

In his position as a lobbyist and spokesman for labor, Stanton Smith encountered a number of Tennessee delegates in the Congress. Some were antagonistic to organized labor. Others were more exasperating than hostile. Kefauver was a pleasant contrast. The former unionist explained:

> Stewart was an interesting person. I would write and ask him for his vote and support on a number of matters of concern to organized labor. He would always write me back and say, "Your views shall get my serious attention." But we never got any votes from him. All we got from him was a lot of "serious attention."

> With Kefauver it was so different. This man was truly a good listener. It really meant something for him to give a matter some serious attention. This did not mean that you always got his vote. He was never a stooge for labor. He was not 100% labor. But when we disagreed we could talk about it.

> And Kefauver had strong influence on the rest of the Tennessee delegation after the '48 election. People saw that

labor had a big victory in '48. So when Taft-Hartley came up
for repeal or amendment in '49, Tennessee had ten pro-labor
votes. (McKellar switched his vote in the Senate.) McKellar
is quoted as saying, "Well, I guess labor had its field day!"[13]

The record of Estes Kefauver as a member of the U.S. Senate and a
friend and champion of all the people needs no detailed recital here—
his exposure of the corrupting effects of organized crime in the nation,
his fight against monopolies, his role as a consumer advocate, his
advocacy of procedural reforms to make Congress responsive to the
needs of modern times, and his inquiries into the operations of the
drug industry are among the more dramatic highlights of this successful public servant.

Tennesseans re-elected Kefauver to the Senate in 1954. The senator
campaigned for the presidential nomination in the pre-convention
periods of both 1952 and 1956. At the 1956 convention he was selected
to run on the same presidential ticket with Illinois' Adlai Stevenson.
The Democratic ticket failed to carry Tennessee in 1956, due mainly to
the popularity and incumbency of President Dwight Eisenhower. In
the general election four years later, Kefauver was re-elected to his
third term in the Senate.

As historians and biographers reflect on Kefauver's career, they are
struck with a sense of paradox. As a progressive on civil rights and
racial justice, the late senator won the endorsement and confidence of
conservative Tennesseans in an age when racial segregation received
major support. As a consistent champion of civil liberties, he first went
to the Senate at the height of anti-communist hysteria. From a state
which typically opposed the goals of organized labor and which was
leery of his enthusiastic support given by the unpopular CIO, Kefauver
courageously voted against anti-labor legislation and sided on most
issues with the wage-earning, production workers of the country.
Clearly, Estes Kefauver was not a "professional politician." Yet he was
one of the most effective legislators who has ever served in Washington.

The secret of Kefauver's success is not easily determined. Friend
and foe alike concur that the tall, almost clumsy, bespectacled cam-
paigner who occasionally wore a coonskin hat possessed charisma, a
special quality which won him the admiration and respect of the
mythical man and woman. His successful political career confirmed
the reassuring fact that his fellow Tennesseans could recognize great-
ness in a public servant.

TEAMSTER TROUBLES IN TENNESSEE

Concern about violence and corruption in organized labor around the nation deepened during the 1950s. Political leaders and newspaper editorial lists were calling for action against such activities. The U.S. Senate then responded by creating in 1957 the Select Committee on Improper Activities in the Labor or Management Field.

The committee, headed by Senator John L. McClellan of Arkansas, was composed of a small but remarkable membership. Among those serving on the committee were John F. Kennedy, destined soon to win the Democratic nomination and election to the U.S. presidency and fated for assassination; Sam Erwin, Jr., destined to national fame as the grandfatherly statesman presiding over the first Watergate hearings; Barry Goldwater, later to be the Republican nominee for president, vanquished by incumbent Lyndon B. Johnson; the controversial Joseph McCarthy, whose reputation as red-hunter had already been established; Pat McNamara and Frank Church, prominent senators. A young Robert F. Kennedy, destined to suffer the same fate as his presidential brother, was the chief counsel for the committee.

The public hearings of this committee shocked the country. The committee's study of union corruption took investigators all over the country and into several unions, but one of the chief targets of the investigation was the Teamsters' Union. The committee was especially startled by its investigation of Teamster president David Beck, who seemed arrogant and disdainful of the committee's powers. The evidence against Beck forced him to relinquish his union presidency and led to his indictment. The committee also linked James R. Hoffa with a number of corrupt activities and reported that the new president was running "a hoodlum empire."[14]

The committee devoted strong attention to union activities in Tennessee and its Interim Report devotes a section to "Organized Violence in Tennessee and Adjacent States." The report gives a tabulation of acts of labor violence committed in the states of Tennessee, Kentucky, Georgia, Ohio, and North Carolina from 1953 to the time of the hearings. The committee placed the total of such acts, described as minimal, at 173, and the property and profit loss to victims was placed conservatively at more than $2 million.[15] The committee noted despairingly that only eight of the 173 criminal incidents had been solved.

The 173 acts of violence cited by the committee were varied: windows smashed, tires slashed, trucks and autos stripped, car windows smashed, offices set afire, men attacked and beaten, shots fired at passing cars, trucks shot at, nails scattered on driveways, cars blown up, milk cartons punctured in a Nashville grocery, and one man pelted with stones. Referring to "specific cases of violence in Tennessee and environs," the committee stated: "one overriding fact which soon emerged was that no target was too insignificant, no situation too minor, to escape the Teamsters' vengeful attentions."[16] Barber shops and trucking firms were major targets of the violence.

The committee investigators concentrated in Tennessee on Nashville's Teamsters Local 327, Knoxville's Teamsters Local 621, and Teamsters Local 515 in Chattanooga. The Teamsters' mode of operation, according to the committee, was: to go into a company; claim that majority of the workers wanted a union; have the manager call an election; refuse any election defeat as valid; throw up pickets around the work area; and initiate violence.[17]

Several names cropped up continually in the ongoing investigation, names such as Perry Canaday, Cocky Ellis, and W. A. "Hard of Hearing" Smith, members of a "professional and highly mobile goon squad, ready, willing, and eminently able, at any time or place, to perpetuate brutalities of any degree desired."[18] The committee defended its use of the slang term "goon" by citing a dictionary definition of a goon as "one hired as a slugger, bomber, incendiary by racketeers or outlaw unionists for terrorizing industry or workers"; supposedly, a cartoonist originated the word to describe some "subhuman creatures" in his comic strip.[19]

The committee proceedings were often characterized by arrogance and contempt on both sides of the table. Understandably, some witnesses were reluctant to testify. The Senate questioners often felt frustration as some of the witnesses continually invoked the fifth amendment against self-incrimination to avoid answering specific questions. On one occasion, the chairman quizzed Perry Canaday, for whom Nashville attorney and long-time friend of labor Cecil D. Branstetter was counsel, using a biting sarcasm: "Have you ever been given any reward or citation from the union for your heroic beating up of people?" The witness then claimed his constitutional right to silence.[20]

The McClellan Committee's wrath was not reserved wholly for the Teamsters. It concluded that law enforcement agencies at each level in Tennessee had been "shockingly derelict" in handling union corruption.[21] Criticism was leveled against sheriffs in several counties and against municipal officials in Nashville and Knoxville. The most celebrated and controversial of the accused officials, however, was Hamilton County's Judge Raulston Schoolfield, whose alleged corrupt involvement with Teamster officials led to impeachment and conviction and to disbarment.[22]

The disclosures of the committee, it should be remembered, while alarmingly credible and serious, involved only a handful of the labor unions in the nation and at the state level. Still, they cast a cloud over the entire labor movement and placed its leaders on the defensive. On Labor Day, 1957, the *Nashville Tennessean* editorialized that, despite achievements of the past, "unionism celebrates in a changed climate. The revelations of racketeering and hoodlumism brought out by Senate hearings on the Teamsters' Union have had an impact on the public mind," but "it is important that the public remember that the vast majority of unions are honestly run by men who bear no resemblance to Mr. Dave Beck and that organized labor must not be penalized by the actions of a few."[23]

Some five years after the McClellan Committee began its investigation, an event occurred in Nashville which was to keep the Teamsters' Union and corruption linked in the minds of many Tennesseans. On Sunday evening, October 21, 1962, President John Kennedy spoke to the nation on television, informing Americans of the presence of Soviet missiles in Cuba and of his decision to blockade any future deliveries. The following day, James Riddle Hoffa, president of the International Brotherhood of Teamsters, went on trial for conspiracy in the Federal Building at Eighth Avenue and Broadway in Nashville. The trial set in motion a chain of events that would not, and did not, end for months, perhaps years.

In the trial, Charles Shaffer and James Neal represented the government in a contention that Hoffa and other Teamsters had participated in a plan whereby Hoffa would be continuously paid off by an employer. At one point a young man strolled into the courtroom and pulled a gun on Hoffa and fired; it turned out to be an air pellet gun. Nashvillians seemed to be uninterested in the trial until December 14 when Hoffa took the witness stand before a packed courtroom. Though Neal cross-examined Hoffa effectively, the trial ended with the jury deadlocked.

In May 1963, Hoffa and five others were indicted in Nashville for jury tampering. Hoffa's new trial was moved to Chattanooga and began in early 1964. In this trial the jury was sequestered during proceedings. Hoffa's defenders, such as William Loeb, blamed the union chief's problems on Robert Kennedy. In the jury tampering trial, the prosecution's major witness, Grady Partin, gave telling, persuasive and devastating evidence which linked Hoffa to every phase of the activities of the other defendants. On several occasions, Hoffa seemed to be attempting to intimidate Neal in the courtroom. On the witness stand, Hoffa was cross-examined by John Hooker. When Hoffa accused the young attorney of shouting at him, Hooker replied, "You're not used to being shouted at, are you Mr. Hoffa?"[24]

When James Neal led off his summation of the prosecution's case, he called the activities in Nashville in 1962 "one of the greatest assaults on the jury system the country has ever known."[25] Defense counsel James Haggerty called the trial a "foul and filthy frame-up." The jury later found Hoffa and the other Teamsters being tried as guilty on several counts of jury tampering. On March 7, 1967, some three years and three days after his conviction, Hoffa surrendered himself to authorities and entered the federal penitentiary at Lewisburg, Pennsylvania. On December 23, 1971, the Teamster chief walked out of that penitentiary as a free man, the beneficiary of an executive grant of clemency from President Richard Nixon.

Despite the damaging publicity given the Teamsters, union locals in Tennessee remained strong during the modern era. Teamster local membership at Local 327 in Nashville, for example, held at 5,200 members in early 1966 when 2,200 members were transferred to a new local, No. 480, which included drivers, desk workers and clerical personnel employed in the freight industry.[26] In October 1966 a strike for a modest wage increase and for health care benefits by Local 327 against five Nashville construction firms called some 7,750 workers of various unions off of an estimated 75 construction jobs, including the construction work on Percy Priest Dam near Nashville. The strike ended in ten days with a new contract which was satisfying to union workers.[27]

Membership totals of the Teamsters remained high in Tennessee and solid gains in bargaining had been registered through the late 1980s when the door was opened to the controversial union to return to the AFL-CIO house of labor.

FIRE IN THE HOLE AND ON THE MOUNTAIN

The Cumberland Plateau mountains of Grundy County provided the setting for some of the most intense labor-management conflicts in

all of Tennessee labor history. It was one day after Christmas—
December 26, 1962—when the labor war began in the coalfields of
southeast Tennessee and continued for several years until it was eventually moved to a federal courtroom in Chattanooga. When the coal
dust of the sixties turmoil had settled, the United Mine Workers of
America, once having enjoyed a solid foothold in Tennessee, had been
all but run out of the Volunteer State.

In some ways, the coalfield warfare which was waged in Grundy
County during the sixties was not greatly different from the warfare
which rumbled throughout the southern Appalachian mountains
since the end of World War II, when automation began taking the jobs
of thousands of miners. But Grundy countians were, as a whole,
already poverty-stricken before their mining jobs were threatened.

The labor dispute began that cold December day in 1962 when
some 600 UMW miners struck the southeast Tennessee mine shafts.
The mine owners were determined to keep the shafts open. In 1963 a
Tennessee Consolidated Coal Company subsidiary, the Grundy
Mining Company, opened its mines without a UMW contract. The
legal situation was clouded by the appearance on the scene of the
Southern Labor Union which claimed the allegiance of both the company operators and the miners. In reality, only a small percentage of
the miners seemed to have supported the Southern Labor Union, an
Oneida, Tennessee-based organization which claimed to represent
coal miners in seven states.

From that bleak winter day that the Grundy UMW miners refused
to enter the mine shafts, passions were inflamed. As the days of the
strike turned into weeks and weeks into months, incidents of violence
became more frequent. By 1965 the citizens of Palmer were particularly hard hit by the violence. After a series of explosions which
rocked the town and destroyed the movie theatre, a service garage,
the barber shop, the post office, and the general store, reporters called
Palmer "practically a ghost town." Later, Palmer's water tower was
dynamited, spilling 200,000 gallons of water from the storage tank.
The headquarters of the Tennessee Consolidated Coal Company was
also turned into rubble. A number of UMW meeting halls were
burned during the height of the labor trouble.[28]

Violent incidents were even more commonplace away from town.
Throughout the area, trucks and private homes were dynamited or
fired on. Men on both sides armed themselves for outdoor business.
Several people were ambushed. Three men were slain in the summer

of 1963. The morale of Grundy countians began to lower as the strike and the violence drug despairingly on.

In the fall of 1965 the labor war moved to a federal courtroom in Chattanooga. Some thirty coal operators sought $15 million in damages from the United Mine Workers Union, which they accused of conspiring with large mine owners in Kentucky to gain a monopoly on the Tennessee Valley Authority coal marked. The court's ruling in the $15 million suit was that the union was not liable for general damages and that the problems of the Grundy mines were the result of pyramiding land leases, low grade coal, and irregular coal seams.

The United Mine Workers had gained a victory in the courtroom, but in the coal fields of southeast Tennessee it was another story. Organizing drives by the UMW were hampered not only by the company-supported SLU, but also by the UMW's failure to stir much enthusiasm. Management, too, had its own problems, finding itself caught in the squeeze of a coal market glut caused by foreign imports of cheap coal and increased competition from UMW producers.[29] The picture had become vividly clear—coal mining was no longer a viable means for Grundy County men to earn a living and provide for their families. The stark specter of poverty would continue to hover over the scenic county.

THE WAR AT THE PRESS

One of the greatest tests of strength between a labor force and its management took place in the mid-sixties in the upper eastern Tennessee city of Kingsport. In a matter of a few weeks after the strike by allied union workers at the Kingsport Press began, the impact of the strike was felt well beyond the border of the Volunteer State. As the days and weeks of the bitter strike turned into months and years, that test of strength also became a test of endurance.

At 6:00 A.M. on March 11, 1963, about 1,650 production and maintenance employees of Kingsport Press went on strike against their employer. (The press employed an additional 800 clerical and supervisory personnel.) The collective bargaining talks, which had continued since the previous December 1, centered on the typical kinds of issues: a wage increase, reduction of the work week, seniority, and the manning of equipment.[30] Wages constituted the main issue in the strike and the Kingsport workers noted that their wages were about twenty percent below the industry's norm.[31]

Producing a published book is no simple process. It involves the coordination and teamwork of several groups of highly skilled workers. Understandably, this strike involved not simply one union, but five: International Printing Pressmen and Assistants Union, Local 336; International Typographical Union, Local 940; International Stereotypers and Electrotypers Union, Local 175; International Association of Machinists, Lodge 1694; and International Brotherhood of Bookbinders, Local 82. All were affiliated with the AFL-CIO.

The strike had an immediate impact on company operations. Orders which had been placed with the press from textbook companies facing fall deadlines were placed in other printing plants. The unions soon opened a boycott campaign to urge supporters not to purchase some of the better known Kingsport products, such as World Book Encyclopedia and the Great Book Series published by Encyclopedia Britannica. Later, the national office of the AFL-CIO joined the allied unions in urging a nationwide boycott of Kingsport Press books.

The dark side of the "mess at the press," as some called it, was the considerable violence. Almost each day of the early weeks of the strike several new incidents of violence were reported in the *Kingsport Times-News*. The local press, which tried to be objective during the labor battle, decried the violence early in the strike.

The strike at Kingsport Press was widely publicized, both in Tennessee and among labor leaders generally. Early in the strike, the Executive Council of the Tennessee State Labor Council made a resolution declaring its support for the union cause.[32] One reporter filed a substantial report on the strike which was published in a Sunday edition of the *New York Times*.[33] From Washington George Meany wrote national and international unions and AFL-CIO central bodies declaring that the 1,600 union members "deserve the support of the whole labor movement" in the "intense struggle" which would "have a profound effect on the future pace of union progress in the South."[34] Union workers in the Knoxville-Oak Ridge area joined a drive to collect toys and other items to make a brighter Christmas for striking workers and their families.

Within a few months after the walkout the Kingsport Press was operating at near capacity. The management's position throughout the strike was that the company had made reasonable concessions, that wages were close enough to industry standards elsewhere, that the unions did not understand the company's labor costs, and that talk about wages should have included the company's generous plan for profit sharing (which supposedly took 30 cents per hour out of the

Kingsport Press union workers on strike, 1963. (Courtesy—Southern Labor Archives, Special Collections Department, Georgia State University)

company till). The strikers' position was that the company had stubbornly and arrogantly maintained at all costs a union-busting attitude throughout the dispute—an attitude which was a direct throwback to the earliest days of trade union struggles in the United States. The original strike issues, however, seemed to have been lost to one main concern on which labor and management could not concur—the right of remaining strikers to return to the plant and resume jobs which had already been filled by replacement workers.

Any real hope for the allied unions winning their strike was probably abandoned within the first few months of the strike in 1963. Four years later, however, the National Labor Relations Board wrote the final chapter of the fated strike effort when it decertified the unions in an election in which the unions charged that replacement non-union workers were permitted to vote. Feelings of bitterness and resentment persisted.

A postscript to the Kingsport Press labor dispute occurred exactly twenty years after decertification. In one of the largest victories in a

Tennessee union election supervised by the NLRB, graphic artists, pressmen, and bindery workers at the Arcata Graphics (formerly Kingsport Press) plant in Kingsport and in Churchill, Tennessee, voted by better than a two-to-one margin for membership in the Aluminum, Brick, and Glass Workers.[35]

The May 1987 victory was a stunning reversal of fortunes for the labor movement and for skilled workers in Tennessee's largest printing firm. The new union became ABGWIU Local 299. Richard Duncan was elected president of the new local. A new contract was signed between the company and the union in January 1988. The memories of the bitter conflict of the sixties still lingered, but clearly a new day had dawned.

TIMES OF CONFLICT AMONG TENNESSEE LABOR

In the sixties, thousands of Tennessee's production workers were idled because of strike activity. In 1963, for example, Tennessee had 52 strikes which idled 18,200 workers, according to the U.S. Department of Labor.[36] There were 49 strikes in the state in 1962.[37] The number of new strikes beginning in Tennessee in 1969 topped all years since 1952; there were 133 new strikes in 1969, compared with 146 in 1952, which idled 37,800 workers (down from 43,600 in 1968).[38]

Employment in the sixties in Tennessee, on the other hand, was consistently high. Jobs were plentiful with the new industries that were locating within the state. The relatively low unemployment, a tradition of low industrial taxes, and the availability of cheap labor constituted three conditions which spawned labor unrest. Given the fact that the labor movement in Tennessee and other southern states had lagged behind the union movement in the northern and midwestern regions, labor disputes and strike activity among Tennessee workers may be viewed as a sign of the "coming of age" of the state's labor movement.

Most of the strikes of the sixties in Tennessee revolved around increased efforts by union leaders to organize the labor pool. Often there was management resistance when organizers worked to establish a union among workers in a plant for the first time. Early organizing efforts were a matter of "breaking the ice" with company management and perhaps with an entire community. On the other hand, in larger companies where the union movement had been entrenched and accepted, negotiations and collective bargaining tended to proceed much more smoothly.[39]

The Teamsters' strike against Murray Ohio in Lawrenceburg in April, 1965, occasioned considerable disorder and violence. Governor Frank Clement placed Highway Patrol Chief Greg O'Rear in charge of units dispatched to the strike scene. (Courtesy—Tennessee State Library and Archives)

Prosperity at home, the coming of new industry to the state, the availability of jobs, the emergence of a strong labor union in the southern region, the perception that company owners were reaping handsome profits, in summary, such were the diverse factors which contributed to Tennessee labor unrest in the modern era. In addition to the long strike at Kingsport Press, a number of strikes among Tennessee unionists gained notice beyond the state's borders.

Did the Teamsters' Union validly and legally represent the production workers at the Murray Ohio facility in Lawrenceburg? Answers were emphatic. Management said no. The union said yes. Many workers in the small, south central Tennessee town were caught in the middle of the dispute. For several weeks in 1965, the strident voices and violence in Lawrenceburg captured the attention of the media in one of the most publicized strikes of Tennessee in the 1960s. Teamster tactics

evoked in time and response from Governor Clement and his Tennessee
Highway Patrol units; 183 strikers were arrested, one of whom was a
brother of THP Chief Greg O'Rear. The Teamsters lost this battle.

THE MEMPHIS GARBAGE WORKERS STRIKE OF 1968

The most dramatic incident which ever occurred in a Tennessee
labor development—an incident which focused the eyes of all
Americans and many foreign observers on Memphis—involved
both a national reform leader and 1,300 of the lowliest workers in
the state's labor force. The struggle was not only for union recognition and bargaining rights, but for the dignity of human beings in a
black community.

Memphis of the sixties had the largest black population among
Tennessee cities. While desegregation policies of the past had been
legally ended, desegregation without adequate economic opportunities proved to be a hollow victory for Memphis blacks. There was one
job considered appropriate by many Memphians for black residents—
picking up the garbage and trash. The Memphis sanitation workers
received little in cash and nothing in status for their services. There
was talk among the workers about organizing a union and collective
bargaining from a position of strength.

Memphis had elected a new mayor, Henry Loeb III, who took
office on January 1, 1968, though his rise to power in city hall was
made with very few of the 80,000 votes cast by the city's blacks. The
following month, the new mayor was confronted with a storm which
had been gathering for months. The city's 1,300 sanitation workers,
virtually all of whom were black, had organized a labor union. The
nascent union was ready to press its demands.

The issues which concerned Memphis Local 173 of the American
Federation of State, County, and Municipal officials were threefold:
(1) recognition of the union local 1733 as the bargaining agent for the
workers; (2) a dues check-off system, whereby, with the employee's
permission, the city of Memphis would deduct union dues from his
paycheck; (3) higher wages. In the matter of wages, the union
presented demands for hourly increases averaging 40 to 45 cents for
workers who were paid from $1.55 to $2.10 per hour, a wage scale
considerably lower than in other major cities in the nation.

Simmering below the surface, of course, was the race issue. When
a settlement could not be reached and the strike began on February 12,

civil rights leaders began talking about blocking any garbage truck that tried to roll and staging an all-night vigil at city hall. The NAACP charged the city of Memphis "with racial discrimination in the treatment of the sanitation workers." Civil rights leaders outside Tennessee saw the dispute as something more than a breakdown in labor-management relations and began planning to offer support to the beleaguered workers.

Meantime, Mayor Loeb dug in for a fierce battle. While the garbage piled up on the streets, the mayor asserted that he would consign "exclusive" bargaining rights to no group or union. Loeb reiterated his belief that each man should be able to consult with a mayor at any time and claimed that his "open door" policy allowed the sanitation workers full access to his attention. Union president Jerry Wurf called such a policy "serfdom," consigning each worker to the role of a "supplicant or beggar, depending on the largesse of the king."[40] The mayor also rejected outright the notion of the dues check-off and claimed that his budget for the 1969 fiscal year provided for a five percent raise for all city employees.[41] Loeb could rightly claim that Tennessee law did not authorize collective bargaining for state or municipal employees;[42] and the fact that Memphis was different in this respect, he contended, was the "tough luck" of other cities and such a difference made him "proud."

Through February and March Memphis was astir. Over one hundred new men were recruited to replace the strikers, but public works management was hard pressed to get many trucks on city streets. Two of the garbage trucks were set afire and the refuse had to be dumped from the trucks in order to get the fire extinguished.[43] On one occasion, after Councilman Fred Davis accused the strikers of not speaking, more than a thousand striking union members marched in force on a city meeting. P. J. Ciampa of the AFSCME's international office told the press: "They wanted bodies so we got them bodies." As it was apparent that the hall would not accommodate all of the union visitors, Tommy Powell, president of the Memphis Labor Council, gestured to the crowd and asked Davis, "Is this enough?"[44]

As the days of the strike passed, interest in the worker's struggle continued to draw attention. A February 23 march, formed by black ministers who supported the strike, brought a direct confrontation between the city and the union when a police cruiser edged over into the group of marchers; when the crowd tried to move the police car away from the demonstrators, the police responded by spraying the marchers with mace. The ministers later met with Mayor Loeb, but his

position was non-yielding. Striking sanitation workers began
marching to city hall carrying signs which read "I AM A MAN." In
early March, over one hundred strike supporters were arrested by
local police while engaging in a sit-in at city hall.

A hard-liner Mayor Loeb was making progress, or so it seemed, in
helping the city win the strike. He announced that garbage collection
would be restored on a once-a-week basis. He further stated that
many strikers had returned to their jobs, some never had left them,
and 156 replacement workers had been hired.[45] The image of the
mayor was that of an official fully in control.

As the strike continued with little prospect of a settlement completely satisfactory to the union, labor and civil rights leaders sought
the involvement and support from outside forces. Coming to Memphis
to boost the morale of the strikers and enhance the coverage by the
national media were Roy Wilkins of the NAACP and Bayard Rustin of
the A. Philip Randolph Institute, both addressing a rally of over 9,000
people. Given the success of this rally, plus the belief that this strike was
the death struggle of the Memphis black community, strike leaders then
invited an even more effective spokesman to visit the community.
Dr. Martin Luther King, Jr., accepted the invitation immediately.

On his first appearance before thousands King told the workers
and their supporters to hold firm in their struggle, that they were
fighting for the right to organize and that organization was the way to
gain power. Though the Memphis press depicted the civil rights
leader as an interfering intruder in the internal affairs of the city, King
returned a week later to lead a large march on city hall. Pressure
began to build on Mayor Loeb, who had already acceded to the
union's demands for formal recognition and the dues check-off.
Negotiations continued but with very little progress.

On March 28 King led another march against the city administration, accompanied by 5000 union supporters. Shortly after the march
began, violence broke out when teenagers began breaking windows
of establishments on Beale Street. The police began using tear gas to
quell the eruption. King announced the next day that he deplored the
violence and that he would return to Memphis the following week to
lead a peaceful demonstration. The emotions of Memphians, black
and white, were at a peak.

King felt that it was important to return to Memphis and prove
that he could lead a non-violent march. At the time he was planning
a Poor People's March on Washington to be held later in the year.

King's critics questioned whether any large demonstration could remain peaceful. A successful Memphis march would set the stage for a grander march in Washington.

King arrived in Memphis on April 3 to finalize plans for the march two days later. The night of his arrival, the civil rights leader addressed a crowd of more than 2000. "Well, I don't know what will happen. We've got some difficult days ahead," King intoned almost prophetically. "But it really does matter with me now. Because I've been to the mountain top. I won't mind. . . . We, as a people, will get to the promised land. So I'm happy tonight." Meantime, city officials and local businessmen continued to express their fears about King leading another march in Memphis.

Most Americans know the outcome of King's last visit to Memphis. While standing on the balcony outside of his motel room that fateful April 4, King was shot and killed by a sniper. While neither the martyred victim nor his alleged assassin was a Memphian, the tragic incident turned the eyes of the nation and much of the western world to Tennessee's largest city. Instantaneously, millions were informed of the Memphis garbage workers' strike. Their cause was weighed in the court of national public opinion. King's assassination sparked racial disturbance and violence, not simply in Memphis but throughout the nation's largest cities. Curfews were imposed in many cities. Estimates of property damages from the racial riots ran into the millions of dollars.

Immediately after the King assassination various groups throughout both Memphis and Tennessee began to call for the resignation of Mayor Loeb, many of whom blamed him for the city's disturbance. Nearly all groups wanted the strike settled immediately for various reasons. The mayor continued to display firmness, but, with King's death, the situation had changed dramatically. Local union leaders were shattered by the tragic incident, but the AFSCME held firm to the cause they had shared with their slain friend and leader. Eventually, the city council approved a resolution by 7-6 which gave the AFSCME tacit recognition.

After over two tumultuous months, the sanitation workers returned to their jobs. Their wages had been raised. More importantly, their union had been recognized. At a terrible cost, a sense of human dignity and a national consciousness had been raised. Within the next decade, the AFSCME became the city's largest and most politically powerful civil rights organization, as well as a union organizing force for blue-collar workers.[46]

SATURN LANDS IN TENNESSEE

"We wanted the best place to build the highest quality car at the lowest cost so we could compete with the Japanese. We liked Tennessee's location and work environment." Thus explained Saturn president Bill Hoglund in his first Nashville press conference in 1985 as to why General Motors was making a $3.5 billion investment in Tennessee.[47]

In 1982 General Motors set out to create the "automobile plant of the future." The result was the Saturn Corporation. The new corporation would manufacture an entirely high-tech automobile, one designed to perform and sell competitively with the popular Japanese models. The next step was a corporate decision on where to locate the new manufacturing facility. Winning the location would have been a real plum for any one of the 37 states which sought the Saturn plant—projections held that the first auto assembly plant would employ 6,000 workers directly and supply an additional 10,000 supply jobs in the vicinity.[48]

Though some states offered more specific, short-term benefits and incentives to the newly created operation than did Tennessee, General Motors announced in July 1985 that it would locate in Spring Hill, Maury County, Tennessee. The seemingly sudden decision hit the town's 1,200 or so citizens, according to author Peter Jenkins, who had recently selected Spring Hill as an ideal site for a quiet home and farm, "with about the same impact of a UFO landing and colonization attempt."[49] Prior to the monumental General Motors decision, the most exciting dream for most Spring Hill residents would have been for their Class A Raiders to win a state football championship, a feat the team accomplished the following year.

Lamar Alexander hailed the General Motors-Saturn decision, the largest new investment in the world, as the ultimate evidence that Tennessee had arrived in the new age of science and human and mechanical technology. With a triumphant elation, the governor spoke of Tennessee as maintaining "yesterday's values while getting tomorrow's jobs." The governor then secured a full-page advertisement boasting about the Tennessee work environment and work force which was published in state and national newspapers.

The Saturn project aimed at introducing several innovations into traditional American labor-management relations. Through a General Motors-United Auto Workers Union agreement, both active and laid-off GM-UAW employees were to be given an opportunity of

Left, view of powertrain building which will produce engines and transmissions for the Saturn car. Right, a section of the Body Systems building in which the body would be assembled and painted. (Courtesy—Saturn Corporation, Spring Hill, Tennessee)

joining the new corporation (a controversial agreement which withstood legal challenges from a right-to-work group). The company planned to introduce a management style much like the Japanese system, with heavy financial investment in exceptionally motivated people, more intensively trained workers, smaller work groups with employees given more of a voice in how jobs should be done, and a minimum number of job classifications and traditional work rules, and with set salaries plus a performance bonus such as the ones given to managing executives.

Within months of the decision to come to Spring Hill, second thoughts about the Saturn dream began to be voiced. As the large trucks rolled into town on Highway 31W, and the noise of dynamite explosions breaking up rock and soil began to be heard, Maury countians started wondering if they wanted their community to be turned into a "little Detroit." From the company's side, which had promised that GM Chairman Roger Smith's pledge to drive a new Saturn off the assembly line before he retired in August 1990 would be kept, new reservations emerged. Could the price of a new Saturn automobile be kept as low as originally promised? Can GM build a 50-mile-per-gallon performance engine? Will American car buyers see the Saturn product as a bold, new automobile or as a slightly different Chevrolet?

By the mid-nineties Saturn was providing some highly satisfying answers to those questions. Performance testing and customer satisfaction surveys have proven that, from a quality of product standpoint, the Saturn is the one U.S. manufactured automobile that consistently ranks as high as Japanese and German-built autos. Undoubtedly, the presence of the new automobile manufacturer in the midst of the rolling hills and valleys which generations of Maury countians had used only for crops and pasturing was a bold experiment which could have an impact on Tennessee workers and their lifestyle for generations to come.

FOREIGN INVESTORS/TENNESSEE LABOR

The 1980s brought to Tennesseans some decisions and some strategic moves that are bound to affect their lives and those of generations to come. The most significant trend of this decade, a trend which impacted heavily on both the state's business community and its labor force, has been the investment of foreign capital in Tennessee industry.

In 1980 the Nissan Corporation announced that it would locate a truck manufacturing facility in Smyrna, Tennessee. The necessary acquisition of land and removal of other hurdles which enabled Nissan to come to middle Tennessee was made possible by state officials serving in the Lamar Alexander administration. From the very beginning, the Nissan operation in Smyrna was intended to be a formidable one. Spokespersons in both Japan and Tennessee boasted that the new, 3.4 million-square-foot Nissan plant in Smyrna would be the largest single Japanese investment in the United States.

Groundbreaking for the new plant was held in February 1981. The first light, American-manufactured Nissan pickup truck, a product of Tennessee handiwork, rolled off the assembly line in Smyrna in June 1983. The production of the first U.S.-made Nissan Sentra was achieved in March 1985. The one-hundred-thousandth truck arrived in October 1984. In March 1987, Nissan's 3,300 workers celebrated the company's production of its five-hundred-thousandth vehicle with a special party and visit by Governor Ned Ray McWherter.[50]

The fact that nags at union leaders and organizers is that Smyrna's Nissan plant remains non-union, despite intensive organizing campaigns by the United Auto Workers. Feeling has been intense on both sides. From the company's side, the Smyrna operation was intended to be and has succeeded as a model of labor-management cooperation. Japanese management style, the firm contends, precludes the need for labor union protection.

Despite all the attention given to the Japanese investors in Smyrna and some sixty other Japanese-owned operations in the state,[51] Nissan is not the largest foreign employer in Tennessee. Tennessee's small cities which are close to interstates have been preferred by foreign investors.

When foreign investors talk about advantages for manufacturing, they usually speak of five factors which separate Tennessee from other states: geographic location as a center for distribution; a strong work ethic; lower taxes; lower land costs; and lower labor costs.

Labor leaders have appeared to be in a minor quandary when speaking of the "foreign invasion" of Tennessee. On the one hand, new jobs for the state's labor force are welcome. In previous generations, reaching adulthood often meant "travelin' on" to find steady work and a decent wage—many west Tennesseans moved to Chicago, many middle Tennesseans to Detroit, and many east Tennesseans to Cleveland. Now the exodus has ended and, in fact, been reversed by the influx of American workers from other states seeking new manufacturing jobs. On the other hand, many old line jobs held by Tennesseans for generations (shoe manufacturing and clothing manufacturing, to cite two examples) have been eliminated due to imports and the subsequent plant closings. The U.S. trade imbalance continues to be an issue that concerns labor spokespersons.

THE TENNESSEE INDUSTRIAL AND LABOR SCENE IN MODERN TIMES

Tennessee of the 1970s and 1980s was a state which had traveled an impressive distance in labor and industrial relations since World War II. During the two decades, the list of large employers had grown both long and impressive: Nissan, Ford Motor, General Motors, Bowaters Southern Paper, Firestone (the later Bridgestone), Union Carbide, DuPont, Peterbilt, Levi Strauss, Mead, Alcoa, ITT, Goodyear, Tennessee River Pulp and Paper, Eastman Kodak, Arcata Graphics, Stokely-Van Camp, Jack Daniel, Carrier, Acme Boot, OshKosh B'Gosh, and Holiday Inn.[52]

The heart and energy of Tennessee workers during the seventies and eighties were, perhaps, tied up less with these large firms or their branch plants than with the schools, the centers of research and development, government services, the farms, and other manufacturing enterprises such as food product plants, timber and forestry operations, mining operations, small textile mills, and small shop operations. The work ethic had been alive and well in the Volunteer State.

If modern Tennessee, given the absence of certain labor legislation and the presence of the nettlesome "right-to-work" law, was hardly a pro-labor union state, it could no longer be claimed that the 500-plus mile parallelogram of territory from Memphis to Bristol could be called anti-union territory. For the fact that Tennessee citizens had at least made their peace with, if not embraced, the labor movement, the evidence is abundant.

Though literature from manufacturing interests and even from the state's Department of Economic and Community Development boasted of an average hourly wage that was over a dollar lower than the national average and a union membership which was almost five percent lower than the national average, the fact remained that Tennessee union membership was as strong and even slightly higher than most other southern states. Union membership in Tennessee in 1976 among nonfarm workers, according to the Bureau of Labor Statistics, ranked twenty-eighth in the nation at 18.3 percent, but ranked second in the South only to Alabama at 19.0 percent. In 1980, Tennessee trailed only Kentucky and Alabama in unionization of its labor force with 19.3 percent of state workers in unions. If labor's image in Tennessee needed some polishing, it was far brighter than its image in other places, say, Texas or the Carolinas.[53] Growth in Tennessee manufacturing jobs in 1987 was the best since 1973 with 24,737 new jobs and $1.7 billion in new or planned investments announced.[54]

Still more evidence that Tennessee and labor unionism are at peace with each other is the fact that the middle sector of the state has in recent times become headquarters for three historically different international unions. The United Furniture Workers Union, now a division of the International Union of Electronic, Electrical, Technical, Salaried, Machine and Furniture Workers (IUE) following a merger in January 1987, located in Nashville in June 1979—thus the first international union to put its headquarters in Nashville. The Furniture Workers Division, headed by Carl Scarbrough as president, had been in New York since 1937. When it merged with IUE, it contributed some 20,000 members to the 200,000-member international organization.[55]

The United Paper Workers International Union, representing 300,000 paper workers in almost every state in the United States and in Canada, moved to Nashville in 1981 and constructed an impressive office building adjacent to Interstate 24 south of the city. The facility housed a library and small museum. A central location to the UPIU locals was a key consideration in coming to Music City.

The United Garment Workers of America, founded and headquartered in New York City since April 1891, made its one and only move in coming to the Nashville area in 1984. The UGWA boasts of having

Samuel Gompers as a former organizer who traveled throughout the South on behalf of the union. The noted labor leader may have wielded a strong influence in helping to establish a union shop at Nashville's O'Bryan Brothers, President Earl Carroll pointed out, as that firm had a contract with the oldest UGWA union in Tennessee.[56] The O'Bryan Brothers Company, with a founding which dates back almost to the end of the Civil War, once maintained factory operations on the square in Nashville. While the UGWA is small in Tennessee, union-made Duckhead overalls and work slacks are worn throughout the country.

Economic trends and decisions made far away from Tennessee's borders in the seventies and eighties have affected profoundly one segment of the state's labor force—the textile, apparel, and leather industries which collectively employed over 100,000 Tennesseans in the early eighties. Traditionally, the garment industry has been one of Tennessee's healthiest industries. It has also been one of the state's most conspicuous industries, with more than 500 apparel manufacturers statewide; in fact, nearly every town in middle Tennessee has at least one garment factory.[57]

Labor-management strife in Tennessee is still capable of eliciting front-page headline media coverage. Case in point: the seven and one-half month warfare between Pirelli Armstrong and five hundred United Rubber Workers in Madison, Tennessee, a strike which was settled in March, 1995. The dispute, which began July 15, 1994, centered primarily on retiree health benefits, but it became bitter with the passage of time; "permanent" replacement workers, the ugly verbal showdowns, and scattered rock-throwing and other violence which drew dozens of police all served only to exacerbate the conflict.[58] Eventually, however, union forces could validly claim a victory: the NLRB sided with the union on the issue of replacement workers, strikers were returned to their jobs, and retirees were given their health benefits through a judge's ruling. "The Pirelli strike was a long, hard battle that the rubber workers finally won," offered James Neeley. "The unionists paid a price for this hard-fought victory, but at least they protected the principles of the trade union movement."[59]

The trade union movement, though still controversial in many circles, has been alive and well in the Tennessee of the eighties and nineties. The whole movement is, in the view of James Neeley, adapting effectively to changing economic and work force trends. "Labor has had some solid election victories, such as the U.A.W. victory at Murray Ohio," noted labor's top leader at the state level. "And other good things are happening, such as UAW's decision to re-locate their regional headquarters from Baltimore to Lebanon, Tennessee. This speaks highly of UAW strength in Kentucky and Tennessee."[60]

Tennessee is a part of a larger labor picture which is changing almost simultaneously with the re-structuring of business corporations at both the national and international level. Just as corporations have merged, so have international unions. "This is the trend that I am confident will continue: The number of international unions will be downsized and more aligned with the industries they represent," Neeley predicted. "This will give the unions greater negotiating strength and leverage in a changing economic world."[61]

Though leaders in the city central councils have sometimes found themselves overwhelmed with work, lacking in support for special drives and programs by the rank-and-file, and often under-funded, a number of strong union locals have continued their proud heritage: Consider, for example, Local 175 of the International Brotherhood of Electrical Workers, chartered June 26, 1912, and effectively serving members in twenty-one counties and three states in the Chattanooga area. Or the teamwork between UAW production workers and Peterbilt in the Nashville area. Or the long-standing relationship between Alcoa and the United Steelworkers Local 309. Or the long-standing relationship between Carrier management and the United Steelworkers Local 7655 in Collierville near Memphis. Or, finally, consider the positive relations maintained in middle Tennessee by United Food and Commercial Workers, with several thousand members in two locals, with Kroger, one of the nation's best-known food chains.

That the UFCW was the largest union in Nashville in the eighties and nineties (followed distantly by the IAM, the CWA, and UAW) may not simply be coincidental—one major division of the large international union was the 450,000-member Amalgamated Meat Cutters and Butcher Workmen of North American which was founded in Nashville in 1896 to improve the hazardous working conditions in the slaughterhouses and meat packing plants and to remedy work-related destructive diseases.[62]

Tennessee has changed a great deal since the noted Spanish explorer, Hernando de Soto, looked out over the Mississippi River in 1541. The Tennessee which was the home for some of the great names of American legend and folklore—Daniel Boone, Davy Crockett, John Sevier, and Andrew Jackson—has long ceased being a land of virgin forests, unbroken soil, vast wilderness, and sparse, pioneer population.

The new age arrived, thanks to the coming of the Tennessee Valley Authority during the Roosevelt era as much as to any other development. The landscape then suddenly and steadily gave way to TVA lakes and reservoirs, expansive farms, new industrial highways and even more new businesses and housing developments.

In the mid-nineties Tennessee construction workers toiled in the sun and dirt of the acreage north of the state capitol to re-locate Nashville's farmers' market and to build a new mall and exhibit area to celebrate the bicentennial of statehood.

Alas, the computer age with its information highway of fiber optic communications has arrived. The twenty-first century seems already to have pushed its way into the lives of Tennesseans, just as it has with most other Americans. The rich diversity of change in modern times is reflected in the diversity of jobs which Tennesseans have held. Most Tennesseans are aware of this past and are anxious to preserve the memory of it for future generations. Through it all, like many other Americans in other states and regions, they have learned a meaningful work ethic and have advanced the nobility of honest toil.

NOTES

1. Anecdote told in Wilma Dykeman, *Tennessee: A History* (New York: W. W. Norton, 1975), 189.

2. Corlew, *Tennessee*, 501.

3. Ibid., 515-16.

4. Ibid., 522.

5. Dykeman, *Tennessee*, 189.

6. *Tennessee Blue Book*, 1987-1988, compiled by Gentry Crowell, Secretary of State, 276.

7. *Merger Agreements and Constitution; Tennessee State Labor Council, AFL-CIO*.

8. Minutes of regular meeting, Knoxville Central Labor Council, March 25, 1957.

9. Quoted in Joseph Bruce Gorman, *Kefauver: A Political Biography* (New York: Oxford University Press, 1971), 370.

10. Charles L. Fontenay, *Estes Kefauver: A Biography* (Knoxville: University of Tennessee Press, 1980), 72.

11. Interview by Perry Cotham with Stanton Smith, Chattanooga, Tennessee, Dec. 17, 1987.

12. Fontenay, *Kefauver*, 121.

13. Stanton Smith interview.

14. Dulles, *Labor in America*, 398.

15. *Interim Report of the Select Committee on Improper Activities in the Labor or Management Field*, United States Senate (Washington: U.S. Government Printing Office, 1958), 330-31.

16. Ibid., 336.

17. *Hearings Before the Select Committee on Improper Activities in the Labor or Management Field*, 85th Congress (Washington: U.S. Government Printing Office, 1958), 7067.

18. *Interim Report*, 331.

19. Ibid.

20. *Hearings*, 7390.

21. *Interim Report*, 368.

22. Opinion is still divided on the justice of these actions. For the Schoolfield story, see Lee Seifert Greene, *Lead Me On: Frank Goad Clement and Tennessee Politics* (Knoxville: University of Tennessee Press, 1982), 247-72.

23. Editorial reprinted in *East Tennessee Labor News*, Sept. 5, 1957.

24. Walter Sheridan, *The Rise and Fall of Jimmy Hoffa* (New York: Saturday Review Press, 1972), 348. (This source was helpful in presenting a narrative of Hoffa's trials in Nashville and Chattanooga.)

25. Ibid., 351.

26. *Columbia Democrat*, Jan. 7, 1966.

27. *Nashville Banner*, Oct. 12, 1966.

28. See feature by Hamilton Gregory, *Nashville Banner*, June 28, 1965.

29. *Chattanooga Times*, Oct. 21, 1986.

30. *Kingsport Times-News*, March 11, 1963.

31. *East Tennessee Labor News*, May 2, 1963.

32. *East Tennessee Labor News*, May 23, 1963.

33. *New York Times*, Oct. 27, 1963.

34. *AFL-CIO News*, Sept. 14, 1963.

35. *AFL-CIO News*, June 6, 1987.

36. *Nashville Tennessean*, June 5, 1964.

37. Ibid.

38. *Memphis Daily News*, July 17, 1970.

39. *Chattanooga Times*, June 21, 1965; *Nashville Tennessean*, June 20, 1965.

40. *Murfreesboro Journal*, Feb. 21, 1968.

41. Ibid.

42. In 1957 the Tennessee State Supreme Court ruled in *City of Alcoa v. the International Brotherhood of Electrical Workers* that strikes by government employees were illegal. This was a precedent which guided Memphis city officials.

43. *Memphis Press-Scimitar*, Feb. 19, 1968.

44. *Memphis Press-Scimitar*, Feb. 22, 1968.

45. *Memphis Press-Scimitar*, March 12, 1968.

46. King's fatal visit to Memphis is reported in Lester C. Lamon, *Blacks in Tennessee*, 1791-1970 (Knoxville: University of Tennessee Press, 1981), 111-13. In addition to the newspaper coverage cited in the previous notes, a most helpful source in preparing the narrative of the Memphis garbage workers' strike and the assassination of King has been Earl Green, Jr., "Labor in the South: A Case Study of Memphis—The 1968 Sanitation Strike and Its Effect on an Urban Community" (Ph.D. diss., New York University, 1980). King's visit to Memphis and his status in the black community is discussed in Jim Bishop, *The Days of Martin Luther King, Jr.* (New York: G. P. Putnam's Sons, 1971), 3-46.

47. Quoted in Lamar Alexander, *Steps Along the Way* (Nashville: Thomas Nelson, 1986), 131.

48. See article by Scott Hodge in *Reason*, March 1986, and reprinted in the *Nashville Banner*, March 11, 1986.

49. From Jenkins' feature in *Nashville Tennessean*, Sept. 6, 1987.

50. *Nashville Tennessean*, March 31, 1987.

51. See the twelve-page special feature on Tennessee's partnership with Japan by journalist Jerry Buckley entitled "How Japan is Winning Dixie: The Tennessee Story," in *U.S. News and World Report* (May 9, 1988), 43-57.

52. For a report on Tennessee and other southern states in the mid-seventies, see *Southern Exposure*, vol. 4, nos. 1-2, 194-96.

53. "Unions Still Find South A Tough Row to Hoe," *U.S. News and World Report*, June 2, 1982, pp. 62-63; Scott Derks, "Unions: Turning Them Out," *The South Magazine*, November 1979, pp.39-40.

54. Based on figures compiled by the Tennessee Department of Economic and Community Development and reported in *Nashville Tennessean*, March 1, 1988.

55. *Nashville Business Journal*, June 1-5, 1987, pp. 19-f.

56. Personal interview by Perry Cotham with Earl Carroll, Nashville, Tennessee, Sept. 3, 1987.

57. Linda Dono Reeves, "State Garment Plants Fare Better than Most," *Nashville Business Journal*, Oct. 27-31, 1986, pp. 3f.

58. *Tennessean*. March 10, 1995, p. 1.

59. Interview by Perry Cotham with James Neeley, Nashville, Tennessee, May 1, 1995.

60. Ibid.

61. Ibid.

62. *Label Letter*, Union Label and Service Trades Department, AFL-CIO, July-August, 1988, pp. 1+6.

12

Building Trust and Creating Future

Labor Educates and
Cares for Its Own

"Education" is a term with precise meaning for most readers. "Nurturance" is a much broader term with wider connotation. Educators do nurturing, to be sure, but the concept of nurturing encompasses much more than the inculcation of facts. To nurture is to provide education, training, counsel, and concern. Indeed, nurturance is the sum of the influences which modify the thinking and behavior of an individual or group to maintain positive health and growth.

In modern times, the most progressive labor leaders have understood the value and importance of educating working women and men in areas that affect their working conditions and lifestyle. Elsewhere in this volume (chapter 9) we have chronicled the establishment of the AFL's Labor's League for Political Education (LLPE) and the emergence of the Committee on Political Education (COPE). Also elsewhere (chapter 8) we have discussed the Highlander idea, conceived mainly by Myles Horton, which led to the establishment on Tennessee soil of one of the most radically creative and courageous laboratories in adult education ever initiated in American history—an experiment so stirringly innovative that national best-selling author Studs Terkel once declared: "Were I to choose America's most influential and inspiring educator it would be Myles Horton of Highlander."[1]

IMPRESSIVE PRESSMEN

Perhaps no labor union in Tennessee history has demonstrated any greater concern for the training and welfare of its membership than has the International Printing Pressmen and Assistants' Union of

North America (IPPAU-NA), an organization of thirteen locals which splintered from the International Typographical Union (ITU) in 1889. In time the International Printing Pressmen and Assistants' Union was destined to become the largest printing trades union in the world with more than 125,000 members.[2]

In 1907 George L. Berry was elected president of the pressmen's union. Berry, born near Rogersville in Hawkins County, Tennessee, as an adolescent worked in the newspaper and printing businesses in Jackson, Mississippi, St. Louis, Denver, and San Francisco. While in San Francisco, Berry became highly interested in union activities. After his election to the union presidency at a New York convention, Berry returned to Tennessee on a union business trip. He was so impressed with the beauty and location of the valley in Hale Springs that he put up $8,000 of his own money to secure the property for use by his union. Berry was originally interested in the property because he was convinced that it was an ideal location for the proposed sanatorium and retirement home, but the 1910 delegation decided also to move both the union's headquarters from Cincinnati and the proposed technical school from Chicago to Hawkins County.[3]

The property that Berry had sited was eventually and appropriately called Pressmen's Home. Union leaders had wisely perceived a need developing for training their members in the skills of the newly emerging system of offset printing. The appearance of the offset press soon demonstrated superior printing methods to the widespread use of indirect transfer. If union members could get a "jump start" on training to use the new offset method they would gain a clear advantage over non-union printers who were content to utilize the old letterpress machines. Chicago-based architects designed the new building. The school was opened in 1912; and in the first year two courses, one in offset and the other in letterpress, were offered for $30 each. Residence room and board was offered for six dollars per week.[4]

The Pressmen's Training School was clearly successful. It operated year-round and in two shifts of instruction. In the peak years of the 1960s the school employed 25 instructors on faculty. Recreation and entertainment were provided for the resident students. In September 1948 the union dedicated a new, million-dollar, four-story trade school building, housing the largest printing technical trade school in the world.[5] By 1963 enrollment had reached 233 students with a waiting list of applicants for future enrollment.[6]

In April 1967, due to the tremendous cost of operation and maintenance of properties at the Tennessee location, the union relocated its international headquarters to Washington, D.C., from Pressmen's Home. In September 1967 the technical school was closed. Both decisions were the result of changing times and changing conditions. The foresight and vision of union president George L. Berry was the guiding force in 3100-plus printers being trained in offset, letterpress, camera, color, platemaking, and stripping.[7]

The story of the International Pressmen and Assistants' Union of North America is incomplete without reference to its sanatorium for the care and treatment of its own union members afflicted with tuberculosis. Until the development of effective vaccination, tuberculosis was a major scourge of both young men and young women. The death rate from "TB" was high. By the turn of the century unions had already expressed social concern for their members; the ITU, for example, had established both a home for aged and indigent union members and a hospital and tuberculosis sanatorium, all in Colorado Springs, Colorado.[8]

George L. Berry served as the chief force in guiding his union's leadership to place its new sanatorium in a valley in the mountains of east Tennessee. The new structure was designed to accommodate 150 patients; it had four stories and a center section with four connecting wings. When construction work halted in spring of 1912, Berry sought and received approval for aid from the state legislature (over Governor Ben Hooper's veto), but political wrangling kept the union from receiving the funds. Finally, in June 1916, construction on the sanatorium was completed.[9]

Patients at the sanatorium were treated in the early years with bed rest, fresh air, and a nutritious diet. New treatments and medications were used as they were made available. "While it may have operated at a loss," Jack Mooney, historian of the Pressmen's union in Tennessee, points out, "the sanatorium maintained a high standard of medical and personal care."[10] In March 1961 the Pressmen's Union Sanatorium was closed and the thirteen remaining patients were placed in private homes and hospitals; the union graciously continued to provide for their care. The equipment and furnishings of the sanatorium were donated to other professional care operations.

CONCERN ABOUT WORKER SUBSTANCE ABUSE

In the 1980s and 1990s the consensus of both business and labor leaders is that employees enter the workplace as total entities. The use of their knowledge and skills on company time cannot be totally divorced from their emotions or from the personal and relationship issues and lifestyle outside the workplace. Increasingly, drug and alcohol abuse emerged as a major social and work-related concern which was vitally linked with job performance, job satisfaction, and quality of workplace relationships.

In the early nineties the late Ray Graves, member of CWA Local 3808, and Mary Ann Quirk, a former assistant to Nashville mayor Beverly Briley, initiated an educational program in drug and alcohol abuse. The Alcohol and Drug Council of Middle Tennessee, also a United Fund agency, has become, in the words of James Neeley, "one of the best educational programs on alcohol and drugs of any state council."[11] The program, now under the direction of Quirk, sponsors conferences, seminars, and workshops all over Tennessee and makes referrals for workers to receive professional treatment. No worker has been left without treatment for lack of medical insurance.

TENNESSEE CENTER FOR LABOR-MANAGEMENT RELATIONS

> There is hereby established within the Tennessee department of labor, an institute for labor studies, which shall operate to develop an association between labor land higher education for the development and delivery of relevant, comprehensive, education services to workers through the state of Tennessee. This institute will function to facilitate uniformity in:
> (1) Broader understanding and meaningful perspectives of societal issues, including union and worker roles;
> (2) Comprehensive educational opportunity for individual worker growth and advancement; and
> (3) Improvement of individual technical skills related to union and civic responsibility, especially those required in an urban setting."[12]

Thus did the Tennessee General Assembly establish an institute to serve the both broader and specific educational needs of working Tennesseans in 1978, at first called the Tennessee Learning Center. The Assembly had passed the above legislation, introduced by Representative John Bragg and Senator Douglas Henry, with only one dissenting vote.

The primary architects of the new program included James Neeley, commissioner of labor, along with Eddie Bryan, assistant commissioner, Chancellor Charles Smith of the University of Tennessee, Nashville, and the university's dean of Public Service and Continuing Education, Dr. John Crothers with his assistant Wayne Fisher. These men were joined by Matt Lynch, president of the State Labor Council, AFL-CIO, the secretary/treasurer of the Council, Lee Case, and the district director of the United Steel Workers of America, Bruce Thrasher. Together these men directed the governance of the new program and collaborated in selecting its new director.

Applicants for the directorship were numerous. A field of sixty-three applicants was reduced to three finalists who were interviewed by the board: Dr. John Remington, director of the Labor Studies Center for the state of Florida, Dr. Everett Miller from Maryland, and Dr. Douglas Davis who was serving as an associate professor at the University of Alabama. Davis was selected to direct the new program and began his duties at the University of Tennessee on September 1, 1978. The new director reported to Dean Crothers in the university's structure, and Chancellor Smith served as chairperson of the governing board. Later chairpersons included Bruce Thrasher and James Neeley. Mr. Neeley has continued to serve as the board's chair and has been actively involved with the Center since its inception. Neeley and Bryan have given countless hours to insure the effectiveness of Center programming and its service to the working men and women of Tennessee.

The appropriation of the new program was $150,000; thus the staff was limited. Pam Beyer was chosen to assist Davis in the beginning, and the following year an instructor was added. Beyer remained with the program for four years prior to moving to Washington, D. C. During the early eighties reduction in funding forced Davis to work alone with only a secretary. Sue Glore joined the Center staff as assistant to Davis in 1985 and continues to serve the Center in that capacity.

Lamar Alexander had succeeded Blanton as governor of the state, revenue collections were short, and the new administration questioned the need for this new state agency. Funding was decreased to a level that threatened the continued existence of the program. Davis and Crothers met with the governor and his deputy Tom Ingram three times to plead and negotiate. But it was through the lobbying efforts of James Neeley and Eddie Bryan, and with the help of Bruce Thrasher and the USWA along with Eddie Collins of the UFCW and others in the statewide union community, that the administration chose to join with the legislature to increase funding to an appropriate level.

The Center's first program was a six-weeks course called "Steward's Training" sponsored by the Nashville Central Labor Council and conducted in the old Labor Temple; 103 people completed the course and Center programs were firmly launched. The Memphis Central Labor Council turned out 115 in November 1978 for a similar program. The United Food and Commercial Workers Local 1557 with Eddie Collins as

Douglas Davis. (Courtesy—Tennessee Center for Labor-Management Relations)

president conducted their annual stewards' conference at the university in October 1978 and Dr. Davis taught communications and steward's behavior and thus began a lasting relationship with that union. The Center has been involved with seventeen conferences for Local 1557 in addition to staff training and special classes. President Collins proved to be an unusual supporter for the Center, served on its board of governors, and his successor, President Rosemary Geddes, continued the supportive tradition.

John Crothers had given the program its identification by calling it the "Learning Center." LEARNING was an acronym for "Labor Education And Remedial Negotiating." In 1983 Davis proposed a name change to "The Tennessee Center for Labor-Management Relations." The adoption of the new name by the governing board was supported by the introduction of a new program the previous year.

One of the earliest programs of the Center had been a joint training program of managers and union leaders sponsored by the Service Employees International Union at the state's mental health facilities. These proved to be beneficial in improving working relationships, and in 1982 Davis introduced a new program that he called "T.R.U.S.T.," another acronym for "Tennessee Relational Union/Supervision Training." The TRUST seminars were to be a joint training experience that would help unions and companies improve working relationships. During early years of the eighties, little was being said about

labor-management cooperation and partnerships. The TRUST program was not only a major deviation from traditional programming of
labor education, but it was immediately suspect from both sides.

Davis reports that the selling job was one of the greatest challenges
of his career. A pioneer struggle with a slow beginning, the TRUST
seminars grew into one of the most effective offerings of the Center.
By the mid-nineties approximately 400 two-day sessions have been
conducted across the state of Tennessee with some of Tennessee's
major industries and unions. The seminars drew national attention
and Davis conducted the seminars in nine other states. TRUST continued to meet the needs of organizations seeking movement from
traditional labor-management confrontation to relationships of
mutual respect, mutual gain, and peace.

In 1987 Nanette Brittain-Gore joined the Center staff and in 1995
was named assistant director, thus succeeding Rick Gregory, who had
left the Center to accept the position of director of education and
Research with the United Food and Commercial Workers, Local 1557.
"Nanette has also diversified our offerings, she has developed effective presentations on such subjects as 'sexual harassment', 'violence in
the workplace', 'substance abuse' as well as continuing the bread and
butter courses of labor education," reported Davis. "She has been
responsible for coordinating a number of conferences and we are
especially proud of the 'Leadership' conference sponsored each year
by the State Labor Council and community service group. We believe
the Center is fulfilling its commission. I hope others agree."

The work of a labor educator hardly fits the traditional mold of
university classroom teaching. The labor specialist typically travels to
a meeting place on site. He/she typically carries enough instructional
aids and audio-visual equipment—flip chart and pad, overhead projector, movie projector and screen (more recently video-cassette player
and monitor), markers, handouts, etc.—to turn a union hall, a factory
break area, an abandoned room in some old building, perhaps even a
factory floor into an acceptable learning environment. Usually, the
labor educator or trainer cannot predict the noise level, room temperature, or other distractions which must be factored into the learning
environment. The schedule, attitude and mood of all the participants,
as well as the group dynamics of each class, are probably the greatest
variables. Alas, the teaching effort can be the best of all learning experiences or it can be the most challenging of teaching experiences.

As an effective speaker and educator before working men and
women, Douglas Davis is unequaled. With a dynamic and booming

voice which has been heard also by general radio audiences and by church audiences, Davis has addressed literally thousands of gatherings, large and small, of labor and management groups throughout the United States. His uncanny ability to place major concepts into acronyms for easy remembrance, his ability to address the level of his audience and speak its language, and his love for telling stories, especially about that wise sage of a possibly fictional relative named "Uncle Mort," keep most of his audiences riveted in attention to every word.

Reflecting on nearly two decades of labor-management education and consulting experiences, Davis reminisced freely:

> The past seventeen years have provided me with some of the most fulfilling and pleasant memories of my career. I have never regretted moving to Tennessee. My experiences have been varied and my feelings diverse. Certainly, there were times of great stress and anxiety but there were more times of personal fulfillment and satisfaction. We came to Tennessee to do a job and I gave it my best shot. I hope we have made working life better and more rewarding for some of Tennessee's citizens.
>
> I've had some harrowing experiences. I remember staying in a dingy motel once with a shag carpet on the floor that had glued itself together in clumps of dirt and waste. I was afraid to walk on it and the staff member with me claims to have jumped from the door to the bed. If I recall correctly, my bed was not so clean either.
>
> One night Beth [Dr. Beth Halteman-Harwell, once on the TCLMR staff and currently in the state legislature] and I drove from Memphis in a blinding snow storm. We left Memphis after completing our work about 5:00 P.M. and arrived in Nashville about 3:00 A.M. and did not stop once. We moved slowly, passing dozens of jack-knifed trucks, abandoned and ditched vehicles. We had no dinner, no food, but I think we must have been the only ones who made the journey that night.
>
> Not everyone coming to our classes was glad to be there. In the TRUST seminars, salaried people were scheduled to come and they had no choice and it was up to me to make them glad they came. Union stewards didn't enjoy sitting in a room with their supervisors . . . often there was not a very positive relationship . . . and I had that negative response to overcome. I remember through the years that perhaps about

a dozen participants announcing, most of them in graphic words for all to hear, that they did not want to be there. On every occasion I have quietly suggested they return to work. Only two ever left our seminars. But overall, in our evaluations, we have been given a 99+ rating. I feel good about that. That means more than 99% of TRUST participants not only enjoyed the experience but saw the value. And, of course, that includes those who were quite negative at first.[13]

The picture of organized labor is quite different today. This is true nationally. The picture has changed for Tennessee as well. Working men and women still struggle, of course, for their share of the American dream and just to maintain a reasonable standard of living. On the other hand, labor no longer must cast itself in dramatic defensive postures against the power of management or the power of the state.

What brought about the change in this picture? Have labor leaders made wise decisions? Have economic realities been factors? What about foreign manufacturing competition? Are there other influences?

Finally, what role have labor education, training, and caring played in producing a greater measure of peace and understanding between parties whose common goals and mutual interests are greater than their differences?

The Center for Labor-Management Relations, as well as other educational arms and outreaches of individual unions and management teams, may fairly be appraised as an idea whose time had arrived—preaching the gospel of professional conduct in union affairs; preaching the gospel of industrial peace; and introducing the concept of labor-management cooperation and partnership before many people were thinking about it.

Union leadership is changing. A new generation is rising. Many in the new generation of leadership have not experienced the trials and battles of hard times. Their thinking will likely be different. Not wrong. Just different.

Not all labor leaders have learned the lessons of the past. Not all have moved away from the confrontational mode. Many have moved away from the old mind-set, however, and Tennessee is better for it.

NOTES

1. Horton, *The Long Haul: An Autobiography*, quotation on dust jacket.

2. Jack Mooney, "The Establishment and Operation of the Technical Training School of the International Printing Pressmen and Assistants' Union in Tennessee, 1911-1967," *Tennessee Historical Quarterly*, Vol. 48 (No. 2; Summer, 1989),111.

3. Ibid., 114.

4. Ibid., 111-15.

5. Ibid., 117.

6. Ibid., 118.

7. Ibid., 119.

8. Jack Mooney, "The Sanatorium of the International Printing Pressmen and Assistants' Union of North America, 1910-1961, at Pressmen's Home, Tennessee," *Tennessee Historical Quarterly*, Vol. 48 (No. 3; Fall, 1989), 163.

9. Ibid., 164-65.

10. Ibid., 169.

11. Interview with James Neeley, May 1, 1995.

12. Acts 1978 (Adj. S.), ch. 840 1; T. C. A., 4-3201.

13. Interview with Douglas Davis, May 12, 1995.

Bibliography

Among the women and men who have taken the time to discuss with me either their role in the Tennessee labor movement or their impressions of same, most of whom have graciously invited me into their homes or offices, are: Eugene Anderson, Betty Barber, George Barrett, Cecil Branstetter, Iva Brooks, Eddie Bryan, Earl Carroll, Jack Comer, Douglas Davis, Richard Duncan, John Glen, Senator and Mrs. Albert Gore, Sr., Johnny Hall, Myles Horton, Mr. and Mrs. Charles Houk, Calvina Little, Maud (Mrs. Matthew) Lynch, Eula McGill, Jay Meyer, Mr. and Mrs. Jack Morris, James Neeley, Dot Pomeroy, Clyde Smith, Mr. and Mrs. Stanton Smith, Geneva Sneed, Howard Strevel, Lucille Thornburgh, Joe Welch, Billy Willis, and Mr. and Mrs. Harold Woods.

Primary source material was searched among Special Collections, Southern Labor Archives, Georgia State University, and at the Tennessee State Library and Archives, especially the Highlander Folk School Collection and in original manuscript materials pertaining to the Old Hickory powder plan. Additionally, the manuscript material, especially correspondence and documents produced by the state labor council, as preserved by the Tennessee State Labor Council, AFL-CIO, was highly useful. Finally, a number of secondary sources were consulted and utilized.

One of the satisfactions of preparing this bibliography has been the opportunity it affords to share with readers those books and articles that have been especially helpful. Also, however, this bibliography provides the opportunity to suggest additional readings for those who seek more breadth or depth. Since there is such variety in the following materials, I have occasionally added notes which might guide the reader in making selections.

The books and articles cited below have been divided into two broad categories: general American labor history and Tennessee labor history. Quite naturally, there will be some overlapping of the categories. Books which deal with the South as a region are placed in general American labor history category, though some of these works contain highly specific information about Tennessee.

United States Labor History

Abernathy, Thomas P. *The South in the New Nation, 1789-1819*. Baton Rouge: Louisiana State University Press, 1961.

"A Short History of American Labor," an article excerpted from the AFL-CIO publication by the same name, prepared for the 1981 Centennial of American labor.

Beardsley, Edward H. *A History of Neglect: Health Care for Blacks and Mill Workers in the Twentieth Century South*. Knoxville: University of Tennessee Press, 1987. Beardsley focuses on health care practices for workers, but illuminates the entire social and political landscape.

Bernstein, Irving. *The Lean Years: A History of the American Worker, 1920-1933*. Baltimore: Penguin Books, 1966. The definitive study of the struggle of American Working people during the 1920s.

Bernstein, Irving. *The Turbulent Years: A History of the American Worker, 1933-1941*. Boston: Houghton Mifflin, 1970. The definitive work on unionism in the 1930s.

Brody, David. *Workers in Industrial America: Essays on the 20th Century Struggle*. New York: Oxford University Press, 1980.

Brooks, Thomas R. *Toil and Trouble: A History of American Labor*. 2nd ed. New York: Dell Publishing Company, 1971. Highly readable, useful survey of labor's struggles in the U. S.

Cash, W. J. *The Mind of the South*. New York: Doubleday and Company, 1941. The traditional and long-renowned study of southern intellectual and cultural history.

Caudill, Harry M. *Night Comes to the Cumberlands: A Biography of a Depressed Area*. Boston: Little, Brown, and Company, 1962. While written mainly about Kentucky miners' work and lifestyle, the book rings so vividly true for Tennessee's Cumberland plateau miners.

Cohen, Sanford. *Labor in the United States*. 3rd ed., Columbus, Ohio: Charles E. Merrill, 1970.

Collins, Herbert. "The Southern Industrial Gospel Before 1860." *Journal of Southern History*, vol. 12 (1940): 386-402.

Cornfield, Dan, ed. *Workers, Managers, and Technological Change: Emerging Patterns of Labor Relations*. Foreword by Ray Marshall. New York: Plenum, 1987. Consists of two general chapters on the history of collective bargaining in the United States, especially as it pertains to the labor issues of technological change, and also brings together fourteen case studies of the history of collective bargaining in several major U.S. industries; editor is a Vanderbilt University sociology professor.

Cotham, Perry C. *Handbook of Labor History: The Tennessee Edition*. Nashville: Tennessee Center for Labor-Management Relations, 1989. A compilation of overviews, timetables, and personalities.

Cotham, Perry C. "Harry L. Hopkins: Spokesman for Franklin D. Roosevelt in Depression and War." Ph. D. diss. Wayne State University, 1970.

Cutler, Addison T. "Labor Legislation in Thirteen Southern States." *Southern Economic Journal*, vol, 7 (1941): 297-316.

Davidson, Elizabeth. *Child Labor Legislation in the Southern Textile States*. Chapel Hill: University of North Carolina Press, 1939.

Doyle, Don H. *New Men, New Cities, New South: Atlanta, Nashville, Charleston, Mobile 1860-1910*. Chapel Hill: University of North Carolina Press, 1990.

Dulles, Foster Rhea. *Labor in America: A History*. 2nd ed. New York: Thomas A. Crowell Company, 1960.

Dunbar, Anthony P. *Against the Grain: Southern Radicals and Prophets, 1929-1959*. Charlottesville: University of Virginia Press, 1981. Gives considerable attention to radical labor educators and leaders, including Tennessee's Myles Horton.

Egerton, John. *Speak Now Against the Day: The Generation Before the Civil Rights Movement in the South*. New York: Alfred A. Knopf, 1994. A volume of great substances which discusses the connection between labor, especially the CIO, and civil rights in the years before the *Brown* decision and Martin Luther King, Jr. Gives attention to Myles Horton and the more influential instructors at the Highlander Folk School.

Eller, Ronald D. *Miners, Millhands, and Mountaineers: Industrialization of the Appalachian South, 1880-1930*. Knoxville: University of Tennessee Press, 1982.

Ellis, John H. *Yellow Fever and Public Health in the New South*. Lexington: University of Kentucky Press, 1992. Explores the impact of the 1878 epidemic upon New Orleans, Memphis, and Atlanta.

Fink, Gary, and Reed, Merl, eds. *Essays in Southern Labor History*. Westport, Conn.: Greenwood Press, 1976. Contains two chapters on textile workers' woes and a chapter on labor's political involvement by Tennessean Daniel Powell.

Fink, Gary M. *Labor Unions* (The Greenwood Encyclopedia of American Institutions). Westport, Conn.: Greenwood Press, 1977. Contains historical sketches of more than two hundred national unions and labor federations that have been a part of the American labor movement.

Flint, J. Wayne. "The New Deal and Southern Labor," in *The New Deal and the South*. Ed. James C. Cobb and Michael V. Namorato. Jackson: University Press of Mississippi, 1984.

Filippelli, Ronald L. *Labor in the USA: A History*. New York: Alfred A. Knopf, 1984. A highly readable and up-to-date survey of American labor history with special features inserted on interesting personalities in American labor.

Foner, Philip S. *History of the Labor Movement in the United States*. Four volumes. New York: International Publishers, 1947, 1955, 1964, and 1965. A highly detailed and thorough history of the American labor movement.

Foner, Philip S. *Organized Labor and the Black Worker, 1619-1973*. New York: Praeger, 1974.

Green, Archie. *Only a Miner: Studies in Recorded Coal-Mining Songs*. Urbana: University of Illinois Press, 1972. Readable and interesting accounts of coal miners adventures as reflected in their music; discusses some Tennessee stories in Anderson and Grundy Counties.

Grubbs, Donald H. Cry. *From the Cotton: The Southern Tenant Farmers Union and the New Deal*. Chapel Hill: University of North Carolina Press, 1971.

Hall, Jacquelyn Dowd, with James Leloudis, Robert Korstad, Mary Murphy, Lu Ann Jones, and Christopher B. Daly. *Like a Family: The Making of a Southern Cotton Mill World*. Chapel Hill: University of North Carolina Press, 1987. A vivid portrayal of life among cotton textile workers; discusses the plight of Elizabethton, Tennessee mill workers in the late twenties.

Haskins, Jim. *The Long Struggle: The Story of American Labor*. Philadelphia: Westminster Press, 1976. Brief and readable survey of American labor history for students in seventh grade and up.

Hodges, James A. *New Deal Labor Policy and the Southern Cotton Textile Industry, 1933-1941*. Knoxville: University of Tennessee Press, 1986. Hodges argues that despite the traditional view of the New Deal as a period of good things happening, the mill workers did not have such a pleasant life or good work experience. The book highlights the failure of the New Deal policy.

Leuchtenburg, William E. *Franklin D. Roosevelt and the New Deal, 1932-1940*. New York: Harper and Row, 1963. Gives considerable attention to labor issues.

Jones, Mary. *Autobiography of Mother Jones*. Rprt. New York: Arno and the *New York Times*, 1969. Perspective on American labor from a worker and labor reformer; scant mention of time spent in Memphis.

Marshall, F. Ray. *History of Labor Organizations in the South*. Cambridge: Harvard University Press, 1957.

Marshall, Ray. *Labor in the South*. Cambridge, Mass.: Harvard University Press, 1967. Begins the story of southern labor in the late-nineteenth century and emphasizes the growth of unionism in the South since the 1920s and 1930s.

Marshall, Ray. *The Negro and Organized Labor*. New York: John Wiley and Sons, 1965. Deals mainly with the experience of black workers and unionism in the twentieth century.

Mason, Lucy Randolph. *To Win These Rights: A Personal Story of the CIO in the South*. New York: Harper and Brothers, 1952.

Meltzer, Milton. *Bread and Roses: The Struggle of American Labor, 1865-1911*. New York: Alfred A. Knopf, 1967.

McLaurin, Melton A. *The Knights of Labor in the South*. Westport, Conn.: Greenwood Press, 1978.

McLaurin, Melton A. *Paternalism and Protest: Southern Cotton Mill Workers and Organized Labor, 1875-1905*. Westport, Conn.: Greenwood Press, 1971.

Miller, Mark S. *Working Lives: The Southern Exposure History of Labor in the South*. New York: Pantheon Press, 1981. A collection of articles in southern labor history which have appeared in *Southern Exposure* and dealing mainly with labor stories of the early and mid-twentieth century. One Tennessee story is included—the saga of the Davidson-Wilder miners and Barney Graham.

Mitchell, Broadus. *The Rise of Cotton Mills in the South*. Gloucester, Mass.: Peter Smith, a 1966 reprint of Johns Hopkins Press edition, 1921.

Mitchell, Broadus, and Mitchell, George Sinclair. *The Industrial Revolution in the South*. Baltimore: Johns Hopkins Press, 1932.

Mitchell, George S. *Textile Unionism in the South.* Chapel Hill: University of North Carolina Press, 1932.

Morris, Richard B., ed. *A History of the American Worker.* Princeton, N. J.: Princeton University Press, 1983.

Morris, Richard B. *Government and Labor in Early America.* New York: Columbia University Press, 1946.

Morris, Richard B., adv. ed. *Labor and Management.* New York: Arno Press, 1973. A collection of photocopied *New York Times* news articles on events in the history of American labor-management relations.

Morris, Richard B., ed. [The U.S. Department of Labor History of] *The American Worker.* Washington, D. C.: U.S. Government Printing Office, 1977. A collection of readable essays, poetry, photographs and paintings in both color and black-and-white.

Piven, Frances Fox and Cloward, Richard A. *Poor People's Movements: Why They Succeed, How They Fail.* New York: Vintage, 1979. Concerned with worker protest movements that erupted among lower-class groups in the United States during the middle years of the twentieth century; discusses the economic modernization of the South and the civil rights movement.

Rogers, Daniel. *The Work Ethic in Industrial America, 1850-1920.* Chicago: University of Chicago Press, 1978.

Schumway, Harry. *I Go South: An Unprejudiced Visit to a Group of Cotton Mills.* Boston: Houghton Mifflin, 1930.

Shapiro, Henry D. *Appalachia On Our Mind: The Southern Mountains and Mountaineers in the American Consciousness, 1870-1920.* Chapel Hill: University of North Carolina Press, 1978.

Terkel, Studs. *Hard Times: An Oral History of the Great Depression.* New York: Pantheon Books, 1970.

Terkel, Studs. *Working.* New York: Pantheon Press, 1974. Draws heavily from oral history offered by American blue-collar working people.

Tindall, George. *The Emergence of the New South, 1913-1945.* Baton Rouge: Louisiana State University Press, 1967. For a general history, Tindall gives considerable attention to labor events and worker problems.

Tippett, Tom. *When Southern Labor Stirs.* New York: Jonathan Cape and Harrison Smith, 1931. Tells the story of the Elizabethton, Tennessee, millworkers' strike of 1929.

Wertheimer, Barbara M. *We Were There: The Story of Working Women in America.* New York: Pantheon Press, 1977. A highly readable account of the significant movement; heavy attention is paid to women garment and textile workers; tells the story of the founding of Amalgamated in Nashville.

Woodward, C. Vann. *Origins of the New South, 1877-1913.* Baton Rouge: Louisiana State University Press, 1971. Gives attention to the child labor issue and other labor concerns in the South.

Zieger, Robert H., ed. *Organized Labor in the Twentieth-Century South.* Knoxville: University of Tennessee Press, 1991. A collection of ten scholarly essays in southern labor history.

Tennessee Labor History

Abernathy, Thomas P. *From Frontier to Plantation in Tennessee: A Study in Frontier Democracy.* Chapel Hill: University of North Carolina Press, 1932. Reprinted Southern Historical Publications, no. 12. Tuscaloosa: University of Alabama Press, 1967.

Adams, Frank. *Unearthing Seeds of Fire: The Idea of Highlander.* Winston-Salem: John F. Blair, 1975.

Alexander, Lamar. *Steps Along the Way.* Nashville: Thomas Nelson, 1986. The former governor discusses the coming to Tennessee of Nissan and Saturn.

Anderson, Jack and Blumenthal, Fred. *The Kefauver Story.* New York: Dial Press, 1956.

Ansley, Fran and Bell, Brenda. "Strikes in the Coal Camps: Davidson-Wilder, 1932." *Southern Exposure,* vol. 1 (Winter, 1974): 113-36.

Armes, Ethel M. *The Story of Coal and Iron in Alabama. Birmingham:* Chamber of Commerce, 1910. Portions of this work deal with Southern Tennessee and the Tennessee Coal, Iron and Railroad Company.

Arnow, Harriette Simpson. *Flowering of the Cumberland.* New York: Macmillan Company, 1963.

Bailey, Robert E. "The 1968 Memphis Sanitation Strike." M. A. Thesis, Memphis State University, 1974.

Bailey, Thomas E. "Engine and Iron: a Story of Branchline Railroading in Middle Tennessee." *Tennessee Historical Quarterly,* vol. 28 (1969): 252-68.

Barclay, R. E. *Ducktown Back in Raht's Time.* Chapel Hill: University of North Carolina Press, 1946. The best study of early copper mining in Tennessee.

Barnett, Paul. *Industrial Development in Tennessee: Present Status and Suggested Programs.* Bureau of Research, School of Business Administration. Study #11, Knoxville: U. T. Division of University Extension, 1941.

Belissary, Constantine S. "Industry and Industrial Philosophy in Tennessee, 1850-1860." East Tennessee Historical Society's *Publications,* Vol. 23 (1951): 46-57.

Belissary, Constantine S. "Behavior Patterns and Aspirations of the Urban Working Classes of Tennessee in the Immediate Post-Civil War Era." *Tennessee Historical Quarterly,* Vol. 12 (1955): 24-42.

Bergeron, Paul H. *Paths of the Past: Tennessee, 1770-1979.* Knoxville: University Tennessee Press (Three-star Series), 1979. A brief overview of state history.

Biles, Roger. "Ed Crump Versus the Unions: The Labor Movement in Memphis During the 1930s." *Labor History,* Vol. 25 (Fall, 1984): 533-52.

Biles, Roger. *Memphis in the Great Depression.* Knoxville: University of Tennessee Press, 1986. Contains the same material on Crump and industrial unionism as in the previous source.

Bishop, Jim. *The Days of Martin Luther King, Jr.* New York: G. P. Putnam's Sons, 1971. Discusses King's fatal visit to Memphis.

Bledsoe, Thomas. *Or We'll All Hang Separately; The Highlander Idea.* Boston: Beacon Press, 1969.

Born, Kate "Organized Labor in Memphis, TN, 1826-1901." West Tennessee Historical Society's *Publications,* Vol. 21 (1967): 60-79.

Brown, Virginia. *The Development of Labor Legislation in Tennessee*. Thesis, University of Tennessee: also Knoxville: Bureau of Public Administration, University of Tennessee, 1945.

Brown, Virginia Holmes. "The Development of Labor Legislation in Tennessee." Thesis, University of Tennessee, 1945.

Burran, James A. "The WPA in Nashville, 1935-1943." *Tennessee Historical Quarterly*, vol. 28 (Fall, 1975): 293-306.

Buckley, Jerry. "How Japan is Winning Dixie: The Tennessee Story." *U. S. News and World Report*, May 9, 1988, pp. 43-57.

Capers, Gerald, Jr. *The Biography of a River Town*. Chapel Hill: University of North Carolina Press, 1939. A story of Memphis.

Carr, John. *Early Times in Middle Tennessee*. Nashville: E. Stevenson and F. A. Owen, 1857. Rpt. Nashville: Parthenon Press, 1958,

Carrier, Ronald E. and Schriver, William R. *Problems Faced by Manufacturers in Tennessee*. Memphis: Memphis State University, 1966.

Carriere, Mark Jr. "Blacks in Pre-Civil War Memphis." *Tennessee Historical Quarterly*, Vol. 48 (Spring, 1989): 3-14. Discusses work life among slaves; racial attitudes; the problem of slaves hiring themselves out to others besides their owners.

Carter, Deborah. "The Local Union as a Social Movement Organization: Local 282, Furniture Division, IUE, 1943-1988." Ph. D. diss., Vanderbilt University, 1988. Contains much oral history in its study of a Memphis local union founded in May 1943 and affiliated with the CIO because of its nondiscriminatory policies. Due to the impact of the black civil rights movement, the local membership expanded dramatically in the sixties and seventies.

Chamberlain, H. S. "Early Tennessee Iron and Steel Industry." *Manufacturer's Record*, Vol. 66 (1914): 41-42.

Changtrakul, Sasithorn. "Patterns of Industrial Growth in the Tennessee Valley States, 1939-1960." Thesis, University of Tennessee, 1964.

Chronology and Documentary Handbook of the State of Tennessee. Robert I. Vexler, state editor; William F. Swindler, series editor. (Chronologies and documentary handbooks of the states, 42.) Dobbs Ferry, N. Y.: Oceana Publications, 1979.

Clouse, R. Wilburn. "The Impact on Workers of an Industrial Plant Shutdown: A Case Study of DuPont's Rayon Plant Shutdown at Old Hickory, Tennessee." Thesis, Middle Tennessee State University, 1968.

Coppock, Helen and Crawford, Charles W., eds. *Paul R. Coppock's Mid-South*. Memphis: West Tennessee Historical Society, 1985.

Coppock, Paul R. *Memphis Memoirs*, Memphis; Memphis State University Press, 1980.

Corlew, Robert E. *Tennessee: A Short History*. 2nd ed. Knoxville: University of Tennessee Press, 1981. The standard college textbook in Tennessee history.

Crabtree, Font F. "The Wilder Coal Strike of 1932-33." Thesis, George Peabody College, 1937.

Crooke, Jonas Boyd. "The Labor Characteristics of Low-wage Manufacturing Industries in East Tennessee: The Berkline Corporation." Thesis, University of Tennessee, 1967.

Crew, H. W. *History of Nashville, Tennessee.* Nashville: Methodist Publishing House, 1890; Charles Elder, Bookseller. Chapt. 10, pp. 214-41, contains a discussion of early Nashville manufacturing, replete with names, prices, receipts, and dates.

Crowe, Jesse C. "The Origin and Development of Tennessee's Prison Problem, 1831-1871." *Tennessee Historical Quarterly,* Vol. 15 (June, 1956): 111-135.

Crutchfield, James A., ed. *The Tennessee Almanac and Book of Facts, 1989-1990.* Nashville; Rutledge Hill Press, 1988.

Daniel, Pete. "The Tennessee Convict War." *Tennessee Historical Quarterly,* Vol. 34 (Fall, 1975) : 273-92.

Davis, J. Treadwell. "Nashoba (near Memphis, Tennessee): Frances Wright's Experiment in Self-Emancipation." *Southern Quarterly* (Oct., 1972): 63-90.

Deaderick, Lucille, ed. *Heart of the Valley: A History of Knoxville, Tennessee.* Knoxville: East Tennessee Historical Society, 1976.

Deaton, Laura A. "Service Does Not Mean Solitude: The Story of the 1966 Hospital Worker's Strike, Oak Ridge, Tennessee." Nashville: Service Employees International Union Local 205 and copyright by Deaton, 1988.

Delfino, Susanna. "Antebellum East Tennessee Elites and Industrialization: The Examples of the Iron Industry and Internal Improvements." East Tennessee Historical Society's *Publications,* Vols. 56-57 (1984-85): 102-19.

Dew, Charles B. "Black Ironworkers and the Slave Insurrection Panic of 1856." *Journal of Southern History,* Vol. 41 (Aug., 1975): 321-338.

Dick, Everett. *The Dixie Frontier.* New York: Octagon Books, 1974.

Dodd, James Harvey. "The Development of Manufacturing in Tennessee Since the Civil War." Thesis, George Peabody College, 1925.

Donovan, William F. "The Growth of the Industrial Spirit in Tennessee, 1890-1910," Dissertation, George Peabody College, 1955.

Doran, William A. "The Development of the Industrial Spirit in Tennessee, 1910-1920." Diss. George Peabody College, 1965.

Douglas, Richard. "Logging in the Big Hatchie Bottoms." *Tennessee Historical Quarterly,* vol. 25 (Spring, 1966): 32-49. Early twentieth century logging in west Tennessee.

Doyle, Don H. *Nashville in the New South, 1880-1930.* Knoxville: University of Tennessee Press, 1985.

Doyle, Don H. *Nashville Since the 1920's.* Knoxville: University of Tennessee Press, 1985.

Dykeman, Wilma. *The French Broad.* (Rivers of America Series) reprinted Knoxville: University of Tennessee Press, 1965.

Dykeman, Wilma. Tennessee: *A Bicentennial History.* New York: W. W. Norton, 1975. A brief, readable one-volume survey of Tennessee history.

Eberling, Ernest J. *Population and Labor Force Changes During the 1960s: The U. S. and Tennessee.* Nashville: Department of Employment Security, 1960.

Egerton, John. *Shades of Gray: Dispatches From the Modern South.* Baton Rouge: Louisiana State University Press, 1991. Contains in pp. 58-76 "The Trial of Highlander Folk School" as originally published in Southern *Exposure,* vol. 6 (Spring, 1978): 82-89.

Egerton, John. *Visions of Utopia: Nashoba, Rugby, Rushin, and the New Communities in Tennessee's Past.* Knoxville: University of Tennessee Press, Tennessee Three Star Series, 1977.

Emerson, O. B. "Frances Wright and Her Nashoba Experiment." *Tennessee Historical Quarterly,* vol. 6 (Dec., 1947): 291-314.

Federal Writer's Project. *The WPA Guide to Tennessee* (Knoxville: University of Tennessee Press [a reprint of the 1939 WPA publication by Viking Press, originally entitled *Tennessee: A Guide to the State]*) 1986.

Fertig, James Walter. "The Secession and Reconstruction of Tennessee." Dissertation, University of Chicago Press, 1898: reprinted New York: AMS, 1972.

Fontenay, Charles L. *Estes Kefauver: A Biography.* Knoxville: University of Tennessee Press, 1980.

Fuller, Justin. "History of the Tennessee Coal, Iron and Railroad Company, 1852-1957." Dissertation, University of North Carolina, 1966.

Garrison, Joseph Yates. "Paul Revere Christopher: Southern Labor Leader, 1910-1974." Ph. D. diss., Georgia State University, 1976.

Gifford, James Maurice. "Montgomery Bell, Tennessee Ironmaster." Thesis, Middle Tennessee State University, 1970.

Glen, John M. *Highlander: No Ordinary School, 1932-1962.* Lexington: University Press of Kentucky, 1988. Glen's volume, based on numerous interviews and private manuscript collections, is the definitive volume on the first thirty years of Highlander's turbulent history.

Goehring, Eleanor E. *Tennessee Folk Culture: An Annotated Bibliography.* Knoxville: University of Tennessee Press, 1982.

Goodspeed Publishing Company. *A History of Tennessee from the Earliest Times to the Present.* 6 vols. Nashville: Goodspeed, 1886, 1887; reprinted Nashville: Elder, 1972.

Gorman, Joseph Bruce. *Kefauver: a Political Biography.* New York: Oxford University Press, 1971.

Gorman, Joseph Bruce. "The Early Career of Estes Kefauver." East Tennessee Historical Society's *Publications,* vol. 42 (1970): 57-84.

Govan, Gilbert E. and Livingood, James W. *The Chattanooga Country, 1540-1976.* 3rd edition; Knoxville: University of Tennessee Press, 1972.

Grantham, Dewey W. Jr. "Black Patch War: the Story of the Kentucky and Tennessee Night Riders, 1905-1909." *South Atlantic Quarterly,* vol. 59 (1960): 215-25.

Green, Earl, Jr. "Labor in the South: A Case Study of Memphis—The 1968 Sanitation Strike and Its Effect on an Urban Community." Ph. D. diss., New York University, 1980. An excellent study of the garbage strike.

Green, Lee Seifert. *Lead Me On: Frank Goad Clement and Tennessee Politics.* Knoxville: University of Tennessee Press, 1982. Highlights the reasons for Clement's appeal to Tennesseans; discusses the problems of Tennessee Teamster leaders and the McClelland hearings.

Gregg, Robert. *Origin and Development of the Tennessee Coal, Iron and Railroad Company.* New York: Newcomen Society, 1948.

Gresham, Mary Richardson. "The History of the Textile Industry Tennessee."
    Thesis, George Peabody College, 1930.
Hale, Will T., and Merritt, Dixon L. *A History of Tennessee and Tennesseans: The
    Leaders and Representative Men in Commerce, Industry, and Modern Activities.* 8
    vols. Chicago: Lewis, 1913.
Harris, W. B. "Splendid Retreat of Alcoa." *Fortune* (Oct., 1955); 114-22.
Haskins, Katherine B. *Anderson County.* Memphis: Memphis State University,
    1979. Contains information on Coal Creek and Anderson County miners.
*Hearings Before the Select Committee on Improper Activities in the Labor or
    Management Field, 85th Congress.* Washington: U.S. Government Printing
    Office, 1958.
*History of Local 309: United Steelworkers of America, AFL-CIO, Alcoa, Tennessee, 1933-
    1977.* Based on research by Sammy E. Pinkston and compiled by Craig
    Billingsley. Alcoa: Local Union 309, 1976.
Hodges, James A. "Challenge to the New South: The Great Textile Strike in
    Elizabethton, Tennessee, 1929," *Tennessee Historical Quarterly,* Vol. 23 (1964):
    343-57.
Hodges, James A. "The Tennessee Federation of Labor, 1919-1939." M.A. Thesis,
    Vanderbilt University, 1959.
Holly, J. Fred. "The Co-operative Town Company of Tennessee: a Case Study of
    Planned Economic Development." East Tennessee Historical Society's
    Publications, Vol. 36 (1964): 56-69.
Holly, J. Fred and Mabry, D. Bevars. *Protective Labor Legislation and Its
    Administration in Tennessee.* Knoxville: University of Tennessee Press, 1955.
Holt, Albert C. "The Economic and Social Beginnings of Tennessee." Dissertation,
    George Peabody College, 1923.
Honey, Michael Keith. "Labor and Civil Rights in the South: The Industrial Labor
    Movement and Black Workers in Memphis, 1929-1945." Ph. D. diss.,
    Northern Illinois University, 1988.
Honey, Michael K. *Southern Labor and Black Civil Rights: Organizing Memphis Workers.*
    Urbana and Chicago: University of Illinois Press, 1993. Scholarly historical
    analysis of labor and civil rights struggles in Memphis in the 1930s and 1940s;
    demonstrates the connection between issues of labor, race, and economic justice.
Horton, Myles, with Judith Kohl land Herbert Kohl. *The Long Haul: An
    Autobiography.* New York: Doubleday and Company, 1990.
Horton, Myles. "Witch-hunt in Tennessee: Highlander Folk School." *New Republic*
    (March 9, 1959): 23.
Hoskins, Katharine. *Anderson County.* Memphis: Memphis State University Press,
    1979. Tells the story of coal miners in Briceville and Coal Creek.
Howard, Patricia Brake. "Tennessee in War and Peace: The Impact of World War
    II on State Economic Trends." *Tennessee Historical Quarterly,* Vol. 51 (No. 1;
    Spring, 1992): 51-65. Speaks of the transformation of the Tennessee labor
    force during World War II, especially in Memphis, Chattanooga, and
    Knoxville, and of the emergence of Kingsport and Oak Ridge as vital cities.
    Howard points out that Nashville was not impacted as much as were the

other major cities, although the apparel industry in the Nashville-area dou-
bled during the war. Howard also points out that the forties was a decade of
great growth and that by 1947 the value of Tennessee manufacturing and
products totaled over $2 billion, two times greater than pre-war figures.

Hunt, Robert F. "The Pactolus Ironworks." *Tennessee Historical Quarterly*, Vol. 25
(1966): 176-96.

Hutson, Andrew Carter, Jr. "The Coal Miners' Insurrection, 1891-1892." Thesis,
University of Tennessee, 1933.

Hutson, Andrew Carter. "The Coal Miners' Insurrection in Anderson County,
Tennessee." East Tennessee Historical Society's *Publications*, Vol. 7 (1935):
103-21.

Hutson, Andrew Carter. "The Overthrow of the Convict Lease System in Tennessee."
East Tennessee Historical Society's *Publications*, Vol. 8 (1936): 82-103.

*Interim Report of the Select Committee on Improper Activities in the Labor or
Management Field. 85th Congress, 2nd Session, Report No. 1417.* Washington: U.
S. Government Printing Office, 1958. Contains a section entitled "Organized
Violence in Tennessee and Adjacent States," pp. 330f.

Isaac, Paul. *Prohibition and Politics: Turbulent Decades in Tennessee, 1885-1920.*
Knoxville: University of Tennessee Press, 1965.

Jenkins, Gary C. "The Mining of Alum Cave." East Tennessee Historical Society
Publications, No. 60 (1988): 78-87. Early 19th century mining in a Smokey
Mountain cave.

Johnson, Rayburn. "Population Trends in Tennessee from 1940-1950," *Tennessee
Historical Quarterly*, Vol. 11 (Sept., 1952): 254-62.

Jones, James Boyd, Jr. "The Memphis Firefighters' Strikes, 1858 and 1860." East
Tennessee Historical Society's *Publications*, Vol. 49 (1977): 37-60. Jones tells an
interesting story of how an early firefighters' strike was precipitated by
muddy Memphis streets in which equipment bogged down.

Junkerman, John. "Nissan, Tennessee: It Ain't What It's Cracked Up to Be." *The
Progressive*, June, 1987, pp. 16-19.

Kephart, Horace. *Our Southern Highlanders*. Intro. by George Ellison. Knoxville:
University of Tennessee Press, 1976.

Killibrew, Joseph J. *Knoxville as an Iron Center*. Nashville: Travel, Eastman and
Howell, 1880.

Lambert, Robert S. "Logging in the Great Smokies." *Tennessee Historical Quarterly*,
Vol. 20 (1961): 350-63.

Lambert, Robert S. "Logging on Little River, 1890-1940." East Tennessee
Historical Society's *Publications*, Vol. 33 (1961): 32-42. Discuss ways in which
the timber was delivered to the saw mills. The Little River Lumber Company,
near the Smokey Mountains, estimated that some 560,000,000 board feet of
timber were consumed at the mill.

Lamon, Lester C. *Blacks in Tennessee, 1791-1970*. Knoxville: University of
Tennessee Press (Tennessee Three Star Series), 1981.

Lee, David D. *Tennessee In Turmoil: Politics in the Volunteer State, 1920-1932.*
Memphis: Memphis State University Press, 1979.

Majors, William R. *Change and Continuity: Tennessee Politics Since the Civil War.* Macon, Georgia: Mercer University Press, 1986. A fresh interpretation in readable prose.

Majors, William R. "Gordon Browning and Tennessee Politics, 1937-1939," *Tennessee Historical Quarterly*, Vol. 28 (Fall, 1975): 293-306.

Majors, William R. *The End of Arcadia: Gordon Browning and Tennessee Politics.* Memphis: Memphis State University Press, 1979.

McDonald, Kenneth M. "Milling in Tennessee, 1780-1860." Thesis, Vanderbilt University, 1939.

McDonald, Michael J. and Wheeler, William Bruce. *Knoxville, Tennessee: Continuity and Change in an Appalachian City.* Knoxville: University of Tennessee Press, 1983.

McDonald, Michael J. and Muldowny, John. *TVA and the Dispossessed: The Resettlement of Population in the Norris Dam Area.* Knoxville: University of Tennessee Press, 1982.

McGee, Gentry R. *A History of Tennessee from 1663 to 1900 for Use in Schools.* New York: American Book, 1900, 1911; revised edition, 1919; revised and enl. edition   C. B. Ijams, 1924; 1930; reprinted Nashville: Elder, 1971.

McKelway, A. J. *Child Labor in Tennessee. National Child Labor Committee, 1911.* The historic document of 16 pages points out that, while there were not many Tennessee children in the mines, there were a number of children (mainly girls) in the textile mills. The average work week of such children was 62 hours. The publication contains a number of pictures of children at work in 1910-1911. Only one copy of this work has been located in a national search and it is secured at the Tennessee State Library and Archives.

McMurtrie, Douglas Crawford. *An Early Tennessee Paper Mill.* Chicago: Privately Printed, 1933.

Miller, William D. *Memphis During the Progressive Era, 1900-1917.* Memphis: Memphis State University Press, 1957.

Miller, William D. Mr. *Crump of Memphis.* Baton Rouge: Louisiana State University Press, 1964.

"Mining and Minerals and Manufacturing in East Tennessee." *Debow's Commercial Review,* Vol. 17 (1854): 302-03.

Minton, John Dean. "The New Deal in Tennessee, 1932-1938." Ph. D. diss., Vanderbilt University, 1959.

Mooney, Chase C. "Some Institutional and Statistical Aspects of Slavery in Tennessee." *Tennessee Historical Quarterly*, Vol.1 (Sept., 1942): 195-228.

Mooney, Jack. "The Establishment and Operation of the Technical Training School of the International Printing Pressmen and Assistants' Union in Tennessee, 1911-1967." *Tennessee Historical Quarterly*, Vol. 48 (Summer, 1989): 111-22.

Mooney, Jack. "The Sanatorium of the International Printing Pressmen and Assistants' Union of North America, 1910-1961, at Pressmen's Home, Tennessee." *Tennessee Historical Quarterly*, Vol. 48 (Fall, 1989): 162-73.

Moore, John Trotwood, and Foster, Austin P. *Tennessee: The Volunteer State, 1769-1923.* 4 vols. Nashville: Clarke, 1923.

Moore, William H. "Preoccupied Paternalism: The Roane Iron Company in Her Company Town—Rockwood, Tennessee." East Tennessee Historical Society's *Publications*, Vol. 39 (1967): 56-70.

Nall, James O. *The Tobacco Night Riders of Kentucky and Tennessee, 1905-1909.* Louisville: Standard, 1939.

Nicholson, James L. *Grundy County.* Memphis: Memphis State University Press, 1982.

Owsley, Frank L. and Owsley, Harriet C. "Economic Basis of Society in the Late Antebellum South." *Journal of Southern History*, Vol. 6 (1940): 24-45.

Owsley, Frank L. "The Economic Structure of Rural Tennessee, 1850-1860." *Journal of Southern History* (May, 1942): 161-82.

Parker, Russell D. "Alcoa, Tennessee: The Early Years, 1919-1939." East Tennessee Historical Society's *Publications*, Vol. 48 (1976): 86ff.

Parker, Russell D. "Alcoa, Tennessee: The Years of Change, 1940-1960," East Tennessee Historical Society's *Publications*, Vol. 49 (1977): 99ff.

Pease, William and Pease, Jane H. "A New View of Nashoba." *Tennessee Historical Quarterly*, Vol. 19 (June, 1960): 99-109.

Perry, Jennings. *Democracy Begins at Home: The Tennessee Fight on the Poll Tax.* New York: J. B. Lippincott, 1944.

Perry, Vernon F. "The Labor Struggle at Wilder, Tennessee." Thesis, Vanderbilt University, 1934.

Pessen, Edward. "The Workingmen's Movement in the Jackson Era." *Mississippi Valley Historical Review*, Vol. 43 (1958): 428-43.

Pessen, Edward. *Jacksonian American: Society, Personality and Politics.* Homewood, IL: Dorsey, 1969.

Pessen, Edward. "The Workingman's Party Revisited." *Labor History*, Vol. 4 (1963): 203-26.

Petrie, J. C. "Memphis Makes War on CIO." *Christian Century* (Oct. 13, 1937): 1273.

Petro, Sylvester. *The Kingsport Strike.* New Rochelle: Arlington House, 1967.

Phelps, Dawson A. and Willett, John T. "Iron Works on the Natchez Trace." *Tennessee Historical Quarterly*, Vol. 12 (1953): 309-22.

Pinkston, Sammy E. *History of Local 309, United Steelworkers of America, AFL-CIO, CLC, 1933-1977.* Compiled by Craig Billingsley. Knoxville: Keith Press, 1976.

Putnam, Albigence W. *History of Middle Tennessee: or, Life and Times of General James Robertson.* Tennessean Edition. Knoxville: University of Tennessee Press, 1971.

Ralph, J. "Industrial Region of Northern Alabama, Tennessee, and Georgia." *Harper's Monthly Magazine* (March, 1895): 607-26.

Report of the Joint Committee on Highlander Folk School, 81st Session of the General Assembly of the State of Tennessee. Nashville: State of Tennessee, 1959.

Robison, Dan M., ed. "Andrew Johnson on the Dignity of Labor." *Tennessee Historical Quarterly*, vol. 23 (1964): 80-85.

Rogers, Wiliam Flinn. "Life in East Tennessee Near the End of the Eighteenth Century." East Tennessee Historical Society's *Publications*, Vol. 1 (1929): 27-42.

Rothrock, Mary U., ed. *The French Broad - Holston Country: A History of Knox County, Tennessee.* Knoxville: East Tennessee Historical Society, 1946.

Rothrock, Mary U., and Smith, Sam B. *This is Tennessee: A School History*, 2nd ed. Nashville: Rothrock and Smith, publishers, 1973. Readable and interesting general state history for middle school students on up.

Satz, Ronald M. *Tennessee's Indian People: From White Contact to Removal, 1540-1840*. (Tennessee Three Star Series) Knoxville: University of Tennessee Press, 1979.

Schulman, Steven. "The Lumber Industry of the Upper Cumberland River Valley." *Tennessee Historical Quarterly*, Vol. 32 (Fall, 1973): 255-64.

Sharpe, Joseph A. "The Farmer's Alliance and Tennessee Politics, 1890-1892." Thesis, University of Tennessee, 1931.

Sharpe, Joseph A. "The Entrance of the Farmer's Alliance into Tennessee Politics." East Tennessee Historical Society's *Publications*, Vol. 9 (1937): 77-92.

Sharpe, Joseph A. "The Farmer's Alliance and the People's Party in Tennessee." East Tennessee Historical Society's *Publications*, Vol. 10 (1938): 91-113.

Sheridan, Walter. *The Rise and Fall of Jimmy Hoffa*. New York: Saturday Review Press, 1972. Gives considerable detail on the Hoffa trials in Nashville and Chattanooga.

Smith, Marion O. "The C. S. Nitre and Mining Bureau of East Tennessee." East Tennessee Historical Society *Publications*, No. 61 (1989): 29-47. Tells about saltpeter mining operations in east Tennessee during the Civil War. Workers were offered $15 a month, soldiers' rations, and exemption from military service "to all men who work faithfully."

Smith, Sam B., ed. and comp. *Tennessee History: A Bibliography*. Knoxville: University of Tennessee Press, 1974. An indispensable reference work for research in Tennessee history.

Special Report of the Commissioner of Labor and Inspector of Mines. Nashville: Marshall and Bruce, 1891.

Spoone, Janice Harrison. "The Textile Industry of Tennessee." Thesis, University of Tennessee, 1964.

Stanfield, J. Edwin. *In Memphis: More Than a Garbage Strike*. Atlanta: Southern Regional Council, 1968.

Steinbach, Carol. "Smokestacks to Bootstraps: An Economic Agenda for Tennessee's Future." *Tennessee Illustrated* (Sept.- Oct., 1988): 13-25.

Tennessee Blue Book, 1987-88. Compiled by Gentry Crowell, Secretary of State. A fact-filled reference book.

"Tennessee Coal and Iron Company Deal and the Panic of 1907." *Nation* (June 15, 1911): 594.

Thomas, Hulan Glyn. "The Highlander Folk School: The Depression Years." *Tennessee Historical Quarterly*, Vol 23 (Dec., 1964): 358-71.

Tilley, Bette B. "The Spirit of Improvement: Reformism and Slavery in West Tennessee." West Tennessee Historical Society's *Papers*, Vol. 28 (1974): 25-42.

Tootle, Margaret Marie. "A History of Old Hickory, Tennessee." M.E. Thesis, George Peabody College for Teachers, 1953. A valuable source for background study on the coming of DuPont and the powder plant to middle Tennessee.

Tucker, David M. *Memphis Since Crump: Bossism, Blacks and Civic Reformers, 1948-68*. Knoxville: University of Tennessee Press, 1980.

Warren, Robert Penn. *Nightrider.* Boston: Houghton, 1939. Rpt. New York: Random House, 1948. A work of fiction set during the Tennessee-Kentucky conflict. Warren, born in the area, had first-hand knowledge of the situation and hostilities.

Westphal, Corrine. "The Farmer's Alliance in Tennessee." Thesis, Vanderbilt University, 1929.

Wheeler, William Bruce and McDonald, Michael J. *TVA and the Tellico Dam, 1936-1979*. Knoxville: University of Tennessee, 1986.

White, Charles P. "Early Experiments with Prison Labor in Tennessee." East Tennessee Historical Society's *Publications*, Vol. 12 (1940): 45-69.

Williams, Samuel C. "The South's First Cotton Factory." *Tennessee Historical Quarterly*, Vol. 5 (1946): 212-21.

Williams, Samuel C. "Early Iron Works in the Tennessee Country." *Tennessee Historical Quarterly*, Vol. 6 (1947): 39-46.

Wilson, B. M. "Tennessee Workman's Compensation Law." Thesis, East Tennessee State University, 1952.

Winters, Donald L. *Tennessee Farming, Tennessee Farmers: Antebellum Agriculture in the Upper South*. Knoxville: University of Tennessee Press, 1994.

Wrenn, Lynette Boney. "The Impact of Yellow Fever on Memphis: A Reappraisal." Western Tennessee Historical Society *Papers*, Vol. 51 (Dec., 1987): 4-18.

York, Max. "Labor's Tall Man on the Hill." *Nashville Tennessean Magazine* (July 1, 1962): 9-15.

Index

Index

Photo page numbers are in bold type.